T0320073

GOVERNING THE ENERGY CHALLENGE:
CANADA AND GERMANY IN A MULTI-LEVEL REGIONAL
AND GLOBAL CONTEXT

As energy prices continue to soar, there is a growing interest in how to better manage and regulate energy sources and their production. *Governing the Energy Challenge* is a comparative study between Canada and Germany that features essays by leading energy and public policy specialists from both countries. It identifies numerous strategies to produce more efficient and sustainable energy by revealing the ways in which Germany, as a member of the European Union, is more advanced in dealing with multi-level governmental tensions and sustainability constraints than Canada is as a member of NAFTA.

Paying particular attention to the relationship between environmental study, climate change issues, and economic market reforms, this volume analyses the influence that the energy sector and multi-level institutional arrangements have on energy governance. The contributors provide valuable information on the formation of energy policy, offering insights into the growing differences between countries that are members of NAFTA and those that are members of the European Union.

BURKARD EBERLEIN is an assistant professor in the Schulich School of Business at York University.

G. BRUCE DOERN is a professor in the School of Public Policy and Administration at Carleton University and in the Department of Politics at the University of Exeter.

BURKARD EBERLEIN AND G. BRUCE DOERN,
EDITORS

Governing the Energy Challenge

Canada and Germany in a Multi-Level Regional and Global Context

UNIVERSITY OF TORONTO PRESS
Toronto Buffalo London

© University of Toronto Press Incorporated 2009
Toronto Buffalo London
www.utppublishing.com
Printed in Canada

ISBN 978-0-8020-9305-9

Printed on acid-free paper

Library and Archives Canada Cataloguing in Publication

Governing the energy challenge : Germany and Canada in a multi-level
regional and global context / Burkard Eberlein and G. Bruce Doern, editors.

Includes bibliographical references.
ISBN 978-0-8020-9305-9

1. Energy policy – Canada.   2. Energy policy – Germany.   3. Energy
industries – State supervision – Canada.   4. Energy industries – State
supervision – Germany.   5. Energy industries – Environmental aspects –
Government policy – Canada.   6. Energy industries – Environmental
aspects – Government policy – Germany.   I. Doern, G. Bruce, 1942–
II. Eberlein, Burkard

HD9502.C32 G69 2009   333.790971   C2009-901215-4

University of Toronto Press acknowledges the financial assistance to
its publishing program of the Canada Council for the Arts and the
Ontario Arts Council.

University of Toronto Press acknowledges the financial support for its
publishing activities of the Government of Canada through the
Book Publishing Industry Development Program (BPIDP).

Contents

Preface

This book originated in the Transatlantic Energy Conference hosted by the Canadian Centre for German and European Studies (www.ccges.ca) at York University, Toronto, 9 and 10 September 2005.

The conference brought together an interdisciplinary group of leading energy scholars and experts from Canadian and European universities, research institutes, and governmental and non-governmental bodies. More than twenty presentations (papers and deck-based commentaries) and lively discussions revolved around current challenges for energy policy from a comparative, transatlantic, and multi-level perspective, with a special focus on Germany and Canada.

The discussion greatly benefited from the input of those who attended the conference. Several York colleagues from Environmental Studies, Osgoode Hall Law School, Political Science, and the Schulich School of Business generously contributed their intellectual input and time. Many thanks are due to all these individuals who helped this book project to emerge and develop.

Ten of the chapters in the book were presented and discussed as initial drafts at the Transatlantic Energy Conference. Other conference presentation decks were not converted into chapters because of their authors' time and scheduling constraints. Another chapter was presented at the conference but dropped from the book for reasons of space and in order to make room for two additional chapters suggested by the reviewers of our initial manuscript. These chapters were those on German and Canadian nuclear policy and on German climate change policy.

The discussions at the conference were instrumental in identifying the key issues, debates, and questions that inform this book. Further joint work by the editors and contributors helped to substantially advance the conceptual framework and refine the empirical analysis, so that this book should be considered a second – and in many ways new – product.

We owe special thanks to the University of Toronto Press external assessors for their extremely useful and constructive comments and suggestions. Members of the University of Toronto Press manuscript review committee also offered very helpful suggestions. Both of these forms of peer review have considerably strengthened the final product.

We would like to personally thank Siemens Canada Limited, and former president and CEO, Albert Maringer, for very generous funding without which the conference could not have taken place. Special thanks are also due to the German Academic Exchange Service, which provided additional funding.

We are particularly indebted to the then co-director of the Canadian Centre for German and European Studies at York University, Mark Webber, who opened many doors and was extremely supportive and generous as plans for the conference emerged and materialized. Anita Szucsko, program assistant at the centre, was an enthusiastic and effective manager of all organizational aspects of the conference, as usual well beyond the call of duty. Birgit Armstrong and Nicole Andrée provided valuable assistance around the conference as well.

Needless to say we are especially indebted to our contributing authors for their research and analytical insights and to our colleagues at the Schulich School of Business and the Canadian Centre for German and European Studies at York University, the School of Public Policy and Administration Carleton University, the Carleton Research Unit on Innovation, Science and Environment, and the Politics Department, University of Exeter, for their continuous support and encouragement.

Burkard Eberlein and G. Bruce Doern
March 2009

Abbreviations

ACCOES	Advisory Committee on Competition in Ontario's Electricity System
AECL	Atomic Energy of Canada Limited
AES	Alberta Electric System Operator
ANWR	Alaska Natural Wildlife Refuge
BDI	Bundesverband der Deutschen Industrie (Federal Association of German Industry)
BMU	Bundesministerium für Umwelt
BMWi	Bundesministerium für Wirtschaft
BNetzA	Bundesnetzagentur für Elektrizität, Gas, Telekommunikation, Post und Eisenbahnen
BP	British Petroleum
CAGPL	Canadian Arctic Gas Pipeline
CANDU	Canada deuterium uranium (reactor)
CCGT	Combined cycle gas turbine
CDM	Clean development mechanism
CHP	Combined heat and power (generation)
CNSC	Canadian Nuclear Safety Commission
COP	Conference of the Parties
CSR	Corporate social responsibility
CUFTA	Canada-U.S. Free Trade Agreement
DEHSt	Deutsche Emissionshandelsstelle
DSO	Distribution system operator
EECP	European Climate Change Programme
ERGEG	European Regulators' Group for Electricity and Gas
ETS	Emission Trading Scheme

EU	European Union
FERC	Federal Energy Regulatory Commission (U.S.)
GATT	General Agreement on Tariffs and Trade
GHG	Greenhouse gases
IAEA	International Atomic Energy Agency
IEA	International Energy Agency
IMO	Independent market operator
IOU	Investor-owned utility
IPCC	Intergovernmental Panel on Climate Change
ISO	Independent system operator (U.S.)
JI	Joint implementation
LCA	Life cycle assessment
LDC	Local distribution company
LNG	Liquefied natural gas
MDC	Market Design Committee
MLG	Multi-level governance
MPMA	Market Power Mitigation Agreement
MVP	Mackenzie Valley Pipeline
NAERC	North American Electricity Reliability Council
NAEWG	North American Energy Working Group
NAFTA	North American Free Trade Agreement
NAP	National Allocation Plan
NEB	National Energy Board
NEP	The National Energy Program (of 1980)
NERC	U.S. National Electricity Reliability Council
NGOs	Non-governmental organizations
NRAs	National regulatory authorities
NRCan	Natural Resources Canada
OEB	Ontario Energy Board
OECD	Organisation for Economic Co-operation and Development
OPEC	Organization of the Petroleum Exporting Countries
OPG	Ontario Power Generation Inc.
PEMEX	Petroleos Mexicanos
PUCs	Public Utility Commissions (in United States)
PURPA	Public Utility Regulation Policies Act (U.S.)
R&D	Research and development
RES-E	Renewable energy sources for electricity (generation)
RPS	Renewable Portfolio Standard
RRO	Regulated rate option

RTG	Regional transmission grids
RTOs	Regional Transmission Organizations
SD	Sustainable development
TPA	Third party access
TSO	Transmission system operator
UNFCCC	United Nations Framework Convention on Climate Change
US NEP	U.S. National Energy Policy (of 2001)
VDEW	Verband der Elektrizitätswirtschaft
WTI	West Texas Intermediate
WTO	World Trade Organization

GOVERNING THE ENERGY CHALLENGE:
CANADA AND GERMANY IN A MULTI-LEVEL REGIONAL
AND GLOBAL CONTEXT

1 German and Canadian Multi-Level Energy Regulatory Governance: Introduction, Context, and Analytical Framework

BURKARD EBERLEIN AND G. BRUCE DOERN

The purpose of this book is to investigate and compare the dynamics of multi-level energy regulatory governance in Germany and Canada. Regulatory governance is a response to energy policy challenges that include a renewed emphasis on energy security as well as on environmental sustainability in a global and competitive resource economy. We argue that today's energy policy faces unprecedented challenges that arise from mounting tensions between core policy goals in a context of increasing interdependence and fast-changing internationalization. The governance of these challenges increasingly involves multi-level patterns of interaction across established territorial and functional boundaries.

The basic logic of the book's analytical journey is captured in figure 1.1. The theoretical roots of the endeavour reside in conceptual work on multi-level governance and multi-level regulation, neo-institutional theory, and the nature of energy resources and policy. These lead us to see regulatory governance as being shaped by two key factors: the substantive energy policy structures, issues, and properties; and multi-level institutional patterns in the two countries. The former includes the endowments of the energy field in the two countries. The latter includes the specific incentives and constraints of the multi-level institutional settings of energy policy, in which public and private actors interact on the basis of their resources, interests, and strategies, set in the larger array of macro political institutions that govern Germany and Canada.

Energy governance, in other words, is not focused upon institutions and processes, or politics and economics somehow disembodied from the substance and content of the energy field. It may seem surprising

Figure 1.1: Governing the energy challenge in Germany and Canada: Theoretical roots, key factors, thematic framework, and book structure

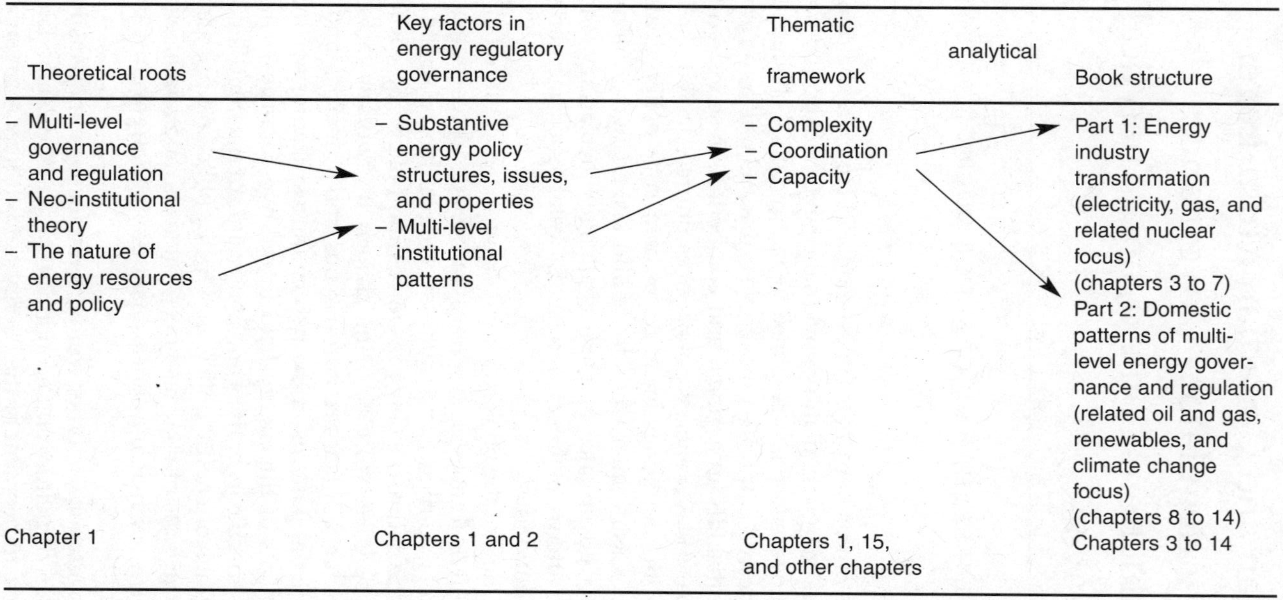

Theoretical roots	Key factors in energy regulatory governance	Thematic framework	analytical	Book structure
– Multi-level governance and regulation – Neo-institutional theory – The nature of energy resources and policy	– Substantive energy policy structures, issues, and properties – Multi-level institutional patterns	– Complexity – Coordination – Capacity		Part 1: Energy industry transformation (electricity, gas, and related nuclear focus) (chapters 3 to 7) Part 2: Domestic patterns of multi-level energy governance and regulation (related oil and gas, renewables, and climate change focus) (chapters 8 to 14)
Chapter 1	Chapters 1 and 2	Chapters 1, 15, and other chapters		Chapters 3 to 14

to have to state and re-emphasize, but many analyses of multi-level regulation are often so focused on institutional niceties that actual policy-field substantive realities and challenges take a decidedly second place position or barely register.

As figure 1.1 shows, the deliberate integration of multi-level institutional patterns and substantive policy structures and properties is reflected in our thematic analytical framework. It consists of three themes that emerge from and structure the material: *complexity, coordination*, and *capacity*. We preview these briefly here and will see them in different ways in the chapters by our contributing authors but reserve our main more detailed discussion of them to our conclusions in chapter 15.

Complexity captures the two dimensions of energy policy: substantive and institutional. In substantive or material terms, energy policy deals with 'large technical systems' (Hughes 1987) that combine technical complexity with high potential for politicization. This makes the management of change susceptible to design flaws, volatility, and unintended consequences. In institutional terms, complexity captures the increasing horizontal and vertical differentiation or fragmentation of the policy arena, characterized by a high degree of dispersion of resources (authority, information, material) required to address governance challenges.

Coordination refers to patterns of multi-level interaction and is fundamentally concerned with the form and effectiveness of coordination between different actors and levels involved in multi-level energy policymaking. Where conditions are complex, coordination involves navigating complex layers of regulatory regimes across territorial and sector boundaries. Negotiation is the dominant mode of interaction in non-hierarchical multi-level systems where authority is dispersed. The specific coordination profile of a multi-level system is shaped by power relations, actor orientations and strategies, and institutional rules and norms (Scharpf 1997).

Capacity, finally, is the ability of jurisdictions and institutional arrangements to meet the substantive challenges of today's energy world as previewed in this chapter and as discussed in more detail in chapter 2 and in others that follow. We use the term *capacity* in the broader sense of institutional capacity. This involves the delicate balance of goals that are often in conflict but also the technical ability to make energy systems effectively deliver the needed mix of energy services.

The book's analytical journey then branches out into two main analytical parts. Part 1 focuses on energy industry transformations, in particular recent industry restructuring and market reforms, and on comparative multi-level regulatory governance in both continents. The focus in part 1 is initially on electricity, nuclear energy, and natural gas, the three fuel sources that are still mainly national or regional and continental, compared to the global markets for oil. However, as an initial analytical entry point, electricity and natural gas immediately require consideration of the role of nuclear power, which in turn raises issues of broader fuel sources and their capacities to meet particular kinds of energy needs in relation to national energy and resource endowments.

The key political role of oil and gas industry interests is also introduced later in this chapter and is discussed in more particular ways in chapter 2 and in other chapters in part 2, such as the Cameron, Theobald, Rivers and Jaccard, and Weidner and Eberlein chapters (7, 10, 11, 12). While the governance of oil extraction and processing follows rules different from those in the production of fuels that are more typically used in electricity generation, the geopolitics of oil is also central to every other aspect of energy policy, since, as chapter 2 shows, it underpins the governance of energy in both the Germany–European Union and Canada–North America clusters we are examining (Noreng 2006). These fuel sources and mixes are first examined in part 1 in terms of explicit comparative multi-level regulatory governance features of the German and Canadian energy polities, functioning within the EU and North American institutions respectively, and are then explored in chapters in part 2 as well.

In part 2, however, the focus shifts in relative terms to domestic patterns of multi-level energy governance and regulation in the two countries. Since Canada and Germany are governed by federal arrangements, multi-level energy governance is still central, as local and regional governments play a crucial role in shaping energy governance. Environmental policy, climate change, crucial oil and gas links, emission trading and renewable energy, and energy efficiency are also brought into the multi-level energy regulatory mix.

We believe that the substantive and institutional complexity of energy policy calls for a multi-disciplinary analysis of governance challenges and policymaking. Our contributing authors focus on multi-level institutional analysis but from a variety of disciplinary perspectives in political science and public policy, law, and economics, and also as regulatory and policy practitioners and advisors in a German-EU and Canadian–North American context.

The selection of Germany (in the EU) and Canada (in the North American Free Trade Agreement) as the comparator countries in part reflects the research interests and backgrounds of the editors, but the value of such a comparison goes well beyond this initial analytical impetus. The two jurisdictions offer contrasting profiles in the two key factors that shape energy regulatory governance: substantive policy structures and resource endowments on the one hand, and institutional patterns of multi-level coordination and management on the other.

As chapter 2 shows overall, and as later chapters show in more detail, each country has a contrasting mix of current and potential future energy sources, with Germany being more dependent on imported sources of supply but also more advanced on alternative energy sources, and Canada having a more plentiful mixture of domestic supply but also a need for U.S. markets and capital and weaker political and economic support and policies for sustainable alternative energy sources and supply.

In terms of multi-level regulatory patterns, the two countries provide major points of institutional difference in the architecture of international embeddedness, of national electoral competition and party systems, structures and traditions of federalism, the relative reliance on sectoral versus horizontal regulatory bodies, core energy business interests and overall corporate political representation, and the composition and structure of environmental non-governmental organizations and public opinion. This chapter draws out these differences in an overall initial portrait, with more detailed analyses emerging in later chapters.

Thus, the two jurisdictions can be considered, within the group of developed industrial societies, as two 'most different systems' (Hay 2002; Przeworski and Teune 1970), the comparison of which allows us to draw conclusions about common features of contemporary energy regulatory governance. These features should hold for other jurisdictions in the OECD world, even if their differences are not as great as our two comparator countries. In different ways, they face the same broad task of meeting the current and future energy needs of their citizens, industries, and internal regions at reasonable prices, through efficient markets, and in ways that meet security concerns and minimize environmental impacts.

At the same time, the focused comparison of Germany and Canada offers the opportunity to study the policy effects of contrasting combinations of the key determinants of energy regulatory governance: Germany with a rather weak natural resource base but a more developed multi-level institutional framework, compared to energy-rich Canada with a more fragmented institutional setting.

This comparative approach and perspective also emerged from discussions at the Canadian Centre for German and European Studies (CCGES) Transatlantic Energy Conference, on which this volume is based (see preface). A key concern raised by several speakers on the podium and in the audience was the need to integrate the analysis of substantive structures and properties of the energy sector with careful attention to the differences in the institutional environment of both countries. Too often, these elements are separated, with economists and energy specialists focusing exclusively on the former and political scientists and country specialists on the latter.

Furthermore, we are convinced that the study of energy policy, through a German-Canadian comparison and from a multi-level regulatory vantage point, offers fruitful perspectives on the general transformation of governance, beyond the case of energy policy, in countries affected by increasing interdependence and internationalization. In this broader governance perspective, we view our investigation into an advanced field of multi-level and internationalized governance in two contrasting settings as a critical case study that has the potential to uncover dynamics and pathways of broader relevance and to generate hypotheses for future research (George and Bennet 2005).

The remainder of this introductory chapter is devoted to previewing the key issues, context, and core concepts of the comparison of German and Canadian energy multi-level regulatory governance. We first set out definitional and theoretical anchors for the book: the nature of energy policy, regulation, and regulatory governance, and neo-institutional theory. We then profile and preview the nature and evolution of the German and Canadian energy regulatory governance regimes, respectively, in the context of their political systems.

Our main conclusions in chapter 15 stress four substantive results from the German and Canadian comparison:

• Energy policy is confronted with a very complex technical system in a highly political environment. As the study of market liberalization and integration in both countries demonstrates, these features invite design flaws, ad hoc political intervention, and unintended consequences, which often translate into disappointing reform outcomes.

- Energy policy is truly multi-level in character. Energy policymaking in Canada and Germany involves practically all territorial levels, from international trade and market integration under NAFTA and EU respectively, to the local community or municipal level of land-use management or alternative energy use.
- Energy policy is also highly multi-level in functional terms, as it reaches into and is in turn affected by multiple policy regimes: environment and trade are most prominent, but other areas include consumer, Aboriginal, and regional policies. This complex territorial and functional layering of levels and policy regimes involves cooperation and collision between different actors and domains, raising the question of how the tensions of 'complex interdependence' can, if at all, be managed.
- Our comparison of institutional coordination mechanisms in the two jurisdictions reveals that Germany and the EU offer a constellation of actors and institutional rules and norms that is more conducive to consensual and productive management of multi-level tensions than Canada and NAFTA. In the latter case, the asymmetrical nature of US-Canadian relations and the domestic institutional setting (a conflict-prone mix of partisan politics and executive federalism with federal-provincial bilateralism) militate against high levels of coordination. Conflicts are exacerbated by major cleavages between energy producer and consumer regions. In contrast, Germany has, for lack of abundant natural resources, avoided these producer-consumer cleavages, And, more importantly, it features an institutional system geared to patient consensus-building – although the corporatist style of government-industry relations can be a source of stalemate, and tensions between the energy provision regime and the environmental regime are far from absent. The EU, finally, is an international arena with a much greater balance of power and higher capacity to manage conflicts than NAFTA. And, unlike Canada, Germany has been able to upload many of its concerns and policy models onto the supranational level.
- Our study finds that this marked difference in institutional capacity to deal with the multi-level nature of energy policy has significant impact on the ability to meet substantive challenges of energy pro-

vision and resource management. Two sets of capacity determine
the overall ability to meet the energy challenge: first, the material
capacity that is mainly a function of resource endowment but also
includes the properties of energy sources as well as energy-specific
expertise and innovative capacities of a country; and second, the
political-institutional capacity of multi-level management. We find
Canada and Germany at opposite ends in a comparison of the
countries and the two kinds of capacity. Whereas Germany combines low material capacity (in terms of resource endowment) with
high institutional capacity, Canada shows the reverse combination.
Germany has been able to leverage its high institutional capacity to
mitigate its inherent absence of abundant oil and gas resources
(while energy dependence on foreign suppliers, Russia in particular, loom large). As a matter of fact, Germany's poor natural
resource base compelled it earlier to search for wider energy
options and build strong institutional and environmental capacities,
to develop alternative energy technologies in particular. Canada's
poor institutional capacity, by contrast, has led to relative under-
performance, considering its strong material resource base. In fact,
abundance of resources may also present a burden and inhibit the
development of new (material and institutional) capacities, especially when it comes to innovative climate policy. Canada's energy
riches have not only fuelled conflicts between producer and consumer regions that have surfaced again over the issue of burden-
sharing regarding the reduction of Canada's GHG emissions.
Canada's abundant resource base, combined with a strong orientation towards securing market-driven exports to the United States,
has also deflected attention from exploring alternative energy
options (except for nuclear energy). In this perspective, our study
underscores the observation that energy riches do not necessarily
translate into strong capacity or successful energy policy.

Key Definitional and Theoretical Issues

The Nature of Energy Resources and Energy Policy

As figure 1.1 indicates, one of the theoretical roots for the book is published conceptual work on the nature of energy resources and resource
endowments and on the related domains of energy policy. Energy
policy as a whole refers to policies aimed at influencing and shaping
the supply of energy sources and fuels, demand for them by users of

energy, and, ever more importantly, the environmental impacts of energy use. Energy policy thus covers energy resource domains, sources, and fuels such as oil and natural gas, coal, hydroelectricity, nuclear energy, and a host of alternative or renewable sources such as biofuels, fuel cells, solar energy, wind power, and biomass, and also energy efficiency and conservation measures and activities. Energy policy also involves global, national, and regional politics where past and current conflicts over prices and security influence views of what future policy should and should not be.

Energy policy and its complex governance system seeks to influence behaviour at numerous stages of production and consumption, from research and development, exploration, and initial extraction, to processing, transportation, use in homes, public institutions, and commercial establishments, and the disposition, reduction, management, and remediation of wastes, effluents, and emissions. Finally, energy policy, at legislative and regulatory levels, involves the use of all the main policy instruments: regulation, persuasion or voluntary approaches, spending (mainly on science, technology, and innovation), and taxation.

After the 1980s and 1990s, when energy policy was dominated by the liberalization of energy markets and when energy prices were low or even declining in real terms, the first decade of the twenty-first century has ushered in a more complex array of energy concerns and interdependencies among countries and regions (Doern 2005; Helm 2003, 2005; Jaccard 2006).

Oil prices tripled and then fell by 50 per cent, energy security has loomed ever larger, and climate change and other aspects of sustainable development and environmental impacts have dramatically gained in prominence. The vast growing economies of China and India are making major demands on the global supply of energy fuels. New technologies offer opportunities for lower or non-carbon futures through renewable energy sources and production processes but also bring back the potential for nuclear power and second-generation reactors.

For developing countries, and indeed for much of the world, coal is by far the most plentiful fuel but also emits the most carbon. Oil is still what puts the 'geo' into the geopolitics of world energy, with the Iraq war and the struggle over Middle East supplies further escalating conflict in the post-9/11 world of terrorism and fears of terrorism, including energy terrorism. The oil sands of Alberta have become officially recognized as a Saudi Arabia–sized source of oil and related fuel reserves, now coveted by the United States as a new strategic source of energy security, especially since President Bush declared that the United States is 'addicted' to oil. Under President Obama, a serious interest in reducing oil emissions changes the dynamics in a major way.

In a nutshell, the new energy world is characterized by increasing tensions between the three goals of the energy magic triangle: energy security, environmental sustainability, and economic efficiency of supply. The *main current line of conflict runs between energy security and sustainability*, both of which have recently dominated the political agenda. Nevertheless, market forces both as drivers of industry change and as governance instruments remain a core component.

The current transformations of the energy arena are essentially driven by four factors, three of which have broader relevance for other economic sectors as well. First, a demand-supply squeeze (and associated price increases) and the environmental costs of a rapidly growing, energy-hungry global economy set a large part of the current energy agenda. However, the 2008–2009 global recession has also wreaked havoc.

Second, while technological change has perhaps been less prominent than in sectors such as telecommunications or financial services, it has nevertheless been instrumental in making small-scale and renewable forms of fuels and generation more accessible and competitive, which paved the way for a broader and potentially more sustainable palette of energy sources. Liquefaction technology has underpinned the rise of natural gas as a global energy source, in an increasingly internationalized energy market.

Indeed, and third, internationalization can be considered a prime force of change. To be sure, important elements of energy supply were 'globalized' long before the term had entered our everyday vocabulary, in particular the oil and coal trade. Yet a number of indicators point to a new scope and quality of internationalization that renders a closed, national-container perspective on energy policy more obsolete than ever. These indicators include the increase in cross-border trade of energy fuels, and dispatch of electricity and of services as part of more complex global, regional, and subregional supplier links, which include the electric and gas utilities; and the rapid integration of energy markets through mergers and acquisition on the company level and through the creation of cross-border, integrated markets as evident in Europe and North America.

Finally, the global liberalization and restructuring of infrastructure industries has profoundly affected the electricity and gas industries. Local and national monopolies have been replaced by open markets that reach across national borders. This transformation towards cross-border markets has opened new avenues for corporate and regulatory strategies: utility companies have engaged in vertical and horizontal mergers, and the EU, for example, is pushing for new supranational mechanisms to regulate the emerging European energy markets.

Multi-Level Governance and Multi-Level Regulatory Governance

Multi-level regulation involves interacting, reinforcing, and colliding rule making and governance at the international, national, sub-national (provincial, state, etc.), and city, local, and community levels or other connected and overlapping spatial realms (such as electricity grids). However, multi-level *regulatory* governance is a part of the even broader study of *multi-level governance* (Doern 2007; Wilks and Doern 2007).

At the heart of the multi-level governance concept is the dispersion of political authority across multiple centres as part of a larger recon-figuration of political authority (Grande and Pauly 2005). Multi-level governance is best defined as non-hierarchical, negotiated exchange between different actors across multiple, interdependent, and overlapping (functional) arenas or territorial levels (e.g., Bache and Flinders 2004; Hooghe and Marks 2003; Peters and Pierre 2001). It explicitly rec-ognizes the participation of non-state, private actors in public policy-making, and it includes informal dimensions of decision-making.

Multi-level governance (MLG) originated in the study of the Euro-pean Union as a novel type of multi-level polity that is less than a state but more than a complex international organization or regime (Marks, Hooghe, and Blank 1996). However, MLG has more broadly emerged as a distinct subject, largely because the conventional approaches to understanding politics – national politics, comparative politics, and international relations among states – simply do not adequately capture the kinds of politics and governance extant in the early twenty-first-century world (Bache and Flinders 2004; Doern and Johnson 2006; Hooghe and Marks 2003).

Multi-level governance is part of a debate that seeks to go beyond existing concepts of statehood and of political authority, by overcom-ing distinctions built around the nation-state container: distinctions between national and international, between public and private, and between formal and informal institutions (Eberlein and Grande 2005, 147). New forms of governance identified under the lead of the MLG label transcend these established dichotomies.

These governance features are now increasingly identified and discussed in the international or global governance literature, especially in patterns of transnational policymaking and regulation (e.g., Braithwaite and Drahos 2000; Held et al. 1999; Koenig-Archibugi and Zürn 2006).

However, it was indeed the formation and expansion of the European Union as a novel multi-level architecture of governance that has been the critical catalyst to think about multi-level governance on its own terms rather than as national politics, comparative politics, and international relations.

The North American Free Trade Agreement has had some similar effects in North America but obviously not on the same scale or depth of political-institutional change (Hoberg 2002; Hufbauer and Schott 2005). This is because, in terms of depth of regional integration, the EU clearly has strong supranational features, in particular regarding the supremacy of EU law, including effective dispute resolution. NAFTA, in this regard, remains a more intergovernmental arrangement – notwithstanding the quasi-constitutional entrenchment of free trade principles (also see below and Clarkson, chapter 4).

The concept of multi-level regulatory governance must also grapple with the notion of regulation as a core policy instrument (along with taxation, spending, and persuasion). One basic definition of regulation is that it is a rule of behaviour backed up by the sanctions of the state (Doern et al. 1999). However, such rules are variously expressed through laws, delegated legislation (or the 'regs'), guidelines, codes, and standards, and thus there are levels and many types of rule-making even in the core definitions of regulation.

Guidelines, voluntary agreements, and memoranda of understanding, as well as codes, for example, are often seen as realms of 'soft law' or rule-making in the shadow of the law. Multi-level regulation also includes complex systems of emissions trading where challenges arise in combining market and democratic systems of legitimization (Baldwin 2008). Multi-level regulation also involves rules that are imbedded in the transfer of funds from one level of government to another, so-called conditional grants or levered-partnered funding. Regulation is a key instrument of policymaking, but it is, in the above ways, increasingly linked to the use of complex mixes of instruments including spending, but also taxation (rules about revenue collection from individuals and corporations) and persuasion (Eliadis, Hill, and Howlett 2005).

The analysis of multi-level energy regulatory governance must also be cognizant of the institutional forms it takes. Such regulatory regimes increasingly involve a series of joint actions between the public and private sectors, including various kinds of self-regulation such as in North American electricity grids and in the use of voluntary codes (Braithwaite and Drahos 2000; Jordana and Levi-Faur 2004).

A focus on regulatory governance recognizes that regulation has to be conceived as rule-making processes, outputs, compliance, and outcomes that can emerge from top-down, bottom-up, and negotiated processes within the state, among states, among provinces or Länder and cities, and among private, economic, and social interests. Thus, multi-level regulatory governance is less broad than multi-level governance overall, but it remains complex and cannot be simply reduced to 'government' or 'public policy.'

Rooted mainly in a political science and public policy discipline, the book is premised on a recognition that multi-level energy regulatory governance has in one sense always been an issue in any kind of political system. It has certainly always been a central feature of federalism in countries such as Germany and Canada where challenges regarding both regulatory competition and cooperation among national and subnational governments is well documented (Burgess 2000). Whereas it was once common to think of regulatory levels mainly in terms of federal and sub-national jurisdictions, it is now important to layer in the international levels of regulation and dispute settlement both in trade and in sectoral realms.

It is also important, as in this book, to refer to local or city-metropolitan rule-making where front-line and spatial/regional competences and jurisdiction are crucial and increasingly linked to all the other senior levels of regulation and governance. For example, in Germany, as the chapter 14 by Mez shows, the progressive take-up of alternative energy sources was in part begun at local levels and also made more feasible by requirements and actions by municipalities to identify sites in local planning where wind power would be allowed to be installed.

Furthermore, it is crucial to incorporate the allocation of authority 'sideways' and 'outwards' from the central state, to private actors who take on public functions. As Theobald documents in his chapter 10 on

German energy regulation, private energy companies and industry associations played an important role in a self-regulatory arrangement that governed access to the electricity and gas networks.

To this can be added new realms of Aboriginal governance: in Canada, Aboriginal communities are granted legal standing and are constituencies with which provinces and the federal government need to negotiate, notably in terms of northern energy development. In addition, rule-making as well as 'levels' arise from shared public and private regulation, self-regulation, and new definitions of space and territory (such as eco-systems), which produce rules and levels that do not obey conventional national, provincial or Länder or international, and local boundaries and jurisdictions (Doern 2005).

Regulatory coordination problems among departments and agencies of a single government such as the national government are not technically an issue of 'levels' of government but to most citizens it may seem much like a levels problem, simply because citizens do not always know that they may be dealing with one government. Internal fragmentation and lack of coordination can lead to turf wars and policy inconsistencies, which in turn shape policy processes and outcomes. Thus issues, decisions, and processes vary in how competition, energy, environment, trade, and health regulators interact within one level of government on energy matters.

Often these are collisions and interactions as well among so-called sectoral regulators and horizontal framework regulators at national, sub-national, and supranational levels (EU, NAFTA). As we shall see below, German energy policymaking has formally been anchored more in its central economics ministry rather than in an energy department, whereas Canada's energy policy nationally has been focused in a national energy department and in sectoral energy regulatory bodies.

Multiple levels of rule-making and the potential and actual coordination and congestion challenges they create are seen by many economic interests as inhibitors of economic growth, efficiency, and innovation in global markets and in 'internal markets.' But such levels are also arenas and avenues to enhance democracy, to experiment with new solutions, and to pursue health, safety, environmental, and fairness-related public interest purposes (Palast, Oppenheim, and MacGregor 2003). They can also potentially increase or confuse basic aspects of democratic accountability, trust, transparency, and legitimacy (Doern and Gattinger 2003; Flinders 2002).

Neo-Institutionalist Theory

Our conceptual perspective of multi-level regulatory governance, further developed in the three-part framework of complexity, coordination, and capacity, is anchored in neo-institutionalist theory (for an overview, see Peters 2005).

The key tenet of neo-institutionalist theory is that formal and informal institutions are rule systems that mediate processes and outcomes of political behaviour and policymaking. Rational choice institutionalism views institutions as intervening variables, offering incentives and imposing constraints on actors in pursuit of exogenous preferences. Sociological institutionalism considers institutions rather as independent variables, shaping or even constituting actors' preferences and normative orientations. Historical institutionalism is concerned with how institutional configurations emerge from historical processes (at critical junctures) and are sustained through sequencing and lock-in effects, resulting in path-dependent trajectories (Hall and Taylor 1996; Lowndes 1996).

We view institutions primarily as intervening variables that act as incentives and constraints for the strategic behaviour of actors. However, we also recognize that powerful norms such as the 'need to protect the Earth's atmosphere' can reorient or even constitute distinct policy preferences. We thus draw on these different traditions in our analysis of how institutional legacies and configurations in our two jurisdictions constitute, shape, and mediate actors' orientations and strategies in energy policy. We view both interest-based strategies and rule-based orientations as contributing to observed policy processes and outcomes.

We are aware of the limits of neo-institutionalist analysis. As stressed earlier, we give equal weight to the substantive or material dimension of policymaking when explaining processes and outcomes. Furthermore, institutionalist approaches have been criticized for their inability to explain or understand change, unless the notion of major crisis is introduced. They seem better able to explain why change may be difficult and why inertia and stability (equilibrium) are strong features of policy and governance. As recognized in more recent work in this tradition, however, change is not necessarily paradigmatic or radical. It may be more cumulative and layered. This more incrementalist perspective allows analysts to incorporate gradual transitions over time in an institutionalist framework (Streek and Thelen 2005).

Our approach in this book by no means fully addresses or solves the problem of dealing with institutional change, or resolving the thorny question of the relative causal effect of institutions in determining policy outcomes. But key aspects of change and continuity in the two countries' energy governance are certainly traced and related to institutional configurations and substantive structures and properties. The dynamics of change and continuity is made more understandable by using a multi-level regulatory governance lens. Both change and continuity are also more likely to be addressed by examining the evolution of the two countries in their regional settings through the complexity, coordination, and capacity framework.

Mapping the German and Canadian Multi-Level Energy Regulatory Regimes in the Context of Their Political Systems

As a final contextual analytical step, we now present an initial mapping of the basics of the German and then the Canadian multi-level energy regulatory regimes. Regulatory regimes and their goals, procedures, policies, and outcomes are shaped by two factors: the structural, substantive features of the sector in a given jurisdiction, and the broader institutional and political economy of the two countries in the context of their political systems.

The German Multi-Level Energy Regulatory Regime

Germany is poorly endowed with natural resources and is therefore highly dependent on foreign energy sources (International Energy Agency 2007; Jochem, Gruber, and Mannsbart 1996). It imports about 30 per cent of the coal it consumes and 82 per cent of natural gas (International Energy Agency 2007, 171). Imported oil represents about 40 per cent of its total primary energy supply. Accordingly, its core energy-industry politics domestically are not driven by oil industry producers as in Canada, but rather, as several chapters show, by electricity and gas business interests, and increasingly also by renewable energy interests. This key difference was also highlighted in conference discussions when Canadian observers were puzzled by the relative success of Germany's environmental sustainability strategy. It became clear that Canada's oil industry is a much more formidable political obstacle to policy changes towards greater sustainability than the German coal and utility lobby.

The government's decision to phase out nuclear power by 2025, among other factors, is projected to result in a further increase in Germany's reliance on imports of coal and natural gas, with the largest share of its foreign supplies coming from Russia.

As a result of these dependencies, Germany's energy policies put a primary emphasis on security of supply. A key part of Germany's energy security policy centres on measures to develop domestic fuels (such as coal and lignite), renewables, energy end-use efficiency, and also, very crucially, on fostering good relations with its energy supplier neighbours and exporters.

Germany is a densely populated and industrialized country in the heart of Europe that is exposed to a high level of environmental risk, including risk from energy production. In contrast to Canada, it does not have regions that are major producers of oil and natural gas, and that defend interests diverging from those of consumer regions. However, Germany has had a small version of producer versus consumer regional contest in matters of domestic coal production and use. Vocal environmental movements had fought against the expansion of nuclear energy technology since the 1970s, and nuclear power was rejected by the broad public after the Chernobyl disaster in 1986. This constellation has helped to foster broadly based environmental sensitivities and advocacy, resulting, inter alia, in sustained public support for renewable energy sources and climate change policies (Jänicke and Weidner 1997; Rüdig 2003; Weidner and Eberlein, chapter 12).

The difficult process of German unification, when the East German regions rejoined the German nation state, also had some implications for the energy-environment nexus. The disastrous environmental legacy of communism highlighted the urgency of environmental measures, and unification extended the strict West German norms and rules to the East. At the same time, the rapid deindustrialization of East Germany conveniently helped a united Germany to meet its ambitious Kyoto emission-reduction targets, as many outdated coal-fired plants in the East had to shut down (chapter 12 by Weidner and Eberlein).

Given the institutionalist perspective adopted in this book, it becomes crucial to understand the broader political system and its key institutionalist features that shape energy policy and governance. In the German case, these are (1) 'cooperative federalism,' including strong municipal self-government, (2) coalition governments, (3) the strong role of organized interests under sectoral corporatism, and (4) the heavy reliance on competition law and courts as opposed to sector-specific economic regulation (Green and Paterson 2005; Sturm and Pehle 2005). Finally, and crucially, (5) the domestic institutional context is increasingly being influenced and reshaped by Germany's integration in the EU policymaking framework (Dyson and Goetz 2003).

COOPERATIVE FEDERALISM AND LOCAL GOVERNMENT

One core element of the German political system is the post-war constitution (Basic Law of 1948), under which Germany continues a peculiar kind of cooperative and intermeshed federal system of government that in its essence goes back to the diplomatic representation of powerful individual states under the Imperial Diet (Lehmbruch 1989). This 'joint' or 'interlocking' federal system of government (Scharpf, Reissert, and Schnabel 1976) stands opposite the 'dual federalism' found in Canada. German federalism puts strong emphasis on joint decision-making between the federal level and the executives of the sixteen Länder – the regional states of the German federation. There are two key linkages between the states and the federal level, or Bund: first, the representation and participation of states in federal legislation through the upper house of the German parliament, the Bundesrat, whose consent is required to pass about two-thirds of all federal legislation; second, as a rule, the Länder governments implement federal legislation, enjoying discretion in the execution. This 'interlocking' nature of German federalism implies that in many regulatory areas federal legislation will have to accommodate regional concerns, and that regulatory implementation will as a rule be under the control of Länder governments, which, for example, limits federal powers over the design and setting up of regulatory agencies.

Thus, the fact that, unlike in Canada, energy policy legislation in Germany is planned and adopted at the federal level, under the guiding responsibility of the Federal Ministry of Economics, should not be interpreted as a centralization of powers. In addition to legislative input in federal energy policy, Länder ministries or regulatory departments have, for example, traditionally supervised the legal obligation of local and regional monopoly suppliers in their jurisdiction to supply household consumers, and they regulated household electricity tariffs. Länder authorities also maintain local anti-trust agencies or competition bureaus to monitor the abuse of monopoly power by energy (or any other) companies operating within state boundaries.

Furthermore, it should be noted that, under the federal framework, Länder governments can initiate individual legislation and programs to promote energy efficiency, conservation, and the use of renewable energy sources, on the basis of their extensive environmental policy powers.

The territorial picture of energy governance also needs to recognize the strong position of municipalities in the federal edifice. Although the municipalities are technically a part of, and subordinate to, the state governments, they enjoy important powers of self-government, based on the constitutional guarantee of 'municipal self-administration,' which includes the right to manage infrastructure services (notably energy, water, and transport). Local authorities collect concession fees for granting right of way for transmission and distribution grids and pipes. And municipally owned and run energy distributors (*Stadtwerke*) traditionally play an important role in the electricity and gas industries. Local authorities exert significant political influence on the federal stage through their *Land* governments.

These core features tend to weaken the central policymaking capacity of the federal government, as it needs to accommodate regional and local interests. However, the territorial distribution of power has also been a source of innovation as local and regional authorities have been often successfully experimenting with alternative energy sources and policies (Monstadt 2004). Local utilities have been, for example at the forefront of innovative combined heat and power (CHP) projects designed to increase energy efficiency. The bottom-up development, injection, and diffusion of environmental policies from the local and *Land* level (in)to the federal arena is an essential factor in accounting for Germany's relative success as an environmental pioneer.

The Federal Ministry of the Environment, Nature Conservation, and Nuclear Safety, which was first established in direct response to the Chernobyl nuclear disaster in 1986, is the administrative sponsor of environmental policies in the federal Cabinet. It has responsibilities for environmental policies, climate change mitigation, and nuclear facilities and radioactive waste disposal.

More often than not, its positions diverge from the policies advocated by the Federal Ministry of Economics, which holds the energy portfolio and is traditionally close to industry and producer interests. This inter-ministerial turf war intensifies and makes a coherent federal policy even more difficult to emerge, if the two ministries are headed by ministers drawn from different political parties, as was typically the case under coalition governments. This tension has been a constant feature of federal politics at the energy-environment nexus. The Chancellor's Office plays an important role in adjudicating between conflicting positions; sometimes detailed coalition agreements provide for resolutions.

COALITION GOVERNMENTS

Indeed, a further constraint on executive federal policymaking results from the fact that German politics functions under a system of proportional representation and thus the federal government is typically a coalition government. This engenders compromise and consensus-seeking and often gives disproportionate influence to smaller parties required to form a winning coalition.

This constellation recently resulted in a party coalition that included the German Green Party, which was in charge of the Ministry of the Environment. This particular Red-Green coalition (in power from 1998 till 2005) produced key energy decisions, including the decision to phase out the use of nuclear energy, and helped underpin the strong environmental orientation of recent energy and environment policies in Germany.

Because of these factors, as Weidner and Eberlein show in chapter 12, Germany was far faster off the mark than Canada in greenhouse gas emission reductions and overall climate change policy. Under the Kyoto Protocol, Germany voluntarily took the largest share (almost 75 per cent) of the EU-15 reduction burden, by committing to a 21 per cent reduction of CO_2 emissions compared to 1990 levels by the period 2008–2012. In 2000 a National Climate Change Protection Program was introduced. It included an eco-tax, the promotion of co-generation and renewables, fuel switching, energy efficiency improvements in buildings, and industrial voluntary agreements. By 2004, CO_2 emissions had been cut by 17.4 per cent already. The decision in 2002 to phase out nuclear power was significant, since nuclear power at the time covered 30 per cent of electricity generation and 13 per cent of primary energy supply.

SECTORAL CORPORATISM

Of crucial importance to the political economy of German energy governance is the role of powerful energy companies and their industry associations that are granted privileged access to government policy formulation in the sector. As indicated above, the Federal Ministry of Economics traditionally views itself as sponsor of the energy industry, and there are strong ties between several Länder governments and large energy utilities that are based in the regions. As stressed above, oil energy interests per se are not at the core of Germany's energy industry lobby, as they are in Canada. National ownership of energy industries or *dirigiste* state intervention into energy markets never played a role in Germany. Energy supply and use was, in principle, left to market forces (Jochem, Gruber, Mannsbart 1996; McGowan 1996). In practice, however, government intervention was widespread, and there has been a long-standing consensus between the government and producer industries about the main directions of energy policy. In the 1960s this entailed the development of nuclear power technology, and later the protection of the domestic coal industry.

At first sight, the fragmented structure of the electricity and gas industry in particular, reflecting the historical heritage of decentralized federalism, seems to suggest that industry influence might be mitigated by fragmentation. As a matter of fact, in contrast to centralized and public monopolies (such as the large hydro companies of Canadian provinces), Germany's electricity system has traditionally been characterized by a mix of private and public ownership and by fragmentation, with over nine hundred electric utilities on three different territorial levels, the majority of which (some eight hundred) are municipal utilities (Ortwein 1996; Sturm and Wilks 1997). Prior to liberalization, the national territory was divided into regional and local supply monopolies, exempted from general anti-trust rules.

However, through various capital market links and cross-ownerships (the energy variant of the Deutschland AG*), there was a much higher degree of concentration than the fragmented structure suggested. And the three biggest market players alone accounted for 65 per cent of electric power sales. Also, private producer interests were strongly intermingled with state and municipal bodies that played an active ownership and/or management role.

---

*Deutschland AG is the tight network (of cross-ownership, in particular) of finance, banks, and industry in post-war Germany. Cross-ownerships would protect German industry from foreign influence/takeover, often as a short-hand for 'Rhenish capitalism.'

The intermeshing of public and private interests ensured that the formal oversight by Länder authorities never constituted a regulatory threat to the flow of monopoly profits. Against this background, the entire electricity industry was often regarded as 'an economic and political power cartel' (Mez 1997, 231). Thus, the industry not only enjoyed monopoly protection from competition but also benefited from exclusive access to political decision-making in sector governance.

Typical for German-style sectoral corporatism, industry associations were granted a major role in the governance of the sector (Padgett 1990), in exchange for delivering on the broad energy policy goals such as energy security, or the support of domestic coal under generous subsidy arrangement. Industry agreements between the peak association of electric utilities and the association of industrial energy producers and consumers, for example, would set policy and foster sector cohesion. The Federal Ministry of Economics would see its role more as a sponsor and partner of the energy industry rather than its regulator. More broadly, the federal government prefers to negotiate voluntary agreements with the industry. This is true not only for the nuclear phase-out. Another good example is the voluntary commitment agreement on climate change, negotiated between the government and the Federal Association of German Industry (BDI) in 1995. However, as developed in chapter 12 by Weidner and Eberlein, voluntary approaches yielded disappointing results in climate policy and have lost in importance.

Market liberalization in 1998 destabilized some key elements of these arrangements for the energy market (Bartle et al. 2002; Coen and Héritier 2006; Eising 1999). The new competitive order undermined sector solidarity between local utilities and the larger energy companies. Market opening triggered a wave of mergers and acquisitions. The number of market players has been reduced significantly, and after the mega-merger of E.on and Ruhrgas in 2003 (forming the biggest supplier of gas and electricity in the EU), the electricity and gas markets have been more closely integrated than ever under a tight oligopoly of four internationally active energy companies: E.ON, RWE, EnBW, and Vattenfall (see chapter 10 by Theobald).

Yet the regulatory governance of liberalized energy markets was, until recently, characterized by surprising continuity. In tune with corporatist traditions, industry associations governed the post-liberalization access of new market entrants to the electricity grid and gas pipelines under voluntary 'Associations' Agreements' (Eberlein 2000).

The federal ministry deliberately stayed on the sidelines of market consolidation and avoided regulatory intervention – but it actively supported the E.ON-Ruhrgas merger, presumably to foster a national energy champion able to thrive in international supply markets, thus enhancing energy security.

COMPETITION LAW AND *ORDNUNGSPOLITIK*

This regulatory gap reflects yet another key feature of regulatory energy governance – the reliance on broad competition rules and court adjudication rather than on sector-specific regulation. This is, more broadly, a reflection of an economic governance approach ('the social market economy') that rejects direct state intervention but insists on government protection of the ordering principles of a market economy (*Ordnungspolitik*), while also allowing for the compensation of undesirable effects of markets by social policy.

In contrast to Canada, Germany has no administrative tradition of establishing sectoral energy (and other) regulators, such as a German equivalent of Canada's National Energy Board (Döhler 2002). Energy markets in Germany were liberalized by simply abolishing the antitrust exemption for the energy sector, but without further structural or regulatory measures such as vertical de-integration.

Instead, building on the tradition of limiting state intervention to uphold the ordering principles of a market economy, Germany's competition regulator, the Federal Cartel Office, assisted by the Länder competition bureaus, was to monitor compliance with competition rules, especially in regard to grid access. But as a rather small and generalist agency, the Cartel Office lacks the necessary resources and expertise to comprehensively monitor individual, complex markets and to directly enforce orders. As a result, many regulatory issues arising in the liberalized market had to be settled in the courts, stalling market competition and favouring market incumbents over new entrants (Eberlein 2000).

It was only under the pressure of EU legislation that the federal government finally established sector regulation in 2005, under the auspices of the new, multi-sector Bundesnetzagentur (Federal Network Agency), whose mandate in the energy sector is limited to regulating grid access and setting of grid access tariffs, as Theobald further explains in his chapter. It will be difficult for this regulatory agency to reinvigorate, by virtue of network access regulation alone, the moribund state of competition in the German market.

EUROPEAN UNION INFLUENCE

From a broader, multi-level perspective, EU-level momentum and influence has indeed been crucial for the more recent trajectory of German energy regulatory governance (Bulmer et al. 2003). More broadly, it is crucial to fully understand the implications of sovereignty transfers to the supranational EU level for the direction of German policy in many sectors (Dyson and Goetz 2003; Featherstone and Radaelli 2003). Under the European treaties and their sweeping interpretation through European Court of Justice rulings, the principle of the free movement of goods and services in a single European market essentially overrides national 'obstacles' to free trade, unless the industry is explicitly exempted or domestic constraints on free trade can be shown to protect key safety concerns with regard, for example, to health. In many sectors, the EU typically pushes market opening and integration by way of binding legislation, in the form of so-called directives that need to be implemented by member states, although national authorities enjoy some discretion in how they implement the goals stated in the directive. But in single market legislation, the EU can also pass regulations that are directly applicable and enforceable in the domestic context. While EU legislation is often the result of intense contestation and negotiation between powerful member states and supranational interests, it is fair to say that EU legislation and policy constitutes a fundamental constraint on domestic policy, not least in energy policy.

One cornerstone of EU energy policy is indeed the intent to complete market liberalization and to create an integrated European market for electricity and gas, as further discussed in chapters 6 and 7 by Froschauer and Cameron. EU pressures for reform were a major factor, if not the crucial one, in Germany's (and France's) decision to liberalize energy markets (Eising 2002).

Furthermore, as Cameron discusses in chapter 7, the EU framework entails rules for the domestic governance of energy markets, and the requirement to establish sectoral regulators, which the EU seeks to network throughout Europe, with the intent to harmonize national regulatory practices, in the absence of a federal energy regulator on the EU level (Eberlein 2005). As noted above, EU legislation forced Germany to adopt a regulatory-agency model of economic governance for the electricity and gas industry – a model that is alien to the competition-policy culture and the corporatist tradition of government-industry relations. As a matter of fact, this new independent-agency type of regulatory infrastructure may contribute over time to an erosion of some corporatist elements of the Germany regulatory framework. Also, EU-level competition policy increasingly seeks to monitor and enforce compliance of national authorities with Single Market rules in the energy market, which may affect the national sponsorship of domestic energy companies. Finally, as chapter 13 by Ziesing shows, German climate change policy (and environmental policy more largely) has also been 'Europeanized.' The EU emission trading system sets mandatory, albeit broad, guidelines for the allocation of emission permits to German companies.

All these examples illustrate how deeply national systems of energy governance and regulation are penetrated and shaped by EU influence.

More details of the German multi-level energy regulatory regime are discussed in the chapters to follow. But it is sufficient here to stress in summary that Germany's inherent absence of an abundant oil and gas resource base compelled it to search for wider energy options. The 1986 Chernobyl disaster profoundly discredited the nuclear option and accelerated the pursuit of alternative energy supplies and policies. It would also appear that energy policy debate and then consensus was somewhat easier to achieve in Germany than in Canada. This is not only because German politics is generally more driven by consensus. It is also because of the broad strength of environmental interests, including a coalition green party in power and in charge of the environmental ministry, and because energy policy was lodged constitutionally and in other respects with the federal government.

Finally, Germany has had no major producer regions of oil and natural gas to oppose the environmental turn of federal politics. At the same time, it is important to recognize that federal policymaking capacity in Germany, while higher than in Canada, is severely constrained by federalism, the strong role of organized economic interests, and increasingly by EU policymaking.

The Canadian Multi-Level Energy Regulatory Regime

With the exception of being a federal state as well, Canada as a jurisdiction is 'most different' from Germany in all key institutional features of the political system.

FEDERALISM
Even the Canadian federal system is strikingly different from German-style interlocking federalism. Federal and provincial competences,

bodies, and arenas are separated under a dual federalism system, as further spelled out below. There is, for example, no provincial implementation of federal legislation. The upper house or second chamber, the Senate, is appointed, not elected and can only nominally be considered to represent provinces and regions. In contrast to the German Bundesrat, the Canadian Senate does not provide institutional access for regional interests to the federal decision-making arena, and there is no other institutional mechanism to link and reconcile federal and provincial politics. Rather, intergovernmental relations take the form of direct federal-provincial and interprovincial negotiations. This arena of non-intermediated 'federal-provincial diplomacy' is combined with partisan party politics, unmitigated by the compromise requirements of coalition government, as found in Germany, to produce so-called executive federalism in energy policy and other political disputes (Doern and Gattinger 2003).

WESTMINSTER PARLIAMENTARY AND MAJORITY GOVERNMENT
Indeed, Canada's national governance structure, in contrast to Germany's, is centred in a system of Cabinet-parliamentary government where majority governments are historically the norm, although less so in recent years. Under a first-past-the-post electoral system, smaller parties such as the Green Party stand little chance to gain significant parliamentary representation and can be dispensed with in the formation of a government. Policy conflicts are fought along strongly partisan-political lines by a small number of large parties, with little regard to minority opinions and little need to compromise. Depending on the electoral base of the party in government, certain provinces and regions may be sorely underrepresented or overrepresented in federal policies.

PLURALIST BUSINESS LOBBYING
In contrast to the corporatist arrangements in Germany, representation of Canadian interests is characterized by more direct lobbying of the energy industry (and other) business. The regional concentration of the oil and gas business has given industry representation and influence a distinctly regional overtone, adding to the conflictual character of federal energy policymaking, as further developed below.

REGULATION AND COMPETITION POLICY
Competition policy and regulation is mainly a federal responsibility, though the provinces can still build barriers and thus lessen competition

in Canada's internal market. Energy policy was never overtly assigned to the Canadian Competition Bureau, as was the case in Germany where, as we have seen, there has not been a national sectoral regulator until recently. Energy regulation has thus not been constrained by concerns about the proper role of government intervention (as in Germany) but rather by federal-provincial conflicts over jurisdiction.

REGIONAL INTEGRATION UNDER NAFTA

Trade policy is a federal responsibility but also depends on some reasonable level of provincial agreement when trade agreements include subjects under provincial jurisdiction. As indicated earlier and developed more fully in chapters 4 (Clarkson) and 6 (Froschauer), NAFTA is a much less legalized and developed framework than the supranational EU. NAFTA does not produce supranational legislation or impose specific regulatory institutions or procedures. However, as Clarkson's analysis in chapter 4 makes clear, free trade agreements can severely limit domestic (energy) sovereignty as well: the Canada-U.S. Free Trade Agreement and the later NAFTA agreement, which added Mexico, were centrally based on a core energy bargain between the oil and gas producing provinces of Canada (Alberta in particular) and the federal government (and the United States). It ensured energy pro-market free trade and pro-rated security of supply for the United States. For Alberta, as the chapter by Clarkson also shows, the initial Canada-U.S. free trade agreement provided a guarantee that the previous 1980–4 interventionist federal National Energy Program (NEP) could never occur again. It virtually 'constitutionalized' North American energy free trade between Canada and the United States (but not between Mexico and the United States, where Mexico insisted on more protection for its largely state-owned oil and gas industry [Hufbauer and Schott 2005]).

It is important to further clarify how Canadian energy policy (in contrast with Germany's) has been forged in a federal constitution where most of the jurisdiction over energy policy resides with the provinces which own most of the reserves of oil and natural gas or of hydro power and have primary regulatory jurisdiction. Federal jurisdiction centres mainly on interprovincial energy trade, energy in the northern territories, and energy imports and exports. Federal jurisdiction is the primary one for nuclear energy safety and also for uranium and international nuclear proliferation. The main federal authorities involved in energy policy are departments such as Natural Resources

Canada and Environment Canada, between which turf and policy wars are the norm rather than the exception (Doern and Gattinger 2003; VanNijnatten and MacDonald 2003), and the two main energy sectoral regulators, the National Energy Board and the Nuclear Safety Commission. But, of crucial importance, each province and territory also has a separate sectoral energy regulator as well as environmental regulator, making up a total of over thirty 'energy' regulatory bodies.

When environmental and other framework rules are added to the policy and regulatory mix, the jurisdictional split and overlap is even more complex. Environmental policy is de facto an area of concurrent powers between the federal government and the provinces, with both providing environmental assessment and legislation on air and water, and both needing each other to ensure ultimate efficacy on climate change commitments.

Canada's energy policy has gone through four main phases of evolution and change (Brownsey 2007; Doern 2005; Doern and Toner 1985). From the 1950s to the late 1970s, federal energy policy was broadly market oriented and also geared to such nation-building activities as pipeline construction, nuclear reactor technology, and northern development. The period from 1980 to 1984, following the oil crisis of 1979, was characterized by massive federal intervention via the Trudeau Liberals' National Energy Program (NEP), a policy strongly opposed by energy interests in Alberta and Western Canada overall. From 1985 to about 2001, federal energy policy was decidedly pro-market but augmented by the discourse, if the not the actions, of sustainable development. Since 2001, federal policy has taken on what appeared to be stronger commitments to climate change but also strong federal support for oil and gas exports (see more below).

Canada's internal energy politics has always been influenced profoundly by conflicts between major energy *producer* regions/provinces (and related energy business interests whose centre of power has been in the oil and gas sector and now in particular, the oil sands sector) and other more populous consumer regions, provinces, and interests (especially Ontario and Quebec). These clashes have been especially important when energy prices have risen suddenly and sharply, as they did in 1973 and 1979 and again in recent years. They have also surfaced in a very central way over Canada's climate change policies and the issue of burden sharing among provinces and their main industries (Doern 2005). As chapter 5 by Mez and Doern shows, inter-regional pressures also have arisen over nuclear energy. Canada's CANDU reactor was developed through federal support for research and development, but actual reactor sales and use have been overwhelmingly confined to Ontario, Canada's main nuclear province (Bratt 2006; Doern, Dorman, and Morrison 2001).

As stressed above, Canada's energy industry business lobby has been centred primarily in oil and gas, in keeping with the dominance that oil and gas has in overall Canadian energy production (Brownsey 2006; Krywulak 2007). Seventy-five per cent of energy production comes from the oil and gas sector, and in 2005, of the total of 2.5 million barrels per day (bd), 1.36 million bd were from conventional oil and 1.14 million bd were from the oil sands (Brownsey 2007). Atlantic Canada offshore oil amounted to about 313,000 bd. Production from the Alberta oil sands looms ever larger and will soon surpass conventional oil. In addition, Alberta accounts for about 77 per cent of Canada's natural gas production.

The oil and gas industry overall is very much Alberta-centred, with extremely strong links to the Alberta provincial government, where the governing Conservative Party has been dominant for decades. The oil and gas lobby group – the Canadian Association of Petroleum Producers (CAPP) – is based in Calgary, Alberta, as is the main national energy regulator, the National Energy Board (NEB).

The Canadian energy business lobby is also characterized by divisions between powerful multinational oil companies (the majority U.S. foreign owned) and the more numerous smaller oil and gas companies, which tend to operate at the exploration phase of oil and gas development. Core links to the U.S. energy industry lobby are thus built in within Canada's energy politics, all the more so as the U.S. government and American multinational oil firms have their eye firmly on Alberta's oil sands as a key part of current and future strategic energy supply for the United States. The ever-growing level of Canadian natural gas exports to the United States also ensures a central U.S. market and lobbying presence in Canada's internal energy industry politics.

Canadian energy policy and regulation is also very much influenced by the different energy endowments of its diverse regions and provinces. As chapter 9 by Pineau shows, provinces such as Quebec, Manitoba, and British Columbia have major hydroelectric resources, whereas Alberta has oil and gas riches. Moreover, it is important to note that Canada has very little interprovincial electricity trade or east-west connecting grids. Provinces typically have greater grid and trade links with immediate subregional U.S. border states.

When one adds the international level to the energy regulatory governance picture, bilateral relations with the United States are dominant. As chapter 4 by Clarkson makes clear, the United States has seen Canada historically as its hinterland supplier of oil and gas, all the more so now that the vast Alberta oil sands have now been established as officially confirmed and recognized reserves.

Canada-U.S. energy relations were once characterized by U.S. protectionist policies, but for the last three decades they have been dominated by guaranteed policies and rules about free trade and secure trade. For its part, Canadian policy (with the brief exception of the 1980–4 NEP) has needed U.S. energy markets, U.S. energy capital, and often U.S. energy regulatory approval before key energy projects could proceed.

In recent years, the extent of cross-border energy interdependence has increased in several ways, including the growing application of U.S. rules by the Federal Energy Regulatory Commission (FERC) to Canadian gas and electricity markets, the need to better manage the reliability of North American electricity grids, and the need to have Canadian climate change policies and actions or lack of action take into account the fact that the United States was not a Kyoto signatory and thus its industries had a comparative economic advantage over Canadian firms, which were being asked (albeit very gradually) to comply with Canada's Kyoto signatory obligations.

Conclusions

This chapter has introduced and previewed the key issues, context, and core concepts of the German and Canadian energy multi-level regulatory governance comparison. It has first set out the main definitional and theoretical underpinnings of the analysis, centred on the general nature of energy policy, national and regional multi-level energy governance and regulation regimes, and neo-institutional theory. It then profiled the nature and evolution of the German and Canadian energy governance and regulatory regimes anchored in the different core structures of the energy business lobby in each country.

The discussion in this chapter represent the editors' views on key contextual features and factors in global, German, and Canadian energy policy and governance over the last two decades. However, the authors whose analyses follow have much more to say on the multilevel regulatory governance realms they examine, and of course, each has individual views about German and Canadian energy policies and regulatory governance.

We examine in much greater detail in our conclusions in chapter 15 our triad of analytical themes (complexity, coordination, and capacity) only briefly introduced here. They are essential to giving more depth to the understanding of energy regulatory continuity and change. They are also crucial in ensuring that multi-level energy regulatory governance is anchored not only in political institutions but also in the substantive problems of energy supply, demand, and use in national, regional, and global contexts.

REFERENCES

Bache, Ian, and M. Flinders, eds. 2004. *Multi-level governance*. Oxford: Oxford University Press.

Baldwin, Robert. 2008. Regulation lite: The rise of emissions trading. *Regulation and Governance* 1:1–23.

Bartle, Ian, Markus M. Müller, Roland Sturm, and Stephen Wilks. 2002. *The regulatory state: Britain and Germany compared*. London: Anglo-German Foundation for the Study of Industrial Society.

Braithwaite, John, and Peter Drahos. 2000. *Global business regulation*. Cambridge: Cambridge University Press.

Bratt, Duane. 2006. *The politics of CANDU exports*. Toronto: University of Toronto Press.

Brownsey, Keith. 2006. Canadian energy policy: Supply, sustainability and a policy vacuum. In *How Ottawa spends 2006–2007: In from the cold; The Tory rise and the Liberal demise*, ed. Bruce Doern, 73–94. Montreal and Kingston: McGill-Queen's University Press.

– 2007. Energy shift: Canadian energy policy under the Harper Conservatives. In *How Ottawa Spends 2007–2008: The Harper Conservatives; Climate of Change*, ed. Bruce Doern, 143–60. Montreal and Kingston: McGill-Queen's University Press.

Bulmer, Simon, David Dolowitz, Peter Humphreys, and Stephen A. Padgett. 2003. Electricity and telecommunications: Fit for the European Union? In *Germany, Europe, and the politics of constraint*, ed. Kenneth Dyson and Klaus Goetz, 119–32. Oxford: Oxford University Press for the British Academy, Proceedings of the British Academy.

Burgess, Michael. 2000. *Federalism and European Union: The building of Europe, 1950–2000*. London: Routledge.

Coen, David, and Adrienne Héritier, eds. 2006. *Refining regulatory regimes: Utilities in Europe.* London: Elgar.

Doern, G. Bruce, ed. 2005. *Canadian energy policy and the struggle for sustainable development.* Toronto: University of Toronto Press.

– 2007. *Red tape, red flags: Regulation for the innovation age.* Ottawa: Conference Board of Canada.

Doern, G. Bruce, Arslan Dorman, and Robert Morrison, eds. 2001. *Canadian nuclear energy policy: Changing ideas, institutions, and interests.* Toronto: University of Toronto Press.

Doern, G. Bruce, and Monica Gattinger. 2003. *Power switch: Energy regulatory governance in the 21st century.* Toronto: University of Toronto Press.

Doern, G. Bruce, Margaret Hill, Michael Prince, and Richard Schultz, eds. 1999. *Changing the rules: Canada's changing regulatory regimes and institutions.* Toronto: University of Toronto Press.

Doern, G. Bruce, and Robert Johnson, eds. 2006. *Rules, rules, rules, rules: Multi-level regulatory governance.* Toronto: University of Toronto Press.

Doern, G. Bruce, and Glen Toner. 1985. *The politics of energy: The making and implementation of the national energy program.* Toronto: Methuen.

Döhler, Marian. 2002. Institutional choice and bureaucratic autonomy in Germany. *West European Politics* 2:101–24.

Dyson, Kenneth, and Klaus H. Goetz, eds. 2003. *Germany, Europe, and the politics of constraint.* Oxford: Oxford University Press for the British Academy, Proceedings of the British Academy 119.

Eberlein, Burkard. 2000. Institutional change and continuity in German infrastructure management: The case of electricity reform. *German Politics* 9 (3): 81–104.

– 2005. Regulation by cooperation: The 'third way' in making rules for the internal energy market. In *Legal aspects of EU energy regulation,* ed. Peter Cameron, 59–88. Oxford: Oxford University Press.

Eberlein, Burkard, and Edgar Grande. 2005. Reconstituting political authority in Europe: Transnational regulatory networks and the informalization of governance in the European Union. In *Complex sovereignty: Reconstituting political authority in the twenty-first century,* ed. Edgar Grande and Louis Pauly, 146–67. Toronto: University of Toronto Press.

Eising, Rainer. 1999. Reshuffling power: The liberalisation of the EU electricity markets and its impact on the German governance regime. In *The transformation of governance in the European Union,* ed. Beate Kohler-Koch and Rainer Eising, 208–28. London: Routledge.

– 2002. Policy learning in embedded negotiations: Explaining EU electricity liberalization. *International Organization* 56 (1): 85–120.

Eliadis, P., Margaret Hill, and Michael Howlett, eds. 2005. *Designing government: From instruments to governance.* Montreal and Kingston: McGill-Queen's University Press.

Featherstone, Kevin, and Claudio M. Radaelli, eds. 2003. *The politics of Europeanization.* Oxford: Oxford University Press.

Flinders, Matthew. 2002. *The politics of accountability in the modern state.* Aldershot: Ashgate.

George, Alexander, and Andrew Bennett. 2005. *Case studies and theory development in the social science.* Cambridge, MA: MIT Press.

Grande, Edgar, and Louis W. Pauly, eds. 2005. *Complex sovereignty: Reconstituting political authority in the twenty-first century.* Toronto: University of Toronto Press.

Green, Simon, and William Paterson, eds. 2005. *Governance in contemporary Germany: The semi-sovereign state revisited.* Cambridge: Cambridge University Press.

Hall, Peter, and Rosemary Taylor. 1996. Political science and the three new institutionalisms. *Political Studies* 44:936–57.

Hay, Colin. 2002. *Political analysis: A critical introduction.* London: Palgrave.

Held, David et al. 1999. *Global transformations.* London: Polity.

Helm, Dieter. 2003. *Energy, the state and the market: British energy policy since 1979.* Oxford: Oxford University Press.

– , ed. 2005. *Climate change policy.* Oxford: Oxford University Press.

Héritier, Adrienne, ed. 2002. *Common goods: Reinventing European and international governance.* London: Rowman and Littlefield.

Hoberg, G., ed. 2002. *Capacity for choice: Canada in a new North America.* Toronto: University of Toronto Press.

Hooghe, Liesbet, and Gary Marks. 2003. Unraveling the central state, but how? Types of multi-level governance. *American Political Science Review* 97 (2): 233–43.

Hufbauer, Gary, and Jeffrey Schott. 2005. *NAFTA revisited: Achievements and challenges.* Washington, DC: Institute for International Economics.

Hughes, Thomas P. 1987. The evolution of large technological systems. In *The social construction of technological systems: New directions in the sociology and history of technology,* ed. Wiebke E. Bijker, Thomas P. Hughes, and Trevor J. Pinch, 51–82. Cambridge, MA: MIT Press.

International Energy Agency. 2007. *Energy policies of IEA countries: Germany 2007 review.* Paris: International Energy Agency.

Jaccard, Mark. 2006. *Sustainable fossil fuels.* Cambridge: Cambridge University Press.

Jänicke, Martin, and Helmut Weidner. 1997. Germany. In *National environmen-*

tal policies: A comparative study of capacity-building, ed. Martin Jänicke and Helmut Weidner, 133–55. Berlin: Springer.

Jochem, Eberhard, Edelgard Gruber, and Wilhelm Mannsbart. 1996. German energy policy in transition. In European energy policies in a changing environment, ed. Francis McGowan, 57–87. Heidelberg: Physica-Verlag – Springer.

Jordana, Jacint, and David Levi-Faur, eds. 2004. The politics of regulation: Institutions and regulatory reforms for the age of governance. London: Elgar.

Koenig-Archibugi, Mathias, and Michael Zürn, eds. 2006. New modes of governance in the global system: Exploring publicness, delegation and Inclusiveness. London: Palgrave Macmillan.

Krywulak, Tim. 2007. Fuelling progress: One hundred years of the Canadian Gas Association. Toronto: Canadian Gas Association.

Lehmbruch, Gerhard. 1989. Institutional linkages and policy networks in the federal system of West Germany. Publius: The Journal of Federalism 19:221–35.

Lowndes, Vivien. 1996. Varieties of new institutionalism: A critical appraisal. Public Administration 74 (Summer): 181–97.

Marks, Gary, Liesbet Hooghe, and Kermit Blank. 1996. European integration from the 1980s: State-centric vs multi-level governance. Journal of Common Market Studies 34:343–77.

McGowan, Francis, ed. 1996. European energy policies in a changing environment. Heidelberg: Physica-Verlag – Springer.

Mez, Lutz. 1997. The German electricity reform attempts: Reforming co-optive networks. In European electricity systems in transition: A comparative analysis of policy and regulation in Western Europe, ed. Atle Midttun, 231–52. London: Elsevier.

Monstadt, Jochen. 2004. Die Modernisierung der Stromversorgung: Regionale Energie- und Klimapolitik im Liberalisierung – und Privatisierungsprozess [The modernization of electricity supply: Regional energy and climate policy in the process of liberalization and privatization]. Wiesbaden: VS Verlag für Sozialwissenschaften.

Noreng, Oystein. 2006. Crude power: Politics and the oil market. London: Tauris.

Ortwein, Edmund. 1996. Die Ordnung der deutschen Elektrizitätswirtschaft [The structure of the German electricity supply industry]. In Wettbewerbspolitik und die Ordnung der Elektrizitätswirtschaft in Deutschland und Grossbritannien [Competition policy and the structure of the electricity supply industry in Germany and Great Britain]. Ed. Roland Sturm and Stephen Wilks, 77–131. Baden-Baden: Nomos.

Padgett, Stephen. 1990. Policy style and issue environment: The electricity supply sector in West Germany. Journal of Public Policy 10 (2): 165–93.

Palast, Greg, Jerrold Oppenheim, and Theo MacGregor. 2003. *Democracy and regulation: How the public can govern essential services.* London: Pluto.

Peters, Guy B. 2005. *Institutional theory in political science: The 'new institutionalism.'* 2nd ed. London: Continuum.

Peters, Guy B., and Jon Pierre. 2001. Developments in intergovernmental relations: Towards multi-level governance. *Policy and Politics* 29 (2): 131–35.

Przeworksi, Adam, and Henry Teune. 1970. *The logic of comparative social inquiry.* London: Wiley-Interscience.

Rüdig, Wolfgang. 2003. The environment and nuclear power. In *Developments in German politics.* 3rd ed. Ed. Stephen Padgett, William E. Paterson, and Gordon Smith, 248–68. Durham, NC: Duke University Press.

Scharpf, Fritz W. (1997). *Games real actors play: Actor-centered institutionalism in policy research.* Boulder, CO: Westview.

Scharpf, Fritz W., Bernd Reissert, and Fritz Schnabel. 1976. *Politikverflechtung: Theorie und Empirie des kooperativen Föderalismus in der Bundesrepublik* [Joint decision-making: Theory and practice of cooperative federalism in the Federal Republic]. Kronberg/Taunus: Scriptor Verlag.

Streek, Wolfgang, and Kathleen Thelen, eds. (2005). *Beyond continuity: Institutional change in advanced political economies.* Oxford: Oxford University Press.

Sturm, Roland, and Heinrich Pehle. 2005. *Das neue deutsche Regierungssystem* [The new German political system]. 2nd ed. Wiesbaden: VS Verlag für Sozialwissenschaften.

Sturm, Roland, and Stephen Wilks. 1997. *Competition policy and the regulation of the electricity supply industry in Britain and Germany.* London: Anglo-German Foundation for the Study of Industrial Society.

VanNijnatten, Debora, and Douglas MacDonald. 2003. Reconciling energy and climate change policies: How Ottawa blends. In *How Ottawa spends 2003–2004: Regime change and policy shift,* ed. Bruce Doern, 72–88. Toronto: Oxford University Press.

Wilks, Stephen, and Bruce Doern. 2007. Accountability and multi-level governance in UK regulation. In *Regulatory review 2006–2007,* ed. Peter Vass, 341–72. Bath, UK: Centre for the Study of Regulated Industries, University of Bath.

2 Mapping the Energy Challenges: Germany and Canada in Comparative Context

G. BRUCE DOERN AND BURKARD EBERLEIN

As a broad context for the chapters that follow, this chapter maps and examines the overall nature of the energy challenges underpinning contemporary multi-level energy regulatory governance. As stressed in chapter 1, the prime focus of energy governance is not on institutions and processes or politics and economics somehow disembodied from the substance and content of the energy field. Accordingly, this book's conceptual framework – centred on complexity, coordination, and capacity – seeks to include real-world energy capacities: to deliver useable and reliable mixes of energy goods and services to citizens of nation states and their regional neighbours at reasonable cost.

In this chapter we examine several such energy challenges in a global context and also within the specific German and Canadian energy systems functioning within their EU and North American milieus. These energy challenges include future prices, demand, and supply for oil and other fuel and energy sources; broadening notions of energy security; oil and natural gas, including liquefied natural gas as a global energy source; climate change and the Kyoto Protocol and beyond Kyoto; electricity and industry restructuring; alternative energy sources and energy efficiency; and nuclear energy. Table 1 provides a visual guide to the overall analytical narrative to follow.

In one sense there is a consensus among energy economists and some national energy policymakers about what the optimum energy system for a country ought to be in the first decade of the twenty-first century (Helm 2003, 2005a). Ideally, all energy sources and supplies

Table 2.1 Energy policy challenges in Germany and Canada

Energy policy challenge	Germany	Canada
Global energy supply and demand projections/choices: Continuing dominance of oil and gas – Growing energy demand: 50% by 2030 – 50% growth in CO_2 emissions – High sustained oil prices, tripled in recent years but also price volatility – 50% growth in natural gas, with LNG accounting for 80% of increase in traded gas – Nuclear energy capacity to increase slightly – Global oil business being transformed from an exploration industry to a manufacturing industry	– Higher prices and supply affected by growing demand by China and India but also by expanded EU member countries – Reasonably good consensus-based approach to energy policy, with long-standing emphasis on security of supply and diversification of energy sources in a corporatist political economy supportive of producer interests, but also of strong environmental policies	– Higher prices and supply affected by growing demand by China and India, but also by growing U.S. demand – Emergence of Alberta oil sands as proven Saudi-Arabian sized reserve – Strong east-west political controversies and conflict in domestic energy policy
Energy security – Traditional security via diversity of supply – Expanded notions of security – Terrorism and physical security of entire energy supply chain – Electricity grid reliability – Security margin/flexibility – Integration – Supply and demand information and analysis	– German historic and current dependence on foreign sources of oil and gas – Security concerns about natural gas reliance on Russian gas via monopoly firm Gazprom – Increased support for EU energy policy with a more explicit focus on security issues (EU Green Paper on Energy Policy, March 2006) – Foreign policy support for good relations with energy exporter nations (e.g., government support for German-Russian Baltic Sea gas pipeline project between E.on, BASF, and Gazprom)	– Security of national supply a key feature of interventionist 1980 to 1984 Liberal National Energy Program – 1985 to 2008 focus on pro-market approach as best guarantee of security of supply – Canada-U.S. free trade as form of security of supply for the U.S. – North American security of supply plus anti-terrorism and security of supply chain in 2005 border, trade, and security pact – Electricity grid security and reliability after major 2003 blackout

Table 2.1 (*continued*)

Energy policy challenge	Germany	Canada
Oil, natural gas, and lique-fied natural gas and core energy business interests – Higher price of oil and gas – Greater use of gas in electricity production – LNG makes it a global market – Varied degrees of gas market liberalization – Oil as globally priced product – Relative centrality of oil versus gas interests in national politics	– No significant national oil production – Natural gas plays growing role in German supply with above-noted increased dependence on Russian supply – Import dependence leads to strategic view on need to diversify supplies from variety of countries/regions – Schröder government supported E.ON-Ruhrgas merger to bolster international weight and bargaining position of German 'champion' E.ON – Domestic gas market remains highly concentrated and difficult to penetrate (EU liberalization slower than in electricity) – Sees LNG as development that will help security of supply – Natural gas and linked electricity business interest groups and firms are dominant – Growing strength of renewable green industry lobby groups	– Conventional oil, offshore oil as major energy source – Oil sands growing and soon to be the major source for Canada and for U.S. as 'secure' supply – Elevated rhetoric by federal government on Canada as a new 'energy superpower' – Gas as growing part of Canadian energy business and of key exports to U.S. – Oil and natural gas more high cost to produce and price increases for gas due also to increased use in electricity supply – Access to northern gas supply hampered by sluggish pipeline development – LNG of marginal interest in Canada but may affect and compete with Canadian gas in U.S. and other markets – Oil and gas business interest groups are dominant part of energy industry lobby – Some divisions between dominant multinational (mainly U.S.) firms and more numerous smaller Canadian firms focused in exploration sector – U.S. firms are strong influence within the Canadian energy lobby

Table 2.1 (*continued*)

Energy policy challenge	Germany	Canada
Electricity	– German electricity restructuring quite well developed (full market opening), but gaps in German and EU electricity regulatory regimes (lack of unbundling, and of vigorous anti-trust and regulation) undermine competition and have allowed high market concentration (oligopoly), cross-border competition is limited – Phasing out of nuclear energy by 2025 – Greater need for new investment in plants (coal-fired and others) over next decade – Opposition to coal-fired plants due to its heavy carbon footprint	– Canadian electricity restructuring (in Alberta and Ontario) quite sluggish and ill-planned – Political intervention if prices become unacceptably high – Plans in Ontario for greater renewables in supply but also some increase in nuclear reactors – Absence of an east-west interprovincial grid – Canadian electricity providers increasingly subject to de facto regulation by U.S. FERC – Differences between U.S. and Canadian approaches to grid reliability governance – Coal resources are ample and coal exports have been increasing – Alberta's use of coal-fired plants and also interest in clean coal technology due to strong links to U.S. interest in clean coal – Ontario seeking to wind down coal plants for electricity production

Table 2.1 (*continued*)

Energy policy challenge	Germany	Canada
Renewable energy and energy efficiency policies and the strength of environmental NGOs	– Leads world in promotion and use of renewables such as wind and solar – Energy-efficiency gains have been steady for 15 years and are central part of climate change targets and goals – Strong national environmental NGOs forged around anti-nuclear and pro-renewables agenda – Strong local municipal pressures	– Weak efforts in renewables but recent initiatives at provincial level – Energy use per capita has increased, not declined, but some selected efficiency measures announced recently regarding the auto sector – Big hydro use in some provinces but seldom seen as a true renewable because of damage in building dams – Weaker NGOs nationally and far less persistent, continuous pressure
Climate change	– Strong climate change emission reduction policy since early 1990s – Strong renewable energy incentives and market-creation – Has reduced emissions from 1990 levels by 17.4 per cent (2004) – Stringent 'beyond Kyoto' GHG emission reduction commitments (but benefited from 'wall-fall' effect) – Taking part in EU emissions-trading system – May need to use more coal because of decision to phase out nuclear energy	– Weak climate change emission reduction policy since 2002 signing of Kyoto Protocol – Weak renewable energy incentives and market-creation – Increased emissions from 1990 levels by 25 per cent in 2005 – 2006 Conservative government adopts slower Kyoto pace and indicates support for U.S. Bush-led coalition of voluntary and R&D first approach for the current and 'beyond Kyoto' phase – In 2007 Conservative government commits Canada to a 20 per cent reduction below 2006 levels by 2020 through a direct regulatory approach

(*continues on next page*)

Table 2.1 (*continued*)

Energy policy challenge	Germany	Canada
		– Province of British Columbia announces first carbon tax in North America – Several provinces joining U.S. states to form regional emissions-trading systems – Overall pro-export and development policies for vast Alberta oil sands and their high GHG emissions
Nuclear energy – Possible comeback in use as part of fight against climate change – Still serious problems in long-term storage of wastes	– 2002 decision to phase out nuclear energy use by 2025 – 1986 Chernobyl disaster had major impact on German public opinion	– Canadian CANDU reactor–centred industry in doldrums since early 1980s – Second-generation CANDU reactors developed – Industry and use in electricity focused mainly in one province (Ontario) – 2006 Ontario plan to increase nuclear/refurbish aging reactors

should be fully costed, including the internalization of environmental costs in market prices. Then, under a market system, but with vigilant regulators, all sources should be allowed to compete on a level playing field with incumbent suppliers having no contrived forms of protection and new entrants allowed entry into markets. In principle, oil, gas, coal, nuclear, hydro, and alternative energy such as wind power, solar power, and biomass would compete openly and fairly. This would mean not only that alternative energy suppliers would not be prevented by traditional energy source incumbents but that particular 'forms' of alternative energy would also not have an unfair status over other forms of alternative energy.

Each form of energy would of course have its own inherent technical and physical advantages and disadvantages as an energy source. And the demand side of the energy equation would be anchored in normal market behaviour, with no concentrations of buying power, and with open and fair overall market prices as well good information about energy product quality.

Overall the energy system would regulate aspects that are monopolistic and leave competitive forces to operate where energy truly functioned competitively, like any other market good. It would also regulate the industry through good environmental regulation and good and open competition law and trade law.

While many of these aspirations of a good energy system garner considerable policy and institutional support, the real world of energy governance has not yet reached this state of affairs, and might well never do so. Yet it is of great value to have a clearly articulated concept of an optimal energy system, so as to be able to benchmark real-world systems against a coherent 'yardstick.'

We return to this difficult issue in chapter 15. Not surprisingly, the gap between ideal and real-life energy systems is due not only to the imperfections of markets but also to conflicting interests and fundamental power relations, in a context where governments, companies, and individuals as citizens and consumers compete, cooperate, and collide in complex ways. It is in this important sense that we examine the diverse energy challenges confronting Germany and Canada in their regional contexts and in a larger global political economy.

Price, Supply, and Demand Projections and Choice: The Continuing Dominance of Oil and Gas

Both of our core countries and their regional partners must locate their energy governance policies and choices in the context of ongoing forecasts of energy supply and demand. In this section we note key findings of the International Energy Association's World Energy Outlook of 2004, 2005, and 2006, the scenarios for which each projects ahead to 2030 (IEA 2004b, 2005b, 2006b). Various scenario assumptions are posited in these forecasts, but several key findings are clear.

- If policies remain unchanged, world energy demand is projected to increase by over 50 per cent between now and 2030.
- World energy resources are adequate to meet this demand, but investment of $20 trillion will be needed to bring these resources to consumers. There is no guarantee that all of the investment will be forthcoming.

- Energy-related CO_2 emissions also climb – by 2030, they will be 50 per cent higher than today. These projected trends have important implications and lead to a future that is not sustainable – from an energy security or environmental perspective.
- Lack of investment in upstream and downstream capacity has contributed to the extreme tightness in the global oil market.
- Rising oil and gas demand, if unchecked, would accentuate the consuming countries' vulnerability to a severe supply reduction and resulting price shock.

These findings complement data in the IEA's 2006 outlook, which projected that fossil fuels will continue to dominate global energy use, accounting for 83 per cent of the *increase* in world primary demand (IEA 2006a). The 2008–2009 recession will restrain these forecasts, but not their basic·trajectory.

Two-thirds of the increase in global demand will come from developing countries, especially from Asia, where the booming Chinese and Indian economies are a key feature. It is also noted that, as international trade expands, the risks will grow of a supply disruption at the critical choke-points through which oil must flow.

Projections also show that worldwide consumption of natural gas will almost double by 2030, overtaking that of coal within the next decade. Liquefied natural gas (LNG), most of which is used for electricity production, will account for most of the increase in traded gas. By 2030, just over half of all inter-regional gas trade will be in the form of LNG, up from 30 per cent at present – provided land use limitations can be managed. Worldwide electricity demand is projected to double between now and 2030, with most of the growth coming in developing countries.

Nuclear capacity is projected to increase slightly but the share of nuclear in the total electrical grid will decline. Nuclear power capacity will increase most in key Asian countries. Renewable energy sources as a whole are forecast to increase their share of electricity generation with renewables other than hydroelectricity (mainly biomass and wind) tripling from 2 to 6 per cent by 2030.

In these mixes of supply and demand, sustained higher energy prices are projected overall. For most of the 1980s and 1990s, world oil prices hovered near $20 a barrel. But from 2002 to 2006, the price tripled to more than $70 a barrel and climbed to over $140 in the summer of 2008 before falling to about $40 early in 2009. The increased prices were seen as being due to the aforementioned lack of investment in upstream and downstream infrastructure (see more below) rather than to an absolute decline of supply or proven global reserves. Sustained higher prices are also seen as a key part of the solution to projected problems and challenges since they can act as incentives to invest in new capacity and in conservation (Maugeri 2006).

Also a part of the art and science of energy forecasting have been debates about 'peak oil,' where some forecasters argue that oil reserves are depleting (Leggett 2005). The evidence for this view is partly that big oil firms are finding it difficult to replace reserves. Pro-market analysts refute this pessimism and cite evidence that the world still has vast supplies of oil, including of course reserves such as the Canadian oil sands, and that when oil and other energy prices rise, more supply will be found in places such as in the Arctic.

One further area of the energy forecasting arts is the need to capture new technological changes and to estimate their effects on demand and supply (IEA 2006a). The *Economist*'s assessment of the oil industry includes a view that 'the global oil industry is on the verge of a dramatic transformation from a risky exploration business into a technology-intensive manufacturing business,' with the latter focused on greener fossil fuels such as biofuels centred on ethanol production but with technology related to clean coal and energy sequestration also included (*Economist* 2006).

As indicated above, looming problems in energy security are also central to current projections of energy futures. But for our purposes, these deserve a separate brief discussion since they change further and deepen the nature of multi-level energy regulatory governance.

Energy Security in a Changed Global Political Economy

Energy security has always been a key feature of national and regional energy policies. But in the early years of the twenty-first century, it has taken on a much broader set of meanings and dimensions (Yergin 2006). Energy security has always meant security of supply at reasonable prices and since the supply shocks of 1973 and 1979–80 has also involved mechanisms to deal with supply shocks and disruptions through international cooperation to share supply during such crises. But in the post-9/11 world, energy security has expanded to issues of terrorism and the physical safety of energy infrastructure and, most importantly, the security and functioning of the entire supply chain, a supply chain that has become ever more global (in terms of oil) and increasingly for natural gas as well (see more below).

Security concerns have also extended to electricity and to cross-border and regional electricity grids. And hurricanes Katrina and Rita delivered in 2006 what Yergin characterizes as 'the world's first integrated energy shock, simultaneously disrupting flows of oil, natural gas and electric power' (2006, 70).

In recent years, with the massive growth of the economies of China and India, energy security has also had to encompass the notion of 'demand shocks,' and for exporting countries there is even the notion of 'security of demand' for their energy exports (e.g., the United States for Canadian oil and gas). The Katrina and Rita hurricane impacts and other developments including high energy prices also drew attention to a particular feature of the supply chain: the absence of refining capacity and in particular a major disjuncture between product requirements demanded by consumers and the capacities of refiners to deliver (Maugeri 2006).

These refining capacity gaps were brought on in turn by 'years of low oil prices, inadequate investment in infrastructure, and producers' fears of surpluses' (Maugeri 2006, 149). Last but not least, energy security has been affected in recent years by the return of energy nationalism, particularly by Venezuela under Hugo Chavez, but also by Russia (Hoyos and Blas 2006).

National, regional, and global energy security regimes were largely forged in the wake of the 1970s supply crises, but current circumstances necessitate a broadened regime that takes into account the new realities of global markets and politics. Yergin suggests the need for such a regime to be governed by several principles: (1) diversification of supply, the oldest notion of security; (2) resilience or a 'security margin' in the energy supply system; (3) the reality of integration; and (4) the importance of information about well-functioning markets, such as that supplied by the International Energy Agency (IEA) and the newly formed International Energy Forum (Yergin 2006, 75–7).

Both Germany and Canada are increasingly affected by this expanded regime and also involved in shaping it. As a non–oil producer, Germany has always been sensitive to its dependence on foreign sources of supply, and in recent years its dependence on Russian natural gas and oil has heightened these concerns, including supply chain protection and reliability. European energy policy had first been linked mainly to establishing liberalized electricity and gas markets, as part of the EU Single Market agenda and this has remained a cornerstone of EU policy (see more below).

Yet, more recently, liberalization has lost some momentum in EU policy, much as 'deregulation' in the United States and Canada lost steam after some sobering experiences, beginning with the widely publicized California power crisis in 2001. In 2003 severe power failures hit Italy, Denmark, Sweden, and other European countries. Also, progress with and results of market liberalization did not meet expectations, especially when electricity prices began to rise after 2001. These developments have moved security of supply back up to the top of the agenda.

Fresh initiatives for greater supply security (in physical, investment, and supplier relation terms), were put forward, resulting first in a new EU directive (2005/89/EC) designed to safeguard security of electricity supply and infrastructure investment. The European Commission, in its 2006 Energy Green Paper (Commission of the European Communities 2006), built its case for a more rigorous, common EU energy policy to a large extent on the pressing need to tackle energy security, and, increasingly, to fight climate change. In March 2007, the spring European Council endorsed the launch of a common energy and climate change package and adopted a comprehensive energy action plan for 2007–9. In January 2008, the European Commission put forward an integrated climate and energy package that features legislative proposals on CO_2 burden sharing under the EU emission trading system and on renewable energies. The March 2008 EU Summit agreed to adopt the package by the end of 2008. Climate change and security of supply lie at the heart of this major reorientation of European energy policy. Obviously, the recent energy sabre-rattling rhetoric between Russia and the Ukraine had helped to give energy security per se a heightened profile in EU energy circles.

Meanwhile in Canada and North America, energy security of this broadened kind moved front and centre after the events of 9/11 and after the Bush energy review was published in 2001.

Canada-U.S. energy security encompassed a greater awareness by the United States of Canada's vast oil sands reserves and of their importance to U.S. security of supply. Energy security also took on a full continental flavour in that it quickly became a key appendage to the North American border and security agenda precipitated by U.S. concerns about protection from terrorism.

Some key initial cross-border anti-terrorism and secure border governance structures later became a core part of the basis for the even broader 23 March 2005 Security and Prosperity Partnership of North America (SPP) announced in Waco, Texas, by the three leaders of the United States, Mexico, and Canada. Dealing with security, trade, and energy, this agreement contained provisions that embraced the broadened notions of energy security (Prime Minister's Office 2005) and of enhanced multi-level regulatory governance and policy development.

Oil, Natural Gas, and Liquefied Natural Gas and Core Energy Business Interests

As noted above, oil and natural gas are the dominant global fuels and are projected to remain so. Natural gas has assumed a growing portion of energy supply, partly because of its growing availability but also because it is a lower carbon emitter, per unit of energy, than oil and coal. It has also expanded because of its increased role in the relatively inexpensive gas-fired turbines used in the generation of electricity. As previously mentioned, natural gas has historically been a regional energy market rather than a global one. In these terms, Russia has become a dominant source of natural gas for Germany and for much of Europe, with Russian supply held under the monopoly control of Gazprom, and with Gazprom in turn seen as an instrument of Russian foreign policy and international economic policy and power (Stern 2006).

With respect to oil, chapter 1 has already shown that conventional oil and increasingly the massive oil sands of Alberta are central to Canadian energy supply. In addition, the core oil industry lobby – both its foreign multinational component and its Canadian component – is firmly anchored in Alberta's oil patch and dominates national energy politics. Chapter 1 has also shown that Germany's core energy sources are not oil-centred but rather are centred in natural gas and electricity. Germany's core energy business lobby is therefore centred in major utilities but also consists of a growing renewables industry and lobby.

In North America, Canada's ample natural gas supplies were forming an ever-larger share of U.S. imports. As a result, and in concert with overall energy market tightness, natural gas prices also increased considerably between 2002 and 2007.

The development of liquefied natural gas (LNG) has been a major change in the natural gas market and is rapidly making natural gas into a truly global product. LNG production and transportation began in the 1960s. However, in the last decade LNG has taken off and is expected to remain high the next decade, with demand growing at 8 per cent a year. Nonetheless, despite billions being invested annually in new facilities, there is a time lag before facilities actually come on stream, caused by cost inflation, budget overruns, and shortages of specialized labour and speciality materials (Catan 2006; Cambridge Energy Research Associates 2006).

Despite these difficulties, some energy market forecasters see LNG as the 'oil of the twenty-first century' and others see an eventual natural gas-LNG version of OPEC emerging. Interestingly, a 2005 publication of the Canadian Gas Association scarcely mentions LNG but focuses instead on the value of Canadian natural gas on overall reliability and affordability, and its argued environmental acceptability (Canadian Gas Association 2005). Canadian energy policymakers do envisage possible LNG import terminals on Canada's east coast. Prime Minister Stephen Harper and Russian Premier Vladimir Putin discussed joint Russian-Canadian private ventures that would bring Russian LNG to eastern Canada. But, overall, these kinds of developments are not a central feature of projected Canadian energy supply. LNG may, however, loom larger in terms of U.S. imports and thus effect Canada's longer term position as the favoured or main natural gas supplier for the United States. Germany is more likely to take early advantage of these kinds of supplies (including Norwegian sources of LNG) than is Canada because of its concerns about security of supply.

In an overall sense, the two countries have a quite different strategic view of their oil and gas needs and therefore their oil and gas policies overall. As noted above, Germany imports virtually all of its oil supply but does so for strategic reasons on an array of suppliers, 45 per cent of which comes from OECD countries, 33 per cent from Russia, and only 14 per cent from OPEC countries but with Russian supply growing rapidly in recent years (IEA 2007, 85). The transport sector accounts for about half of oil consumption but there has been a longstanding German policy to promote the use of diesel in passenger vehicles and as a result a quarter of all cars and almost half all new cars purchased are fuelled by diesel (IEA 2007, 92). Germany is also heavily dependent on natural gas imports, although it does have domestic natural gas supplies that satisfy about 18 per cent of domestic demand. Once again, the strategic view of natural gas is to garner supply from an array of countries and areas including the North Sea area, the

Netherlands, and Russia. Security of gas supply is based not only on diversity of suppliers but also on storage, transportation routes, and long-term gas supply agreements (IEA 2007, 95–6).

Canada's overall strategic view of its oil and gas needs and policies is that of an oil and gas exporter essentially feeding the U.S. market while exhibiting deep-seated faith in markets to meet all of Canada's domestic oil and gas needs. The Harper Conservative government has in particular elevated its energy policy rhetoric by characterizing Canada as a global energy superpower because of the massive reserves now proven and recognized in the burgeoning Alberta-based oil sands (Brownsey 2007). As noted above, there may be some federal strategic concerns about natural gas supplies, given their much greater use in electricity generation in Canada and the United States, but there is no indication that this will bring back policies from the pre-1980s in which designated reserves of natural gas had to be held back before exports were allowed. Market-based signals and resulting investment are cast as the ultimate guarantor of longer-term supplies of both oil and gas.

Both countries, of course, have a market-led base to their strategic view of oil and gas, but the German view is much more nuanced and reflective of its role as importer but also as a transit way for European supply, compared to Canada's buoyant export market–led view elevated by the oil sands boom. Both countries also have had to recognize the interactions between oil and gas policy and climate change as discussed further below, but again the national responses are vastly different in the kind and degree of recognition and response.

Electricity and Choices in Supply and Production

The IEA's summary view of electricity demand globally is that it is expected to double by 2030 and that it will have absorbed 60 per cent of total energy investment needed to supply that demand (IEA 2004b). It also stressed that the electricity supply industry was set for further restructuring and more far-reaching regulatory reforms. It concluded,

Reforms in the OECD have yielded positive results, but many challenges remain to be met. Blackouts in 2003 and 2004 highlighted the importance of adequate reserve margins, the need to improve the resilience of networks and the importance of providing adequate regulatory incentives for investment. (IEA 2004b, 34)

Within this compact summary paragraph lies a complex set of realities about electricity and multi-level energy governance.

In the 1990s, the electricity supply industry experienced profound regulatory changes in the broader context of neoliberal policy reforms. The neoliberal agenda entailed efforts to reduce government ownership and regulation and give market mechanisms a greater role in the governance of previously state-run or heavily regulated economic sectors such as in the case of infrastructure industries (for electricity, see Cameron 2001; Csamanski 1999; Gilbert and Kahn 1996; IEA 2005a). The United Kingdom – the first major OECD country to fully deregulate and liberalize its electricity industry in 1990 – and the United States were pioneers and drivers of pro-market electricity restructuring (Helm 2003; Hirsch 1999). The apparent success of electricity liberalization in Britain served as an important 'anchor' and provided a welcome reform template that was 'uploaded' to the EU level (Padgett 2003). For Canada, as chapters 3, 4, and 6 by Dewees, Clarkson, and Froschauer respectively show, U.S. deregulation and reciprocity requirements for Canadian provinces that export into the liberalized U.S. wholesale markets were an important factor for electricity restructuring. More radical reforms, however, including retail market liberalization, have been implemented only in Alberta and Ontario, where provincial governments pursued a neoliberal agenda.

Electricity restructuring, as the chapters by Dewees and Froschauer show, involves efforts to recognize and operationalize the fact that not all components of the electricity system are natural monopolies (Hunt 2002). The generation and supply of electricity (but not transmission and distribution over a single, monopoly network connection) can, to some extent, be treated as a marketable commodity.

At the same time, electricity is not like other normal products in that it cannot be stored but rather involves instant transmission and use, according to the laws of physics. Moreover, electricity continues to be considered as an essential service for the citizens of any modern country (Doern and Gattinger 2003; Palast, Oppenheim, and MacGregor 2003).

Restructuring therefore involved aspects of deregulation, to allow new producers of electricity supply to enter the market; new or expanded regulation to coordinate market operations and ensure that anti-competitive behaviour did not occur; and privatization and/or the breaking up of previous monopoly companies. And all of these varied potential acts of change were also occurring as the environmental and sustainable development debates and pressures proceeded apace.

Because of these complex linkages, and despite some examples of progress through market-oriented restructuring (IEA 2005a), electricity is still seen as different from oil and gas, where market-oriented approaches have been dominant for the past two decades. Moreover, market design, which means in essence still-regulated managed markets, is highly complex and therefore problematic. It depends on complex local-regional situations and circumstances, politically, economically, and institutionally.

Recent experiences in both Europe and North America have tempered enthusiasm for market reforms in electricity: a number of local and regional blackouts (though not necessarily attributable to liberalization), price volatility after liberalization, and general price increases have not been well received by consumers, especially household consumers. Reforms that are not institutionally embedded or protected, such as the EU reforms, run the risk of not surviving the difficult transition period when costs may outweigh benefits to the majority of consumers.

Moreover, unlike in oil and natural gas, there is no continent-wide sense of Canada-U.S. or Germany-EU markets in electricity, only contingent cross-border grids whose management as grids policymakers are only beginning to address. Cross-border trade of electricity in Europe continues to be hampered by insufficient transmission capacity and by inadequate rules for capacity allocation and for infrastructure investments, at national borders.

As the Dewees chapter shows, electricity restructuring in its ultimate form would establish a competitive wholesale power pool that sets an hourly (more or less) spot price and/or allow retail competition. Dewees argues that the primary driver for restructuring in the United States was the high prices charged by regulated utilities in the 1990s as they recovered the cost of investments in expensive facilities, when falling natural gas prices and increased efficiency of combined cycle gas turbine (CCGT) plants reduced the cost of new generation. He also argues that 'in practice, introducing competition in electricity has been more difficult than for railroads, trucking, airlines, natural gas, and long distance telephone rates, because of politics, starting points, and neighbours.' This was certainly true in the case of both Alberta and Ontario, where 'politics' referred to the intervention of politicians when energy prices increased in politically unacceptable ways and governments introduced price freezes or subsidies. These actions meant that markets could not work, and investment and supply shortfalls were the result.

'Starting points' in the Dewees analysis refer to the differences that emerged when Alberta began with an already private sector industry, whereas Ontario had a monopoly publicly owned utility. And 'neighbours' introduced the importance of neighbouring jurisdictions and their possible role as a supplier of excess electricity but also of imported pollution.

Analyses of European electricity restructuring as driven by EU liberalization reveal some similar complexities of electricity restructuring (see Glachant and Finon 2003; Finon and Midttun 2004; Jamasb and Pollit 2005). They show that the creation of true competition and of an integrated EU-wide market have been elusive goals. European electricity markets are plagued simultaneously by market concentration and regional fragmentation. These analyses also draw attention to the costs of implementing market competition, and to their potential negative effects on other sector goals such as equity and security of supply (investment incentives).

It must also stressed that the energy and governance challenges of the electricity sector are immediately entwined with the discussion above of natural gas. This is because CCGT technology brought natural gas to the fore in electricity supply and thus greatly increases the overall global, North American, and European demand for natural gas. It is also linked to the discussions below in the next two sections on alternative energy sources and on nuclear energy, where Canada and Germany have forged, or have had thrust upon them, quite different choices and challenges arising from previous energy endowments and policies and from different political and institutional forces and sources of inertia and change in their multi-level energy governance and regulatory regimes.

Finally, the role of coal in electricity generation options warrants mention, again with significant differences between the two countries. Coal is a plentiful resource in Canada, with significant export markets. Alberta uses coal-fired plants in its electricity mix, but Ontario is on a path to end the use of such plants because of their high greenhouse gas (GHG) emissions. There has also been considerable interest in clean coal technology in Alberta, in part because of its industry's close links with coal interests in the United States, where clean coal and the fostering of more research on clean coal was a key part of U.S. energy policy under the Bush administration and remains so under the Obama administration.

In the case of Germany, as we have already seen, imported and domestic coal in electricity generation (and the utility and coal lobby) has been a feature of German energy policy, but there have also been strong pressures to wean Germany off coal, pressures linked to the broader development of alternative energy sources and to the strong environmental movement.

Alternative Energy Sources and Policies, Energy Efficiency, and Environmental NGOs

Alternative energy sources, linked to strong energy efficiency measures, are the preferred energy option of most environmental lobby groups and of green parties in countries such as Germany. Environmental non-governmental organizations (NGOs) include green lobby groups per se but also unions and consumer groups as well. In both Canada and Germany, such groups consist of nationally known major NGOs and unions but also, crucially, very active smaller regionally and locally based lobby groups. The green lobby also includes firms in the so-called environmental industries sector, which includes firms that make their living out of developing new environmental technologies or are progressive practitioners of sustainable development in their own internal production (Doern 2005, 40–4; Toner 2006). German environmental lobby pressure has been stronger than that in Canada, largely because it is anchored in a green party that has actually held office in a coalition government and also because, as chapter 5 by Metz and Doern shows, the Chernobyl nuclear reactor disaster in 1986 galvanized the German green lobby.

The green lobby in both countries strongly opposes current energy policies focused on coal, oil, natural gas, and nuclear energy. Alternative sources to oil, natural gas, and nuclear energy include low impact renewables such as some biofuels, wind, solar, biomass, and small hydro (with big hydro often excluded in Canada as a 'renewable' because of its major impacts in creating huge hydro dams). Measures to promote energy efficiency are also seen as closely supportive policies through proper full pricing of energy sources and through rules mandating technical standards for electricity and energy using appliances, products, and production processes.

Policies on alternative energy are seen by advocates as policies that will meet multiple objectives of sustainable development, climate change reduction and protection, air quality, and – because of their much more decentralized nature – energy security. Because they involve new technologies, they are also often advanced as a part of national industrial and innovation policies (IEA 2006a). The general public's view of alternative energy sources is mixed. Wind power is supported, but often only as long as proposed wind turbines are not in one's proverbial backyard as an environmental eyesore. For others, renewables in public opinion are vaguely small, popular, and pricey.

As noted above, alternative energy policy (and also key aspects of the climate change debate) are rooted in the paradigm of sustainable development (SD) policy. SD policy refers to policies whose intent is to ensure in any number of areas of governance that the environment and its ecosystems are left in at least as good a state for the next generation as they were for the current generation (Lafferty and Meadowcroft 2000). Cast somewhat more loosely, such policies are often seen by governments as those that take into consideration the economic, social, and environmental effects of policies, the so-called triple bottom line (Toner 2000).

In more specific energy policy terms, sustainable development is also initially tested against the basic concept of whether countries such as Canada and Germany have made progress in energy efficiency, such as by reducing per capita energy use over the past twenty years, or as evidenced by other measures of energy efficiency. The basic policies for energy efficiency in Canada have not been updated in any overall sense since the mid-1990s. The federal government has initiated some measures to increase energy efficiency in the auto industry (Toner 2008, chapter 1), and of course very high oil and gas prices between 2006 and 2008 themselves produce some efficiency gains. Since in Canada per capita usage has actually increased marginally or has produced only sluggish gains in some sectors but not others, there is clearly much more to do (Doern 2005, chapter 1).

This is not the case in Germany, where energy use per capita has been declining (IEA 2007, 53). Germany's energy intensity (energy consumed per unit of economic output) has improved by 1.8 per cent annually on average between 1990 to 2005, one of the best records among industrialized countries. Greater energy efficiency targets are also a central part of Germany's climate change policy, where an annual increase of 3 per cent per year is the goal to meet an overall doubling of energy productivity by 2020 (IEA 2007, 53–4).

When the Kyoto Protocol and its requirements for reductions in greenhouse gas emissions are added as a core test of sustainable development, the Canadian record, as we shall see below, is still inferior in basic energy terms.

Policies on renewables turn on mixtures of regulatory 'push' to require targets and requirements for the feed-in of such sources into electricity grids, and subsidies through pricing or front-end innovation and incentives for research and development and innovation. Clearly the extent to which such renewables are fostered in different countries is a product of the relative power and influence of incumbent energy suppliers and providers, compared to those of these new supplier industries, allied with environmental groups, environmental industry lobbies more generally, and party and public opinion nationally and sub-nationally (especially in a federation).

Local municipal pressure can also be at play here, in the form of community group advocacy of alternative energy. This is especially where municipal electricity utilities are owned and operated by municipalities. But despite considerable lobbying and some governmental support, renewables are still seen to be a small (but growing) share of world energy supply. As noted earlier, IEA forecasts see it tripling by 2030 but still even by then occupying only 6 per cent of use globally.

As the Mez analysis in chapter 14 shows, Germany is pre-eminent in the promotion of renewable energy sources for electricity generation (Reiche 2005). By 2005, Germany had installed wind power capacity of 18,427.5 megawatts (MW) and photovoltaics of 1,537 MW, compared to Canada's 683 for wind and 14.9 for photovoltaics. Installed wind power capacity in Germany reached 22.25 MW by the end of 2007, compared to 1.84 MW in Canada. Germany started its alternative energy promotion policy after the first oil price crisis. And then after policy breakthroughs in 1998 and then 2002, Germany was a world leader in installed wind power capacity and ranked first in photovoltaics.

Meanwhile, in Canada, alternative energy was barely visible in energy policy practice. In part this was due to strong provincial governmental control over electricity policy and also to the fact that there was limited federal leverage because there is scarcely any east-west electricity grid through which some federal policy influences might have effect. But even if there had been such pan-Canadian imperatives, it is unlikely that federal initiatives would have emerged.

Federal policies were focused upon oil, gas, and nuclear power, as we have seen, for most of the 1980s and 1990s, based on strong support for liberalized markets – a view that did not extend to the necessary practical task of 'creating' markets for alternative energy. In the early years of the twenty-first century, some provincial initiatives for so-called green power began to emerge in Ontario, Quebec, and Prince Edward Island (Lipp 2007). These are likely to grow and to receive increased technology and innovation funding as well. But overall the place of alternative energy in Canada has been very marginal in the face of interests and governments whose priorities have been else-where. Even Canada's large hydro power sources are now often not cast as real renewable sources. In Quebec, Aboriginal peoples are still engaged in lawsuits against Hydro Québec and the Quebec provincial government for the damage caused by the earlier building of huge hydroelectric dams. Only small hydro projects, which are less disruptive to the environment, fit the current definition of renewable energy.

Climate Change, Kyoto, and beyond Kyoto

Climate change policy with a focus on the 1997 Kyoto Protocol has been the centrepiece of the core interactions between energy policy and regulation and environmental and sustainable development (SD) policy and regulation. The analysis by Rivers and Jaccard in chapter 11, and in chapter 12 by Weidner and Eberlein, shows the variety of commitments made by signatory countries to reduce their greenhouse gas emissions through a variety of domestic measures or through the arrangement of credits for reductions achieved in other countries.

Overall, the politics of Kyoto since the early 1990s has been forged around the refusal of the United States to sign the protocol and to opt instead, in the George W. Bush administration, for a technology-first approach rather than regulatory intervention. In February 2002 the United States announced its own unilateral alternative to Kyoto centred on voluntary approaches for U.S. energy producers and incentives for new technology development on alternative energy technologies (Schelling 2002; Victor 2001).

This policy fitted in directly with the Bush National Energy Policy (NEP). Drafted by Vice-President Dick Cheney in an administration whose Cabinet contained several ex–energy industry executives, the Bush NEP is unabashedly a supply-driven and -dominated policy (Government of the United States 2001). The policy was crafted in the midst of rapidly rising gas prices at the pump and in home heating fuel and was forged in the midst of the electricity crisis in California, where electricity prices were soaring and blackouts frequent (Jaccard 2002). The central features of the Bush NEP were as follows:

- Ease restrictions on oil and gas development on public lands;
- Open part of the Arctic National Wildlife Refuge in Alaska for drilling;

- Reconsider requirements for 'boutique' gasoline blends that contribute to supply shortages;
- Streamline the approval process for siting power plants;
- Create government authority for takeover of private property for power lines;
- Provide tax breaks for developing clean coal technologies;
- Ease regulatory barriers, including clean-air rules to speed expansion or build new plants;
- Speed nuclear safety reviews in the re-licensing of reactors and the licensing of new plants;
- Limit industry liability from a nuclear accident.

The Bush NEP also included some tax breaks for renewable energy and conservation but these were decidedly secondary in the plan as a whole. However, following Bush's 2006 State of the Union address in which he emphasized American's unhealthy 'addiction to oil,' the Bush administration further increased its funding for research and development to energize its alternative Kyoto approach.

The overall politics of the Kyoto Protocol also centred on the fact that developing countries were not a part of the protocol on the grounds that it was essentially the developed Western countries that had created the problem and that, moreover, developing countries would need expanded energy growth as they themselves grew and hopefully prospered economically. Increasingly, by mid-decade, and following the 2005 Gleneagles G8 summit, the Bush administration, backed by big U.S. energy interests, began forging an alternative and also 'beyond' Kyoto small coalition around the Asia-Pacific Partnership on Clean Development and Climate. It consisted of Kyoto non-signatory countries, which crucially included China and India – the two developing but dynamic and fast-growing economies whose energy needs were insatiable but whose rapidly increasing GHG emissions could also negate climate change progress in other ways. Indeed, key advocates of the Kyoto Protocol saw it, even if implemented, as merely the first in a series of steps to tackle climate change in the decades beyond the protocol end date of 2012 (Grubb, Vrolijk, and Brack 1999; Houghton 1997; Muller 2005). The Bali UN Climate Conference in December 2007 was mired in conflict but reached a consensus on a post-Kyoto road map: a new global regime is to be put in place by 2009. Canada, with Australia, Japan, and Russia, joined the United States in opposing mention of specific emissions reduction targets for industrialized countries (20 to 40 per cent below 1990 levels by 2020), a proposal that the EU countries vigorously campaigned for. Future developments will essentially hinge on the evolving U.S. position after a new administration takes power in early 2009.

Current and near-term energy policies are clearly being influenced by the climate change debate, but such policies are always partly premised on long-term energy projections and scenarios already sketched out above. A central question in assessing these scenarios is whether countries are planning for, or moving towards, a low carbon economy. The notion of what *low carbon* means and whether it can be achieved is of course itself contentious.

Some argue that the past patterns of change in fuel use have been steady progress towards a *lower* carbon economy, in that the movement from wood to coal to oil to gas, etc., has involved a movement from high carbon to lower carbon emissions per unit of energy (Dunn 2001). But of course economic and population growth means that carbon emissions have been growing to the point where climate change effects became a serious global issue.

The term *low carbon economy* also implies the question of how fast such a movement or progression might occur. The speed of the transition to 'low(er) carbon' is driven by the power of established producer interests, their alliances with governments, and the counter-pressure of new energy-producer and manufacturing interests, environmental lobbies, and their alliances with governments.

This book's two climate change chapters (11 and 12) show that in Germany and Canada the Kyoto and climate change policy and implementation story could not be more starkly different. Germany had succeeded by 2003 in reducing its GHG emissions by 18.5 per cent since 1990, and Canada's had increased by 24.2 per cent (Mittelstaedt 2005). As Rivers and Jaccard show in chapter 11, the Canadian underperformance was largely due to policy and regulatory failures on actions that really began to be implemented only in 2002 and later. But it was also due to Canada's higher population growth and also better overall economic growth (Jaccard 2007). Germany, meanwhile, as Weidner and Eberlein show in chapter 12, achieved its significant reductions partly through better policies on climate protection and through its world leading policies in the use of non- or low-carbon alternative energy sources (see chapter 14), but also because, after German unification, the absorption of the weaker former East German economy meant that Germany's overall economic growth faltered, and outdated Eastern coal-fired plants had to close, thus also reducing GHG emissions.

The German and Canadian institutional contexts for climate change policy and governance also differ because of the much greater progress in the EU on emission trading than has been the case for Canada in North America. Chapter 13 by Ziesing shows the development of emission trading and national allocation plans for the initial allocation period (2005–7) with a focus on Germany. As further discussed in his chapter, there have been serious growing pains for Germany and other countries (Benoit and Minder 2006), but progress has been virtually non-existent for Canada, although this may eventually change under the Harper Conservative government.

In 2005 and 2006 Germany and Canada began governance periods with conservative-led governments in power (in coalition and minority governments, respectively). For Canada, its already weak Kyoto implementation record has been weakened further. The Conservative government of Prime Minister Harper has its power base in Alberta, Canada's oil and oil sands heartland, and it has spoken openly about alternatives to Kyoto in two senses (Calamai 2007). One sense is its view that Canada's current Kyoto policy is based too much on foreign credits rather than on actually taking actions in Canada. Accordingly, it has called for a 'made in Canada' policy that would take action on energy and clean air and would also foster more voluntary approaches in close consultation with the provinces and industry (Curry 2006). It initially cancelled several previous Liberal government Kyoto funding initiatives but then crafted its own alternatives and in 2007 announced its own regulation-centred approach but with required emissions based on a 20 per cent reduction below 2006 levels by 2020 (Canada 2007; Toner 2008). The second sense of having an alternative to Kyoto has come in the form of declarations that Canada will link with the Bush 'second front' coalition of countries referred to above (Fraser 2006), a coalition that would favour a technology-first approach. An anti-Kyoto and beyond-Kyoto position is also inherent in Prime Minister's Harper declaration that he believes that Canada is, and will be under his government's pro-energy policies, a global 'energy superpower' (Calamai 2007). Harper's first summit with President Obama led to an agreement to have a clean energy 'dialogue,' a process that may result in more substantive change.

But these are not the only dynamics at play in Canada. Several provinces are strongly pro-Kyoto as are the three main federal opposition parties. British Columbia announced in 2008 that it would impose a carbon tax, the first jurisdiction in North America to do so. Quebec has announced that it will introduce a carbon tax in that province. Several provinces have decided to join nearby U.S. state governments in creating regional emissions-trading systems. City governments have also announced a pro-Kyoto alliance of actions.

For Germany, the underlying politics for even its new grand coalition, conservative-led government is quite different. As chapter 12 shows, the German government continued the earlier Red-Green coalition policies that put in place strong initiatives on energy alternatives and climate protection. Germany is also committed to making extensive use of progressive instruments (such as auctioning of permits) under the second (and improved) phase of the EU's emissions trading system (2008–12). Germany's energy politics does not have to factor in the presence of a strong producer region as Canada does with Alberta, and it is accustomed to crafting energy policies knowing that it has always been dependent on foreign sources of supply. As we see further below and in chapter 5, Germany also does not have a domestic nuclear reactor industry with its own home-grown preferred reactor technology, and thus for this and other crucial reasons, its domestic politics produced the decision in 2002 to phase out nuclear energy in electricity production.

The international context of climate change policy shifted and broadened further in 2006 and 2007. The U.K. Stern Report broadened the debate through its quite extensive, though controversial, assessment of the economics of climate change (HM Treasury 2007). The G8 Heiligendamm (Germany) Summit also managed to ease the United States into a broader acceptance of the science of climate change, though not of any hard regulatory approaches. U.S. politics had also changed when the 2006 mid-term elections resulted in the Democratic Party taking control of both houses of the U.S. Congress and, in the process, exerted new pressure – mainly positive – on the climate change file. This change followed pressures and actions in numerous U.S. states, in particular aggressive measures by California's Republican governor, Arnold Schwarzenegger, under the Global Warming Solutions Act of 2006 (Assembly Bill 32). The election of President Barack Obama promises a new impetus to tackle climate change but in as yet unclear ways.

A Comeback for Nuclear Energy?

Last but not least in the set of energy challenges is the issue of nuclear energy. The twentieth anniversary of the Ukraine's Chernobyl nuclear disaster was marked in 2006. Since its occurrence and the earlier U.S. Three Mile Island nuclear accident, the nuclear power industry had been largely dormant, with very few new reactors built and existing reactors aging and in need of more frequent repair and refurbishment

(Grimston and Beck 2002). Among Western countries, only France maintained a strong defence of nuclear energy as its primary energy source. For other energy ministers, nuclear energy became for most of the 1980s and 1990s an energy policy option with only political downsides and no upsides. It was a political 'lose-lose' realm where even the politically brave did not tread (Doern, Dorman, and Morrison 2001).

Its main political-economic characteristics as a power source for electricity have not changed. Its liabilities are still centred on concerns about reactor safety and nuclear proliferation and hence linked to seemingly immovable and unfavourable public perceptions among citizens. They are also centred on the still unresolved issues of how to deal with the long-term storage of nuclear reactor wastes. Moreover, if states want to consider new nuclear plants, the time frames for developing and approving reactors and their high costs loom large.

The advantages of nuclear power were still argued for and supported by the nuclear industry in OECD countries. These were its advantages as a baseline source of power, its role as part of a country's technology policy, and its actual safety as opposed to its perceived lack of safety. Its role as a source of no- or low-carbon emissions was also stressed more in the industry's lobbying and communications campaigns with governments. The nuclear industry was, also during the period of nuclear energy decline, working on new and more efficient reactor technologies.

From 2000 to the present, the nuclear energy option moved from being a 'precarious opportunity' in the future energy mix to a potential opportunity. The more that Kyoto and climate change policy emerged, the more nuclear energy interests could trumpet nuclear energy as a part of the low or lower carbon future.

The more that energy security issues were raised, the more that nuclear could be presented as a reliable national source of energy, provided of course that countries had good access to uranium supplies. The more that the oil and gas pricing system did not factor in its full environmental costs, the more that nuclear power interests could argue that its pricing did (as long as decommissioning and long-term storage costs were kept out of the equation). And the more that some nervous national energy ministers and governments did not want to be the ministers who failed to keep their nation's lights on, the more nuclear energy became a kind of political and energy 'security blanket' of a different kind.

The Mez and Doern analysis in chapter 5 shows that, in our two countries the trajectories of nuclear energy played out in very different political-economic-energy settings. In Germany, nuclear energy continued its rapid phase-out. Influenced partly by Green Party presence in the governing coalition, but also the strong underlying environmental movement in Germany, the nuclear option had few friends and strong public opposition. As a result, in 2002 Germany decided to phase out nuclear power over twenty years, as current nuclear power plants reach the end of their useful life.

Moreover, as we have seen above, because Germany had always been more dependent on foreign sources of energy, it developed alternative energy sources and technologies to a far greater extent than Canada and also in comparison with many fellow EU member countries (Beam 2006; Helm 2005a). For example, in Britain, as the changed realities of energy governance emerged in the early years of the twenty-first century, the Blair Labour Government first refused to rule out more nuclear power and then increasingly and openly endorsed it as a part of the United Kingdom's projected energy mix (Blitz 2006).

In Canada, the nuclear industry had been on political life support for some time, but now, as the Mez and Doern analysis in chapter 5 suggests, it is making a comeback of sorts. Here the core governance coalitions are at the provincial level and mainly in one province, Ontario. As Canada's main nuclear province using Canada's nationally developed CANDU reactors, Ontario also saw the need for nuclear energy in its long-term energy mix and announced in June 2006 that it would build new reactors and refurbish old ones, albeit as a part of a package of energy initiatives that would also see an increased share of energy being supplied by alternative energy sources (Ferguson and Benzie 2006). A federal environmental body also supported greater nuclear energy use in Canada, essentially as the lesser of two evils, with the other evil being the greater use of coal-fired plants (National Roundtable on the Environment and the Economy 2006).

North America was also more favourable to nuclear energy because the U.S. energy policy of 2001 and also later Bush government policy pronouncements also preferred nuclear options for reasons of national energy security, among others. In larger global terms, China's interest in nuclear energy to help fuel its ferocious appetite for energy also added to a more positive nuclear energy climate, with important effects in Canada, for example, because of Canada's (mainly Saskatchewan's) ample supplies of uranium.

Conclusions

This chapter has set out the key energy policy and governance challenges: global future prices, demand, and supply for oil and other fuel and energy sources; broadening notions of energy security in a post-9/11 world; natural gas, including liquefied natural gas, that is fast transforming natural gas from a regional to a global energy source; electricity industry restructuring; climate change, the Kyoto Protocol, and debates about the post–Kyoto Protocol era when even larger GHG emission reductions are needed; alternative energy sources and the need to create markets; and nuclear energy as a low carbon alternative but with its own serious environmental liabilities. These challenges and choices were examined in their own terms as global and regional energy challenges but also through a closer look at Germany and Canada in response to each challenge, and in relation to the significant differences in the structure of core energy business interests and environmental NGOs.

The chapter has shown that, while many of the core aspirations of a good market-driven competitive and environmentally costed energy system garner considerable policy and institutional support, the real world of energy governance has not reached this state of affairs. The imperfections of markets, fundamental conflicts of interest and power relations, and the complexities of competing, cooperating, and colliding governments, companies, and individuals as consumers and citizens produce a quite imperfect energy world.

The remaining chapters in part 1 explore these realms of multi-level energy regulatory governance in their national and regional multi-level contexts, and then the chapters of part 2 will probe the energy governance within Germany and Canada as differently constructed and evolving federations and political systems.

REFERENCES

Beam, Rebecca. 2006. We see the dawn of an atomic age? *Financial Times*, 30 May.

Benoit, Bertrand, and Raphael Minder. 2006. Berlin accused of capitulating to industry in carbon emission targets. *Financial Times*, 29 June.

Blitz, James. 2006. Blair gives full backing to new generation of plants. *Financial Times*, 28 April.

Brownsey, Keith. 2007. Energy shift: Canadian energy policy under the Harper Conservatives. In *How Ottawa spends 2007–2008: The Harper Conservatives; Climate of change*, ed. Bruce Doern, 143–60. Montreal and Kingston: McGill-Queen's University Press.

Calamai, Peter. 2007. The struggle over Canada's role in the post-Kyoto world. In *Innovation, science, environment: Canadian policies and performance*

2007–2008, ed. Bruce Doern, 32–54. Montreal and Kingston: McGill-Queen's University Press.

Canadian Gas Association. 2005. *A sustainable energy future: The role of natural gas*. Toronto: Canadian Gas Association.

Cambridge Energy Research Associates. 2006. LNG supply build on track despite growing pains. Press release. Cambridge: Cambridge Energy Research Associates (CERA).

Cameron, Peter D. 2001. *Competition in energy markets*. Oxford: Oxford University Press.

Canada. 2007. *Turning the corner: An action plan to reduce greenhouse gases and air pollution*. Ottawa: Environment Canada.

Catan, Thomas. 2006. LNG: Worries grow over supplies. *Financial Times*, 30 May.

Commission of the European Communities. 2006. Green paper: A European strategy for sustainable, competitive, and secure energy (COM 2006, 105 final). Brussels, 8 March 2006.

Csamanski, Daniel. 1999. *Privatization and restructuring of electricity provision*. Westport, CT: Praeger.

Curry, Bill. 2006. Ottawa wants Kyoto softened. *Globe and Mail*, 12 May.

Doern, G. Bruce, ed. 2005. *Canadian energy policy and the struggle for sustainable development*. Toronto: University of Toronto Press.

Doern, G. Bruce, Arslan Dorman, and Robert Morrison, eds. 2001. *Canadian nuclear energy policy: Changing ideas, institutions and interests*. Toronto: University of Toronto Press.

Doern, G. Bruce, and Monica Gattinger. 2003. *Power switch: Energy regulatory governance in the 21st century*. Toronto: University of Toronto Press.

Dunn, Seth. 2001. Decarbonizing the energy economy. In *State of the world 2001*, ed. Lester Brown, 83–101. London: Norton.

Economist. 2006. Steady as she goes: Why the world is not about to run out of oil. 22 April.

Ferguson, Rob, and Robert Benzie. 2006. Ontario opts for nuclear plants. *Toronto Star*, 13 June.

Finon, Dominique, and Atle Midttun, eds. 2004. *Reshaping European gas and electricity industries*. London: Elsevier.

Fraser, Graham. 2006. Harper praises non-Kyoto group as 'the kind of initiative the world needs. *Toronto Star*, 20 May.

Gilbert, Richard J., and Edward P. Kahn, eds. 1996. *International comparisons of electricity regulations*. Cambridge: Cambridge University Press.

Glachant, Jean-Michel, and Dominique Finon, eds. 2003. *Competition in European electricity markets*. Cheltenham, UK: Elgar.

Government of the United States. 2001. *Reliable, affordable and environmentally sound energy for America's future*. Washington DC: U.S. Government Printing Office.

Grimston, Malcolm C., and Peter Beck. 2002. *Double or quits: The global future of civil nuclear energy*. London: Earthscan.

Grubb, Michael, with Christiaan Vrolijk and Duncan Brack. 1999. *The Kyoto Protocol: A guide and assessment*. London: Royal Institute of International Affairs.

Helm, Dieter. 2003. *Energy, the state and the market: British energy policy since 1979*. Oxford: Oxford University Press.

– , ed. 2005a. *Climate change policy*. Oxford: Oxford University Press.

– 2005b. European energy policy: Securing supplies and meeting the challenge of climate change. Paper prepared for the U.K. presidency of the European Union.

Hirsch, Richard F. 1999. *Power loss: The origins of deregulation and restructuring in the American electric utility system*. Cambridge, MA: MIT Press.

HM Treasury. 2007. Stern review on the economics of climate change. Cambridge: Cambridge University Press.

Houghton, John. 1997. *Global warming: The complete briefing*. 2nd ed. Cambridge: Cambridge University Press.

Hoyos, Carola, and Javier Blas. 2006. Oil wrestling: How nationalist politics has muscled its way back into world energy. *Financial Times*, 5 May.

Hunt, Sally. 2002. *Making competition work in electricity*. New York: Wiley.

IEA. *See* International Energy Agency.

International Energy Agency. 2004a. *Energy policies of IEA countries*. Paris: International Energy Agency.

– 2004b. *World energy outlook 2004*. Paris: International Energy Agency.

– 2005a. *Lessons from liberalised electricity markets*. Paris: International Energy Agency.

– 2005b. *World energy outlook 2005*. Paris: International Energy Agency.

– 2006a. *Energy technology perspectives: Scenarios and strategies to 2050*. Paris: International Energy Agency.

– 2006b. *World energy outlook 2006: Summary and conclusions*. Paris: International Energy Agency.

– 2007. *Energy policies of IEA countries: Germany 2007 review*. Paris: International Energy Agency.

Jaccard, Mark. 2002. California shorts a circuit: Should Canadians trust the wiring diagram? *C.D. Howe Institute Commentary* 159.

– 2007. *Designing Canada's low-carb diet: Options for effective climate policy*. Toronto: C.D. Howe Institute.

Jamasb, Tooraj, and Michael Pollit. 2005. Electricity market reform in the EU: Review of progress towards liberalisation and integration. Special issue, *Energy Journal* 22 (2): 11–43.

Lafferty, William M., and James Meadowcroft, eds. 2000. *Implementing sustainable development*. Oxford: Oxford University Press.

Leggett, Jeremy. 2005. *Half gone: Oil, gas, hot air and the global energy crisis*. London: Portobello Books.

Lipp, Judith. 2007. Renewable energy policies and the provinces. In *Innovation, science, environment: Canadian policies and performance 2007–2008*, ed. Bruce Doern, 176–99. Montreal and Kingston: McGill-Queen's University Press.

Maugeri, Leonardo. 2006. Two years for expensive oil. *Foreign Affairs* 85 (2): 149–61.

Mittelstaedt, Martin. 2005. Canada's greenhouse-gas emissions rise. *Globe and Mail*, 28 November.

Muller, Benito. 2005. Climate change post-2012: Transatlantic consensus and disagreements. *Journal for Energy Literature* 11 (1): 22–33.

National Roundtable on the Environment and the Economy. 2006. *Advice on long-term strategy on energy and climate change*. Ottawa: National Roundtable on the Environment and the Economy.

Padgett, Stephen. 2003. Between synthesis and emulation: EU policy transfer in the power sector. *Journal of European Public Policy* 10 (2): 227–46.

Palast, Greg, J. Oppenheim, and T. MacGregor. 2003. *Democracy and regulation: How the public can govern essential services*. London: Pluto.

Prime Minister's Office. 2005. Security and prosperity partnership of North America established. News release. 23 March.

Reiche, Danyel, ed. 2005. Handbook of renewable energies in the European Union: Case-studies of the EU-15 states. 2nd ed. Berlin: Lang.

Schelling, Thomas C. 2002. What makes greenhouse sense? *Foreign Affairs* 81 (3): 1–9.

Stern, Jonathan. 2006. *The future of Russian gas and Gazprom*. Oxford: Oxford Institute of Energy Studies.

Toner, Glen. 2000. Canada: From early frontrunner to plodding anchorman. In *Implementing sustainable development*, ed. William M. Lafferty and James Meadowcroft, 98–125. Oxford: Oxford University Press.

– , ed. 2006. *Sustainable production*. Vancouver: UBC Press.

– , ed. 2008. *Innovation, science, environment: Canadian policies and performance 2008–2009*. Montreal and Kingston: McGill-Queen's University Press.

Victor, David G. 2001. *The collapse of the Kyoto Protocol and the struggle to slow global warming*. Princeton: Princeton University Press.

Yergin, Daniel. 2006. Ensuring energy security. *Foreign Affairs* 85 (2): 69–82.

PART ONE

Industry Transformations and
Comparative Multi-Level Regulatory
Governance

3 Electricity Restructuring in the Provinces: Pricing, Politics, Starting Points, and Neighbours

DONALD N. DEWEES

Economists like restructuring because it should improve efficiency. Competitive forces in the generation sector should squeeze the inefficiency out of monopoly generators, while market discipline should lead to better investment decisions. The wholesale price should reflect marginal cost, and passing this price to consumers should lead to optimal energy use and conservation, allowing the price to equate supply and demand in every hour of every day. But competitive electricity markets are artificial markets with extensive rules for all participants arising from the complex interconnections of the electricity network. Governments or regulatory agencies oversee market design and the operation and maintenance of the market, so market design is necessarily a political process involving technical and political capacity.

This chapter explores the institutional side of electricity restructuring. We review the history of restructuring in Ontario and, more briefly, in Alberta. We examine the criteria for electricity pricing in competitive markets and the impact of prices on participants in the electricity system. We evaluate the political forces that have operated on restructuring in Canada, particularly in Ontario, their effects, and the implications of those forces for future market design. Letting a competitive market set the price means that governments cannot ensure a specific future price level, and both theory and experience tell us that prices may increase after restructuring. This makes it difficult for elected leaders to sell restructuring to consumers, who will be more interested in lower prices than in efficiency.

We explore the ways in which institutional starting points influence what is politically feasible. The problems are different and more complex if one begins with a Crown monopoly than if one has investor-owned utilities; if expected prices are higher than recent prices rather than lower; if governments have been deeply involved in the electricity sector rather than distant from it; and if the public has experience with stable electricity prices rather than fluctuating prices. Ontario started with a popular Crown monopoly, prices below cost, government involvement, and prices frozen for a decade – not a strong foundation on which to build competition.

Finally, we look at the importance of neighbouring jurisdictions for the operation of an electricity market and for the competitive design that might be feasible. Are neighbouring prices higher or lower than domestic prices? Can neighbouring generators contribute to a competitive structure? Will electricity imports bring imported pollution? We conclude that successful restructuring requires the pursuit of economic efficiency, but that equal attention must be paid to the politics, the starting points, and the neighbours.

Electricity restructuring requires the elimination of the traditional statutory monopoly on generation and allowing competition in generation as well as requiring the transmission owners to transmit power from generators to their customers. It may go further and establish a competitive wholesale power pool that sets an hourly (more or less) spot price or allow retail competition.[1] Joskow has argued that the primary driver for restructuring in the United States was the high prices charged by regulated utilities in the 1990s as they recovered the cost of investments in expensive facilities, when falling natural gas prices and increased efficiency of combined cycle gas turbine (CCGT) plants reduced the cost of new generation (Joskow 1997, 123). In practice, introducing competition in electricity has been more difficult than for railroads, trucking, airlines, natural gas, and long distance telephone rates, because of politics, starting points, and neighbours.

History of Restructuring in Ontario and Alberta

Ontario

A century ago the government of Ontario created the Hydro-Electric Power Commission of Ontario, which Sir Adam Beck developed into the provincial Crown corporation responsible for generation, transmission, and distribution of most of the electricity in the province. In the first half of the twentieth century inexpensive hydroelectric power from the Niagara River provided low-cost electricity. In the 1950s and 1960s HEPCO built coal-fired generating stations and in the 1970s and 1980s it added nuclear generation, both of which cost much more than hydro power. The *Power Corporation Act* required Ontario Hydro, as HEPCO was renamed in 1972, to provide 'power at cost,' which has become part of the lore of electricity supply in Ontario. The utility did not pay taxes or generate profits. The government of Ontario appointed the directors of Ontario Hydro; guaranteed all of its debt, and through the minister of energy could issue policy directives to Ontario Hydro. Ontario Hydro set its own rates, subject to review but not amendment by the Ontario Energy Board (OEB). With a headquarters close to the provincial Parliament buildings, Ontario Hydro was always close to the government, and there has been debate whether the government controlled Ontario Hydro or vice versa.[2]

As chapter 5 on nuclear power by Mez and Doern shows, the high cost of the Darlington nuclear station drove up prices by 30 per cent in the early 1990s as Ontario Hydro rolled the costs into its rates. The resulting public outcry led the government to freeze the price in 1993 somewhat below actual costs, a freeze that lasted until 2002. In 1995, the government of Ontario appointed a committee chaired by Donald Macdonald to study options for competition in Ontario's electricity system. The committee's report, *A Framework for Competition*, was issued in 1996 and recommended the establishment of wholesale electricity competition. Retail competition, in which distributors would manage a portfolio of supply contracts for customers who did not choose a retailer, was to follow. Ontario Hydro's generation assets were to be divided among competing units: four separately operated nuclear entities with a single owner; the fossil fuel plants to be operated as independent units, and the hydroelectric facilities to be established as separate entities for each river system (ACCOES 1996, 58–61). The government responded with a White Paper on electricity reform in November 1997, which suggested that Ontario Hydro should be divided into a generation company (now Ontario Power Generation, or OPG) and a transmission company (now Hydro One) (Ontario 1997, 18). There was no suggestion of breaking up or selling off the generation assets of Ontario Hydro. The white paper proposed to achieve full wholesale and retail competition by 2000 (ibid., 16). The government then appointed the Ontario Market Design Committee, which worked through 1998 to recommend an initial market design and a set of market rules (OMDC 1999). The MDC was given to understand that it should not recommend breaking up and selling off the generation assets of Ontario Hydro, so it designed an alternative mechanism to achieve a competitive result, the Market Power Mitigation Agreement (MPMA). The wholesale price, which had been around 4.3 cents/kWh was expected to be about 3.8 cents/kWh when the electricity market opened, although independent power producers complained that new investment in generation required much higher prices. Ontario Hydro's average total cost was thought to be in the vicinity of 4.5 cents/kWh, so a 'stranded debt' charge of 0.7 cents would be required on top of the market price.

Legislation divided Ontario Hydro into a transmission company and a generation company, and established the Independent Market Operator and the framework for a competitive wholesale and retail market.[3] Because OPG generated 90 per cent or so of the electricity in Ontario, the MPMA provided a revenue cap for OPG at 3.8 cents/kWh, which was to be relaxed as OPG sold or otherwise divested itself of control of generating capacity. The revenue cap would be lifted entirely when OPG controlled only 35 per cent of the generating capacity (OMDC 1999, 2-4 to 2-6). The wholesale market incorporated an hourly spot market managed by the IMO, competition in generation, support for bilateral contracts, and default supply by local distribution companies (LDCs) to customers who do not choose a retail supplier (OMDC 1999, 3-7 to 3-9). The Ontario Energy Board was to regulate the monopoly elements of the system, including distribution and transmission, as well as regulating retailing and other activities.

By 1998 eight nuclear units at Pickering A and Bruce A were out of service for serious maintenance and upgrading. As chapters 1 and 15 argue, such inherent capacity issues or the lack thereof are crucial to energy governance. It was expected that most nuclear units would be back on line before market opening, but in fact none were. OPG had, in 2001, leased the Bruce nuclear station to British Energy/Bruce Power, thus reducing its share of generation to about 70 per cent. Unable to delay any further, the government opened Ontario's competitive market on 1 May 2002, utilizing a mandatory pool and passing the spot price to any consumer who had not signed up with a retailer for a fixed price. About 1 million consumers had signed contracts with retailers for electricity at prices around 5.7 cents/kWh. Consumers without retail contracts would receive a rebate if the revenue received by Ontario Power Generation averaged more than 3.8 cents/kWh over an entire year, with the rebate reflecting the pro-

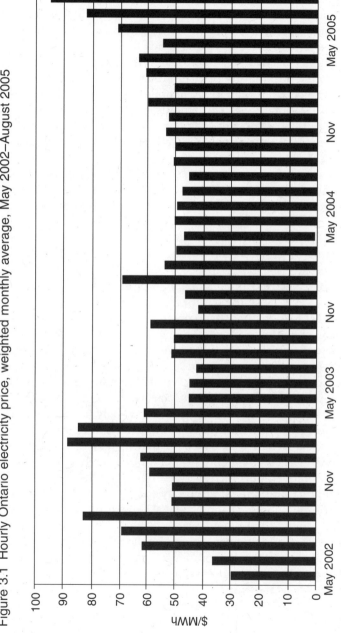

Figure 3.1 Hourly Ontario electricity price, weighted monthly average, May 2002–August 2005

portion of total Ontario generation produced by OPG, expected to be about half in 2002.

Record drought and heatwaves in the summer of 2002 combined with a shortage of nuclear units to spike the peak hourly price to $4.71/kWh on 2 July, more than 100 times the normal price, and a monthly average price for July of 6.2 cents (IMO 2002, 5). September was worse, with a peak hourly price of $10.28/kWh. Monthly average price nearly tripled from May to September (see figure 3.1). The IMO called for conservation to avoid brownouts and blackouts. Consumers, who faced high bills as a result of higher prices and of running their air conditioners heavily during the summer, were outraged. On 11 November 2002 the government announced a price freeze for smaller consumers at 4.3 cents, embracing the second-worst feature of the California market design. The freeze would be retroactive to market opening, so that customers would receive rebates for the high summer prices.[4] The price freeze eliminated the price incentive to conserve electricity and damaged investor confidence, reducing the likelihood of investment in new generation facilities and of being able to sell or lease OPG facilities.

In November 2002 the price since market opening had averaged over 5.5 cents/kWh, close to 50 per cent above the price expected in 1998. Yet the MPMA ensured that consumers would receive a rebate for about half of the excess over 3.8 cents. Moreover the wholesale price represents less than half of the consumer's electricity bill. Table 3.1 shows the components of a typical Ontario consumer's monthly bill and the cost to the consumer per kWh at different wholesale prices. A wholesale price of 5.5 cents would increase the consumer's bill by only 12 per cent, and the net cost after rebate by only 6.2 per cent over the baseline of 4.3 cents. Consumers were actually exposed to very little price risk. The rebate was to be paid at the end of a year, however, and most consumers seemed either ignorant of the rebate or dissatisfied with it. Moreover, bills increased by more than this because consumers used large amounts of electricity for air conditioning during the summer of 2002. Table 3.1 shows that a 20 per cent increase in electricity consumption alone would increase the bill by at least 15 per cent, an increase greater than that caused by the price increase over the first six months of market operation. Consumption was a larger problem than price but consumers seem not to have separated the two.

February 2003 was the worst month yet, with a peak price during a cold snap of $3.75/kWh and a monthly average price of 8.86 cents

Table 3.1 Effect of wholesale price in Ontario residential consumer's bill, 700 kWh, 2002

Monthly average wholesale price (cents/kWh)	4.3¢	5.5¢	8.0¢
Wholesale charges[a] (cents/kWh)	1.32¢	1.32¢	1.32¢
Transmission[b] and distribution[c] (cents/kWh)	2.38¢	2.38¢	2.38¢
Total of per kWh charges (cents/kWh)	8.0¢	9.2¢	11.7¢
Total charge for 700 kWh	$56.00	$64.40	$81.90
Monthly customer charge (fixed)	$14.00	$14.00	$14.00
GST @ 7%	$4.90	$5.49	$6.71
Monthly bill	**$74.90**	**$83.89**	**$102.61**
% bill increase from price > 4.3 cents	0%	12%	37%
Rebate[d]	($1.87)	($6.37)	($15.73)
Net cost after rebate	**$73.03**	**$77.52**	**$86.88**
% net cost increase from price > 4.3 cents	0.0%	6.2%	19.0%
Monthly bill for 20% more electricity	**$86.10**	**$97.67**	**$120.14**
% bill increase for 20% more electricity[e]	15.0%	16.4%	17.1%

[a]Debt reduction charge 0.7; IMO and other charges 0.62/kWh.
[b]Transmission charge 1.04 cents in 2002.
[c]Distribution charges vary among municipalities. Toronto charge was 1.34 cents/kWh.
[d]Assuming that the Market Power Mitigation Agreement rebate equals half of the excess of the wholesale price over the MPMA price of 3.8 cents. Including 7% GST.
[e]Not considering the rebate. % increase in a column compared to the bill with the wholesale price in the same column.

(IMO 2003, 5). The weighted average wholesale price for the first full year of market operation to 30 April 2003 was 6.22 cents/kWh – 64 per cent greater than the expected price of 3.8 cents and 38 per cent above Ontario Hydro's average total cost of a few years previously of 4.5 cents. Small consumers paid 4.3 cents.

In December 2001 the premier had announced his intention to sell the transmission company, Hydro One, but a court challenge led to cancellation of the sale. During the summer of 2002 a scandal erupted over compensation of the CEO of Hydro One, and the government replaced the directors of Hydro One, who fired the CEO, who then sued for millions of dollars in damages for wrongful dismissal (Simon 2002). These gyrations heightened the unease among investors interested in the electricity business in Ontario.[5]

The price freeze was extended to a somewhat larger number of consumers in 2003. To mitigate the cost of subsidising this price, on 1 April 2004 the price cap for small consumers was raised to 4.7 cents for the first 750 kWh consumed in a month and 5.5 cents for any additional consumption. Some nuclear stations were returned to service in 2003 and 2004. Average wholesale prices in 2003–4 fell to 5.07 cents. The summer of 2004 was cool and wet and the average wholesale price in 2004–5 was 5.31 cents (IESO 2005). On 1 April 2005 the price cap was raised to 5 cents for the first 750 kWh and 5.8 cents for any excess; and in November 2005 the threshold for the two prices was modified to 1000 kwh per month for the winter and 600 kWh per month for the summer. In addition, the price that OPG would receive for the output of its nuclear units and its baseload hydroelectric units was regulated by the OEB. In the future the regulated two-tier price for small consumers would be based on the regulated cost of power from prescribed OPG plants, the capped price of power from other OPG assets, the contract cost of power from independent producers, and the forecast spot market price (OEB 2005a, 2005b).

Alberta

In Alberta, there were several integrated utilities, including investor-owned utilities and municipal utilities. Coal was the main fuel, followed by natural gas. The Alberta market began operation 1 January 1996, adopting a mandatory power pool and consumers paying the spot price, with distribution costs and other fees added on.[6] The wholesale price was determined by bids from generators, so the system operators could dispatch plants in merit order. Local distribution utilities retained the obligation to supply customers, and the six largest distributors were assigned a share of the output of the existing generators at a fixed price. Consumers in Alberta were encouraged to purchase hedges to mitigate price fluctuations (Alberta Energy 1997; McNamara 1998). Partial retail access, which allowed customers to purchase directly from retailers or generators rather than taking their LDC's price, began on 1 April 1999, with full retail access in 2001. In 2003 the Alberta Electric System Operator took over the functions of the former Power Pool and the Transmission Administrator. The AESO operates the spot market and plans the electricity system (AESO 2004).

Despite steady economic growth, there was little growth in generation capacity from 1994 to 1998, pending the resolution of some market design issues. Wholesale prices were stable during most of 1996 but rose sharply during the last quarter of 1996, although the average for the year was still only $14.42/MWh. In 1997 prices averaged $20.39, an increase of about 40 per cent over 1996. The price averaged $42.74 in

1999 and rocketed to $133.22 in 2000 (AESO 2005, 2). Consumers complained and the government implemented a consumer protection plan, the Regulated Rate Option (RRO). Residential consumers in 2001 paid a high regulated price – 11 cents/kWh – but received a rebate of $40 per month, yielding an average electricity cost of 6.5 cents/kWh for an average consumer. The RRO set a high marginal price for electricity, preserving the incentive to conserve electricity, but the fixed monthly rebate relieved the financial burden of the high price. For medium and large commercial and industrial customers the price was the same as in the RRO but a per-kWh rebate reduced the net price to 7.6 cents/kWh. Utilities started offering their own RRO rates in 2002, which in November 2002 ranged from 4.8 cents to 6.8 cents/kWh, while retailers offered fixed price contracts.[7] This RRO has apparently brought stability to the Alberta market while encouraging conservation. However, the generation market is highly concentrated, with two firms often setting the price, so a truly competitive result seems improbable.

Electricity Pricing: Volatility

Electricity cannot be stored; it must be generated when it is consumed. Long distance transportation is feasible but costly. A typical service area will have three types of generation facilities. *Baseload plants* have high capital cost and low operating cost; they can be nuclear, run-of-the-river hydroelectric, or coal-fired thermal plants. *Mid-merit plants* have moderate capital and operating costs; they are usually coal- or oil-fired steam turbine plants, or combined cycle gas turbines (CCGT). *Peaking plants* have low capital cost and high operating cost and often rely on a simple gas turbine or storage hydroelectric power. Most electric utilities dispatch plants in merit order, starting with the lowest marginal cost plants, which minimizes the cost of generation. The aggregate marginal cost curve for a typical fleet of plants rises gradually over a range of output as baseload and mid-merit plants are used but rises rapidly as capacity is approached and peaking plants must be run. Complexity and capacity are therefore intricately linked.

Turning from supply to demand, empirical studies have found price elasticities of demand for electricity to be relatively small in the short run and near unity in the long run (Faruqui and George 2002; Ham, Mountain, and Chan 1997). This inelastic short-run demand combined with inelastic short-run supply may cause volatile spot prices for electricity when demand approaches capacity.

Restructured markets that are fully competitive use bids by generators to set a wholesale spot price reflecting the price-setting bid for that hour.[8] If generators cannot exercise market power, this spot price should represent the short run marginal cost of generation. Economists' enthusiasm for competitive markets arises from the use of this price to equate supply and demand in real time; at every moment (or hour anyway) generators and consumers are matching supply and demand at a market price. At the margin, the cost of generation should equal the value of consumption.

Shifts in either supply or demand may substantially increase or decrease the short run marginal cost, and thus the efficient price, especially if the system is close to full capacity utilization. In a competitive market, the spot price will respond at once to these factors. With inelastic demand and supply, the price variation can be considerable. Wolak found that the standard deviation of hourly prices within a year in five restructured markets was sometimes greater than the annual mean, and was at least one-third of the mean in half of the cases (Wolak 2000, 129, 130). If a system experiences a supply-demand crunch, as happened in California in 2000, in Alberta in 2000, and in Ontario in 2002 and 2005, the weekly and monthly average prices may rise substantially. In California, the price rose from an annual average of about $30/MWh in 1998 and 1999 to an annual average of $115 in 2000 (Joskow 2001, table 1). The average Alberta price in the year 2000 was 13.9 cents/kWh, more than five times the annual average in 1996, the first year of market operation. The average price in Ontario during the first full year of market operation was $62/MWh – 38 per cent greater than the average total cost for the preceding several years. Figure 3.1 shows monthly average prices in Ontario for 2002 through 2005. The prices during June, July, and August of 2005 are higher than in the same months in any of the preceding three years.

Charging customers a marginal cost price or the spot price is efficient, but it can lead to variable electricity bills, as was dramatically demonstrated in Alberta in 2000 when high spot prices doubled or tripled normal electricity bills, in California in 2000, and in Ontario in 2002 and 2003. If the utilities had still been under rate-of-return regulation, their cost-based prices would have barely risen in these years. Whether the utility operates its few, high-marginal cost units for 5 per cent of the year or 10 per cent of the year will only modestly affect its total costs. However, if the price for all power generated in an hour is set by the marginal cost of generation in that hour, increasing the time spent at high marginal cost by 5 per cent can substantially increase the generator's revenue and the customer's cost. With marginal cost pricing, small shifts in supply or demand can affect the marginal cost by much more than they affect average total cost.

Restructuring and Politics

The politics of restructuring includes two quite different questions. The first relates to the governance of the independent system operator and other institutions that will manage the market, dispatch the power, and maintain the rules. This chapter addresses a second question: how does a government or regulator approach restructuring and what forces does it respond to? Here the literature is relatively thin. There are at least two broad theories as to how governments would behave in addressing regulatory issues generally and electricity restructuring in particular. The 'public interest theory' assumes that government agencies try to determine what will maximize public welfare and then to pursue policies to achieve this end. This is an attractive theory, except that it seems not to explain much of what governments actually do. Joskow rejects 'public interest' as a major force behind electricity restructuring in the United States, accepting instead special interest pleading, specifically the desire of large customers to pay a price lower than the average cost of generation in jurisdictions where that average cost is high (Joskow 1997, 125–7). The self-interest models assume that policies emerge as the result of the self-interested activities of affected individuals and groups. One such model is the median-voter model, which predicts that voters and their elected representatives will generate policies that reflect the interests of the median voter in the relevant group(s). Stigler (1971) and Peltzman (1976) argue that regulators are captured by the regulated firms; this theory would predict that electricity restructuring would serve the interests of the most powerful stakeholders in the industry. Another set of models looks at the political process, incorporating the preferences of politicians and of agencies, so that policies are affected by the demands of supporters but also by the relationships of individuals within the government (Keohane, Revesz, and Stavins 1998, 554–8). The private interest theories are most persuasive, and the outcome of restructuring can be expected to be shaped largely by the political influence of the major stakeholders and of small consumers/individual voters.

Ando and Palmer (1998) analyse the factors that induce legislators and regulators to adopt retail competition. Factors that increase the likelihood of a state moving toward retail competition include one interest group that dominates the others; high regulated prices; lower prices in adjoining states; and larger price variations among utilities within the state. The last three factors are all indicators that competition might lower prices for consumers as low-price generators outbid high-price generators. Hirsch (1999) finds that the consensus early in the twentieth century that electric utilities were a natural monopoly was displaced in the last quarter of the century with a belief that competition could perform better, given the increasing utility problems of operating nuclear plants and building new plants in the face of strict environmental requirements. White (1996) calculates the expected gains and losses to consumers and utilities in each state and finds that restructuring has proceeded most rapidly where the expected price changes are the greatest.

Ontario's restructuring seems to have been motivated by the government's belief that Ontario Hydro was performing poorly by the 1990s, evidenced by the huge cost overruns at Darlington and consequent price increases (see also chapter 5 by Mez and Doern). ACCOES (1997, 20–4) identified as motivators an increasingly competitive climate for Ontario industry; the steadily increasing price of electricity, which was approaching that of U.S. states; the expectation that electricity competition would lower prices in the United States; the development of efficient small-scale CCGT generators, and the demand for a wider variety of services including metering and energy-management technology. It appears that major power users were strong supporters of competition. It is unlikely that small consumers wanted competition or customer choice, but the government's white paper emphasized choice and the lowest possible prices for consumers as well as increasing jobs.

While the government was attracted by the benefits of competition, it could not bring itself to support the necessary structural changes, mainly separating the control of individual Ontario Hydro generating stations and selling or leasing some of them so they would compete with each other. It compromised by embracing the benefits but not the costs. Here it tried to please two constituencies – consumers (small and large) who wanted lower prices, and those who wanted to build new generation. In practice, the initial high prices displeased consumers and the price freeze on 11 November 2002 displeased generators and would-be investors.

The MDC's recommendation to pass the spot price directly to all consumers was radical, and was agreed upon by the committee only after vigorous discussion. Its advocates liked the efficiency of the price signal that it generated, in addition to which it greatly simplified the administration of retail competition. The MDC felt that the risk of price volatility was addressed by the MPMA rebate, and the government was initially persuaded. In practice, consumers were either insufficiently informed about the rebate or thought it was too late or too little. After six months of market operation, the government could not withstand the public outcry and imposed the price cap, thereby satisfying small consumers but destroying investor confidence in the Ontario market for the foreseeable future. The imposition of the price cap was a political reaction to vigorous demands by an unorganized but large interest group: small consumers. Whether the government understood that this cap would undo all the work of the preceding six years is not clear. If so, it suggests the very short time horizon of the government and its interest in being re-elected, rather than in preserving the new electricity market structure that had been erected at great cost.

The Ontario experience supports the interest group model of political action. Generators and large consumers supported the restructuring and helped push it forward. When small consumers concluded that they were being unfairly treated by the new market, the government stepped in to 'protect' them. The government was the owner and thus had its own interests; it failed to give up its control over much of the generation sector, although this was important for competition. The largest risk in competitive electricity markets may not be power shortages or heatwaves but government intervention – sovereign risk. Thought must be given to processes in which a government could preclude its own future intervention.

Ontario's experience also suggests the difficulty of developing policy in a field in which the underlying assumptions are changing. In the mid-1990s it appeared that competition would lower prices, which caused large consumers to support competition. By late 2002 it was clear that competition could increase prices dramatically, eroding support from large and small consumers alike. While the MDC felt that consumers were protected from priced increases by the MPMA, this protection was not sufficient for the high prices that were experienced.

The influence of interest groups is particularly hard to avoid because of the complexity of electricity markets. The intricate interconnections in an electricity system provide enormous opportunities for market participants to impose externalities on each other (Wilson 2002). Extensive, detailed rules are necessary to minimize these opportunities and to ensure an economically efficient market design.[9]

Yet every jurisdiction is different, so the market must be custom designed each time. Coordination is complex. The market participants must be involved in the design to ensure that it meets local needs, to ensure that they understand it well enough to participate intelligently, and to win their support. How does the government – that is, the Cabinet or premier – resist the pleading of special interests when elected officials are unlikely to understand the technical details of the market and may not trust the political instincts of their staff, only a few of whom are likely to understand it well enough to give advice that is in the public interest?

California is an example of market design where the government did not have a clear vision of efficiency and public interest, or perhaps the necessary expertise. Observers have argued that in California some market participants injected design features that served their private advantage while contributing to the flawed performance of the market as a whole.[10] Subsequent government intervention involved decisions made quickly under great political pressure and without regard to expert advice. This made the problems worse, not better.[11]

The Ontario MDC pursued a design that a majority felt would perform efficiently, only to have the entire market undermined by subsequent government intervention when prices rose. In Ontario's case, the market design relied initially on a rebate from OPG to protect consumers from high prices. At market opening the consumer education program was inadequate to inform consumers of what was to come, especially fluctuating prices. In the white paper the government wrung its hands about Ontario's high prices and said that prices and costs would be driven to the 'lowest possible level,' only technically avoiding an explicit promise of lower prices (Ontario 1997, 11). The full title of the 1998 *Electricity Act* included the phrase 'promoting low-cost energy through competition.' In March 2002, Minister Jim Wilson said that the Ontario Hydro monopoly was responsible for high prices, that consumers would enjoy a safe and reliable supply of electricity at the lowest possible cost, and that Ontario would have a reliable supply of electricity for the next decade (*Globe and Mail* 2002). Nowhere did the government's publicity say that prices might increase significantly, despite the experience in California and Alberta.

This reveals another general political problem: the complexity of selling competition. The public will not easily understand the merits of efficient pricing that involves fluctuating prices, or of high prices at times of power shortage, or even of prices high enough to cover costs. Yet in jurisdictions in which the legacy generation has lower costs than new power sources – and this would include most of Canada if we reject new coal plants – competition and marginal cost pricing will more likely lead to higher prices than to lower prices. So if governments sell competition on the basis of lower prices, the public will feel cheated and demand protection if prices rise.

These political problems must be solved if electricity restructuring is to succeed. The key is to seek market designs that are politically robust as well as being robust to technical failures in the electrical system. This means trying to balance costs and benefits for most participants in most likely scenarios. It means that economists must seek designs that solve political problems as well as market problems. There is much to like in pricing systems for small consumers that yield real-time marginal prices with modest bill variations, such as the Alberta RRO, and the San Diego fixed price for a base amount and market price for deviations from that amount and other combinations of a fixed or regulated price with some form of real-time pricing (see, for example, Borenstein 2001). The cost of electricity retailing seems relatively high, so it may be more important for the distributor to provide an acceptably stable default or regulated price to consumers than to encourage consumers to seek such prices from retailers. Thus far, however, such designs have not been adopted widely. Further work on the political economy of efficient and robust markets is clearly needed.

The Importance of Starting Points

Each jurisdiction will have historic features that will influence the development of a market and the optimal design as well as the feasible design. These starting points are important because people tend to regard their current situation as a right, and while they will accept improvements easily they may resist taking away what they currently have; the disutility of a loss exceeds the utility of a gain of the same magnitude. This is an application of 'prospect theory' articulated by Kahneman and Tversky (1979).

The first starting point is the ownership of the electric utilities by public bodies or by private investors. Ontario had a century-long tradition of provincial ownership of most of the generation and transmission system, and municipal ownership of most distribution not owned by the province. This situation is repeated in much of Canada: provincial and municipal ownership dominate the electricity sector except in Alberta, PEI, Nova Scotia, and Newfoundland and Labrador (Canada 1999). During that century the public perception of Ontario

Hydro as a public servant – powerful, expert, and benevolent – was developed or carefully cultivated. If restructuring requires selling or leasing significant assets that have been publicly owned, the public must be persuaded that this is in their interest, which would likely require a major change in the public perception of the utility. This was not remotely accomplished in Ontario. Despite the well-publicized problems that Ontario Hydro experienced in the 1980s and 1990s, people continued to ask why the government was changing things. The public resistance to breaking up OPG or selling its generating stations is a huge barrier to achieving a competitive market structure (see Gattinger's analysis in chapter 8 on related institutional barriers inherent in Canadian federalism overall).

In Quebec, Hydro-Québec may have even greater cultural and symbolic importance. The creation and growth of Hydro-Québec is closely associated with the economic and political growth of the province. It is hard to imagine any of the major hydroelectric generating stations of Hydro-Québec being privatized and sold off to create a competitive market structure.

Perhaps instead of selling assets of a Crown corporation to private investors, the utility could be divided into separate operating units still owned by the government but with instructions each to behave competitively. Before following this path, one would want reassurance from successful experience with this model in some area of Crown corporation activity.

On the other hand, in a jurisdiction with investor-owned utilities there is often little public affection for the monopoly utility. In such a situation there is little problem with public opinion, and one must only confront the legal and financial issues involved in forcing a firm to divest some of its assets.

A second starting point is whether the public utilities are fully integrated or vertically segregated into generation, transmission, and distribution utilities. Fully integrated utilities must be broken up in order to create competitive entities or conditions: it is crucial to separate generation from the other functions. Ontario's situation was mixed, with Ontario Hydro serving a number of large industrial consumers directly, and providing distribution service to many – particularly rural – areas of the province. In addition, Ontario had over three hundred municipal electric utilities prior to restructuring, the smallest with only 113 customers (ACCOES 1996, 13). Many of these were much too small to afford the conversion of their customer software to that appropriate for a competitive market, and others were too small to acquire the expertise needed to operate in the new environment. Consolidation was needed but it met with considerable resistance from the MEUs and their customers, who disliked handing control of their local utility to strangers. Jurisdictions with vertically integrated utilities will not have to deal with consolidation of the local distribution system, but will have to deal with other issues of disintegration.

A third issue is whether recent electricity prices are above or below average total costs of new plants. Suppose that a jurisdiction has a monopoly electric utility whose assets include very expensive plants, while new generation is expected to involve lower-cost facilities. This was the situation of many U.S. utilities in the 1990s when natural gas was inexpensive, nuclear plants were problematic, and coal plants faced increasing environmental protection costs. The main problem here is to compensate the utility for its 'stranded costs' and to prepare consumers for lower prices ahead. More generally, the challenge of competitive market design raises the question of which role the regulator should play.

In the opposite circumstance, consider a jurisdiction utilizing mainly low-cost hydroelectric generation where all the best sites have been used. Any new generation will have average costs well above the existing system average cost. This would be the situation of HEPCO in 1950 or Hydro-Québec or BCHydro today. The first problem here is to persuade the public that higher prices are a good thing because they will support new generation investment. This is a major challenge, which the Ontario government did not meet prior to restructuring. The second problem is to decide 'who gets the cheap power.' Simply allowing all generators to receive the market price will offer windfall gains to those owning the low-cost assets. One alternative is to offer a two-part tariff in which one block of power is sold at a low price and any additional power commands a high price. This distributes the benefits to all power users yet maintains the efficient high marginal cost price for all.

In much of North America coal is the lowest-cost fuel, if you ignore the harm caused by air pollution discharge, but tough environmental regulations on the traditional pollutants have raised the cost of coal generation significantly, and a serious policy to reduce greenhouse gas emissions would raise coal costs much further. Natural gas emits much less air pollution, although it still emits significant amounts of CO_2, so tough air pollution policies favour gas relative to coal, although they favour renewable power even more. Policies that force significant investment in renewables will increase the cost of power, since renewables are generally more expensive than fossil fuel plants.

A fourth issue is the extent of government involvement in the electricity sector. In Ontario the government traditionally had a close relationship with Ontario Hydro and was accused by some of using it as a job-creation machine, rather than allowing it to focus on producing electricity at the lowest possible cost. One potential benefit of restructuring would be to increase the distance between the government and the utility. This is not a benefit that most governments would welcome, and it is not one that the public would easily understand if it saw the government as the instrument of ensuring that Ontario Hydro served the public interest. After all, the government had 'protected' electricity consumers by freezing prices in 1993. Indeed, when the public complained about high electricity prices in 2002, the government could not resist re-involving itself in defiance of the market it had just established, despite the resulting destruction of that market. Moreover, the government could not resist intervening in the management of Hydro One when an executive's compensation was criticized. The government intervened to bar the sale of some coal-fired power plants that OPG pursued in compliance with the MPMA. The Ontario experience suggests that it should be easier to restructure in a jurisdiction in which there had been little government involvement in the past, because there is less political power for the government to give up.

A fifth starting point is the actual and potential market structure of generation. Without a competitive structure, the risks of market power, market manipulation, and high prices are considerable. Ontario had six thermal plants that were expected to set the price much of the time. The general problem is that control over peak plants (those whose power is needed to satisfy the crucial marginal units of peak demand and clear the market) accords enormous power to manipulate the market, in particular by withholding capacity and driving up the spot market price. To achieve a competitive generation structure the largest of these plants must be owned or at least operated by separate firms, so as to eliminate the potential for market power abuse. Not only must one firm not operate two of them, but the operators should not compete in other markets, lest they compete less here for fear of retaliation there. With the varying size of the six thermal plants, a competitive structure is possible but not easy to achieve.

If a competitive structure will be achieved only with difficulty in Ontario, how can provinces with fewer generation plants achieve competitive structures? Given the vast geography of most provinces and the limited capacity of transmission lines, it will not be easy for generators to compete with each other. This is a substantial challenge to spreading the model of competition in Canada or elsewhere where generation plants are large and widely spaced.

A final starting point is the public's experience with fluctuating prices for other utilities and energy sources. The public in Ontario were accustomed to prices for electricity that were stable for years at a time. The last experience with rising prices was in the early 1990s when the government stepped in and imposed a price freeze. Natural gas prices had been regulated and stable until a decade or so earlier, but by 2002 the public had developed some experience with varying gas prices. Gasoline prices are unregulated, and the public are used to substantial fluctuations, although they routinely complain to the government about upward fluctuations. Interestingly, the increase in gasoline prices in 2005 generated substantial public grumbling, but it did not result in inappropriate government actions – that is, government actions that simply eliminate price formation by markets (even if regulated) and set a politically motivated price below long-run marginal cost, a price that discourages investment, perhaps because there is no historic or natural role for government. So the experience in other markets could have prepared Ontarians for varying electricity prices. It did not. One reason may have been that the public had come to expect lower prices, so upward fluctuations were seen as a breach of promise (see table 3.2 for a summary of starting point information for Ontario, Alberta, and other provinces).

The Importance of Neighbours

In electricity restructuring, as in so much of life, the neighbourhood is important. The price of electricity in neighbouring jurisdictions will have a significant impact on the enthusiasm of various stakeholders for competition. As Pineau's analysis in chapter 9 shows, Canada does not have a developed east-west electricity grid, and thus provincial electricity neighbours are likely to be U.S. states. The extent to which the home jurisdiction shares an airshed with neighbours will affect the jurisdiction's enthusiasm for competition if electricity generation emits air pollutants in both jurisdictions. Finally, the extent and capacity of inter-ties with the neighbours will affect the design of a competitive market in the home jurisdiction.

Regulated monopoly utilities are usually allowed to charge prices that will recover their reasonable costs, while competitive firms will charge what the market will bear. Suppose that the home jurisdiction has low costs and thus low regulated prices, while the neighbours have high costs and prices. Under competition, generators in the home

Table 3.2 Starting points at market opening

	Ontario	Alberta	Other provinces
Ownership	Mostly Crown corporation generation and transmission; municipal distribution utilities	Mostly private utilities, some municipal utilities	Mostly provincial utilities, except private in PEI, NL, and NS
Integration	Mostly integrated generation and transmission, separate distribution	Mostly integrated utilities, some municipal distribution	Mostly integrated utilities, some municipal distribution
Expected market price compared to current price	1995: Expected market price < current 1998: Relationship debated 2002: Market price above pre-restructuring price	1995: Expected market price < current 1997–2000: Market price > pre-restructuring price	
Government involvement	Government deeply involved in planning, prices, investment	Government regulation of utilities, municipal operation of MEUs	Government closely involved with Crown corporations
Generation market structure	Concentrated: 85% Ontario Hydro	Concentrated: Two firms often set price	Generally near monopoly
Past price variability	Electricity: Very stable Gas: Stable, recently variable	Electricity: Very stable Gas: Stable, recently variable	Generally stable

jurisdiction will be free to sell electricity to neighbouring customers, subject to inter-tie capacity and to the obligation to keep the lights on at home. Neighbouring customers will be keen to purchase cheaper electricity from the home jurisdiction. Exports from the low-cost jurisdiction to the higher-cost jurisdiction will increase, raising prices in the low-cost jurisdiction and lowering them in the high-cost jurisdiction. These effects will be welcomed by generators in the low-price jurisdiction and customers in the high-price jurisdiction, while customers in the former and generators in the latter will be worse off. Before embarking on a move to competition, governments in both jurisdictions should understand the likely effects of competition on their average prices, they should prepare their stakeholders for these effects, and they should ensure that they have the political support for restructuring and that they have a market design that will handle the emerging economic flows and political pressures.

Ontario enjoyed prices that were generally lower than those in adjoining U.S. states prior to market opening; indeed, Ontario prices were less than half the average U.S. price until the late 1980s. It was recognized that competition might lead prices to rise to meet those in the United States, so while foreign generators were allowed to bid into the Ontario market, their bids could not set the market price. Instead, the cost of the difference between the foreign bid and the market price went into the 'uplift,' an amount charged (or credited) to all consumers. In this way, the need to take, for example, 2 per cent of Ontario's power from a foreign generator whose bid was 10 per cent above the price-setting bid in Ontario would raise the market price not by 10 per cent, but only by 0.2 per cent.

There appears to be little enthusiasm in Quebec for establishing a competitive market that would tend to force domestic prices up to Ontario or even New York levels. At present Quebec consumers benefit from lower prices, and the provincial government seems happy to leave the benefits with those consumers while extracting the best possible price from exports to New York.

The home jurisdiction can regulate air pollution emissions from its own generators, but usually it has little influence on emissions from generators in neighbouring jurisdictions. In Canada, the dominant regulations are provincial, while in the United States the federal government sets standards that are applicable to many states, but only one state, California, has the authority to exceed them.[12] Suppose that Ontario and Ohio both burn coal in mid-merit plants and both have similar emission rates per kWh produced. In a regulated market with monopoly utilities, both Ontario and Ohio would tend to be self-sufficient in electricity generation. If Ontario imposes strict environmental regulations on its coal-fired stations, this will raise the marginal cost of electricity from those stations, making imports from Ohio more attractive. In a competitive market, imports from Ohio should increase. Emissions from Ontario will be reduced, both because of the lower emission rate and because of reduced utilization of the Ontario stations. Emissions from Ohio will increase, however, and the proportion of Ohio pollution that affects Ontario will offset the Ontario reduction. Thus the ultimate effect of the increased stringency of Ontario air pollution regulations is less than the initial effect calculated in the absence of an import response. More generally, it will be more difficult to control imports and exports in competitive markets than in regulated markets, so pollution control policies in one jurisdiction will have less effect than might be estimated.

In fact, the Ontario government pledged to close down all coal-fired generation in the province by 2007 (now postponed to 2014) and has closed several stations (Ontario 2005). Without adequate replacement power for Nanticoke within Ontario, it is becoming clear that imported power would yield increased pollution from the U.S. Midwest, thus substantially offsetting the reduction from Nanticoke. The shutdown has full effect only if the power is replaced by power from a non-polluting source.

If the pollution rates are different in the home and neighbouring jurisdiction, the calculation is more complicated, but the same forces are at work. Tough regulation of a dirty domestic source that led to imports from cleaner sources would yield benefits that were only modestly offset by the imported pollution. Tough regulation of an already clean source that led to imports from much dirtier sources might completely cancel out the benefits. The more closely coupled the air quality in the two jurisdictions, other things being equal, the greater the offset.

Finally, competitive markets require a competitive market structure. In a jurisdiction where the generation fleet does not yield a competitive market structure, imports may enhance competition, provided that there is sufficient transmission capacity. If a neighbouring jurisdiction has several generators that could bid into the home market, and if the inter-tie capacity is sufficiently great, then competitive prices may be achieved even in a home jurisdiction that is not workably competitive on its own. In the case of Ontario, the MDC recommended that the inter-ties to the United States and Quebec be enhanced specifically to help reduce the market power that OPG would otherwise wield until it had substantially decontrolled. See table 3.3 for a summary of neighbour information for Ontario, Alberta, and other provinces.

Conclusions

The experience with restructuring of the electricity sector in Ontario and Alberta offers lessons for other jurisdictions. Replacing monopoly with competition in generation may lead to more efficient generation, and it may produce a spot price that can be used as the basis for marginal cost pricing of electricity to consumers. However, competition also increases risks, and the system design must recognize the risk tolerance of market participants so that risks are shared appropriately.

Electricity markets are artificial markets with extensive rules for all participants arising from the complex interconnections of the electricity network. The operation and maintenance of the market are necessarily political processes with linked capacity and coordination dimensions. Some of the participants in an electricity market are likely to have substantial political influence. The conceptual design of the market must recognize these political realities so that the political process will not thwart the intended outcome of the market. The prices received by generators and those paid by consumers must transmit accurate market signals, but they must also not impose unpredictable and unacceptable gains and losses on the parties, lest they persuade the government to intervene with price caps if wholesale prices exceed expectations, or with subsidies if they fall short.

Moreover, one should assess, early in the market design process, whether the political landscape will support the development of an efficient market that will serve all stakeholders well. In the case of Ontario, in hindsight, we can see the lack of government will to sell off Ontario Hydro's generation plants to create a competitive structure, arising in part from the lack of public support for such a radical change from the long-standing Crown corporation. There is also reason to doubt the government's willingness to distance itself from the electricity business. While the MDC tried to work around these problems, another jurisdiction might postpone restructuring until there is political support for the essential steps.

The limited ability of small and medium-size consumers to understand changes in the electricity sector, at least in the short run, poses a real constraint on what can be achieved politically. Ontario's market design included a rebate to consumers if prices increased, yet consumers were not aware of the rebate or could not estimate its effect on

Table 3.3 Relations with neighbours at market opening

	Ontario	Alberta	Other provinces
Price relation to neighbours	Ontario price half that of U.S. until 1980s. At opening, close to U.S., > Quebec, Manitoba prices.		Varied. Quebec << U.S.
Sharing airshed	Mixed airshed with U.S. Midwest, NY, Quebec	Airshed isolated from neighbours	Airsheds isolated in west, partly linked in east
Inter-tie capacity	Inter-ties to U.S., Quebec equal 15% of demand	Connections to BC, Saskatchewan	Quebec has large supply connections to U.S., smaller connections to Ontario. Manitoba has major connections to the U.S. and Saskatchewan. Generally inter-provincial connections are weak.

them or simply would not wait until the end of the year. Either more effort should have been put into educating consumers or the refunds should have been more timely, to reduce consumer complaints that the government could not resist. A central challenge for restructuring is to charge consumers a price that reflects marginal generation cost while avoiding excessive bill variability. Several such systems have been devised, but adapting them to a particular jurisdiction, persuading stakeholders to support them, and explaining them to small and medium consumers will be challenging.

A challenge for electricity restructuring is that the starting points differ from one jurisdiction to another, and the starting points matter. The existence of Crown utilities may create public opposition to divestiture of generation and to restructuring in general. A history of low and stable prices provides no motive for consumers to seek changes. A government that has been deeply involved in the power sector may be reluctant to give up that political power. Each of these has implications for the market design and for the feasibility of restructuring.

Finally, the situation in neighbouring jurisdictions matters as well. Restructuring in a low-price jurisdiction surrounded by high prices will increase the prospect of price increases at home, while a high-price jurisdiction is more likely to see its prices decline. If workable competition will be difficult to achieve at home, strong inter-ties to neighbouring jurisdictions can improve competitive performance if the market is appropriately designed. Air pollution, like electricity, moves across borders, so one must assess and evaluate the pollution implications of competition and make appropriate adjustments to the market design.

ACKNOWLEDGMENT

I would like to thank participants in several workshops, including a Canadian Law and Economics workshop and the CCGES Transatlantic Energy Workshop, as well as the editors of this volume, for their comments and suggestions.

NOTES

1. See Hunt (2002, chap. 3) for a categorization and description of restructuring possibilities.
2 For background information, see Daniels and Trebilcock (1996) and ACCOES (1996).
3 *Electricity Act, 1998*, S.O. 1998, c. 15, Sch. A. The full title is *An Act to Create Jobs and Protect Consumers by Promoting Low-Cost Energy through Competition, to Protect the Environment, to Provide for Pensions and to Make Related Amendments to Certain Acts.*
4 Premier's Office, 'Eves Takes Action to Lower Hydro Bills,' press release, November 2002.
5 For a detailed analysis of this period, see Trebilcock and Hrab (2005).
6 *Electric Utilities Act*, R.S.A., 2001, c. E-5.5.
7 See http://www.customerchoice.gov.ab.ca/elect/images/summary _2002.pdf.
8 See Hunt (2002, chap. 7) for a description of several wholesale market arrangements.
9 The Ontario market rules fill more than 20 MB of pdf files. See http://www.ieso.ca/imoweb/manuals/marketingdocs.asp (9 August 2005).
10 'Getting it done fast and in a way that pandered to the many interests involved became more important than getting it right. The end result was the most complicated set of wholesale electricity market institutions ever created on earth and with which there was no real-world experience' (Joskow 2001, 370). 'I said that the split between the ISO and the PX was primarily a device to create business and profit opportunities for middle-

men such as Enron, and that the resulting inefficiencies and gaming would ultimately impose large costs on the market and on consumers' (Ruff 2002, 7). 'The design of the California market embraced the notion that what little the system operator would do should be done inefficiently in order to leave even more coordination problems for the market to solve. This was an unprecedented experiment in markets that did not work in theory. We now know that it did not work in practice either' (Chandley, Harvey, and Hogan 2000, 2–3).

11 For discussions of the California debacle, see Berg et al. (2001), Borenstein (2002), Borenstein, Bushnell, and Wolak (2002), and Sweeney (2002).

12 For an overview of Canadian environmental jurisdiction, see Benidickson (2002, chap. 2); for the United States, see Davies and Mazurek (1998, chap. 1–4).

13 For an elaboration of the argument that continental free trade agreements combined with the World Trade Organization comprise an external constitution for its member states, see Clarkson (2004, 1–31).

14 NAFTA, 609.1

15 *Security and Prosperity Partnership of North America: Report to Leaders.* June 2005, 28–33.

REFERENCES

ACCOES. *See* Advisory Committee on Competition in Ontario's Electricity System.

Advisory Committee on Competition in Ontario's Electricity System. 1996. *A framework for competition.* Toronto: Queen's Printer.

AESO. *See* Alberta Electric System Operator.

Alberta Electric System Operator. 2004. Annual report. http://www.aeso.ca/files/2003_annual.pdf (accessed 25 August 2005).

– 2005. Alberta Electric System Operator corporate profile. http://www.aeso.ca/files/corpprofileJuly05.pdf (accessed 25 August 2005).

Alberta Energy. 1997. *Moving to competition.* Edmonton: Electricity Branch, Alberta Department of Energy.

Ando, Amy, and Karen Palmer. 1998. *Getting on the map: The political economy of state-level electricity restructuring.* Resources for the future DP 98/19, March 1998. Washington DC: Resources for the Future.

Benidickson, Jamie. 2002. *Essentials of Canadian law: Environmental law.* 2nd ed. Toronto: Irwin Law.

Borenstein, Severin. 2001. The troubles with electricity markets and how they

derailed California's electricity restructuring.
http://www.aei.org/past_event/conf010614a.pdf.

Canada. Natural Resources Canada. 1999. *Electric power in Canada, 1997.*
Ottawa: Natural Resources Canada.

Chandley, John D., Scott M. Harvey, and William W. Hogan. 2000. Electricity
market reform in California.
http://www.aei.org/past_event/conf010614b.pdf.

Daniels, Ron, and Michael J. Trebilcock. 1996. The future of Ontario Hydro: A
review of structural and regulatory options. In *Ontario Hydro at the Millennium,* ed. Ron Daniels, 1–52. Montreal and Kingston: McGill-Queen's University Press.

Davies, J. Clarence, and Jan Mazurek. 1998. *Pollution control in the United
States.* Washington DC: Resources for the Future.

Faruqui, Ahmad, and Stephen S. George. 2002. The value of dynamic pricing
in mass markets. *Electricity Journal* 15 (6): 45–55.

Globe and Mail. 2002. Strengthening Ontario's electricity sector. Interview
with Jim Wilson. 11 March.

Ham, John C., Dean C. Mountain, and M.W. Luke Chan. 1997. Time-of-use
prices and electricity demand allowing for selection bias in experimental
data. *Rand Journal of Economics* 28 (0): S113–S141.

Hirsch, Richard F. 1999. *Power loss: The origins of deregulation and restructuring
in the American electric utility system.* Cambridge, MA: MIT Press.

Hunt, Sally. 2002. *Making electricity competition work.* New York: Wiley.

IESO. *See* Independent Electricity System Operator.

Independent Electricity System Operator. 2005. Your road map to Ontario
wholesale electricity prices: May 2004–April 2005.
http://www.ieso.ca/imoweb/pubs/marketReports/MarketYear-
Review_2005apr.pdf.

IMO. *See* Independent Market Operator.

Independent Market Operator. 2002. Monthly market report: July 2002.
Toronto: Independent Market Operator.
http://www.ieso.ca/imoweb/pubs/marketReports/monthly/2002jul.pdf.

– 2003. Monthly Market Report: February 2003. Toronto: Independent
Market Operator. http://www.ieso.ca/imoweb/pubs/market
Reports/monthly/2003feb.pdf.

Joskow, Paul L. 1997. Restructuring, competition and regulatory reform in
the U.S. electricity sector. *Journal of Economic Perspectives* 11 (3): 119–38.

– 2001. California's electricity crisis. *Oxford Review of Economic Policy* 17 (3):
365–88.

Kahneman, D., and A. Tversky. 1979. Prospect theory: An analysis of decisions under risk. *Econometrica* 47:263–91.

Keohane, Nathaniel, Richard Revesz, and Robert Stavins. 1998. The choice of regulatory instruments in environmental policy. *Harvard Environmental Law Review* 22:313–67.

McNamara, Fergal. 1998. Alberta's electricity market: How it works, recent developments, new opportunities. PowerPoint presentation.

OEB. *See* Ontario Energy Board.

OMDC. *See* Ontario Market Design Committee.

Ontario. 2005. McGuinty government unveils bold plan to clean up Ontario's air. Press release. 15 June.

Ontario Energy Board. 2005a. OEB issues reminder on details of the recently announced new price plan. Press release. Ontario Energy Board, 22 July.

– 2005b. *Regulated price plan manual.* Toronto: Ontario Energy Board.

Ontario Market Design Committee. 1999. Final report of the Market Design Committee. Toronto.

Ontario. Ministry of Energy, Science, and Technology. 1997. *Direction for change: Charting a course for competitive electricity and jobs in Ontario.* Toronto: Ontario Ministry of Energy, Science, and Technology.

Peltzman, S. 1976. Toward a more general theory of regulation. *Journal of Law and Economics* 19:211–40.

Ruff, Larry. 2002. Statement of Larry E. Ruff, PhD, on California State Senate bill no. 2000, unlawful electric power and natural gas practices. Before the California Senate Judiciary Committee, 23 April.

Simon, Bernard. 2002. Ambitious plans in disarray at Canada utility. *New York Times.* 27 July 27.

Stigler, George. 1971. The theory of economic regulation. *Bell Journal of Economics and Management Sciences* 2:3–21.

Trebilcock, Michael, and Roy Hrab. 2005. Electricity restructuring in Ontario. *Energy Journal* 26 (1): 123–46.

White, Matthew W. 1996. Power struggles: Explaining deregulatory reforms in electricity markets. *Microeconomics.* Vol. 1 of *Brookings Papers on Economic Activity*, 201–50. Washington, DC: Brookings Institute.

Wilson, Robert. 2002. Architecture of power markets. *Econometrica* 70 (4): 1299–1340.

Wolak, Frank A. 2000. Market design and price behaviour in restructured electricity markets: An international comparison. In *Pricing in competitive electricity markets*, ed. Ahmad Faruqui and Kelly Eakin, 125–52. Dordrecht: Kluwer.

4 The Governance of Energy in North America: The United States and Its Continental Periphery

STEPHEN CLARKSON

Since the North American Free Trade Agreement came into force on 1 January 1994, comparing the two regionalisms on either side of the Atlantic Ocean has become an intellectually tempting but academically risky endeavour. Transatlantic comparisons are intellectually tempting because the European Union and North America are so similar in size (whether measured by population or gross national product) and similar in culture (whether measured by common heritage or linked histories). But such exercises are academically problematic, because the very act of looking at NAFTA in the context of the European Union leads most analysts to assume that the former is an embryonic, institutionally lighter version of the latter. This is a daring assumption, given NAFTA's small membership (three compared to the EU's twenty-seven member states); given its stark asymmetries (the United States is not just overwhelmingly more powerful than its neighbours to the north and south, it is the global hegemon); and given the skewed nature of its two bilateral relationships (rich Canada has long enjoyed a relatively easy, even cosy relationship with Washington, whereas a much poorer Mexico has mostly had to manage a tense, extremely difficult one).

It is well known that the processes forming the European Union constrained the largest power, Germany, from flexing its economic muscles and empowered the smaller members with institutions that offset their low political weight. The EU's highly complex system, which weakened the strong and strengthened the weak, derived from a continental consensus about the need to guarantee intergovernmental peace based on a generous social policy framework. However, if our interest is continental governance in general and energy governance in particular, NAFTA did little to create anything in North America's two bilateral sets of asymmetrical, market-led relationships – between the United States and Canada on the one hand and the United States and Mexico on the other – that resembles the extraordinary model of state-led governance established on a continental scale by the EU. Indeed, much of North America's energy governance – especially in its northern dyad – has been driven throughout the twentieth century by private-sector forces that turned state powers to their service. This is especially the case in oil and gas, although in the electricity-nuclear realms – as chapter 3 (Dewees), chapter 5 (Mez and Doern), and chapter 6 (Froschauer) show – the governance of energy is more complex, and Canadian energy capacities are somewhat stronger and diverse.

This chapter takes the position that the apparently descriptive phrase *North America* actually conceals two parallel but separate realities whose cross-border dynamic is moving the continental model along a path diverging from the one offered by Europe. It makes the case by first establishing the political-economy origin of the first North America made up of the United States and Canada. It then explains how intergovernmental relations on the continent became constitutionalized through so-called free trade agreements. With the extension of free trade redefining North America to include Mexico, we then identify the dimensions of the continent's two petroleum asymmetries. The asymmetry found in U.S.-Canada petroleum relations is indicative of the larger bilateral energy relationship (see chapter 2) and can thus also be applied, with some modifications, to natural gas and electricity, as further developed in chapter 6 (Froschauer) and chapter 8 (Gattinger). Hence, the investigation of oil markets can be an interesting gateway to governance patterns in electricity markets presented later in this volume.

This chapter will close with a speculation about the possibility that the three countries' Security and Prosperity Partnership of 2005 promises to generate a more genuinely trilateral energy integration in North America.

Overall, this chapter uses the petroleum industry to argue that the North American Free Trade Agreement of 1994 did not herald a European-Union-in-the-making. Far from counteracting the asymmetries and levelling the inequalities between member states as the EU has done, NAFTA increased U.S. power over its periphery, with most striking success in Canada whose oil and natural gas sectors have been deregulated internally and integrated externally with their contiguous American markets.

Because national ownership and control of its resources was entrenched in its constitution as one of Mexico's prime revolutionary goals, the continental hegemon has had much less success in forcing energy-policy harmonization with its poor neighbour to the south. Although the state corporation Pemex retains most of its monopoly control, the diversion of its profits to bolster the government's budget prevents the national petroleum industry from adequately financing either upstream exploration and development or needed downstream refining capacity.

Efforts by the George W. Bush administration to promote continental energy integration have moved from establishing the North American Energy Working Group in 2001 to inaugurating the North American Security Prosperity Partnership in 2005, but political resistance in Mexico has restricted this U.S. push towards continental governance for energy to the tri-national harmonization of data.

The Political Economy of First North America

When the smoke of battle had cleared, its territorial wars had been recorded in the history books, and the continent's national boundaries had solidified by the middle of the nineteenth century, North America was left with three sovereign but very different states, each of which stretched from the Atlantic to the Pacific oceans and federated their many subregions, Aboriginal peoples, and immigrant ethnicities in unions of varying coherence.

Dominating the continent from its broad centre at the dawn of the twentieth century was an already imperial United States of America. Rich in its resources, burgeoning in its population, dynamic in its industry, and expansionist in its policies, the United States exerted a powerful push-pull force on its periphery. The push involved American corporations pressing into their neighbouring economies in search of extra markets for their products; the pull was extracting resources for their manufacturing.

Frail rather than robust in population and enterprise, the French- and English-speaking colonies of British North America relied for their survival on maintaining, rather than cutting, their imperial ties. For military security, they depended on the Pax Britannica. For their economic well-being, they relied on importing capital from the mother country and sending back primary products along transportation routes linking the eastern to the western regions of the emerging country.

The significance of this colonial and post-colonial experience for Canada's energy governance was that exporting barely processed raw materials to the imperial centre has always had priority over their use as inputs for national economic development. Since staple exports have been largely developed and transported thanks to large injections of capital from their principal market abroad, Canadian economic elites have tended to identify their own interest with those of their empire. Rather than attempting to maximize their autonomy, their approach reflected a desire to nurture relations and borrow practices from their dominant partner.

Once petroleum was discovered and developed in Alberta, little thought was given to the rapid takeover of domestic oil firms by their American competitors. The immediate significance of a large, U.S.-owned and -controlled presence in Alberta's fledgling petroleum sector was the easy import of a regulatory framework that had first been developed in Oklahoma and Texas. The result was the development of the Canadian oil and gas sector as a northern extension of the geographically contiguous sector in the United States.

With the American government's interests directly represented in Canada through U.S.-owned corporations in Canada, it is not surprising that the economic geography of Canada's petroleum industry was shaped by Washington's Cold War security interests. Already by 1952, the U.S. Paley Report had identified Canada as the most secure resource base for dozens of the strategic raw materials needed by the U.S. military economy. Exploration and development by U.S. firms in Canada was subsidized by American tax incentives (Clarkson 1985, 58–9).

Following recommendations from the U.S. oligopoly, Prime Minister John Diefenbaker's 1961 National Oil Policy gave Alberta the protected right to supply oil to all areas west of the Ottawa River, while Quebec and the Maritimes were to be supplied with oil that U.S.-based multinationals gladly shipped up from Venezuela due to the State Department's fear that their holdings there might be nationalized. In exchange for not extending its Prairie-oil pipeline to Montreal to service its eastern market, Canada was exempted from the tough U.S. oil protectionism (which excluded Venezuelan oil from the Texas market) so that it could offset the cost of importing oil for the Maritimes and Quebec by selling to the sheltered market of the U.S. northwest the maximum possible volume of what was thought to be its permanent surplus of prairie petroleum.

Throughout the rest of the 1960s, as its petroleum became increasingly integrated with the American sector, Canada willingly conformed to U.S. energy demands. The National Energy Board (NEB), the body responsible for enforcing tariffs, overseeing the construction and operation of pipelines in terms of their environmental impact, and regulating imports and exports of oil, gas, electricity, and other petrochemicals (Dybwad 2003) developed a close relationship with its American counterpart, the Federal Power Commission (FPC) and facilitated the proposals of oil and gas exporters, as the FPC relaxed its protectionism (Bradley and Watkins 2003, 15).

After the 1970 Shultz Report updated Paley's advice that the United States help secure its energy supplies by recognizing Canada as a low-risk, reliable, strategically important energy partner, President Richard Nixon declared that imports of oil, natural gas, hydro power, and water from Canada would save the United States from its looming energy crisis (Bradley and Watkins 2003, 60).

The power structure of this informally institutionalized regime came under strain for a decade once the cartel formed by the Organization of Petroleum Exporting Countries (OPEC) quadrupled world oil prices in 1973. To Washington's dismay, the government of Prime Minister Pierre Trudeau responded to this first OPEC-induced energy crisis by raising the export price for petroleum to that of the world market while maintaining domestic prices at a lower level. After several years of growing concern about its energy security and following OPEC redoubling world prices in 1979, Trudeau's government launched the National Energy Program (NEP) in 1980 to reduce its energy interdependence (Bradley and Watkins 2003, 60). With an ambitious medley of interventionist measures, it promoted the pan-Canadian market at the expense of cross-border trade in order to make eastern Canada's economy less vulnerable to fluctuations of the world price and supply of oil and to assure Canada's autonomy by expanding Canadian ownership of the predominantly U.S.-owned industry (Neustaedter 2003).

By early 1981, an outraged American oil and gas industry, which had been a major backer of Ronald Reagan's recently successful campaign to oust Jimmy Carter from the White House, placed mounting pressure on the newly elected president to resist the NEP, which it considered had violated its fifth amendment rights in Alberta by favouring Canadian petroleum companies (Clarkson 1985, 57, 75).

The NEP marked a short-lived experiment in Canadian government intervention to achieve greater autonomy through partial withdrawal from extensive north-south integration and market reregulation. During its eighteen months of existence, Canadian ownership of the industry jumped from 6.7 per cent to 34.7 per cent (Clarkson 1985, 82). Given that the NEP was crafted with almost no provincial or industry consultation, it also created a political backlash from the energy-exporting provinces and private sector in Canada, particularly in the oil- and gas-rich Alberta (Gattinger 2004, 5). In the end, it was collapsing world oil prices that caused the NEP to unravel, but the mutual interests of the Trudeau and Ontario governments in energy nationalism were no match for the combined power of President Reagan's Washington, Premier Peter Lougheed's Edmonton, and the incensed petroleum industry on both sides of the Canadian-American border, which demanded a return to the status quo ante OPEC.

It is, of course, pure speculation to imagine that, had the NEP been designed after OPEC I, when Washington was in turmoil, the buyback of the Canadian petroleum sector could have been handily financed from the economic rents generated by the escalating world price of oil. As it was, Ottawa had retreated well before the election in 1984 of the Progressive Conservative Party, whose leader Prime Minister Brian Mulroney put 'finished' to this episode in national oil autonomy with a 1985 Western Accord that liberalized the Canadian oil sector by reducing federal taxes and accepting market pricing for the commodity (Bradley and Watkins 2003, 4).

On the eve of the free trade era, Canada's oil and natural gas industries were already functioning as territorial extensions of the American marketplace. This was the status quo that 'free trade' was to lock in place.

Continental Constitutionalization through Free Trade

The received wisdom has it that the Canada–United States Free Trade Agreement (CUFTA) was sparked by a request made in October 1985 by Prime Minister Mulroney that Washington negotiate an economic integration agreement. Behind the agency question of who started the actual negotiations is a more structural issue concerning what enabled a project that would have been unthinkable five years before. The United States in the early 1980s was responding to a confidence crisis about the threat to its economic dominance posed by the rise of Europe, Japan, the newly industrialized countries of Southeast Asia, and even fundamentalist Iran whose militants had humbled the United States by taking its diplomats hostage. The United States' globally competitive, knowledge-based industries and service sectors believed they were losing out because their intellectual property was being pirated abroad or they were being denied permission to operate in foreign jurisdictions. For their part, uncompetitive U.S. industries were demanding that Congress provide them with even greater protection against what they deemed unfair competition from importers benefiting from foreign-government subsidies and other manifestations of unfair practices.

Normally such issues would provide the stuff of intergovernmental negotiations at the continuing rounds of the General Agreement on Tariffs and Trade. But because the GATT had become known as the General Agreement to Talk and Talk for its interminable efforts to forge a consensus, Washington added a third prong to its traditional, two-level trade-policy strategy. If multilateral talks at the GATT showed little promise in the mid-1980s and if unilateral actions targeting individual trading partners with retaliatory measures proved counterproductive, there was an intermediate position. Bilateral agreements with compliant partners could set precedents that established the norms Washington wanted to universalize, putting on the wall writing that more recalcitrant competitors would ultimately have to read with care, or else suffer adverse consequences in later negotiations.

The United States' desire to transform the domain of international intellectual property rights, to strengthen the conditions for U.S. transnational corporations operating abroad, and to extend trade-rule protections to cover services required a counterpart need on behalf of potential negotiating partners.

This condition was met on Washington's northern border when the Canadian business community reversed its position concerning its own competitive dilemmas. Ever since the mid-1970s, when Canadian direct investment abroad had begun to exceed foreign direct investment in Canada, business elites had started talking a less protectionist language. A devastating recession in the early 1980s, an increase in the U.S. protectionist measures taken against Canadian exports, and general hostility for the deemed Keynesian policies of Pierre Trudeau's Liberal government combined to give political credence to the dramatic recommendation to embrace free trade with the United States that was made in 1985 by the report of the Macdonald Royal Commission on the state of the Canadian economy.

In the Macdonald Report's analysis, Canada's future economic pros-. perity required enhanced and secure access to the U.S. market. 'Enhanced' meant trade free of tariffs. 'Secure' meant trade unthreatened by anti-dumping duties, countervailing duties, or the legion other measures that Congress had perfected over the years to protect its uncompetitive industries. The Mulroney government initiated one-on-one palavers with the world's toughest trade negotiators with these two objectives as its major goals.

Given the disparity in power between the two sides, it would not have surprised an outside observer that the U.S. agenda prevailed over the Canadian. While tariffs were lowered (Canadian more than American), Canada failed to achieve its prime goal, exemption from U.S. trade protectionism. As a result, CUFTA did not produce the free cross-border trade to which Ottawa had aspired. However, this document, which Ronald Reagan called the 'economic constitution of North America,' did resolve many of Washington's irritants with Canada, its energy concerns *primus inter pares.*

CUFTA locked in the already deregulated nature of trans-border energy flows by establishing norms that would prevent a future Canadian government from affecting the price or supply of its petroleum exports to the United States. With the Canadian state's powers curtailed by this new external constitution, market forces of supply and demand would be free to govern cross-border energy trade.[13] As Gattinger's analysis in chapter 8 shows, the willing compliance of the Mulroney government with these pro-market provisions facilitated bilateral relations by privileging U.S. energy security concerns and the petroleum industry's bottom-line desire for profit maximization over any pan-Canadian interest in energy security and cheaper energy for citizens' needs and domestic industrial inputs.

The U.S. Energy Policy Act of 1992 subsequently served as the fountainhead for the natural gas sector's further liberalization through the Federal Energy Regulatory Commission (FERC) Order 636, which mandated the unbundling of vertically integrated gas utilities to allow more private-sector participation through wholesale competition, access to pipeline infrastructure, and market-based pricing (Natural Gas Supply Association 2004).

Although CUFTA allowed export restrictions in cases of conservation of exhaustible resources, supply shortages, price stabilization, and national security, the Canadian government has chosen not to invoke these conditions (Gattinger 2004, 5). Instead it has voluntarily relaxed its regulation of energy trade.

CUFTA gave it little choice, because Canada had agreed to a 'proportionality' clause to assure the United States that it would not face another period like that from 1973 to 1982. The proportionality provision in Article 605 requires that in any export restrictions justified on the basis of conservation, price stabilization, and supply shortage, 'the share of total supply available for export purchase may not fall below the average level in the previous 36 months' (Natural Gas Supply Association 2004, 5). In other words, no country may reduce the *proportion* of the energy or petrochemicals it exports to the other party. Should Canada raise production in an effort to offset world energy shortages, it would be forced to increase exports to the United States in order to maintain the export proportion. Likewise, should Canada decide to undertake initiatives to increase energy conservation or be faced with energy shortages, it would be unable to cut exports to the United States by a greater proportion than the reduction of its own domestic usage. However, this proportionality clause refers to actions taken by governments restricting exports, not to market forces that serve to limit exports. This means that Canadian – or Chinese – consumers could potentially out-bid Americans even for more than their proportional share of Canadian energy (Natural Gas Supply Association 2004, 208).

Further evidence that CUFTA achieved Washington's goals with Canada, thus increasing its dominance, can be found in the interesting contradiction between the principle of national treatment (which forbids industrial subsidies) and Article 608(1) – which encourages them for energy development. By having CUFTA extend the notion of non-discrimination between domestic and foreign *goods* to apply to *investment*, Washington achieved an important precedent. It had long been trying to prevent foreign governments from pursuing industrial-strategy policies that boosted the competitive capacity of their corporations by offering them subsidies and incentives unavailable to U.S. companies. By accepting the principle of national treatment for investment, Ottawa gave up its long-treasured capacity to promote Canadian corporations.

In the case of energy, however, Article 608(1) states that nothing in the agreement is meant to constrain 'future incentives for oil and gas exploration, development and related activities in order to maintain the reserve base for these energy resources.' Where subsidies would bolster the Canadian capacity to compete with U.S. corporations, CUFTA prohibited them. Where subsidies would bolster U.S. energy security, CUFTA endorsed them. To maintain their reserve base, 608(2) also commits Canada and the United States to sharing their reserve base in case of emergency (Natural Gas Supply Association 2004, 210). As the energy provider in this relationship, this apparently reciprocal clause created a future commitment for Canada to pump up its exports to meet Uncle Sam's needs in a crisis.

CUFTA contributed to the full liberalization of Canada's upstream (exploration and production) gas market (International Energy Agency 2000). Even though the National Energy Board is still mandated to allow the export only of gas that is surplus to Canadian needs, in practice, now that it is headquartered in Calgary, it lets exports be governed by market demand and supply (Bradley and Watkins 2003, 7).

Article 609(1), which defines an energy regulatory measure as behaviour by 'federal or sub-federal entities that directly affects the transportation, transmission, distribution, purchases or sales, of an energy or basic petrochemical good,'[14] ensures that sub-central jurisdictions come under the aegis of the new super constitutionalism (Globerman and Walker 1993, 209), thus compromising provincial and state autonomy over energy resources, even in areas beyond federal government jurisdiction. With the Canadian constitution placing resources under provincial jurisdiction and with Alberta, the major energy producing province, taking the lead in promoting deregulation and privatizing the downstream (distribution and pricing) side of the market, this loss of autonomy is moot. Alberta produces 80 per cent of Canada's natural gas and issues licences for all gas that is removed from the province but does not distinguish between gas for international export and gas for interprovincial trade (International Energy Agency 2000, 11).

In the natural gas sector, Canada and the United States have demonstrated an impressive capacity to plan and invest cooperatively: witness the massive Alliance Pipeline, a bilateral venture that stretches 2,300 miles from western Canada to Chicago (Nivola 2002, 20, 2). The regulatory boards in both countries, FERC and the NEB, cooperate so closely that they hold joint hearings on proposed cross-border projects. This bilateral governance functions so cohesively that it is almost as straightforward to seek approval for a trans-border pipeline as it is for a domestic U.S. trans-state or Canadian interprovincial one. Current gas pipeline infrastructure reflects this integration, as there now exists

Table 4.1 Canada-U.S. oil and gas trade, selected years, 1980–2004

	Imports to U.S. from Canada				U.S. exports to Canada			
	1980	1990	2000	2004	1980	1990	2000	2004
Petroleum (thousand barrels/pd)	455	934	1,807	2,118	108	91	110	141 (2003)
Natural gas (billion cubic feet)	797	1,448	3,544	3,607	0.1	17	73	395

Note: Electricity data from 2003 are preliminary.
Source: Petroleum Supply Annual 2003; United States Energy Information Administration (Annual Energy Review 2003); U.S. Energy Information Administration, Natural Gas Navigator and Petroleum Supply Annual 2003.

an essentially seamless border between the United States and Canada, with pipelines crisscrossing the 49th parallel. As described by FERC Chairman Pat Wood, 'You look at a pipeline map of North America [without Mexico] and it's just no boundaries' (Santa 2003).

Bilateral oil and gas flows between Canada and the United States since the 1980s have been mostly southbound from Canada into the United States. As indicated in table 4.1, the United States does export energy to Canada, its natural gas exports having increased tremendously between 2000 and 2004. Nevertheless, Canada remains an overall energy exporter to the United States, increasing its exports from 455,000 barrels of petroleum per day in 1980, to 2,072,000 in 2003, and from 797 billion cubic feet of natural gas in 1980, to 3,490 billion in 2003. This leaves the United States dependent on Canada for over 27 per cent of its net energy imports (Bradley and Watkins 2003, 6).

By 2003, Canada exported to the United State about 60 per cent of its annual oil production and over half of its natural gas (Bradley and Watkins 2003, 3), making Canada the United States' single largest petroleum supplier. Canada provided only 15 per cent of U.S. natural gas needs, in 2003, but this represented 87 per cent of total U.S. natural gas imports.

The Second North America and the Second Asymmetry

Although the economically liberal presidency of Porfirio Días had developed Mexico in the late 1890s and early twentieth century as another neighbouring site for U.S. direct investment and source of raw materials for the U.S. economy, the abuses and miseries of Porfirio capitalism helped provoke a revolution in Mexico that reasserted national control over the political economy, including its natural resources.

The importance of energy in Mexican politics can be traced back to the 1917 Constitution (Globerman and Walker 1993, 206), whose Article 27 declared the exploration, exploitation, development, and sale of oil and gas, and the generation, transmission, and distribution of electricity to be exclusively under the control of the federal government (North American Energy Working Group 2002a). Mexico's nationalist approach to its energy sector was further entrenched by what was seen as its second declaration of national control over its economic development (North American Energy Working Group 2002a, 7), the 1938 nationalization of foreign oil and gas properties and the establishment of a state-owned oil and gas company, Petroleos Mexicanos (Pemex), to manage its petroleum destiny.

Pemex explores for and develops Mexico's petrochemical reserves, including the management of the downstream facilities needed to refine and market them (Canadian Energy Research Institute 1995, 36). It is the country's largest corporation, has the largest union in the country, and is a vital source of tax revenue, as it is legally required to transfer up to 30 per cent of its earnings to pad the federal government's budget (Nivola 2002).

Because the Mexican government has siphoned off so much of Pemex's profits to pay for state programs, Mexico has not developed the capacity to refine its petroleum into the derivatives it needs for its own economy. This leaves Mexico as a net importer of natural gas from the United States (table 4.2) and also imports refined petroleum products such as gasoline because it lacks the financial capacity and/or technical expertise to develop the facilities needed for refining its sour, heavy crude oil. These limitations, coupled with increasing demand projections, create further pressures for more private and foreign investment and greater deregulation.

Less enthusiastic than Ottawa – President Salinas de Gortari had hoped to achieve economic salvation through an agreement with the European Union – the Mexican government came to negotiate a trade and investment agreement with the United States because it considered that its economic development model had reached an impasse. Once Brian Mulroney joined the negotiations, a new tri-national North America was created by the North American Free Trade Agreement.

Table 4.2 Mexico-U.S. natural gas and petroleum trade, 1980–2004

	Imports to U.S. from Mexico				U.S. exports to Mexico			
	1980	1990	2000	2004	1980	1990	2000	2004
Petroleum (thousand barrels per day)	533	755	1,373	1,642	28	89	358	209
Natural gas (billion cubic feet)	102	0	12	0	4	16	106	398

Source: Adapted from United States Energy Information Administration (2004).

Although the North American Free Trade Agreement's Chapter 6 put a veneer of common governance over the continent's petroleum sector, it actually disguised the perpetuation of two separate bilateralisms. Chapter 6 reiterated Canada's CUFTA commitments to a deregulated, integrated, free-market economy. However, the law that ruled energy matters to the south of the Rio Grande remained Mexican, because, during the negotiations that led to NAFTA, the United States failed in its attempt to loosen Pemex's monopoly hold over the country's oil and gas sectors (Canadian Energy Research Institute 1995, 35).

Mexico made fewer energy-policy concessions in NAFTA than Canada by negotiating significant exemptions from its disciplines. The first article of Chapter 6 stated, 'The Parties confirm their full respect for their Constitutions' (which was code for Mexico's Article 27) and consequently recognized that Mexico retained the right to full national control over the exploration and exploitation of oil and natural gas, along with associated activities such as refining and foreign trade. However, private participation in cross-border trade was accepted, subject to the Mexican government's approval and Pemex's continuing control: 'Where end-users and suppliers find cross-border trade may be in their interests [they] shall be permitted to negotiate supply contracts ... [with] the state enterprise' (Globerman and Walker 1993, 210).

The national-security exception, which is recognized as an appropriate reason for energy-export restrictions, is defined in NAFTA in different ways for Canadian-American relations and for Mexico's relations with the other two signatories. Canada negotiated a narrow definition of national security to protect itself against the United States invoking its security as a justification for imposing arbitrary import restrictions. In contrast, Article 605 gives Mexico the right to restrict exports or imports any time it is deemed necessary to protect what is broadly defined as Mexico's 'essential security interests.'

These differing rules over national security confirm how the energy sector continues to be governed by two separate bilateral regimes. This skewed nature of the two bilateralisms could also be seen in the proportionality provision of the Canadian-American agreement to which Mexico subsequently took an exemption in NAFTA, so that it still only applies to the United States and Canada.

NAFTA did reduce cross-border tariffs, setting Mexico's tariff on natural gas imports at 10 per cent in 1993, with a 1 per cent reduction scheduled for every year. This rate was accelerated in 1998, when the Interstate Natural Gas Association of America successfully lobbied the U.S. government to accept the Mexican government's proposal to hasten the elimination of the tariff on natural gas in exchange for U.S. decreases in tariffs on Mexican chemicals, a reduction that promoted the development of cross-border pipelines (Fossil Energy International 2005).

Currently under the *Regulatory Act of Constitution* Article 27 on Petroleum, 'the exploration, extraction, production activities, and first-hand sales' of natural gas are considered strategic and thus protected, whereas only 'construction, operation, transportation, storage, and distribution' are open to private participation (North American Energy Working Group 2002b, 12).

The march towards natural gas liberalization was boosted by the first ever meeting between FERC and its Mexican counterpart, the *Comisión Reguladora de Energía* (CRE), in February 2003. A further step towards energy liberalization in Mexico can also be seen in the government's reduction of the number of 'basic' petrochemicals (which are constitutionally reserved for state control), by reclassifying them as secondary (and therefore opening them to private participation), thus shrinking the number of primary petrochemicals from fifty to eight.

President Fox's proposed measures to increase privatization in the energy sector met fierce public and political hostility (*Economist* 2002). Lacking requisite support in the Mexican Congress, restructuring efforts were largely unsuccessful. As a result, privatization and deregulation have reached their constitutional limit, leaving Mexico's oil and gas sector by far the most nationally contained and strictly governed in North America. In the nineteenth Assembly that took place in 2005, PRI deputies called for the expansion of state ownership and governance over the energy sector (Gonzales 2005), affirming the need to strengthen Mexico's autonomy in the face of Fox's attempt to introduce private sector control. The lack of political will to restructure Pemex's output abilities and increase its revenue, means that, unless the government leaves Pemex its revenues for reinvestment, it will not be able to keep up with increasing domestic consumption (Weintraub 2005).

Towards Trilateral Integration

Although NAFTA's notionally trilateral umbrella disguised two completely separate sets of bilateral energy relationships, a modest move towards continental governance was set in motion when Vice-President Cheney's 2001 National Energy Policy advocated energy integration and a tripartite energy framework 'to expand and accelerate cross-border energy investment, oil and gas pipelines, and electricity grid connections' (Government of the United States 2001, 14). Using the same logic as the 1952 Paley Report, the Cheney Report emphasized the vulnerability of the United States to disruptions in foreign energy supplies and identified Canadian resources as an element of U.S. security – in this case officially recognizing Alberta's tar sands reserve base of 176 billion barrels as a 'pillar of sustained North American energy and economic security' (Bradley and Watkins 2003, 2). When the 11 September terrorist attacks placed national security at the forefront of the policy agenda, U.S. policy shifted to maximizing domestic energy security and taking greater advantage of its periphery's energy supplies.

This pressure emanating from Washington pushed its two neighbours to formalize cross-border integration planning and envisage a clear regulatory framework for making infrastructure investment decisions. Actual North American energy cooperation was advanced in April 2001 when the three heads of government created the trilateral North American Energy Working Group (NAEWG) at the Summit of the Americas in Quebec City. Building on the already established bilateral yearly energy consultations between U.S. and Canadian representatives, the NAEWG was given a mandate to 'foster communication and cooperation among the governments and energy sectors of the three countries on energy-related matters of common interest and to enhance the North American energy trade interconnections consistent with the goal of sustainable development, for the benefit of all' (North American Energy Working Group 2002b, 2).

As the U.S. ambassador to Canada, Paul Cellucci, put it, through the NAEWG 'our three countries have begun to look at North America's energy market as a unified whole.' (*Energy Processing Canada* 2003, 95).

Still in its infancy, the NAEWG has so far been engaged only in sharing energy data. In 2002 it published a continental self-portrait showing with common statistical units where each country stood in its energy resources, production, consumption, infrastructure, and future requirements (North American Energy Working Group 2002b). In the winter of 2006 it updated that snapshot in a second, trilingual·ninety-four-page report, which showed that progress in cross-border energy cooperation had been incremental in the intervening four years (Dukert 2006, 1; North American Energy Working Group 2006b).

Oil and gas is integrated between Canada and the United States, an example less of government coordination than of a private-sector amalgamation induced by market-friendly policies in both countries. While Mexican integration into the market paradigm has been slow, it is growing. For the first time, in May 2003, representatives from Mexico's CRE attended a meeting with the NEB and FERC, which have been meeting bilaterally to discuss gas policy since the mid-1980s. The meetings were meant to respect the sovereignty of each participant, while coordinating with and learning from each other to increase efficiency. Mexico's participation in the meeting was a symbolically important step towards harmonization with its North American partners.

Action beyond symbolism was taken in March 2005, when the three heads of government recognized and responded to the blow to North American economic development that had resulted from the post–11 September 2001 shift by the United States to a security paradigm. In their North American Security and Prosperity Partnership (SPP) signed in Waco, Texas, the three leaders proclaimed their intention to reinvigorate their commitment to the continent's economic integration. In Ottawa three months later, a trilateral ministerial SPP meeting published a slick trilingual *Report to Leaders* of some 300 measures that had been cobbled together by working groups of bureaucrats from the three governments to constitute an agenda for intergovernmental cooperation.

The *Report to Leaders* energy chapter contained nine commitments: 'expand science and technology collaboration,' 'increase energy efficiency collaboration,' 'increase regulatory cooperation,' 'enhance electricity collaboration,' 'greater economic production from oil sands,' 'increase natural gas collaboration,' 'enhance nuclear collaboration,' 'enhance cooperation on hydrocarbons,' and 'improve transparency and coordination in energy information, statistics and projections.' This very general wish list spoke to the SPP's diplomatic strategy of enhancing continental integration through executive sponsorship of incremental bureaucratic actions, given that political paralysis in the

Mexican legislature prevented a major move towards further energy deregulation or any privatization of Pemex that might divest it of its dominion over the country's petroleum industry.[15]

Meeting in Cancún in March 2006, presidents Fox and Bush along with the newly elected Conservative prime minister of Canada, Stephen Harper, declared the SPP successful after its first year in operation and announced the creation of a big-business North American Competitiveness Council to advise the three executives about how to promote further integration. The notable absence of a bilateral agreement on the management of undocumented Mexican immigrants in the United States or a resolution of the long-standing softwood lumber dispute with Canada was a silent reminder that bilateral issues between the periphery and the centre continue to impede the North American project.

Intergovernmental conflict is inescapable; the question is whether it is resolvable. While the Americans' revolutionary sense of manifest destiny, which still impels the United States to control the entire continent's energy resources, is compatible with Canadians' default position of attachment to empire, it comes up against Mexicans' revolutionary impulsion to resist foreign domination. This conundrum leads two Mexican scholars to conclude that, although the SPP seeks 'the establishment of common principles, the harmonization of energy policies, besides trying to make the normative frameworks of the energy systems converge, this is no easy task in the light of dissimilar political and juridical systems, above all that of Mexico' (Vargas and Rogríguez-Padilla 2006, 158).

Implications for Governance

Under conditions of continually increasing demand (see appendix), the Canada-U.S. oil and gas relationship has become highly integrated in the last twenty years. This integration expanded as further liberalization and tariff-reduction occurred. Although NAFTA enshrines neo-conservative norms, the agreement changed very little in terms of energy integration, because Canadian policymakers had already subscribed to U.S. thinking that pushed for free-market governance and trans-border integration, making north-south integration in North America more extensive than east-west integration within Canada.

But North America is not operating as a single energy system. Strongly nationalistic in its oil and gas governance, Mexico's political sensitivity makes major deregulation unlikely. As a result, the continent's energy governance remains split between a highly deregulated and largely integrated bilateral regime between Canada and the United States and a partially integrated one between the deregulated American industries and Mexico's still regulated system. It remains to be seen how Mexico will participate in this expanding neoconservative regime marked by informal governance.

Conclusions

Returning to our opening reflections, we can see how different North American governance is from European. Far from reducing intergovernmental asymmetries, NAFTA accentuates them by bolstering U.S. power. While power relations are not absent in the European arena, and while there is the external challenge of Russian gas dominance, the North America political economy remains very different from Europe's: the free-trading market in North America favours the most powerful interests, relentlessly driving forward U.S.-defined hegemonification.

The contradictions continue. The two bilateral relationships under NAFTA's umbrella remain skewed, an impoverished, near-democratic Mexico having managed to show greater capacity to resist U.S. demands than a rich compliant Canada. With its constitution sacrosanct in the public mind, Mexico was a stronger defender of its autonomy than Canada, whose negotiators were driven less by the need of the Canadian public than by the greed of Alberta's largely U.S.-owned petroleum industry. Furthermore, what appears as policy coordination when seen from Washington and the petroleum lobby in Calgary is perceived as dictation in the rest of Canada. Berlin may be a co-driver of EU energy governance; Ottawa is little more than a spectator watching the market being driven.

The extraction of petroleum from Alberta's vast tar sands returns us to the intractable trade-versus-environment nexus. Refining tar sands requires enormous inputs of water (which dangerously lowers the level of the area's aquifers) and natural gas (thus burning up other non-renewable petroleum resources) and releases so much greenhouse gases that the corollary of exploiting the tar sands is environmental catastrophe – a prospect that NAFTA's environmental mandate was originally billed as preventing.

In sum, when looking at North America through the lens of its petroleum industries, the imposition on its three countries of a weakly institutionalized, trade- and investment-centred normative regime called NAFTA can hardly be taken as the implantation of an embryonic European Union in the womb of the New World.

APPENDIX

Table 4.3 Energy demand overview in Canada, Mexico, and the United States, 1980–2010

	Canada				Mexico				United States			
	1980	1990	2000	2010	1980	1990	2000	2010	1980	1990	2000	2010
Petroleum (thousand barrels/pd)	1,837	1,527	1,700	1,888	967	1,341	1,728	1,919	17,056	16,988	19,701	22,610–24,130
Natural Gas (billion cubic meters)	56	69	95	112	25	27	45	106	563	530	638	775–825
Coal (million metric tons)	37	49	61	53	5	8	13	28	638	819	981	1,121–1,153
Electricity (terawatt-hours)	339	466	546	623	52	92	155	265	2,092	2,817	3,621	4,084–4,284

Source: Adapted from United States Energy Information Association (2002).

Table 4.4 Energy supply overview in Canada, Mexico, and the United States, 1980–2010

	Canada				Mexico				United States			
	1980	1990	2000	2010	1980	1990	2000	2010	1980	1990	2000	2010
Petroleum (thousand barrels/pd)	3,242	6,130	4,749	9,995	2,129	2,970	3,450	4,616	10,214	8,994	8,110	7,390–7,540
Natural gas (billion cubic meters)	70	99	168	200	37	38	48	90	549	504	549	631–684
Coal (million metric tons)	37	68	69	65	4	8	14	22	753	933	975	1,153–1,186
Electricity (terawatt-hours)	372	474	563 (1999)	656	62	114	193	330	2,286	3,025	3,800	4,552– 4,763

Source: Adapted from United States Energy Information Association (2002).

ACKNOWLEDGMENT

Preliminary research for this article was done by Kate Fischer, whose trip to Washington DC in April 2004 was made possible by funds generously provided by the University of Toronto's Dean of the Faculty of Arts and Science. Funds from the Social Sciences and Humanities Research Council of Canada also made possible further research in Mexico City by the author in the winter of 2006.

NOTES

1 For an elaboration of the argument that continental free trade agreements combined with the World Trade Organization comprise an external constitution for its member states, see Clarkson (2004, 1–31).
2 NAFTA, 609.1
3 *Security and Prosperity Partnership of North America: Report to Leaders.* June 2005, 28–33.

REFERENCES

Bradley, Paul G., and G. Campbell Watkins. 2003. *Canada and the U.S.: A seamless energy border?* Toronto: C.D. Howe Institute.
Canadian Energy Research Institute. 1995. *Towards a continental natural gas market: The integration of Mexico.* Calgary: Canadian Energy Research Institute.
Clarkson, Stephen. 1985. *Canada and the Reagan challenge: Crisis and adjustment 1981–1985.* Toronto: Lorimer.
Dukert, Joseph M. 2006. North American Energy – 2006: Three governments offer a new self-portrait. *CSIS: Centre for Strategic and International Studies, Washington, DC* 3 (March): 161–80.
Dybwad, Carmen. 2003. Energy trade and transportation: Conscious parallelism. Speech to the IAEE North American Conference, Mexico City, 20 October.
Economist. 2002. The Americas: Where energy is sacred; Reform in Mexico. 13 July.
Energy Processing Canada. 2003. Cellucci urges continental energy market. (May/June): 95.
Fossil Energy International. 2005. An energy overview of Mexico. http://www.fe.doe.gov/international/mexicover.html.

Gattinger, Monica. 2004. From government to governance in the energy sector: The states of the Canada–US energy relationship. Unpublished paper, University of Ottawa.

Globerman, Steven, and Michael Walker. 1993. *Assessing NAFTA: A trinational analysis*. Vancouver: Fraser Institute.

Gonzalez, Enrique Andrade. 2005. Mexico still hopes for energy reform. Mexidata.info, 14 March 14. http://www.mexidata.info/id420.html.

Government of the United States. 2001. *Reliable, affordable, and environmentally sound energy for America's future*. Washington, DC: U.S. Government Printing Office.

International Energy Agency. 2000. *Canada review*. Paris: International Energy Agency.

Natural Gas Supply Association. 2004. The market under regulation: Important FERC regulations and orders. http://www.naturalgas.org/regulations/market.asp.

Neustaedter, L. 2003. *The national energy program*. http://pages.cpsc.ucalgary.ca.

Nivola, Pietro S. 2002. Energy independence or interdependence? Integrating the North American energy market. *Brookings Review* (Spring): 116–28.

North American Energy Working Group. 2002a. *North America, subsection Mexico, general outlook*. Washington, DC: North American Energy Working Group.

– 2002b. *North America: The energy picture*. Washington, DC: North American Energy Working Group.

– 2006. *North America: The energy picture II*. Washington, DC: North American Energy Working Group.

Santa, Donald F. 2003. New challenges in the integrated North American energy market. Speech at the Energy in the North American Market Conference, 12 June. http://www.canadianembassy.org/trade/santa-en.asp.

United States Energy Information Administration. 2002. *North America: The energy picture*. Washington, DC: Department of Energy.

– 2003. *Annual Energy Review 2003*. Washington, DC: Department of Energy.

– 2004. *Annual Energy Review 2004*. Washington, DC: Department of Energy.

U.S. Energy Information Administration Natural Gas Navigator. http://tonto.eia.doe.gov/dnav/ng/ng_sum_top.asp.

Vargas, Rosío, and Víctor Rogríguez-Padilla. 2006. La energía en la Alianza para la Seguridad y Prosperidad en América del Norte. *NorteAmérica* 1 (1): 158–58.

Weintraub, Sidney. 2005. Mexico's oil, gas, and energy policy options. *Issues in International Political Economy* 68 (August): 123–34.

5 Nuclear Energy in Germany and Canada: Divergent Regulatory Policy and Governance Paths

LUTZ MEZ AND G. BRUCE DOERN

Chapters 1 and 2 have already briefly noted the different roles that nuclear energy plays in Germany and Canada, with Germany phasing out its nuclear reactors as an explicit policy choice and Canada retaining nuclear power as an option in its energy mix, mainly in Ontario. Dewees' analysis in chapter 3 also showed how nuclear reactor problems in Canada were a part of the eventual restructuring of Ontario's electricity system. In this chapter, we look more closely at how multilevel regulatory policy and governance coordination and the underlying complexity and capacity configurations of the two countries produced these two different nuclear energy paths and whether they will be maintained in the foreseeable future.

Three arguments are central to the analysis. First, the two countries differed in the realms of multi-level governance where nuclear and related energy policy and regulatory decisions were made and coordinated and where accommodations were reached. In Germany they were made for the most part at the national level as part of the coalition party politics and its need for reasonable consensus within the party structure but also to accommodate Germany's sectoral corporatist interest group structure. There was certainly initial federal and Länder involvement, but overall the governance story was a nationally focused public-private one. In Canada, on the other hand, nuclear policy was very much a federal-provincial institutional process, and indeed mainly a bilateral federalism coordination and accommodation between the federal government and the province of Ontario. It was also mainly focused in state enterprises.

The second argument advanced is that in industrial policy, energy policy, and eventually energy and environment policy terms, there was a different level of centrality to nuclear policy in these overall governance agendas, given each country's basic resource endowments and economic and social location and disposition. In Germany, nuclear policy was initially quite central to German industrial policy, then to national energy policy, and eventually also to German environmental policy. The German environmental movement was in many ways based on the anti-nuclear movement.

In Canada, nuclear policy was never a central feature of overall national industrial or energy policy or in any consistent way of national environmental policy (Doern and Conway 1995). Both these relative positionings were a product of Germany's and Canada's situations, as chapters 1 and 2 have shown, regarding resource endowments, with Germany in a much poorer resource situation and more continuously concerned about energy security and about its manufacturing-centred economy, and Canada being resource rich in an economy that was (and is) still a more mixed natural resource and manufacturing economy.

The third argument in the chapter is that environmental concerns were much more deeply embedded in German society and politics nationally and began at a much earlier stage. The Chernobyl nuclear accident galvanized these environmental concerns in a very energy-focused way. While Canada had an anti-nuclear lobby (Martin and Argue 1996), there was no equivalent extent of environmental pressure on nuclear policy in Canada, in part due to the more decentralized and roller-coaster nature of environmental policy and politics in Canada as a whole and its relative lack of centrality to energy policy as noted above.

The structure of the chapter reflects the analytical task at hand. We look first at the origins and historical context of the nuclear option in both countries and how it shaped initial issues of technical capacity. Second, we examine multi-level governance in shaping the trajectory and coordination of nuclear policy. The third section probes the nuclear policy positions of new conservative-led governments elected in each country and their links to the inherent complexity of the politics and governance involved. Conclusions then follow.

Origins and Historical Context

The origins and historical context of German and Canadian nuclear policy and governance reveal initial key differences in technical capacity, policy trajectories, and policy and governance framing. As this section shows, Germany located nuclear policy as a central part of its initial post–Second World War industrial policy. It developed nuclear reactors through public funding and private delivery of the research and development, based on a licensing regime on existing foreign reactor technologies. It pursued more than one such technology. Germany also nurtured ambitions regarding the entire nuclear fuel cycle.

In the Canadian case, nuclear energy was born out of Canada's wartime comparative and strategic advantage in uranium supplies and then evolved into a public sector focus on a single new reactor technology, the CANDU reactor. Canada had no overt ambitions about involvement in the full nuclear fuel cycle, nor was nuclear energy central to either national industrial policy or energy policy.

Germany: Licensed Reactor Technologies, Industrial Policy, and Public-Private Development

In what was then West Germany, the official nuclear policy initiative started in 1955 and was closely tied to concerns about the Cold War relations with the Soviet Union.[1] It was aimed at the development of a nuclear sector, including the production and operation of nuclear power plants (NPPs) as well as all other facilities of the nuclear fuel cycle. Initially, the nuclear program was regarded an integral part of a general industrial policy to re-establish Germany as a viable force in international markets. The German nuclear industry consisted of the electronics industry, the machinery industry, and the chemical sector. They represented the majority in the Deutsche Atomkommission, the main advisory body of the Ministry for Nuclear Questions, founded in October 1955, and the unofficial centre of nuclear policymaking[2] (Keck 1984, 56).

The early nuclear power era in Germany was characterized by an enormous technological optimism, which until the early 1970s was based upon a political consensus among the governing parties. Major financial support for public-private nuclear R&D, for producers and operating companies for individual projects, was central to the German nuclear program.[3]

In 1956–7, the Deutsche Atomkommission started the Eltville Program, as the first official German nuclear program (Prüß 1974, 70). By 1965, five 100-megawatt (MW) nuclear reactor designs were to be developed in parallel. The number five was not the result of scientific considerations, but was due to the number of German company consortia involved in implementing the program. All participants wanted to have a share of the financial support of the German government. Only two of the five planned reactors were built, and already by the end of the 1950s the first nuclear program was dropped in favour of more 'realistic' designs (Mez 1981, 29).

Nuclear power was already on its way when the first nuclear power act of the Federal Republic (*Gesetz über die friedliche Verwendung der Kernenergie und den Schutz gegen ihre Gefahren*) was passed in December 1959. Until then, acts and ordinances of the Länder had regulated economic and public health interests in radiation, nuclear power, and the production of isotopes and their usage.

Despite the partial failure of this program, the early consensus continued. Siemens started the construction of pressurized water reactors (PWRs) on the base of a Westinghouse licence, and AEG, an affiliate of General Electric, started construction of boiling water reactors (BWRs) on a licence base too. In 1958 RWE, the largest utility, ordered, together with Bayernwerk, the nuclear power pilot plant Kahl (15 MW) from AEG, but all nuclear components were delivered by General Electric. Already in 1958 AEG started in cooperation with General Electric and Hochtief AG the planning of a 200-MW NPP for RWE. Construction started at the end of 1962, and in 1967 the 237-MW NPP Gundremmingen was connected to the grid.

The second nuclear program (1963–7) integrated research, development, construction, and operation of pilot plants and of prototypes. The nuclear reactor development strategy tied in with the experiences of the United States. As a short-term strategy it involved the takeover of proven technology and reactor designs, and the development of the high temperature reactor. It also involved an aid program for construction and radiation protection, and a long-term strategy for the development of fast breeder reactors.

Direct subsidies for the nuclear industry were multiplied by a factor of five during the second nuclear program. By the time of the expiration of the program Germany had caught up to international standards of nuclear technology with countries abroad.

Germany strived from the beginning for the establishment of a nuclear fuel cycle in the country. Uranium enrichment technologies had been developed in Germany during the Second World War. After 1955 Germany continued as a partner in the tri-national enrichment company Urenco Ltd. During the 1970s the three partners in Urenco constructed and operated pilot and demonstration plants at Almelo in the Netherlands and at Capenhurst in the United Kingdom.

After analysing several possible sites in Germany, Gronau – near the Dutch border – was selected in 1978 as the site for Urenco's third uranium enrichment plant, which started operation in 1985. Between 1971 and 1990 a pilot reprocessing plant was operated in Karlsruhe. After the chemical sector ceased all activities in the German nuclear industry, utilities championed the construction of a reprocessing plant in Germany. In 1980 sites were developed in Bavaria and Hesse. After the site Volkmarsen in Hesse was dropped, the Bavarian municipality of Wackersdorf was selected to host a reprocessing and fuel production facility. However, the strong local opposition supported by the international anti-nuclear movement forced the nuclear industry to abandon the reprocessing plant project in Wackersdorf in 1989.

Since 1967 AEG and Siemens offered in cooperation with Westinghouse and General Electric developed reactor designs (AEG: boiling water reactor; Siemens: pressurized water reactor) to German utilities. Also in 1967 the nuclear lobby succeeded in having nuclear operators receive subsidies on the same level as the hard coal subsidy scheme. This led to the first commercial orders: AEG constructed the 670-MW BWR in Würgassen, and Siemens the 672-MW PWR in Stade. The two reactors started operation in 1971 and 1972, respectively.

The German nuclear power station manufacturer KWU was created as joint venture of Siemens and AEG in 1967. In 1975 KWU had gathered orders for 30 billion DM (15 billion) and ranked as number three in the world nuclear industry.

The NPP Biblis A was set in operation in 1974. With a capacity of 1,000 MW it was the world's largest nuclear reactor at the time. Furthermore, nuclear export contracts with Brazil, Iran, and Argentina had contributed to the industry's development.

This success was reflected in the government's first energy program of September 1973.[4] The commercial operation of large nuclear power plants in Germany happened to coincide with the first oil price crisis of 1973. Nuclear power became central on the energy policy agenda and the government decided to substitute nuclear power for oil in an ambitious program.

This concluded the first phase of nuclear policy, which, in summary, was largely restricted to one main policy field. It was forged as a key part of German industrial policy. Since this phase was centred on research and development, initially it had few publicly palpable economic and social effects. It involved a relatively restricted circle of political actors, which limited public awareness and debate. Considering the results, one could argue that the early nuclear policies of the German government were straightforward and quite successful in supporting the inception of a German nuclear industry of acknowledged – albeit not indigenous – technical competence.

Canada: CANDU Technology, State Enterprise, and Federal-Ontario Partnership

Canada's nuclear power industry is a mixture of its home-developed CANDU heavy water reactor, its possession of large uranium reserves and exports, and a nuclear medicines component. All three emerged ultimately from the Second World War in which Canada became a strategic player in the U.S.-led war effort to develop the first atomic bomb (Bothwell 1988). The resultant post-war peaceful use of nuclear power emerged through the role of Atomic Energy of Canada Limited (AECL), a federal Crown or state-owned company. The nuclear medicines component of AECL was privatized in the 1990s. The main user by far of CANDU reactors for domestic energy supply has been Ontario, Canada's industrial heartland and largest province. Single reactors are also in operation in New Brunswick and Quebec.

For its first four decades, the primary focus of Canada's nuclear power program was to meet domestic electricity needs, mainly in Ontario. Exports were seen as an additional opportunity and as a way to ensure that the CANDU was competitive. In the early 1990s the domestic market dried up (see further discussion below) and looked as if it would remain that way for decades. Ontario concentrated on trying to run its existing reactors. At the same time, export markets opened up and became AECL's main focus (Bratt 2006; Morrison 2001). But globally, CANDU reactors have a small market share, are competing with larger players, and operate in conditions of other countries' complex assessments of their own energy policy, energy security, and financing needs. AECL's future thus ultimately turns on sales of reactors abroad (Doern, Dorman, and Morrison 2001).

Canada's nuclear policy evolution in overall energy policy has also been transformed across the last six decades. This is because Canadian energy policy itself has evolved from an earlier era of, in effect, 'fuel by fuel' policy (which is related separately to each fuel, such as oil, gas, nuclear, coal, and uranium) to a concern about inter-fuel substitution, which is a 'natural resource' policy in which the focus is on an integrated view of natural resources and sustainable development and full-scale or managed competition. This includes, crucially, the introduction of competitive electricity markets in Alberta and Ontario. It is now a fundamental determinant of the nuclear industry's future in Canada and elsewhere, including Canada's possible links with the U.S. reactor business, as many reactors there undergo refurbishment and as some new reactors seem likely to be built under U.S. energy plans (*Economist* 2006).

With respect to the ever closer links with environmental policy and sustainable development, Canada's nuclear industry faces the proverbial double-edged sword. On the one hand, it faces, as does the global industry, the historic concerns of legitimacy centred on reactor safety, nuclear proliferation globally, and the unresolved and costly issues of the safety and storage or long-term nuclear wastes (Stoett 2003). On the other hand, the climate change debate allows the nuclear industry to position itself more readily as a green energy source compared to carbon-based sources such as oil and gas. This potentially broadens the underlying rationale for government support to preserve and strengthen the nuclear energy industry in Canada, and in other countries that have a nuclear power option, to include environmental factors. But in Canada, this potential has been characterized as a still 'precarious opportunity' (Doern, Dorman, and Morrison 2001, chap. 1) and globally, the *Economist* referred to this potential as 'the ghostly flickers of a new dawn' (2006, 59).

Public opinion polls in Canada indicate majority support for the use of nuclear power, including the refurbishment and continuation of existing nuclear reactors (Atomic Energy of Canada Ltd. 2006). However, the support is invariably conditional on basic public trust in key institutions, including confidence in the ability of the industry and the regulators to manage the safety of ageing nuclear reactors in a more competitive milieu, and to resolve issues such as non-proliferation and long-term management of nuclear wastes, as noted above (Bratt 2006; Doern, Dorman, and Morrison 2001).

Multi-Level Regulatory Governance and Later Nuclear Policy Divergence

The discussion above has shown the regulatory and related governance focal points and dynamics in the two countries, with Germany's focus clearly on national-level accommodations and Canada's on federal-provincial and mainly bilateral processes. In this section, we see these traced out further in the last two decades when nuclear policy divergence between the two countries became even more pronounced. Multi-level regulation and governance also change as a result of global and regional energy developments, including EU energy policy, U.S. nuclear developments, and the politics and economics of climate change.

Germany: Technical Failures, the Chernobyl Accident, and Nuclear Phase-Out

A second phase of Germany's nuclear policy started 1975. This phase was induced by considerable public protests, and the first critical statements were published by the evolving anti-nuclear alliance. The public protests had effects. The planned NPP Wyhl facility in the Upper Rhine Valley in southwest Germany, where in 1975 the movement was conceived, had to be given up, and in Lower Saxony, in 1979, the prime minister declared the plans for a nuclear waste plant in Gorleben impossible to enforce for political reasons.

In 1980 an Enquête Commission of the Bundestag proposed a paradigmatic change in energy policy away from nuclear power. This was only one contribution to a broad shift in German public opinion, the formation of the Green Party, and finally its election to the Bundestag in 1983 (Brand 1986).

Then came the 1986 Chernobyl nuclear disaster in the Ukraine, which far exceeded the residual risk of a maximal credible accident and sparked a major debate about nuclear dangers worldwide. Chernobyl also clarified the economic risks of nuclear power stations for a national economy in a drastic way and stimulated a novel appreciation of nuclear power in politics and industry. However, the termination of the nuclear era in Germany needed more than the Chernobyl disaster to bring it about.

In West Germany the CDU/CSU/FDP-led government reacted to Chernobyl by establishing the Federal Ministry for the Environment, Nature Conservation, and Nuclear Safety (BMU).

Probably no other country has conducted the discussion about nuclear phase-out on as perfect a scenario base as Germany: the confluence of external drivers, technological developments, and alignment of key political forces pushed the debate on nuclear phase-out onto the agenda. The Green Party strived for the immediate shut-down of all nuclear facilities. The SPD resolved the nuclear phase-out within ten years.

In addition, Länder governments, municipalities, parties, and trade unions started to deal with the question of whether the use of nuclear power technology was reasonable and sensible for the future.

Advanced reactor designs in Germany also turned out to be flops. Two fast breeder reactors (FBRs) were built, but both were closed in 1991 without the larger ever having achieved criticality. The small demonstration breeder KNK-II was converted from a thermal reactor, KNK-I, which had been used to study sodium cooling. KNK-II had a capacity of 20 MW and achieved criticality as a fast reactor in 1977. The second fast breeder – a 300-MW sodium natrium cooled breeder, called SNR-300 – at Kalkar was completed in 1985, but was never operated. The SNR-300 was maintained and staffed until a decision to close it was finally made in 1990, and has since been decommissioned. Today it houses an amusement park.

The high-temperature reactor THTR-300 at Hamm-Uentrop was under construction in 1970, started in 1983, but was shut down in September 1989. The THTR was synchronized to the grid for the first time in 1985 and full power operation started in February 1987. The THTR-300 was the German prototype for high-temperature reactors (HTR) and was the first to use a pebble bed design and TRISO[5] fuel. The THTR-300 cost 2.05 billion and is predicted to cost an additional 0.5 billion until December 2009 for decommissioning and associated costs. The novel pebble bed design technology encountered several technical obstacles and failed ultimately because it was considered unsafe: several incidents (among them a serious radioactive gas escape just one week after the Chernobyl disaster) undermined credibility and economic and political viability.

After also having dropped the reprocessing option in Germany, the nuclear industry tried since 1992 to reach an energy consensus with all parties about a 'politically undisturbed' operation of nuclear power plants. It argued that for operator purposes the energy consensus should comprise seven components: the definition of regular service life of nuclear power plants; the acceptance of electricity generation in large power plants; the exclusion of enlarged electricity imports; the abandonment of reprocessing after termination of existing international contracts; processing plutonium for MOx-fuel; the search for an international alternative for final high-level nuclear waste storage; and the availability of two low- and middle-level nuclear waste storage facilities in Germany. In the spring of 1993, consensus talks started, but all attempts failed (Mez 1997, 433).

When the Red-Green coalition took office in the fall of 1998, nuclear phase-out consensus talks had the highest priority on the agenda. The result, after twenty months of negotiations with the nuclear plant operators, was, among others, that the operating licence for nuclear plants was determinable, and that the construction of new reactors and the transportation of spent fuel for reprocessing were prohibited.

The agreement restricts the operating lifetime of the existing reactors, not by restricting the operating licence to a specified year or total number of years but by pinning down total allowed amounts of electricity to be produced by each individual plant. Calculated in years and at current output, German nuclear power plants were allowed total operating times (*Regellaufzeit*) of thirty-two years each. Furthermore, should one plant be closed down early, its leftover share of allowed electricity production could be shifted to another plant.

Thus, from the agreement it is impossible to exactly predict when the plants will be shut down and which company will provide how much nuclear power capacity at which time. However, an approximate calculation shows when the effects of the agreement will come and what their impact will be upon the individual operators. A first effect of the phase-out agreement on the operational nuclear capacity became noticeable after 2006 and the number of shutdowns will accelerate in 2010.

The leading roles of the four largest operators – RWE, E.ON, Vattenfall Europe, and EnBW – will be maintained. However, compared to E.ON and EnBW, who will continue to have greater stakes in nuclear energy, the share of RWE's nuclear production will reduce substantially so that, on the basis of current sales numbers, other electricity sources will become much more important for RWE's supply. Looking at Vattenfall Europe, the share of nuclear production will decrease to less than one-tenth of the current share by 2014, significantly reducing the current importance of nuclear energy for this utility.

By this agreement, followed up by an amendment of the *Atomic Act* in 2002, Germany introduced as the first large industrial country a clear signal to phase out nuclear power by 2023 (Mez and Piening 2006).

The Red-Green federal government had emphasized ecological modernization and climate change policy as well as job creation and socio-economic development in its overall approach, and energy policy was to be a leading example of it. It included tax reform (an eco-tax on energy), phased-out nuclear power, and strengthened renewable energy sources and combined heat and power. Additional reforms followed later when the government implemented the provisions of the new electricity and gas directive of 2003 (2003/54/EC), by setting up an integrated regulatory authority for different network or infrastructure industries: electricity and gas, postal services, telecommunications, and railways (Bundesnetzagentur, see Theobald, chapter 10).

The nuclear phase-out decision reflected the consensus among Greens and many Social Democrats since the Chernobyl accident and was enshrined in the *Nuclear Energy Phase-Out Act*. Licences of existing plants were time limited. The government endeavoured to reach a consensus with nuclear power interests and to avoid legal disputes before the courts, which entailed the withdrawal of regulatory legislation that would have affected the economics of nuclear power (liability insurance, taxation of funds for plant removal and final storage, etc.).

In November 2003 the NPP Stade was the first plant to be shut down according to the nuclear phase-out consensus, and in May 2005 the NPP Obrigheim followed. Four NPPs (Biblis A and B, Neckarwestheim 1, and Brunsbüttel) will reach their limit during the next legislature.

Canada: Reactor Problems, Ontario Electricity Restructuring, and Precarious Opportunity

Multi-level regulation and governance and nuclear policy in Canada is dominated by bilateral federal-Ontario relations. Ontario is the province that has most benefited from Canada's nuclear energy investment, in electricity supply, lessened exposure to carbon emissions over the last three decades, and the private sector nuclear business, consisting largely of technology-based manufacturing, engineering, and consulting firms in Ontario. Moreover, AECL's operations in Mississauga and Chalk River confer major employment benefits in Ontario.

In the 1960s, 1970s, and 1980s, there was an explicitly recognized partnership between federal nuclear policy and activity and the Ontario government, either directly or through Ontario Hydro (Bothwell 1988; Doern and Morrison 1980). As Ontario Hydro built its first CANDU reactors, there was considerable collaboration, including Ontario contributions to the R&D of AECL through joint projects and

through the nuclear fuel waste R&D program. Ontario Hydro also con-
tracted a lot of work on its CANDU stations to AECL, although it took
over more of this work in the late 1970s as AECL became more focused
on markets outside Ontario.

Ontario Hydro as a monopoly utility was clearly a key player in the
earlier development of nuclear power, but in the late 1980s it went
through an institutional crisis as it failed to adjust from a company
used to continuously *building* reactors to one that had to *manage* them
as an efficient operational entity. Ontario Hydro was joined by other
provincial utilities that used nuclear power such as New Brunswick
Power and Hydro-Québec but these were much smaller institutional
players.

As Dewees' analysis shows, in the current era, with Ontario Hydro
broken up into constituent companies, Ontario Power Generation
(OPG) has become the key player, along with the Ontario Ministry of
Energy, Science, and Technology, which influenced and implemented
the major restructuring of the Ontario electricity industry, created the
Independent Market Operator, and reformed the Ontario Energy
Board, which has expanded regulatory responsibilities over energy
sectors in Ontario.

By the mid-1980s, and certainly into the 1990s, the Ontario–federal
relationship became strained by a number of factors, some due to the
pursuit of separate goals, some market and technology-based, and
some political, as both levels of government faced fiscal deficits and a
changing global economy. Ontario Hydro's focus was clearly upon its
investment of tens of billions of dollars in a thirty-year construction
program of twenty nuclear power plants, rather than planning for an
electricity market of lower demand.

Through decades of steady growth in electricity demand averaging
close to 7 per cent per year, Ontario Hydro had invested in expanded
generation capacity using dams, coal-fired generation, and, in the
1960s and 1970s, nuclear power, on assumptions that rested seemingly
on the continuation of this ever-expanding demand (Daniels 1996).
However, the rate of demand growth in electricity consumption fell,
initially in the 1970s and then extensively in the 1980s and 1990s, as a
result of the combined effects of economic recession and effective
energy conservation measures (Ontario 1996).

In the 1990s the intensity of these political-economic pressures
increased. Their political salience was in particular propelled by a 30
per cent increase in power rates for consumers in the early 1990s, at a

time when economic recession and hardship for many ordinary Ontario citizens was present. Ontario's electricity demand remained below its 1989 value for the better part of a decade.

When the Darlington nuclear station with four large CANDU units came on line in the early 1990s, its capacity was surplus to Ontario's needs. The resulting rate increases were a direct result of the inflated debt taken on by Ontario Hydro to pay for the nuclear plants and for other mechanisms to reconcile supply and demand.

Other assessments of the causes of change focused on nuclear power per se. Some authors explicitly linked Ontario Hydro's problems to the over-expansion and related borrowings for its nuclear facilities in the 1970s and 1980s, and to the 'substantial cost over-runs and disappointing operating performance of a number of these facilities, in part itself a function of a federal-provincial industrial strategy to promote the atomic energy sector in Ontario through the Atomic Energy of Canada Ltd.' (Trebilcock and Daniels 1995, 6). This assessment also drew attention, in the economic sphere, to 'an anachronistic regulatory structure characterized by dispersed and fragmented authority that has at times subverted public transparency and fostered government micro-management' (ibid.).

Ontario Hydro's management of its nuclear reactors was severely criticized in August 1997 by U.S. nuclear experts called in by Ontario Hydro's president. The president then resigned, and the U.S. experts were put in charge of the nuclear operations. They decided to shut down seven reactors in order to focus the company's efforts on getting the other twelve operating reactors back up to top performance (Farlinger 1997).

This was a dramatic move, with significant implications for the future of nuclear energy in Canada. Although safety was not an immediate issue, the scope of the problem cast long shadows over the entire Canadian nuclear energy program. The U.S. experts put the blame on management and took great pains to exonerate the CANDU design, but the initiative created federal resentment that Ontario Hydro was damaging the reputation of Canada's nuclear technology.

The anti-nuclear attitude of the NDP provincial government from 1990 to 1995 and the concomitant changes in senior management at Ontario Hydro did not help morale. Work procedures and union rules may have hampered efficient operation and the transfer of staff to high-priority work sectors and locations. Insufficient attention was paid to maintenance and to regulatory concerns at senior management and board levels (Peabody, Andognini, and Machon 1998). A decision was made to shut down seven older CANDU units, in order to focus technical expertise and trained manpower on the twelve newest plants.

In July 2000, OPG announced that it would lease the Bruce A and B nuclear stations – including the four shut-down reactors at Bruce A and four operation reactors at Bruce B – to British Energy until 2018. Such actions are therefore part of a global nuclear industry trend to consolidate plant ownership in fewer but ideally more expert hands.

The key in the new competitive Ontario electricity market is that CANDU reactors will have to compete with newer, mainly gas-fired sources of electricity generation, which will now be able to enter the Ontario electricity market under private ownership. AECL is affected negatively by these choices because domestic CANDU reactor sales seem highly unlikely in this decade, but also positively, because new opportunities for commercial service and refurbishment will emerge as OPG tries to get its nuclear plants into competitive shape, and to penetrate the neighbouring U.S. market.

AECL has certainly sought to keep the CANDU as technologically advanced as possible. Its CANDU 6 power reactors were designed explicitly for electricity production rather than from evolved other uses. They went into service in the early 1980s and were central to exports to Korea and China in the 1990s. A larger ACR-1000 or Advanced CANDU Reactor is being developed for 2016 and is undergoing a pre-licensing review in Canada (Atomic Energy Commission 2006). AECL, in concert with South Korea, is also developing the Direct Use of Spent Pressurized Water Reactor Fuel in Candus (DUPIC), which is intended, through technical changes, to allow countries with pressurized light water reactors (the reactor type mainly in place globally) to use CANDU reactors to recycle spent fuel (Hamilton 2007a). As always in nuclear matters, AECL and Canada must overcome many hurdles to operationalize the two key arguments made about nuclear power. These are that nuclear provides the cheapest, base load generation. (Base load power is power that is on all the time, as opposed to peak load, which is on only part of the time and requires generating plants to be switched on and off.) It is also an energy source that does not emit significant greenhouse gases, even on a life cycle basis (where emissions are assessed at all stages of use). AECL's argument is centred in the latter case on the evidence that each year a CANDU 6 reactor avoids emission of 4.8 million tons of carbon dioxide (AECL 2006).

Conservative-Led National Governments: Policy Change?

In recent years, Canada and Germany have elected conservative-led governments. This raises the question of whether the core nuclear regulatory and governance regimes, including issues such as the siting and operation of nuclear power, will change or continue on their basic path. In Germany, 'conservative-led' means conservative leadership in a traditional German-style coalition government. In Canada, 'conservative-led' means at present a Conservative party in power but in a minority Parliament. Both these changed political contexts are now briefly explored.

Germany: Preserving or Extending the Phase-Out?

Under the impact of the economic crisis in Germany and in particular of rising unemployment and unpopular measures to fight it, support for the Red-Green government declined after 2003. When in the key state of North Rhine–Westphalia a Red-Green Länder government was replaced by a conservative-liberal coalition, Chancellor Schröder called for early elections about a year ahead of schedule. A national conservative-liberal victory was widely anticipated, and it seemed clear that it would make dramatic changes in German energy policy.

At the national level, these two parties talked of reversing the nuclear phase-out law, making policy more favourable to the utilities and industrial interests (in the name of competitiveness), questioning the eco-tax, and replacing RESA by a more competitive system. The Kyoto approach to climate protection was also questioned. On the stock market, the shares of the utilities were boosted by Schröder's election announcement.

The Free Democrats (liberals) emphasized the need to return to nuclear and coal and wanted to subject renewable energy sources for electricity (RES-E) to market discipline. This had already been their approach before 1990, with a liberal minister of economic affairs preventing all substantial measures in favour of RES-E. In 2005, they proposed to install a quota/certificate system for a similar purpose.

The position of CDU/CSU was more complex, partly due to internal conflicts that had not been resolved. Angela Merkel, the conservative leader, had repeatedly made clear that changes in the energy sector would have to be substantial, and she earned high praise from VDEW, the Association of Power Utilities, when she gave a speech on her plans. But several of her proposals lacked specific details.

On nuclear power, she proposed to reverse the phase-out decision but did not say clearly by how long the lifetime of reactors should be extended. Some in the party argued in favour of an extension by eight years (from thirty-two to forty years) and asked the utilities to respond to such a step – which would have increased their profits by 20–30 billion, according to an estimate of the Öko-Institut (iwr 2005b) – by lowering prices for industry. The reaction of the utilities was to issue a statement that price formation should be left to the market and that such a request did not fit with the world of profit-oriented enterprises (iwr 2005a). Merkel also proposed to reduce the support for German hard coal.

When the close results of the 2005 parliamentary election became evident, the pro-RES and anti-nuclear community drew a sigh of relief. A conservative-liberal coalition would not have enough votes in parliament. This led to a coalition between the conservatives and the social democrats. RES and nuclear safety was to stay with the Environment Ministry (under a Social Democratic minister). After weeks of negotiation, the coalition agreement between the CDU, CSU, and SPD made clear that energy policy would continue in the footsteps of the Red-Green coalition.

CDU/CSU and SPD continued to have different opinions about nuclear power. In the coalition treaty, therefore, the following formula was included: 'Hence the agreement between the Federal Government and the energy utilities concluded on June 14, 2000, with respect to the agreed procedures and the amendment of the Nuclear Act cannot be changed.'

But this formula is no guarantee that the nuclear dispute in Germany is settled. It only reflects the fact that pro-nuclear politicians do not have a majority in the Bundestag. The Federal Minister of Economy, Mr Glos (CSU), responsible for general energy policy matters, is using each suitable and unsuitable opportunity to take a pro-nuclear power stance, which is, even in the wording used, pure public relations of the nuclear lobby.

There is now, in light of the climate change challenge, a lively public debate about the possibility to extend the life-span of younger nuclear power plants. The federal Economics Ministry under Conservative minister Glos has developed a proposal to extend the licence of the remaining seventeen plants by eight years (to forty years total), which would delay the completion of the phase-out to 2029 (when the youngest plant to shut down). But this is not the policy of the grand coalition government, as a result of SPD resistance.

The operators of nuclear plants have made several attempts to move the remaining lifetime from newer reactors to the four NPPs scheduled for shut-down during this legislature. The federal minister of the environment, who is responsible for nuclear safety, has turned down all applications and challenged the utilities to take the oldest nuclear power plants off-grid as soon as possible.

As a matter of fact, nearly all remaining German nuclear power plants are located in Länder, which are governed by either conservative-liberal or conservative-social democratic coalitions, or – as in Bavaria – ruled by the CSU alone. In general these Länder governments are essentially in favour of lifetime extension, albeit for different reasons.

Nuclear power is recommended as CO_2-free electricity generation, although the life cycle analyses of nuclear power plants calculate considerable emissions of greenhouse gases. Other arguments offered are the economic advantages of depreciated old nuclear power plants and the outdated age structure of the West German power stations in general, which does not afford the substitution in all plants of renewable energy technology.

The agreement on the phase-out of nuclear energy production that was concluded between the German government and the utilities on 14 June 2000 does not include the nuclear fuel facilities, such as the Urenco Gronau enrichment plant, or the ANF Lingen fuel fabrication plant. Finally, the grand coalition admits national responsibility for the secure final storage of nuclear waste and intends to find a solution during the legislature.

Canada: From Precarious Opportunity to a Potential Nuclear Comeback?

Compared to the previous Liberal governments since 1993, and despite its minority government status, the federal Conservative government in Canada has openly supported nuclear power as a part of Canada's overall energy mix. In Prime Minister Stephen Harper's view, Canada is an 'energy superpower,' in which case Canada's CANDU technology and even its large uranium reserves are seen as a part of the energy mix, including significant future energy exports.

But the willingness to tout nuclear power has also been manifest in more particular ways that link it to climate change and to technology and innovation policy. The federal Minister of Natural Resources Gary Lunn has gone out of his way to support the nuclear option. Lunn has argued, 'I think there are some very good opportunities for nuclear in the future and we're not afraid to talk about them' (qtd in Wattie 2007, 7). He stressed that AECL was working on a 'fourth generation' of nuclear reactors (see more below) that would extract more energy out of nuclear fuel to minimize the storage of radioactive waste. Lunn has also intimated that a nuclear reactor might be used to replace or reduce the large amounts of natural gas now used to generate power and steam in the extraction of petroleum from the vast Alberta oil sands. Some oil sands companies had suggested such a possibility, though it would be many years away from fruition and it would be a highly controversial step nationally and within Alberta (Ebner 2007; Fekete 2007; McCarthy 2006).

Federal nuclear policy, however, took a somewhat peculiar tangent early in 2008 when the federal government demoted the head of Canada's nuclear regulatory body, the Canadian Nuclear Safety Commission (CNSC). The demotion occurred over a dispute about regulatory safety delays regarding one of AECL's research reactors at Chalk River, which was crucial in producing isotopes used in medical diagnosis and imaging of cancer patients. Canada supplied over 70 per cent of the global market for such isotopes (Calamai 2008; MacLeod 2008). A severe shortage of supply was looming. The head of the CNSC argued correctly that her mandate did not deal with the isotopes. The CNSC mandate was only in nuclear reactor safety. The government put its emphasis on the isotope problem and had emergency legislation passed to allow the reactor to resume operations so that the isotopes could be produced.

The controversy over the demotion exposed underlying issues regarding AECL and its relationships with the regulator and the government (Calamai 2008). These relationships centred on government failure to adequately fund AECL's investment needs for current and new reactor development, in part because the Conservative government had concerns about its managerial competence. This in turn fed into the questions, discussed below, about whether AECL ought to be wholly or partly privatized.

The key nuclear link to climate change policy has come, however, from the Conservative view that nuclear reactors must continue to be a key part of Ontario's energy policy. The federal government cannot directly dictate such a policy in Ontario, but it has taken one step in a direction that it must take, regardless of whether or not Canada as a nuclear energy future, which is to deal with the long-term storage and management of nuclear waste, its political Achilles heel.

In June 2007, Lunn announced that he had accepted the federal Nuclear Waste Management Organization's (NWMO) recommended approach for managing used nuclear fuel in Canada (Calamai 2007; Canada, Natural Resources Canada 2007). In particular, the government has accepted the NWMO's Adaptive Phased Management (APM) option, which includes the isolation and containment of used nuclear fuel deep in the earth, with an option for temporary shallow underground storage. The NWMO is now mandated to begin planning and designing a site selection process collaboratively with Canadians, which will take years.

A further potential development under the Conservative federal government has centred on tentative efforts to partially privatize AECL. Discussions are underway to sell a significant share of the state-owned company to one of its global competition firms, such as General Electric (GE) or Areva, the French-owned firm. GE has its own light water nuclear reactor and is one of three main successful global nuclear technology firms, along with Westinghouse and Areva. Light water reactors are by far the dominant reactor technology globally.[6] The CANDU heavy water reactors of AECL have barely 10 per cent of the global market. GE has historically been a competitor to AECL but it has also been involved in significant contract work for and with AECL for decades.

It appears that the goal of these negotiations is to establish a strategic partnership that would be linked to the expected Ontario government decisions to build new reactors as part of its energy strategy. For these negotiations to succeed, each partner and player would need to see strategic advantage. For the federal government, a key virtue is that it could potentially unburden it, and Canadian taxpayers, of some of the annual $100 million in R&D and related funding. It would also cater to its desire to reduce the role of government or at least government ownership. But the federal government would also want to keep the CANDU design and protect Canadian high-tech jobs such as those 4,000 staff who work for AECL. The fact the nuclear industry may be on the verge of a global upswing, albeit a precarious one (see *Economist* 2006) also figures in the federal government calculus.

For these firms the main attraction would be that they would acquire new intellectual property linked to reactor design, waste storage, and fuel recycling, not to mention highly qualified nuclear engineering and research personnel.

The Ontario government's view of such a possible partial privatization is centred on its preference to be able to select the right nuclear reactor technology at the right price and in a competitive market, rather than being pressured simply to buy Canadian and buy Ontario by purchasing CANDU reactors from AECL. A wider range of choice may be available through AECL as a firm partly owned by a competitor. Both AECL as an Ontario-centred company and the Ontario and federal governments would also see advantages if a partially privatized AECL had a second kind of reactor product when it bids in the global market for reactor contracts in the United Kingdom, the United States, and China.

In all of these hypothesized and rumoured arrangements much will depend on the actual structure of the deal, what percentage of the ownership is agreed to by the federal government, what powers over CANDU are left in government hands, and what exactly GE might be buying into and later investing in.

The reason for some federal government optimism or bullishness about nuclear power is also undoubtedly tied to the larger announced Ontario government plan for its electricity sector and also to broader advice it has been receiving on its approach to climate change.

Under Ontario's announced plan, the provincial Liberal government will be moving away from coal in favour of nuclear power and renewable energy (Ontario, Ministry of Energy 2006). The government has directed OPG to undertake feasibility studies to refurbish units at the Pickering and Darlington sites. OPG has also been directed to begin work for an environmental assessment for the construction of new units at an existing nuclear facility. The province projects that nuclear will continue to be the single largest source of electricity in 2025.

At the federal level, the Conservatives have received advice on what a low carbon future might look like for Canada over the next forty-five years (National Roundtable on the Environment and the Economy [NRTEE] 2006). The NRTEE study certainly does not push nuclear as a central part of its two suggested scenarios and strategies (under different assumptions), but under both it sees the need for all existing nuclear plants being replaced/refurbished plus an additional 9200 MW capacity added to Ontario (ibid., 31).

Conclusions

In this chapter we have examined how multi-level governance and regulatory coordination and the underlying complexity and capacity configurations of the two countries produced ultimately two quite different nuclear energy policy paths in Germany and Canada. Both countries began the post–Second World War era with nuclear ambitions, albeit of a very different kind and reflecting quite different choices about technical capacity and alternative or complementary resource and energy endowments.

Both counties encountered reactor performance difficulties and failures and related coordination problems, with Germany then particularly affected politically and in other ways by the 1986 Chernobyl accident. At present, the German nuclear phase-out decision seems likely to hold, and the Canadian decision to keep the nuclear option in Ontario seems likely to be achieved but with several obstacles still to be faced. These obstacles are substantive and political, at the federal level, in Ontario, and vis-à-vis possible exports and U.S. reactor refurbishment opportunities and also in the continuing task of responding to environmental NGOs that concede none of the industry's positive climate change or other environmental claims.

Three arguments have been central to the analysis. First, the two countries differed in multi-level governance coordination, where nuclear and related energy policy decisions were made and accommodations reached. In Germany they were made for the most part at the national level as part of the coalition party politics and its need for reasonable consensus within the party structure but also regarding accommodations with Germany's sectoral corporatist structure of organized interests. There was certainly initial federal and Länder-level involvement, but overall the governance story was a national public-private one. In Canada, on the other hand, nuclear policy was very much a federal-provincial institutional process, and indeed mainly a bilateral coordination and accommodation between the federal government and the province of Ontario. It was also mainly a public sector issue.

The second argument advanced has been that in industrial policy, energy policy, and eventually energy and environment policy terms, there was a different level of centrality to nuclear policy in overall agendas, given each country's basic resource endowments and economic and social location and disposition. In Germany, nuclear was initially quite central to German industrial policy, then to national energy policy, and eventually and crucially also to German environmental policy. In Canada, nuclear policy was never a central feature of overall national industrial or energy policy or in any consistent way to national environmental policy. Both these relative positionings were a product of Germany's and Canada's situations, as chapters 1 and 2 have shown regarding resource endowments, with Germany in a much poorer resource situation and more continuously concerned about energy security and about its manufacturing-centred economy, and Canada being resource rich in an economy that was (and is) still a more mixed natural resource and manufacturing economy.

The third argument made in the chapter is that environmental concerns were much more deeply embedded in German society and politics at an overall national level and began at a much earlier stage. The Chernobyl nuclear accident galvanized these environmental concerns in a very energy-focused way. While there was an anti-nuclear lobby in Canada, there was no equivalent high environmental pressure on nuclear policy in Canada, in part due to the more decentralized and roller-coaster nature of environmental policy and politics in Canada as a whole and its relative lack of consistent centrality to energy policy until the quite recent movement of climate change to a central place on the Canadian agenda.

NOTES

1 In 1955, the Parisian Treaties were signed, which lifted the allied ban of any nuclear (civil and military) research from the losing parties of the Second World War. In the same year, the UN conference on the peaceful use of nuclear energy in Geneva was held, which to the German delegates underlined the urgency of a nuclear program to catch up to international standards (Keck 1984, 52–6).

2 The commission was in place from 1956 until 1971. More than two hundred delegates from industry, research centres, and universities were members of its many working groups, and it thus brought together leading representatives of the German nuclear community.

3 In the course of the four nuclear programs from 1957 to 1976 (beginning with the Eltviller Programm), 10 billion of research funds of the Federal Ministry for Research and Technology (BMFT) were spent. According to one historian, this financial contribution was a precondition for the success of Germany's nuclear industry, since many private investors by

the late 1950s had retreated from the nuclear venture because of low profitability expectations (Radkau 1983, 196).

4 The goal of this program was to increase nuclear capacity twenty-fold by 1985, i.e., to install total nuclear capacity of 40–50,000 MW and supply a share of up to 40 per cent of electricity needs through nuclear energy. This was reconfirmed in 1974 (Deutscher Bundestag 1974).

5 Tristructural-isotropic fuel.

6 Light water reactors (LWR) use ordinary (light) water as neutron moderator, whereas heavy water reactors (HWR) use heavy water as moderator and coolant.

REFERENCES

Atomic Energy of Canada Ltd. 2006. *Annual report: 2005–2006*. Ottawa: Atomic Energy of Canada.

Bothwell, R. 1988. *Nucleus: The history of Atomic Energy of Canada Limited.* Toronto: University of Toronto Press.

Brand, Karl-Werner. 1986. *Aufbruch in eine andere Gesellschaft: Neue soziale Bewegungen in der Bundesrepublik* [Departure to a different society: New social movements in the federal republic]. 2nd ed. Berlin: Campus.

Bratt, Duane. 2006. *The politics of CANDU exports*. Toronto: University of Toronto Press.

Calamai, Peter. 2007. Ottawa approves plan to bury nuclear waste. *Toronto Star*, 15 June.

– 2008. Chalk River crisis sired by AECL. *Toronto Star*, 19 January.

Canada. Natural Resources Canada. 2007. Canada's nuclear future: Clean, safe and responsible. News release. 14 June.

Daniels, Ronald J., ed. 1996. *Ontario Hydro at the millennium*. Montreal and Kingston: McGill-Queen's University Press.

De Souza, Mike. 2006. Tories pledge $520 million to nuclear cleanup. *Ottawa Citizen*, 4 June.

Deutscher Bundestag. 1974. *Erste Fortschreibung des Energieprogramms der Bundesregierung* [First continuation of the energy program of the federal government]. Bonn: BT-Drucksache.

Doern, G. Bruce, and Tom Conway. 1995. *The greening of Canada*. Toronto: University of Toronto Press.

Doern, G. Bruce, A. Dorman, and Robert Morrison, eds. 2001. *Canadian nuclear policy: Changing ideas, institutions and interests*. Toronto: University of Toronto Press.

Doern, G. Bruce, and Robert Morrison, eds. 1980. *Canadian nuclear policies.* Montreal: Institute for Research on Public Policy.

Ebner, David. 2007. Shell eyes nuclear power in oil sands. *Globe and Mail*, 24 May.

Economist. 2006. Nuclear power: The ghostly flickers of a new dawn. 25 November.

Farlinger, William. 1997. Statement by William Farlinger, chairman and interim CEO, Ontario Hydro, re hydro announcement, Toronto, 13 August.

Fekete, Jason. 2007. Dion dismisses nuclear power in oil sands extraction. *Calgary Herald*, 13 January.

Hamilton, Tyler. 2007a. The CANDU edge? *Toronto Star*, 12 February.

– 2007b. Nuclear selloff in the works. *Toronto Star*, 6 July.

iwr. 2005a. iwr news, 9 August. http://www.iwr.de/news/php?id=7684.

– 2005b. iwr news, 13 September. http://www.iwr.de/news/php?id=7774.

Keck, Otto. 1984. *Der Schnelle Brüter: Eine Fallstudie über Entscheidungsprozesse in der Großtechnik* [The fast-breeder reactor: A case study of decision-making processes in large-scale technology]. Berlin: Campus.

MacLeod, Ian. 2008. Harper government fires Linda Keen over isotope crisis. *National Post*, 16 January.

Martin, David H., and David Argue. 1996. *Nuclear sunset*. Ottawa: Campaign for Nuclear Phaseout.

McCarthy, Shawn. 2006. Nuclear power pushed for oil sands production. *Globe and Mail*, 29 September.

Mez, Lutz, ed. 1981. *Der Atomkonflikt. Berichte zur internationalen Atomindustrie. Atompolitik und Anti-Atom-Bewegung* [The nuclear power conflict: Reports on the international nuclear power industry, nuclear power politics and policy, and the anti-nuclear movement]. 2nd ed. Berlin: Rowohlt.

– 1997. Energiekonsens in Deutschland? Eine politikwissenschaftliche Analyse der Konsensgespräche – Voraussetzungen, Vorgeschichte, Verlauf und Nachgeplänkel [Energy policy consensus in Germany? A political science analysis of consensus negotiations: Preconditions, past history, process, and subsequent squabble]. In *Energiepolitik* [Energy policy], ed. Hans Günter Brauch, 433–48. Heidelberg: Springer.

Mez, Lutz, and Annette Piening. 2006. Phasing-out nuclear power generation in Germany: Policies, actors, issues and non-issues. In *Environmental governance in global perspective: New approaches to ecological modernisation*, ed. Martin Jänicke and Klaus Jacob, FFU report 01-2006, 322–49. Berlin.

Morrison, Robert. 2001. Global nuclear markets in the context of climate change and sustainable development. In *Canadian nuclear policy: Changing ideas, institutions and interests*, ed. Bruce Doern, A. Dorman, and Robert Morrison, 34–51. Toronto: University of Toronto Press.

National Roundtable on the Environment and the Economy. 2006. *Advice on a long-term strategy on energy and climate change*. Ottawa: National Roundtable on the Environment and the Economy.

Ontario. 1996. *A framework for competition*. Report of the Advisory Committee on Competition in the Ontario Electricity System to the Ontario Ministry of Environment and Energy.

– 1997. White paper: Direction for change. Toronto: Minister of Energy, Science and Technology.

Ontario. Ministry of Energy. 2006. McGuinty government delivers a balanced plan for Ontario's electricity future. News release. 13 June.

Peabody, Warren, Carl Andognini, and Richard Machon. 1998. Ontario Hydro: Restoring nuclear excellence. Paper presented to 11th Pacific Basin Nuclear Conference, Banff, May.

Prüß, Karsten. 1974. *Kernforschungspolitik in der Bundesrepublik Deutschland* [Nuclear research policy in the Federal Republic of Germany]. Berlin: Suhrkamp.

Radkau, Joachim. 1983. *Aufstieg und Krise der deutschen Atomwirtschaft 1945–1975* [Rise and crisis of the German nuclear power industry, 1945–1975]. Berlin: Rowohlt.

Stoett, Peter. 2003. Toward renewed legitimacy? Nuclear power, global warming, and security. *Global Environmental Politics* 3 (1): 99–116.

Trebilcock, Michael, and Ronald Daniels. 1995. The future of Ontario Hydro. *Utilities Law Review* (Winter): 152–61.

Wattie, Chris. 2007. Conservatives say nuclear power on the table. *National Post*, 24 January.

6 National or Supranational Electricity Governance – NAFTA and the EU: Electricity Market Reforms in Canada and Germany

KARL FROSCHAUER

This chapter examines whether supranational governance allows member states of the EU and NAFTA to make national choices in reforming their electricity markets. Examining the supranational directives and the path of national implementation to reform the electricity sectors in Canada and Germany contributes to understanding to what extent nation states can pattern these reforms. After establishing Germany's and Canada's supranational context, both countries are assessed for reform policy outcomes in national regulation, access to transmission systems, vertical de-integration, and anticipated competition.

The analysis shows that both countries show nationally specific patterns of electricity market reform. This result can be attributed to a combination of different structural sector properties on the one hand and contrasting institutional constellations of multi-level regulatory governance on the other hand, as developed in the overall framework presented in chapter 1 and 15 of this volume. Sector properties and institutional frameworks affect the capacity to provide integrated policy responses to energy challenges. The chapter highlights how institutional and market conditions constrain Canada's capacity to develop electricity market strategies and shows how Germany moves to a more coherent national regulatory system under EU constraints, while maintaining some traditional features of energy regulatory governance.

Some of the literature on energy reforms uses concepts of either intergovernmental or supranational interests to categorize sectoral case studies and to analyse regional coordination of electricity policy (Schmidt 1996). In analysing such international policies for electricity sector integration, an isolated emphasis on the supranational dimension of policies neglects how national interests participate in and are affected by policy formation above the nation state (van den Hoven and Froschauer 2004).

In spite of the significant differences in Canada's and Germany's trading patterns – proximity to a superpower, asymmetry in size and power of trading partners, powerful supranational integration structure, national and sub-national control over electricity market reform and their federal systems – both showed the ability to institute specific patterns of reform. This occurred, in Europe and North America, after participants in trans-governmental networks (that are complex, formal or informal, and extend to the supranational, national, and sub-national level) attempted to advance harmonization of electricity market policy and its implementation (Eberlein 2005; Morales and Higginbotham 2006).

This chapter argues that, in both cases, regional market integration did not erode national choices: Canada (or rather the provinces and the federal government) and Germany exercised discretion when opting for certain regulatory institutions. Both could translate regional integration pressures – more U.S. export-market driven in Canada and more legally and institutionally driven in the German case – into nationally specific patterns of market reform (see table 6.1). National and sub-national choices shaped the implementation of reform policies of these two members of the EU and NAFTA.

As both the Dewees analysis in chapter 3 and the Clarkson analysis in chapter 4 have indicated, several conditions have weakened the authority of Canada's national regulator: (1) U.S. dominance in North America and Canada's reticence stemming from an unequal relationship and historic trade irritants with the United States, (2) the deregulation assumptions behind the NAFTA agreement, and (3) internal sub-national resistance to national Canadian energy policies from Quebec, Alberta, and, at times, other provinces. Canada's specific pattern of market reform was initiated by electricity-exporting provinces that have historically decided the extent to which they were willing to restructure their utilities. Most provinces have merely administratively restructured their electric utilities.

This chapter first sets out the supranational NAFTA and EU contexts, then introduces the relevance of Canada and Germany as case studies, and, thereafter, assesses just how NAFTA and EU electricity policies were formulated and implemented to bring market reforms to the electricity sector at the national level. This chapter traces four

Table 6.1 Patterns of electricity market reform: Canada and Germany

Dimension	Canada	Germany
Supranational context	Canada, Mexico, and the United States sign NAFTA (1992); NAFTA provisions on energy; bi-lateral cross-border trade (U.S.-Canada, U.S.-Mexico); NAEWG – trilateral energy department experts; provincial utilities that export are members of NERC; NERC follows U.S. FERC orders; provincial utility commissions adapt FERC rules in provinces	EU 25 member states; Council, Parliament, and Commission as executive body pass EU legislation: first liberalization Directive 96/92 EC resulted in uneven national implementation; second Directive 2003/54 EC to advance and coordinate internal electricity market reforms: full market opening by July 2007, networking of national regulators to enforce regulated grid access and unbundling (legal, functional, and accounting), increasing role for competition law
National regulation	NRCan, Indian and Northern Affairs Canada, and the NEB hold national authority over energy policy; provinces own energy resources (e.g., gas, oil, hydro power); provincial commissions regulate markets, generation, transmission, and distribution. Provinces tend to follow U.S. FERC regulations orders (e.g., Order # 888, year 1997).	Federal Ministry of Economics and Technology; Federal Cartel Office; Federal Network Agency (electricity, gas, telecoms, postal services, railways); Directive 96/92 EC implemented by the *Energy Industry Act* 1998; Directive 2003/54 EC implemented by the *New Energy Industry Act* 2005; sub-national regulation in federal states of smaller and mid-sized power companies with grid access
Transmission	NEB holds authority over international transmission and inter-provincial transmission, and issues export permits; provinces regulate transmission; inter-provincial grid underdeveloped; twelve-year negotiations over electricity trade internal to Canada incomplete	First phase of reforms failed to regulate firm third-party access to transmission; new Federal Regulatory Authority is to assure third-party access; unbundling of transmission and regulation of tariffs
Vertical de-integration	NAFTA provisions and FERC orders stipulate that, in order to have access to the U.S. electricity market, provinces will reciprocate in unbundling and in allowing access to Canadian transmission lines; most provinces have restructured their vertically integrated utilities through unbundling	In 2000/1 Germany's eight major utilities merged into four, then oligopoly dominated the German electricity market; vertical integration of utilities remains largely intact; rather than competition by a multitude of suppliers, concentration of ownership increased

150   Karl Froschauer

Table 6.1 (continued)

Dimension	Canada	Germany
Competition	Wholesale competition: Alberta and British Columbia 1996; Quebec and Manitoba 1997; Saskatchewan 2001; Ontario 2002; and New Brunswick 2005; retail: Alberta and Ontario; major utilities' ownership is provincial	Germany's electricity market has been fully opened (for wholesale and retail) competition since 1998; most new electricity retailers now bankrupt; oligopoly of E.on, RWE, EnBW, and Vattenfall remains.

Note: German institutions and EU directives in table: Bundesministerium für Wirtschaft und Technologie (Federal Ministry of Economics and Technology); Bundeskartellamt-FCO (Federal Cartel Office); Bundesnetzagentur für Elektrizität, Gas, Telekommunikation, Post und Eisenbahnen (Federal Network Agency); Gesetz zur Neuregelung des Energiewirtschaftsrechts vom 24 April 1998 (E-Directive 96/92 EC implemented by the *Energy Industry Act* 1998); Zweites Gesetz zur Neuregelung des Energiewirtschaftsrechts vom 7.7.2005 (E-Directive 2003/55 EC implemented by the *New Energy Industry Act* 2005).

complex modifications to this sector: strengthening national regulation, access to transmission networks, de-integration of power companies (e.g., by functions, such as transmission from generation), and introduction of more competition by increasing the number of electricity providers and their selection by wholesale and retail customers (table 6.1).[1]

In Canada, electricity generating companies rank among the largest companies in the country and have wielded considerable influence over provincial governments. Similarities become evident when observing that the large provincially owned power utilities have retained large market shares in Canada, as have four large private power companies in Germany. Hydro-Québec, Ontario Power Generation (OPG, Ontario's generating company), Hydro One (transmission and distribution company), and BCHydro are the biggest players among Canada's seventeen provincial utilities. In Germany, E.ON, RWE, EnBW, and Vattenfall dominate the electricity market and are, like Canada's public utilities, vertically integrated, owning or controlling generation and transmission facilities.

Germany and Canada show similarities but also great differences in their electricity sector (for further details on Germany, see Theobald's chapter 10, and table 2.1). For example, Canada and Germany show a different generation mix: Germany's electricity generation in 2004 was based 48 per cent on coal, 28 per cent on nuclear power, 10 per cent on gas, 4 per cent on hydro, 4 per cent on wind, 2 per cent on oil, and 4 per cent on other, whereas Canada's in 2003 was based on 58 per cent hydro, 19 per cent coal, 12 per cent nuclear, 6 per cent natural gas, 3 per cent oil, and 2 per cent other (CEA 2006, 5; VDEW 2005, 1). Thus, Canada relies mostly on hydro, whereas Germany relies primarily on coal for power generation. The amount of electricity they produce, however, is similar: Germany in 2003 generated 595.5 terawatt hours (TWh) of electricity, and Canada 587 TWh (BMWi 2003, 59; IEA 2005, I.32 [table 2]; NAEWG 2006, 15). On the other hand, Canada's trade is more predominantly export-oriented than Germany's. Whereas in 2003 Germany imported 46.8 TWh (or 8 per cent of its generation), Canada imported 24.5 TWh (or 4 per cent of its generation). Both countries, however, exported different portions of their generated electricity in 2003, with Germany exporting 47.2 TWh (or 8 per cent of its generation) and Canada 31.2 TWh (or 5 per cent of its generation) (CEA 2005, 30; IEA 2005, I.32 [table 2]). Germany's electricity trade with its neighbours appears more balanced in its imports and exports.[2] Whereas Germany trades electricity with a number of European countries, Canada trades primarily with the United States.

Germany is the largest electricity market in Europe and the United States is the largest electricity market in North America. Although Canadian power companies' share of the entire U.S. market appears very small – electricity imports from Canada (31.2 TWh) accounted for less than 1 per cent of total electricity consumption (3569.6 TWh) in 2003 in the US – electricity exports from Canada's major utilities are very important for the northern states in the United States and vary considerably from province to province (IEA 2005, I.62, I.67). Canadian exports are primarily base-load. Quebec exports to Vermont, New York, and Maine; Ontario exports to New York and Michigan; Manitoba exports to eleven states, but primarily to Minnesota and Wisconsin; and British Columbia exports to ten states, but predominantly to Washington, Oregon, and California. Quebec, Ontario, New Brunswick, Manitoba, and British Columbia accounted for 98 per cent (42.1 TWh) of all Canadian exports (42.9 TWh) in 2005 (NEB 2005, 30). With important exporting interests at stake, provinces have played an important role in promoting cross-border trade in electricity and have joined U.S. power pools and transmission groups (NEB 2001, 5–6). Their membership in cross-border U.S. organizations made them subject to the U.S. Federal Energy Regulatory Commission (FERC), the implications of which will be developed below.

In North America, stemming from its colonial development history, Canada has continued its resource-export orientation in the energy sector by treating gas, oil, and electricity as export products. Canada's net exports grew substantially from the early 1970s, reaching a peak of 45 TWh in 1987 (CEA and Natural Resources Canada 2000, 62), fluctuating in the 1990s, reaching a peak of 51.0 TWh in 2000, with recent exports of 36.1 in 2002, 31.2 in 2003, 34.4 in 2004, and 42.9 TWh in 2005 continuing the fluctuating trend (between 6 per cent and per cent of its generation) of the previous decade (IEA 2005, I.68 [table 26]; NEB 2005, 30). Whereas in Germany, recent electricity trade, in exports and imports, almost offset each other, in Canada exports continue substantially to exceed imports from the United States.[3]

Canada's Supranational Context

As Stephen Clarkson shows in his chapter 4, neither the bilateral 1988 Canada-US Free Trade Agreement (CUFTA) nor the 1992 North American trilateral United States, Canada, and Mexico Free Trade Agreement (NAFTA) resulted in the same kind of legitimized institutional depth as in the European Union (EU), characterized by the European Council, Parliament, Commission, and Court of Justice. Countries in the NAFTA region have avoided creating permanent supranational institutions but have favoured, instead, trans-governmental working groups and a dispute settlement mechanism. In North America, trilateral electricity sector integration is at only the beginning stage; electricity trade in this region remains bilateral, Canada–United States and United States–Mexico (Pineau, Hira, and Froschauer 2004, 1459).[4]

Although the three countries have made provisions for trilateral electricity trade in NAFTA, each country retains autonomous jurisdictions over regulation. Whereas Mexico's regulation is more centralized, those of the United States and Canada are more decentralized at the national and sub-national levels. In Canada, however, provincial utility commissions tend to imitate U.S. regulatory requirements, but these requirements do not extend to forced vertical de-integration through privatized ownership. In addition, bilateral trade irritants with the United States resurface, such as financial settlements related to British Columbia's electricity exports to California during its major electricity supply crisis (Pineau, Hira, and Froschauer 2004, 1473).

Countries neighbouring the United States, such as Canada and Mexico, experienced pressures from within and from without to integrate their energy markets. In the twentieth century, integration pressures came from British and U.S. energy companies and their Canadian and Mexican subsidiaries to export electricity, oil, and gas from Canadian and Mexican locations in the United States. In Canada, for instance, the reversal of allowing U.S. development of electricity generation on the Canadian side of Niagara Falls for export to the U.S. companies that created shortages in Canada led to the creation of Ontario Hydro (as a principally owned electric utility) and in subsequent decades contributed to the institutionalization of a national export regulator and guardian of Canadian energy policy interests, the National Energy Board (NEB).

Since the 1960s, however, provinces took the lead. British Columbia, Quebec, Manitoba, and Newfoundland and Labrador bought private utilities that had focused mostly on profitable urban markets for a number of reasons: to build large northern power projects; to integrate distant northern, rural, and urban electricity transmission grids; and to export surplus electricity (from oversized hydro projects) to the United States. In Quebec, public ownership of the electric utility – Hydro-Québec – became, and has remained, part of a sovereigntist political strategy, whereby exports of electricity to the United States were seen as part of Quebec's nation-building strategy and as sovereignty assertion over electricity transport across Quebec territory from Labrador to Ontario – a matter that remains highly contentious.[5]

In Canada – in part because of fears that U.S. electrical utilities would become more protectionist and exclude Canada from the U.S. electricity market – federal governments continued to support provincial electricity exports from north to south. By the mid-1980s, Canada was prepared to accept the continentalization of energy markets (Watkins 1997, 32). Before long, energy provisions in the CUFTA and NAFTA would serve as 'conditioning frameworks' to promote continental electricity market integration and neoliberal market-oriented restructuring,[6] including the weakening of Canadian national regulation.

In North America, the electricity provisions in NAFTA, as well as later the 1997 FERC order, became very important for market reform in the electricity sector in Canada (U.S. FERC 1997; van den Hoven and Froschauer 2004, 1087). In 1989, Robert Priddle (1989, 5) then chair of Canada's National Energy Board, captured the new orientation of Canada's electricity export policy by stating that it is 'essentially market-based.' The requirements for export hearings by the NEB were drastically reduced, and the NEB announced that it would be part of

North American Trade Regulation Business (Priddle 1989, 3). The Canada-U.S. Free Trade Agreement, an earlier agreement from which clauses are carried forward into NAFTA, also provides for consultations between Canadian and American electricity market regulators to harmonize their practices (Canada 1988).[7] However, in the absence of supranational NAFTA institutions, national regulators, such as FERC in the United States and the NEB in Canada, did not play the same regulatory role in the harmonization of electricity market reform. The North American framework of regulating the electricity sector privileges the trans-governmental compliance of Canadian provincial regulatory authorities with U.S. national regulatory authority but without institutionalized (trilaterally) supranational leadership in regulation. The result is separate partially liberalized electricity markets, with Alberta and Ontario as leaders of market reforms (for details on differences between provinces, see table 9.5 in Pineau's chapter 9).

Even before NAFTA, electric utilities in Canadian provinces continued to become members in regional councils that are part of the U.S. National Electricity Reliability Council (NERC); after the NAFTA was in force and with the approval of the leaders in the three countries, energy department experts in Mexico, Canada, and the United States formed the North American Energy Working Group (NAEWG). In this institutional way, such participants in trans-governmental networks at the national and sub-national level attempted to resolve issues through consultation, exchanges of information, and informal communication, and to advance the harmonization of electricity market policy.[8] For instance, Canadian power-exporting companies became members of NERC councils (eight regional councils that account for almost all the electricity supplied in the United States from Canada and from a portion of the Baja California Norte in Mexico) and, since the 1990s, Canadian electricity exporters applied to the U.S. FERC to attain the status of U.S. electricity market participants. Soon, in the absence of the Canadian National Energy Board's taking a pan-Canadian regulatory initiative, the Canadian federal government – fearful of the interprovincial conflict generated by being seen as formulating a national energy or electricity policy – did not take the initiative to develop a coherent electricity market reform policy. Given this lack of national reform policy, U.S.-based institutional pressures to adapt to U.S. reliability standards and electricity market reform led provincial electric utility regulators to regulate electric utilities by adapting to FERC orders in a patchwork pattern of unbundling (vertical de-integration of utility structures), transmission access reciprocity, and competition across the country.

Germany's Supranational Context

Twentieth-century Canada feared becoming a satellite of the United States. It feared being overpowered by the United States economically, culturally, and demographically. In contrast, support for economic integration in Europe stems not only from a constructive response to twentieth-century wars in Europe, but also from the post-war rebuilding and post–Cold War unification experiences. Whereas Canada's national regulation of energy originally emerged in response to too much integration with the electricity market of the United States, European national regulation arises from a planned integration following multilateral policy formation. Sector-by-sector integration, such as developing an internal European market for the electricity sector, accelerated in the twenty-five European member states. In these ways European supranational organizations attempted to create a single electricity market. As a supranational organization, 'the European Union is a multilayered governance system that is characterized by shared competencies and joint policy making' (Eberlein 2005, 59).

Three supranational institutions play a major role in the formulation and implementation of EU electricity market policy and in market regulation. The European Council is a meeting of twenty-five heads of state or government of the European Union; it decides on the major directions of EU policy, including energy policy. The Council of Ministers brings together the individual ministers in charge of specific portfolios in their respective countries. The Council of Energy Ministers, assisted by various committees of national policy specialists, legislates, in conjunction with the European Parliament, on energy matters as far as they fall into the EU's legal remit. The European Commission, the EU's executive branch, proposes and executes legislation. Implementation of EU legislation generally lies with the national level. European directives need to be transposed into national legislation. However, the European Commission, as the guardian of the European treaties and representative of the EU 'general interest,' does enjoy certain executive duties and powers, in implementing regulations that specify legislation. Yet these powers are monitored by committees staffed with expert member state officials, under the so-called comitology system.

Two European directives to create a single European market in the electricity sector are worth noting. The first, Directive 96/92 EC, foresaw a partial opening of the electricity market by requiring common rules for the electricity markets in each member state. Peter Cameron identified three main implementation problems: (1) uneven implementation among member states, (2) use of discriminatory methods to manage access to networks and especially interconnections, and (3) high levels of market power of incumbent electricity and gas companies (Cameron 2005, 9).[9]

The second, Directive 2003/54 EC, repealed the first and was expected to resolve some of the problems resulting from the first directive. To overcome the problem of item 1 above – uneven implementation – this new directive proposes institutional enforcement by national regulatory authorities (NRAs) with strengthened policing powers in setting tariffs, access conditions, and advancing an integrated electricity market within the EU (Cameron 2005, 11; Eberlein 2005, 82–3). To remedy item 2 – discriminatory transmission access – clear advocacy of regulated third-party access *ex ante* (TPA) without discrimination by a transmission system operator and distribution system operator is required; that is, new market entrants are to have more effective access (Cameron 2005, 11, 13). And to deal with item 3 – overcome major market power – a regime of legal, functional, or accounting unbundling that removes barriers to access because of vertically integrated power companies is required (ibid., 17–18).[10]

Lessons learned from the implementation outcomes of the first directive also led the European Commission to pursue a strategy of engaging transnational networks, forum discussions, and advisory institutions to coordinate national with supranational electricity regulation policy (Eberlein 2005, 65). The first electricity sector directive had resulted in a European patchwork of national divergences in electricity market reforms and regulatory practices.

Instead of delegating more powers to the supranational level, the commission has sought to achieve European policy coordination by promoting transnational networking of member state agencies, such as the networking among the National Regulatory Authorities (NRA). For instance, the NRAs have an advisory role in implementation of the most recent directive through a newly established institution established by the commission, called the European Regulators Group for Electricity and Gas (ERGEG) (Cameron 2005, 11). It acts as an advisory group to the commission, and its purpose is to contribute to effective market opening in practice by promoting consistent approaches to market regulation throughout the European Union (Eberlein 2005, 83). A detailed account of this decentralized regulatory model by networks is given by Peter Cameron in chapter 7 of this volume.

In a 2007 report, ERGEG (2007) presents progress on one of its most important initiatives to further step-by-step integration – the development of seven regional electricity market projects in the European regions: Central-West, Northern, United Kingdom and Ireland, Central-South, South-West, Central-East, and Baltic. These are intermediary steps of integration before full integration of all regions into one single EU market can be achieved. For instance, Central-West includes the member states Belgium, France, Germany, Luxembourg, and the Netherlands (the lead regulator in this group is Belgium). Because of its central location, Germany, represented by the Federal Network Agency for Electricity, Gas, and Telecommunications, Posts, and Railway (BNetzA), is a member of four different regional initiatives.

Canada's Pattern of Market Reform

In Canada, regional market integration allowed national choices. The provinces and the federal government exercised discretion when opting for federal and provincial regulatory institutions. In this way Canada could translate regional integration pressures (mostly market driven) into nationally specific patterns of market reform in national regulation, transmission access, de-integration, and competition (table 6.1).

National Regulation

Although the provincial, territorial, and federal energy ministers gathered annually at the Council of Energy Ministers to address energy issues at the highest level or to form working groups to address interprovincial issues on electricity, provinces took on the major initiatives to advance market reform through their regulatory practices (for details on Canadian energy regulatory governance, see chapter 1, and also Doern and Gattinger 2003). In Canada's northern territories, however, the federal Department of Indian and Northern Affairs Canada acts on all energy matters in the Northwest Territories and Nunavut. The federal government devolved responsibility for energy matters to Yukon and negotiates such devolution to the Northwest Territories (IEA 2004, 35).

Natural Resources Canada (NRCan) is the primary federal department responsible for general energy policy. The national regulator, the National Energy Board, reports through the minister responsible for NRCan to Parliament. The NEB is an independent national regulatory agency that was established in 1959. Concerning electricity, the NEB regulates and authorizes the construction and operation of interprovincial and international power lines under federal jurisdiction and issues export permits (IEA 2004, 37). The NEB is involved in matters under federal jurisdiction, while provincial energy boards such as the Ontario Energy Board (OEB), Alberta Energy and Utility Board (EUB), and the British Columbia Utilities Commission (BCUC), and the Régie de l'énergie in Quebec play roles in matters of provincial regulatory policy (Richmond et al. 2005, 40).

Most importantly, as the International Energy Agency (IEA) noted, Canadian provinces have more jurisdiction over energy than other sub-national governments of other federated countries. Electricity is almost exclusively regulated at the provincial level (IEA 2004, 35). Provincial utility commissions hold jurisdictional responsibilities for regulating transmission, generation, distribution, rates, and proposals to provincial governments for electricity market reforms, such as the introduction of wholesale or retail (customer-oriented) competition (NAEWG 2002). Therefore, delicate federal-provincial compromises to satisfy diverse provincial and First Nations[11] interests, including strengthening of interprovincial electricity interconnections, have to be worked out (IEA 2004, 45). In Canada, each province has a separate regulator that may operate at arm's length or serve as a policy arm of its respective government.

In this way, rather than Canada's policy and regulatory institutions, such as the Council of Energy Ministers, Natural Resources Canada, or the National Energy Board regulating and designing the new domestic electricity market (90–94 per cent of Canadian electricity generation), in exporting provinces market reforms are driven by U.S. regulatory changes to enable the provinces' major players to be part of the U.S. market (IEA 2004, 147). For instance, provincial utilities are required to follow reciprocity requirements of the American electricity regulator, FERC Order #888 (which includes reciprocal access to cross-border transmission grids), if they want to wholesale their surplus electricity in U.S. states (U.S. FERC 1997).[12] In other words, FERC's regulations and market designs have 'major impacts on policy and regulation of electricity grids and markets in Canada through FERC's control of access of Canadian utilities to the US market (which fluctuates between 6 to 8% of Canadian electricity generation since the 1980s)' (CEA 2005, 5; IEA 2004, 146).

Canadian federal institutions continue to avoid taking the lead in regulating domestic interprovincial or national transmission systems. For instance, in 2006, Canada's Internal Trade Secretariat reports that harmonizing the legal provisions within Canada for the interprovincial trade of energy goods and energy services (including those related to the production and transmission of electricity) are still to be negotiated (Canada 2006). In 2006, after twelve years of federal and provincial negotiations, it appeared that transmission of electricity across provinces to third-party markets had not been resolved (Canada, CMIT 1996, 15). Provincial energy ministers and the Committee on Internal Trade had hoped 'that the energy chapter will provide limited uniform access to cross-territory transmission of electricity. It will also provide a mechanism to settle disputes' (IEA 2004, 129).

Given the Canadian patchwork pattern of provincial electricity market reforms, a C.D. Howe Institute report 'urged the National Energy Board to begin to take a much more active role in the process of increasing the degree of regional integration, at least within the Canadian electricity market' (Pierce, Trebilcock, and Thomas 2006, 23); and a report by the International Energy Agency recommends that the government of Canada should 'take a more active role in initiating cooperation between federal, provincial and territorial governments with a view to formulating national consensus on the goals and implementation of energy policies, where mutually beneficial, e.g., through the Council of Energy Ministers and bilateral and regional meetings of ministers and high officials' (IEA 2004, 11).[13]

Transmission

Although the large utilities in Canada's major electricity-producing provinces – Quebec, Ontario, Manitoba, Alberta, and British Columbia – advocated cross-border electricity market integration with the United States, they only reluctantly opened domestic electricity markets to competition and de-integrated public utilities. Thus, different from the German case, Canadian provincial utilities preferred an export-oriented liberalization model for electricity with strong transmission linkages (licensed by the National Energy Board) in a north-south direction.

The provinces and their utilities adopted their own approaches to opening their transmission systems for domestic and international suppliers, mostly towards the United States, and to 'functionally unbundling' their public monopolies to meet American regulatory directives (FERC). Usually this happened through membership in regional transmission organizations that were regulated by FERC. Manitoba, for example, is a member of a regional council, the Midwest Independent Transmission System Operator Inc., a U.S. FERC–approved regional transmission organization (RTO) that ensures equal access to the transmission system and maintains or improves electric system reliability in the Midwest (Richmond et al. 2005, 38).

Whereas the generation component of electricity rates will be based on market forces, the transmission facilities will continue to be planned. For instance, Alberta Electricity System Operator (AESO) is expected to 'plan transmission facilities to meet the anticipated demands for electricity, generation capacity and reserve margin' (NAEWG 2006, 61). The Ontario Power Authority is required to file an Integrated Power System Plan, which will predict demand by considering generation, transmission, and conservation. The New Brunswick Operator is likewise responsible for developing integrated system plans but cannot directly implement them (ibid.). The difficulty, of course, in planning a suitable transmission system is whether investment in new generation facilities is predictable; for example, investors may displace investments in space and time.

De-integration of Utilities

Provinces and utilities exercised their jurisdiction to implement electricity market reforms by restructuring integrated utilities through unbundling. Rather than succumbing fully to supranational pressure, Canadian provinces have decided the extent to which they were willing to restructure their utilities, and most have merely restructured their utilities administratively. Quebec has only 'functionally unbundled' its provincially owned and vertically integrated monopoly by establishing Hydro-Québec Generation, Hydro-Québec Distribution, and Régie de l'énergie, but retained provincial ownership (CEA 2000, 6). Unlike Quebec, the former Ontario Hydro was restructured into separately managed business entities for future divestment, including Ontario Power Generation Inc. (OPG), Hydro One Inc. (Hydro One), the Independent Electricity Market Operator (IMO), the Ontario Electricity Financial Corporation (OEFC), and the Electrical Safety Authority (NEB 2001, 36). In 1996, Manitoba also 'functionally unbundled' its major provincially owned public electricity utility Manitoba Hydro into distinctly accountable business units: Power Supply, Transmission and Distribution, and Customer Service. Thus, Manitoba Hydro is still a vertically integrated government-owned utility like Hydro-Québec (CEA 2000, 6). With the exception of Edmonton Power, Alberta's major power companies (TransAlta Utilities and ATCO Electric) are privately owned (CEA 2000). In contrast to Alberta, British Columbia's BCHydro was simply 'functionally unbundled' into BC Power Supply, BC Hydro Transmission and Distribution, and the electricity export subsidiary Powerex. BCHydro remains vertically integrated and provincially owned. A recent report by the Canadian Electricity Association shows the ownership structure of utilities has changed little (CEA 2006, 13–40).

Competition

The federal government, but particularly the provinces, exercised discretion when opting for federal and provincial regulatory institutions. For instance, the federal Competition Bureau became involved in deregulation and privatization of some of Canada's provincial electricity markets as an independent party of experts (Southey 2002).

The Competition Bureau reviewed and influenced 'core features of the institutional structure of Alberta's electricity market, including the role of market surveillance and regulation in overseeing competition and the restructuring of other market and system operation institutions' (ibid.).[14] In Ontario, the bureau advocated key regulators, and oversight and market operations features that have become part of this province's market reform. In Nova Scotia, the bureau advocated a 'measured approach towards the introduction of electricity sector competition' (ibid.). In addition, provinces decide on the degree of market reform according to specific circumstances in the province, such as the potential for competition, potential stranded assets, and interconnection with other jurisdictions (CEA 2004, 147).

Thus, in Canada, individual provinces have decided the extent to which they would restructure the ownership of utilities and have chosen to implement the opening of their domestic markets in varying degrees. During the last decade, most provinces have initiated wholesale competition, although at different dates: Alberta and British

Columbia in 1996; Quebec and Manitoba in 1997; Saskatchewan in 2001; Ontario in 2002; and New Brunswick in 2005. By 2006, only Alberta and Ontario have initiated retail competition. Donald Dewees, in his chapter 3 of this volume, provides a detailed account of the process and outcomes of electricity restructuring in these two provinces.

Germany's Pattern of Market Reform

The European Union directives needed to be implemented in Germany through new legislation. Directive 96/92 EC had been implemented in Germany through the *Gesetz zur Neuregelung des Energiewirtschaftsrechts* (*Energy Industry Act* 1998). Its three main features were (1) immediate and full market liberalization, so that all end-users could choose their electricity wholesaler and retailer; (2) no restriction for vertical integration, which was prevalent and increasing in the German electricity sector; and (3) allowance of negotiated Third Party Access to the transmission network (Brunekreeft and Twelemann 2004, 3; also see chapter 1 and Theobald, chapter 10, this volume). However, access to the transmission system, lack of merger control (including continued vertical integration), and an increasingly oligopolistic ownership structures became problematic.

To improve upon the outcome of the first phase of electricity market liberalization, the EC's second directive, 2003/54 EC, repealed the first, and the second directive was implemented in Germany through the *Energiewirtschaftsgesetz* – EnWG (*Energy Industry Act* 2005), and a new federal regulatory authority was created, the Bundesnetzagentur (Federal Network Agency) (for details see Theobald, chapter 10). The second directive requires Germany's 'vertically integrated electricity utilities to unbundle transmission and distribution network activities from other activities' (Scholz and Stappert 2005, 80).

National Regulation

As explained in chapter 1, in Germany, the federal state is primarily responsible for passing energy legislation, and the Länder are responsible for administrative implementation of national law. At the national level, the Bundesministerium für Wirtschaft und Technologie – BMWi (Federal Ministry of Economics and Technology) holds responsibility for energy policy, while environmental aspects of energy use fall under the jurisdiction of the Federal Ministry of the Environment, as developed in chapter 12 on Germany's climate change policy (Weidner and Eberlein). Although the federal government has significant administrative powers, the individual states are also involved in shaping energy policy through co-legislation through the Bundesrat (ministerial-level conferences), a range of joint government and state committees and the working groups recently established at the national energy summit. In addition, competition authorities on both territorial levels and, as noted, a newly created network industries regulator are part of a highly complex regulatory system (also see overview of regulatory structures in IEA 2007, 22).

Christian Theobald provides in chapter 10 a detailed account of this multi-layered regulatory system. Hence, we can limit ourselves to highlighting one key element, the transition from a traditional, corporatist system of industrial self-regulation (by way of industry agreements) to a system of more formal regulation built around the new regulatory agency. Regulation by industry Associations' Agreement, monitored only ex-post by competition law, was characteristic of the first phase of market reform. It has been replaced by a system of public regulation by agency, with ex-ante powers in ensuring non-discriminatory access to the natural monopoly of the electricity transmission and distribution system.

Whereas in Canada the federal government had established a federal regulator in 1959, it was later reluctant to use national regulatory power, in part also because CUFTA and NAFTA provisions were supposed to bring deregulation, and because of provincial resistance. In Germany, the problem was opposition, by the powerful utility industry and the Länder, to establishing such a national regulator (Eberlein 2000). Industry self-regulation based on Associations' Agreements and complemented by oversight through the cartel bureau had proven to be an insufficient implementation of the first directive (96/92 EC). Therefore, the implementation of the second directive (2003/54 EC), through the *Energy Industry Act* of July 2005, resulted in a new national regulatory institution, the Bundesnetzagentur für Elektrizität, Gas, Telekommunikation, Post und Eisenbahnen – BNetzA (Federal Network Agency), which was exclusively responsible for the implementation of the unbundling requirements, the enforcement of EU Regulation 1228/2003 on cross-border electricity trading, and the notification procedure for household customer suppliers (Scholz and Stappert 2005, 83). The requirement for national regulatory authorities in the second directive is indeed more precise: regulatory authorities are to ensure non-discrimination, effective competition, and efficient market functioning. Also the authority must be empowered to ensure *ex ante* access to national networks (Cameron 2005, 20).

Thus, EU legislation has significantly transformed German energy regulation and brought it more into line with the European model of independent agency regulation, without, however, eliminating important traditional features (competition policy, role of Länder).

Transmission

Analysts of electricity market reforms tend to agree that 'due to the peculiarities of all network-bound industries and the former monopolies in supply areas, the prohibition of the abuse of a dominant position (e.g. refusal to grant TPA, excessive or predatory pricing, selective price-cutting, unjustified impairing or hindering of competition) and of any discrimination by dominant enterprises are of particular importance in the electricity sector' (Scholz and Stappert 2005, 83).

In Germany, where, as noted by Theobald in his chapter, transmission activities have been carried out solely by legally unbundled transmission operators of RWE, E.ON, EnBW, and Vattenfall Europe, distribution services have been provided by about nine hundred network operators on the regional or local level (ibid., 80). Although in Europe and North America access to transmission systems has been a contentious policy issue,[15] in Germany the outcomes of the first liberalization took a particular form, as noted earlier, through industrial self-regulation of access to transmission and distribution networks. For instance, issues of access were related to the price of transporting electricity. Brunekreeft and Twelemann assume that 'the fact that in many countries the network is under separate ownership from the competitive activities suggests that the extent of common costs in the vertically related electricity business (between the networks and the competitive businesses) is low' (2004, 14). In Germany, the Bundeskartellamt (Cartel Office) (2001) found transmission 'access charges were [too] high' (ibid., 6). In its review, it found that, although it was the norm that transmission network operators would not unduly discriminate against third parties, in reality genuine price discrimination against third parties (also known as raising rivals' costs or sabotage) did occur (ibid., 70). Squeezing the profit margins of competing electricity providers was made easier by Germany's vertical integration in the electricity sector and the lack of network regulation, which discouraged entry of new firms generating or supplying electricity (Brunekreeft and Twelemann 2004, 2). As noted above, the German legislature eventually opted for the *ex-ante* control of regulated network access, implemented by a new regulatory authority (also see Theobald's chapter).

Vertical De-integration

Whereas the first directives and legislative implementation were to have increased vertical de-integration and a growth in competition, in fact the opposite has occurred: the authorities produced a 'concentration by regulation' (see Theobald's analysis in chapter 10).

Despite the predictions by the German economics minister in 1997 that no major concentration of ownership in the electricity sector would take place, eight major German utilities merged into four (Vorholz 2003, 28). The concentration in generation had increased slowly since the early 1990s but rather steeply around 2000–2001 (Brunekreeft and Twelemann 2004, 4). A strongly criticized merger occurred in 2002 when E.ON merged with Ruhrgas. E.ON is predominantly electricity-based, whereas Ruhrgas is predominantly a gas importer and transporter and highly dominant in the German market. Because access to gas is increasingly in competition with electricity generation, the Cartel Office prohibited the merger because it would substantially lessen competition in electricity. Again having other aims, the minister of economic affairs overruled the Cartel Office as well as his own advisers in the Monopolies Commission, and approved the merger (ibid., 5). As a result, the ownership structure in Germany's electricity sector remained highly concentrated. Because in Germany large-scale private utilities (E.ON, RWE, EnBW, and Vattenfall) control 80 per cent of the domestic capacities and about half of the transmission lines, the unbundling requirement (the vertical de-integration of production from the transmission of electricity) appears to be particularly important (Theobald; Scholz and Stappert 2005, 80).

Competition

During the first liberalization phase, unlike in Canada, wholesale and retail competition, and 'the sale of power was fully open to competition. From the beginning of the liberalisation of the energy sector in

1998, Germany did not make any distinctions as to the eligibility of customers' (Scholz and Stappert 2005, 80). Both retail and wholesale competition suffered. In legal terms, the German market has been fully open to competition since 1998. As a consequence, electricity prices for both industrial and domestic consumers decreased significantly between 1998 and 2000. Because of the negotiated third-party agreements, the profit margins in generation and retail of electricity remained low or below cost in Germany. In 2004,

> Müller and Wienken (2004) estimated that roughly 40% of the household market was below cost. The cumulative switching rates [of customers to new suppliers or retailers] were very low, with less than 5% for households and slightly more than 6% for commercial customers ever having switched. Several initially successful retailers went bankrupt and by 2004 only Yello, which is a subsidiary of EnBW, survived and it was struggling, despite having one million customers. The same picture emerges at the wholesale market. (Brunekreeft and Twelemann 2004, 7)

After the first liberalization implementation, unregulated vertically integrated private monopolies in the German electricity sector and its securing of profits in the provision of high-cost transmission allowed no or only small profit margins for suppliers of electricity that wished to compete. This underscores Theobald's argument in chapter 10 that the EU's and Germany's regulation in the first electricity market reform phase did not result in diversified ownership but instead fostered more concentrated utility ownership, in short, 'concentration by regulation.'

Conclusions

What discretion did Canada and Germany have when they faced international pressures from supranational governance structures? I have argued that although both nations have faced supranational pressures to reform and integrate their electricity markets, Canada and Germany developed *nationally specific patterns of electricity market reform.*

With regard to the overall multi-level regulatory governance approach of this volume, this chapter yields two results. First, it shows that in both national cases, the supranational framework does not determine national reform paths and outcomes but instead provides crucial incentives for reform choices, more market-based in the Canadian and NAFTA case, more institutionally driven in the German and EU case. Second, the chapter illustrates how the interplay of structural sector properties and institutional frameworks yields different capacities of multi-level management in response to energy challenges. Interestingly, though, in both cases, trans-governmental networking plays an increasing role in regional integration.

Different supranational contexts for Canada, as a member state in NAFTA, and Germany, as a member state of the EU, take guidance from different institutions. The EU region has created supranational institutional depth, including the European Commission, Council, Parliament, and Court of Justice, and has practised among member states relatively multilateral power relations in the EU region. The NAFTA region has not created similar permanent supranational institutions, but instead has agreed to working groups and bi-national or tri-national panels that review trade disputes and provide updated information. Although the key ideas to reform the electricity sector and integrated networks within a larger region were similar – including the need for national regulation, allowing access to transmission systems, de-integrating electric power companies, and introducing wholesale and retail competition – the specific patterns of market reforms were different.

Whereas Germany did not develop a national regulatory institution until recently, Canada had instituted a national regulator – the National Energy Board in 1959. Subsequent to the most recent EC directive, the supranational bodies insist that national energy regulatory authorities must have the power and resources to exercise regulatory oversight over national markets. In Canada, on the other hand, especially since CUFA, NAFTA, and ideas of deregulation became prominent as part of neoliberal market reforms, Canada's national energy authority, the NEB, has avoided using its national regulator authority and thereby allowed a kind of institutional neo-colonialism to occur by allowing the U.S. FERC to exercise its powers over Canadian electricity market participants. Whereas Germany moves towards more national regulation in the EU context, Canada avoids national regulatory initiatives; instead, provincial regulators have created a patchwork of provincial electricity market reforms that straddle the Canada-U.S. border.

Although in both countries major power companies also controlled access to the transmission system and access remained a major issue, the integration of provincial transmission systems across the Canada-

U.S. border occurred at the expense of interprovincial transmission. In addition, the *inability* to develop an integrated, internal electricity market within Canada is evident in the Internal Trade Agreement, in which the energy chapter dealing with interprovincial access to transmission lines after twelve years of negotiations is still not resolved, an issue discussed in detail in chapter 9 by Pineau.

Whereas in Canada the unbundling – separate incorporation of sector functions, such as transmission, generation, and distribution of electricity – did occur in different years and to different extents, the electricity sector ownership structure (although more unbundled) has changed little and remains largely in provincial hands. In Germany, vertical integration and high concentration of ownership (four major power companies) remain the key issue. While Germany opened its retail and wholesale market in 1998, only two provinces in Canada did the same (Alberta and Ontario) and electricity rates remain provincially regulated. Whereas the ownership structure in Canada remained roughly the same, Germany achieved ownership 'concentration by regulation' as a result of the first liberalization step, but it is possible that the same mistake could be repeated with implementation of the second directive (see Theobald's analysis in chapter 10). These different outcomes of how directives about reforms including national regulation, transmission, de-integration, and competition have been institutionally implemented shows that in Germany and Canada nationally specific patterns of electricity market reforms did occur.

NOTES

1 Electricity market liberalization can include a number of changes: (1) the introduction of market competition whereby customers of different categories (e.g., wholesale, industrial, small business, and household) can select electricity suppliers, (2) the regulation of transmission systems to give suppliers access to potential customers, (3) the deregulation of prices charged by generating companies so that marketers can conduct arbitrage sales by buying electricity at a low cost in one market and selling it in another at a higher cost, or so that new generating facilities would be built, and (4) the expansion of international trade via exports and imports of electricity (Pineau, Hira, and Froschauer 2004).
2 Germany relies on a more multilateral electricity trade relationship with its neighbours. The total volume of international electricity trade in

Germany amounted to 87 TWh in 2000, with exports and imports almost offsetting each other. The imports essentially came from France (34 per cent), the Czech Republic (20 per cent), Norway (14 per cent), Austria (13 per cent), and Switzerland (12 per cent), and exports went mostly to the Netherlands (40 per cent), Switzerland (24 per cent), and Austria (18 per cent) (IEA 2002, 102–3).

3 Some of these imports can be explained by the power companies' policy of energy banking.

4 We are not focusing in this paper on subregional exchanges, though we recognize that international exchanges can be concentrated in certain subregions of the countries involved.

5 The historical legacy of the long-term Churchill Falls power contract, which allows Quebec to import electricity from this Labrador location (which is part of Newfoundland) and, in turn, profitably export it to the United States (Froschauer 1999).

6 R. Grinspun and R. Kreklewich, cited by Macdonald (1997, 183).

7 See energy trade in Articles 902 through 905 in chapter 9 of the CUFTA.

8 This insight stems from Morales and Higginbotham (2006) and is similar to insights offered by Eberlein (2005).

9 In addition, he listed the factors hindering achievement of an integrated European energy market: lack of transmission and cross-border capacity; lack of transparency in network access; lack of coordination between transmission system operators; and lack of consistency in application of competition law (merger control, anti-trust, etc.).

10 *Legal unbundling* means separation of the transmission system operator and the distribution system operator from the vertically integrated undertaking. *Functional unbundling* refers to separating to get independence from vertically integrated undertaking legally but not by ownership; *accounting unbundling* involves separating company accounts for transmission network activities (Cameron 2005, 17, 18).

11 For instance, interests in Alberta and Quebec opposed to national energy policies, or Aboriginal peoples who are opposed to building hydroelectric projects for export.

12 See also Froschauer (1999) and NEB (2001, 59).

13 In Canada, the federal government avoids painful political decisions on the unsettled borders of Labrador, the Churchill Falls power contract and Quebec export benefits, and the high U.S. ownership of oil and gas companies and their resistance to any national energy policy. The current Harper government, stating a market-oriented energy policy, has argued for more devolution of power to the provinces, which could result in this

federal government not leading in national regulation of the energy sector.

14 Presentation by Sally Southey, assistant commissioner, Communications, Competition Bureau (Canada), 1 November 2002 (http://www.competitionbureau.gc.ca)

15 In the 1960s and 1970s in Canada, Quebec blocked transmission of Labrador electricity to Ontario. In the United States, Bonneville Power, as federal owner of transmission lines to California from the Northwest, gave priority to U.S. over Canadian electricity shipments from British Columbia to California (Froschauer 1999).

REFERENCES

Brunekreeft, G., and S. Twelemann. 2004. Regulation, competition and investment in the German electricity market: RegTP or REGTP. In *Cambridge working papers in economics*, 111–32. Cambridge, MA: Cambridge-MIT Institute.

Bundeskartellamt. 2001. *Bericht der Arbeitsgruppe Netznutzung Strom der Kartellbehörden des Bundes und der Länder* [Report of the Working Group on Network Use in Electricity of the Federal and Länder Cartel Authorities]. Bonn: Bundeskartellamt. http://www.bundeskartellamt.de/wDeutsch/download/pdf/Merkblaetter/Merkblaetter_deutsch/01_Netznutzung.pdf.

BMWi. 2003. Bundesministerium für Wirtschaft und Technologie. *Energieversorgung für Deutschland: Statusbericht für den Energiegipfel am 3 April 2003* [Energy supply for Germany: Report on status quo for the Energy Summit on 3 April 2003]. http://www.bmwi.de.

Cameron, P. 2005. Completing the internal market in energy: An introduction to the new legislation. In *Legal aspects of EU energy regulation: Implementing the new directives on electricity and gas across Europe*, ed. Peter Cameron, 7–39. Oxford: Oxford University Press.

Canada. 1992. North American Free Trade Agreement between the Government of Canada, the Government of the United Mexican States, and the Government of the United States of America. Minister of Supply and Services Canada.

Canada. Committee of Ministers on Internal Trade. 1966. Annual report: The Agreement on Internal Trade, July 1994 to March 1996. http://strategis.ic.gc.ca.

– 2005. Energy (chapter 12). *Annual report: The Agreement on Internal Trade, Annual Report 2004–2005*, 13–14. Ottawa: Industry Canada.

Canada. Department of External Affairs. 1988. The Canada–United States Free Trade Agreement. Ottawa: Minister of Supply and Services.

Canada. Internal Trade Secretariat. 2006. Chapter twelve: Energy (to be negotiated). Agreement on Internal Trade: Consolidated version, 129–30. Internal Trade Secretariat. http://www.ait-aci.ca.

Canadian Electricity Association. 2005. *The integrated North American electricity market: Assuring an adequate supply of electricity through cross-border cooperation and trade.* Toronto: Canadian Electricity Association.

– 2006. *Power generation in Canada: A guide.* Toronto: Canadian Electricity Association.

Canadian Electricity Association and Natural Resources Canada. 2000. *Electric power in Canada 1998–99.* Ottawa: Ministry of Public Works and Government Services Canada.

CEA. *See* Canadian Electricity Association.

CMIT. *See* Committee of Ministers on Internal Trade.

Doern, G. Bruce, and Monica Gattinger. 2003. *Power switch: Nuclear regulatory governance in the twenty-first century.* Toronto: University of Toronto Press.

Eberlein, B. 2000. Institutional change and continuity in German infrastructure management: The case of electricity reform. 2000. *German Politics* 9 (3): 81–104.

– 2005. Regulation by cooperation: The 'third way' in making rules for the internal energy market. In *Legal aspects of EU energy regulation: Implementing the new directives on electricity and gas across Europe,* ed. Peter Cameron, 59–88. Oxford: Oxford University Press.

ERGEG. *See* European Regulators Group for Electricity and Gas

European Regulators Group for Electricity and Gas. 2007. ERGEG regional initiatives annual report: Progress and prospects. http://www.ergeg.org/portal/page/portal/ERGEG_HOME/ERGEG_RI/Progress%20Reports/RegionalInitiati ves%20annual%20report.pdf.

Froschauer, K. 1999. *White gold: Hydroelectric power in Canada.* Vancouver: University of British Columbia Press.

IEA. *See* International Energy Agency.

International Energy Agency. 2002. *Energy policies of IEA countries: Germany 2002 review.* Paris: Organisation for Economic Co-operation and Development and International Energy Agency.

– 2004. *Energy policies of IEA countries: Canada 2004 review.* Paris: Organisation for Economic Co-operation and Development and International Energy Agency.

– 2005. *IEA statistics 2005: Electricity Information.* Paris: Organisation for Economic Co-operation and Development and International Energy Agency.

172   Karl Froschauer

– 2007. *Energy policies of IEA countries: Germany 2007 review.* Paris: Organisation for Economic Co-operation and Development and International Energy Agency.

Macdonald, L. 1997. Going global: The politics of Canada's foreign economic relations. In *Understanding Canada: Building on the new political economy,* ed. W. Clement, 172–96. Montreal and Kingston: McGill-Queen's University Press.

Morales, N., and J. Higginbotham. 2006. 21st century diplomacy: Mapping and understanding trans-governmental networks in Canada-U.S. relations. In *Convergence and divergence in North America: Canada and the United States,* ed. K. Froschauer, N. Fabbi, and S. Pell, 61–72. Burnaby, BC: Centre for Canadian Studies, Simon Fraser University.

NAEWG. *See* North American Energy Working Group.

National Energy Board. 2001. *Canadian electricity: Trends and issues; An energy market assessment.* Calgary: National Energy Board.

– 2005. *Annual report 2005.* Calgary: National Energy Board.

NEB. *See* National Energy Board.

North American Energy Working Group. 2002. *North America: The energy picture.* Ottawa: Natural Resources Canada.

– 2006. Security and Prosperity Partnership Energy Picture Experts Group. *North America: The energy picture II.* Ottawa: Natural Resources Canada.

OECD. *See* Organization for Economic Co-operation and Development.

Pierce, R., M. Trebilcock, and E. Thomas. 2006. Beyond gridlock: The case for greater integration of regional electricity markets. *C.D. Howe Institute Commentary* 228. http://www.cdhowe.org/pdf/commentary_228.pdf.

Pineau, P., A. Hira, and Karl Froschauer. 2004. Measuring international electricity integration: A comparative study of the power systems under the Nordic Council, MERCOSUR, and NAFTA. *Energy Policy* 32: 1457–75.

Priddle, R. 1989. Regulation of Canadian energy exports in the free trade era. Paper presented at 21st Annual Conference of the Institute of Public Utilities, Michigan State University, Colonial Williamsburg, VA, 11 December 1989, p. 5.

Richmond M., K. Sebalj, S. Stoll, and O. Wakil. 2005. *Electricity regulation 2006.* London: Law Business Research.

Schmidt, S. 1996. Sterile debates and dubious generalizations: An empirical critique of European integration theory based on the integration processes in telecommunications and electricity. MPIFG discussion paper 95(6). Munich: Max-Planck-Institut für Gesellschaftsforschung.

Scholz, U., and H. Stappert. 2005. *Electricity regulation 2006.* London: Law Business Research.

Southey, S. 2002. Building a competition culture. Presentation notes. http://seoulforum.ftc.go.kr/ko/data/sally_korea4_.doc-Supplemental Result.

U.S. FERC. *See* United States. Federal Energy Regulatory Commission.

United States. Federal Energy Regulatory Commission. 1997. Promoting wholesale competition though open access: Non-discriminatory transmission service by public utilities. Docket no. RM95-8-001, order no. 888-A, issued 3 March. Washington: Federal Energy Regulatory Commission.

van den Hoven, A., and K. Froschauer. 2004. Limiting electricity sector integration and market reform: The cases of France in the EU and Canada in the NAFTA region. *Comparative Political Studies* 37 (9): 1079–1103.

VDEW. *See* Verband der Elektrizitätswirtschaft.

Verband der Elektrizitätswirtschaft. Zahlen und Fakten. 2005. *Pressegespräch zum VDEW-Kongress 2005.* (VDEW). http://www.strom.de.

Vorholz, F. 2003. Die Illusion vom Wettbewerb [The illusion of competition]. *Die Zeit,* 27–28 April.

Watkins, M. 1997. Canadian capitalism in transition. In *Understanding Canada: Building on the new political economy,* ed. W. Clement, 19–42. Montreal and Kingston: McGill-Queen's University Press.

7 The EU Single Energy Market and Multi-Level Interaction

PETER D. CAMERON

Whereas the previous chapter by Froschauer has presented a comparative overview of how the different supranational frameworks of EU and NAFTA respectively affect electricity reform paths in Canada and Germany, this chapter deals explicitly with the challenge of multi-level governance coordination within the specific EU setting. It explores the complex multi-layered interaction between multiple regulatory bodies and stakeholders in the implementation of EU market reforms.

More specifically, it addresses two themes of the analytical framework developed in chapters 1 and 15 of this volume. It discusses the political *complexity* of energy market reforms in a large and heterogeneous space occupied by twenty-seven nations, where any top-down model of energy reform is bound to fail. And it investigates alternative mechanisms of policy *coordination* that have emerged in the EU regulatory governance system. The chapter deepens the notion suggested in the previous chapter that in complex multi-level settings of fragmented jurisdiction transnational regulatory networks, as a core element of a decentralized regulatory model involving multiple stakeholders, play an increasingly important role in managing multi-level tensions.

The idea that a group of more than two dozen nation states could establish a single regulatory space to promote competition in their key energy industries seems bold, even audacious. Yet, essentially, this is what the European Union has been attempting to achieve in the last decade. The project is still a work in progress but it is beyond doubt that the foundations of a common legal and regulatory structure are firmly in place, making a provisional assessment of the EU model of multi-level governance in energy a feasible goal.

This chapter will look first at the origins and context of the EU regulatory regime for electricity and gas, before examining in the second section the institutional structure of the regime. The third section deals with the relationship between the regulator and the regulated in this structure, and particularly the interplay between formal and informal elements. The tensions within this recently established regime are examined in the fourth section to assess its workability. Finally some conclusions about the future development of the EU model of regulatory governance are made.

It is argued that the decentralized regulatory model chosen by the EU has been favoured largely because the alternative – the creation of a single, centralized regulatory authority – would represent a loss of sovereign control over a key sector that is unacceptable to EU member states. As a result, the model contains considerable potential for instability and a permanent need for harmonization of regulatory practices. From both an academic and a practical point of view, this will require development and application of a comparative method of analysis if the actions of so many different and diverse national practices are to be understood and evaluated.

The Establishment of a Single Energy Market

For almost twenty years the EU has struggled to establish an internal market in energy, particularly in the electricity and gas sectors (Cameron 2002, 2005, 2007). During that time the number of countries involved in the project has grown from twelve to twenty-seven, with several important neighbouring countries significantly affected by it. Inevitably, with such a diverse membership and the social and economic interests at stake, this has been a complex and often controversial process.

The initial goal and driver behind the Single Market concept was largely one of promoting competition in response to an increasingly globalized economy, with energy being part of a wider program for economic reform in the EU. However, as in most other parts of the OECD, this goal of promoting competition has had to be adapted to changing priorities in the policies on energy security and sustainability vis-à-vis the environment. In particular, any program of market opening for energy raises issues about the high (and growing) level of dependence on non-member countries as sources of supply.

This geopolitical dimension highlights the limits to the current legal foundations for a liberalization agenda. Nevertheless, the result of this long period of legislative innovation is that the EU has set up an entirely new legal and regulatory framework to govern the energy sector of its economy. The focus has shifted to implementation, with a view to bringing the economic reality in line with the legal vision and its requirements.

As discussed in comparative perspective by Froschauer in chapter 6, the legal framework for the Single Market in energy comprises a body of secondary legislation of recent origin. Two comprehensive framework laws, called directives, set out the parameters for the electricity and gas sectors respectively, and contained a timetable for market opening (that is, liberalization) that mandated a full opening of EU markets to competition by July 2007 (Commission of the European Communities [CEC] 2003a, 2003b) (see table 7.1). Since then, all residential and industrial consumers are free to choose their supplier, although there remain many obstacles in practice. Each directive was supplemented by a regulation that applies more specific rules to the sectors that are being liberalized (CEC 2003d, 2005b).

In addition, there is a body of binding and non-binding instruments such as guidelines under the regulations, voluntary guidelines developed by the national regulators' common body, the European Regulators' Group for Electricity and Gas (ERGEG) and the Florence and Madrid Forums (discussed below), as well as commission interpretative notes that are not binding on the parties and not enforceable in a court of law.

Under the operation of the subsidiarity doctrine, the implementation of much of this law is left to the individual member state, which recognizes the diversity of circumstances in the energy mix among the member states and the diverse priorities in national policies. However, the European Commission is required to carry out regular assessments of the legislation's impact and make recommendations for its improvement.[1] Typically, this is done on the basis of a comparison of country profiles developed largely from data provided by the regulators themselves.

There are four features of this legal framework that require comment. First, it is still being developed to ensure that its implementation is in line with the original intent. The current legal regime came into force in Europe in July 2004 and has been found to be unsatisfactory in a number of respects. A new package of legislative measures is under discussion to amend it. Second, it requires all member states to

Table 7.1 EU timetable and key events

Date	Event
July 2004	Entry into force of 2003 directives and electricity regulation: market opening for non-household customers and legal/operational unbundling
End 2004	First report under Article 28(1) and 31(1) of the 2003 directives
January 2005	Emissions Trading Scheme commences operation
June 2005	Inquiry launched by commission competition directorate into energy sector November 2005 Adoption of gas regulation
End 2005	Second report from commission under new directives, covering public services issues and matters related to full market opening by 2006/7
February 2006	Commission publishes preliminary findings from competition investigation
July 2006	Entry into force of gas regulation
December 2006	Commission takes policing action against sixteen member states for failures of implementation of European legislation
January 2007	Third energy package announced; final report from Sector Inquiry published
July 2007	Full market opening
September 2007	Legislative proposals for new directive and regulation to amend existing legislation on electricity and gas, including proposals to enhance the powers of NRAs both within member states and in their cross-border competences

establish specialist energy regulators with minimum powers and to ensure that these nationally based entities cooperate with each other on cross-border matters and with the commission. A new 'level' of regulatory competence was thereby formalized as a necessary part of ensuring the capacity of the Europe-wide regime.

A third feature is that the framework is supported by a body of competition law rooted in the primary law of the European communities. The enforcement of the latter is in the hands of both national competition authorities and the commission (a competition network). Finally, the scope of this legal framework extends to all member states of the EU but also those in the European Economic Area (EEA), a body that is significant in this context because it includes Norway (a non-EU member but commercially integrated through the Scandinavian market) as one of its members, and the countries of the European Energy Community, located mostly in the southeast of Europe (CEC 2005b). Each of these features is considered below.

The legal framework established in 2003 is the successor to an earlier, short-lived structure, established in 1996–8, that proved far too modest in scope and aspiration (CEC 1996, 1998). The 2003 regime aimed at accelerating the establishment of a single market in electricity and gas and repealed the preceding framework. An important feature is the requirement that member states designate one or more competent bodies as regulatory agencies, independent of the electricity and gas industries, with minimum powers over a range of matters specified in the legislation.

Implementation of this legislation has been beset with difficulties. The principal legal instrument, known as a directive, is addressed to the member states and fetters their powers by means of binding obligations and prohibitions. However, member states have some discretion over the form and methods of implementation. Evidence that this discretion has led to abuse has quickly mounted. By December 2006 the commission had found it necessary to take policing action against sixteen member states for failure to implement this legislation (CEC 2006a).

One chief concern of the commission, which is charged to monitor implementation, is that the powers of energy regulators are insufficient, in the setting of tariffs for access to networks. Cross-border interconnectors have been found to be particularly vulnerable to the grant of preferential access, which weak regulation has been unable to resist in many cases. In January 2007 the commission published a progress report that was highly critical of the existing regulatory framework. It prefigured a new legislative package, the third since liberalization began.

The introduction of a new level of governance in the energy sector triggered the creation of a number of networks to facilitate cooperation and a harmonization of practices. Several were at the initiative of the commission: the electricity regulatory forum (the Florence Forum); the gas regulatory forum (the Madrid Forum), and the European Regulatory Group for Electricity and Gas (ERGEG). All are discussed later in this chapter. Their existence reflected the necessity of cooperation in a complex regulatory environment rather than a long-term strategy of regulatory control by the commission itself.

The third notable feature is the support given to this framework for liberalization by the pre-existing law on competition contained in the Treaty of Union. While the mechanisms of anti-trust law, merger control, and state aid control have been available for some time, they have played an increasingly important role as the sector has become liberalized, primarily as support measures, but used in an increasingly assertive manner. Indeed, at the time the 2003 legislation was adopted, there was a 're-nationalization' of competition law enforcement and a new regulation on merger control (CEC 2003c, 2004).

These developments have encouraged a view that the competition network could provide valuable support to the regulatory thrust of the new legislation and might even prove decisive in breaking down the remaining barriers to a single market. In late 2004, for example, the Competition Directorate of the European Commission ruled against a proposed merger of two Portuguese energy utilities (CEC 2004a), thereby blocking the emergence of a national champion and sending a clear signal to other member states that the competition rules will be applied vigorously in the energy sector in support of the internal market goal. Other energy cases are pending and are likely to result in approvals subject to certain pro-competitive conditions being satisfied.[2] In 2005–6 the commission's competition directorate carried out a major review of the state of competition in the energy sector, resulting in conclusions that were highly critical of existing practices and triggered new actions by the commission in the sector.[3]

Finally, it should be noted that the legal and regulatory framework that has been adopted in the EU is one that the commission is keen to see adopted in neighbouring states. To date, it has chosen to do so by means of two legal instruments: the EEA Agreement and the Energy Community Treaty.[4] These have acted as vehicles for the export of EU ideas on liberalized energy markets and regulatory governance in non-EU countries as different as Norway and Serbia, Croatia and Albania.

Multi-Level Governance

The key regulatory innovation of the 2003 legislation was the generalization of national regulatory authorities (NRAs) for electricity and gas, with a minimum set of powers, across the EU. In many countries, these had already been established,[5] but they are now mandatory in each member state, as is the grant of a minimum set of competences. The directives expressly require a coordination of NRA activity among states and, importantly, between NRAs and competition bodies. It may be inferred that they aim to establish, albeit implicitly, nothing less than a market-oriented 'regulatory culture' in the EU energy sector (with 'energy' understood as the electricity and gas sectors). These changes serve to underpin the emerging EU regulatory architecture.

While the first directives (1997–8) approached the establishment of a coordinated EU regulatory framework in a way that was both hesitant and imprecise, the second directives more than compensated for this unpromising start by setting out minimum requirements for the functions and competences of sector regulatory bodies charged by the member states with supervising the electricity and gas sectors.

Their independence from the electricity and gas industries has also to be guaranteed by the member states.[6] More than this, they require the NRAs to coordinate with each other and to liaise with the commission from time to time. While member states have discretion at many points about how exactly they meet the requirements (such as over the choice of competent body and its legal status), the outcome is likely to be a very different, more pervasive, and significantly less politicized regulatory environment in the near future – if the member states permit such a loosening of state control.

However, the NRA represents only one layer in a governance scheme that includes a number of other important bodies. In each member state there exists a 'holy trinity' of enforcement agencies, comprising a lead ministry, a sector regulatory agency (the NRA), and a competition authority (sometimes a competition court). The differences in development of their relationships *inter se* and the relative independence of the NRAs from political control may vary considerably from one member state to another. Indeed, there is no requirement to limit the number of energy regulatory agencies to one in each member state; more may be established if it is considered appropriate for reasons of regional policy, for example. In some cases, administrative instruments such as guidelines and concordat-style agreements have been developed in the member states themselves to avoid duplication of effort between the respective authorities and to minimize conflicts over jurisdiction.[7]

In other cases, however, the relationships within government appear to be at an early stage of development. For example, in two very different regimes, Germany and Greece, the regulatory authority is in need of considerable development vis-à-vis the member state ministries to comply with the minimum conditions of powers and independence that are required by the directives. Yet, in spite of the foregoing remarks, the sector regulator has, in a number of countries, already had sufficient roots for the proper exercise of its regulatory powers and, as a result of its published decisions, a distinct body of jurisprudence has begun to build up (Austria, Italy, and Spain are examples, in addition to the Netherlands and the United Kingdom).[8]

A final layer in the levels of public sector governance comprises the role of the courts in reviewing exercises of regulatory authority. In some member states (the Netherlands, for example) this has already played a role in constraining the scope of the regulatory bodies.[9] Where a written constitution provides protection for private property, there may be a basis for challenging the more ambitious attempts to tackle market structure by rigorous unbundling requirements. The European Convention on Human Rights should be noted as an influence on the administrative law framework in which regulators operate. This factor is significant in the United Kingdom, for example, where it represents a very recent addition to the regulatory landscape. The Charter of Fundamental Rights originally contained in the draft Treaty on a Constitution for Europe could also be expected to enhance the legal basis for actions through the courts if included in a new version of the treaty.

As the powers of regulators expand with the implementation of the directives, it can only be expected that they will increasingly be subject to scrutiny by the courts as to their operation and scope (although this is always likely to be more limited in scope and degree than in the North America). As they explore their new powers, the NRAs will find themselves in such new territory.

Before moving on to the relationship of the regulator to the regulated in this structure, it is worth pausing to consider why there is no central regulatory authority in this structure. The commission appears to be the obvious candidate for such a role but is largely restricted to an oversight function, with some policing powers vis-à-vis the progress of liberalization and, under the treaty, in certain competition matters.[10]

Yet if one were asked to identify a single factor responsible for shaping the current EU regulatory framework for the electricity and gas industries, it is the determination of the member states to resist the emergence of a centralized European energy regulatory authority. The heterogeneity of NRAs and the creation of regulatory associations with important coordinating roles is the result of this resounding '*non*' to the idea of a single federal-style regulatory body.

It is hardly an exaggeration to claim that the entire multi-level construction that is being developed gives the lie to any suggestion that a single energy regulator might emerge in the EU in the foreseeable future. However, the member states and all of the parties to that structure of governance have a strong interest in encouraging cohesion and coordination among the diverse elements that make up the complex EU regulatory structure. These include not only the networks of NRAs and national competition authorities but also administrative and quasi-judicial bodies and to an increasing extent the national environmental authorities. Moreover, questions about competence have to take into account the very different stages of maturity of the various bodies with regulatory authority and their relations with their 'host' government departments.

The Role of Industry

For industry, this emerging regulatory structure is a development that has been viewed with some apprehension. An authoritative electricity industry report declared,

> Regulation is the single most important factor facing electricity utilities in the foreseeable future. The action and decisions of these sector specific regulatory authorities affects core company revenue, business processes, customer service, company structure and the nature of competition for most utilities. (Eurelectric 2004, 2)

There is a genuine issue here of whether the expansion of regulatory powers will lead to companies becoming over-burdened with regulation and creating disincentives to the kind of large-scale investment that is increasingly viewed as essential for new interconnectors, LNG facilities, and replacement of ageing infrastructure.

To address concerns such as these, the model of governance has been developed to permit and indeed encourage industry input into the legal architecture. In addition to specific provisions in the legislation such as Article 22 of the Gas Directive, which has facilitated the financing of gas infrastructure, the regulations on electricity and gas include substantive measures in their texts as well as in sets of guidelines in annexes attached to them. They cover very specific matters such as the management and allocation of available transmission capacity of interconnections, congestion management, and the provision of third-party access services.

All of these provisions rely heavily on input from the so-called Florence and Madrid Regulatory Forums on electricity and gas, respectively.[11] This is the principal formal mechanism by which stakeholders in industry can influence the shape of legislative proposals or supplementary measures for their implementation (although there are ample opportunities for contact and indeed 'lobbying' at an informal level between stakeholders and governments, agencies, and the commission itself). The forum concept developed soon after the first directives were adopted in 1997–8, and has therefore been operational throughout the period in which the EU regulatory model has been established.

It has been the principal means through which the market players, usually acting through the associations of transmission system operators (TSOs), producers, consumers, network users, traders, and energy exchanges meet the NRAs, member states, and the commission at roughly twice-yearly intervals to shape measures aimed at deepening the impact of the EU legislation and taking the internal market process forward. The concept was expanded in 2004–5 to permit the holding of small-scale, regional forums on electricity in various parts of the EU on the assumption that progress in certain areas of market reform might be faster if approached from a regional rather than a Europe-wide view, at least in the first instance.[12]

The agreements reached by the diverse participants in the forum process have seemed to justify the term *regulation by co-operation* (Vasconcelos 2001). In this voluntary process, an agenda is set by the commission following consultation with the ERGEG, and discussions with all the parties lead to the allocation of tasks for the following meeting, where progress is monitored.

The limitations of the forum process have shown themselves in different ways in the two sectors. In the gas sector, the reluctance of the industry to make adaptations to the climate created by the first gas directive (1998) drew attention to the absence of teeth in the forum process. Later, there were similar difficulties in making progress with the establishment of guidelines on access to gas storage facilities. In the electricity sector, the impasse reached in 2002 over a set of common rules on cross-border tarification highlighted the difficulties in making progress on an issue when a very few parties were not prepared to make concessions.[13]

Although the issue was subsequently resolved, it was done so largely by the introduction of draft legislation. There are other shortcomings in the forum process as an alternative to legislation. Most importantly, it is slow, with consensus being built up only gradually among participants. However, if the electricity or gas industry and/or other parties do not agree with a proposal, there is always the threat that legislation may be introduced to resolve the deadlock. If they do agree, there is the possibility that the resulting codes of practice or guidelines will be given legislative form by incorporation in an Annex to the Electricity or Gas Regulation in any case to 'consolidate' the regime and to harmonize with existing legislation.

The specific outcomes of the forum processes are now becoming a part of the law applicable to the electricity and gas industries. The adoption of 'soft law' measures such as guidelines, annexed to regulations, should not be underestimated. They are binding on the persons to whom they are addressed (in the case of the Electricity Regulation Guidelines, this category is the TSOs), who have an obligation to implement them. Their interpretation may not be uniform across the EU, a fact that could throw up obstacles to the internal market, but this risk is more likely to arise if the regulations are drafted in general terms.

In the case of the Gas Regulation 2005, in which the drafting of the guidelines is very specific, it is unlikely that many problems of interpretation will arise: after all, the guidelines are based upon the second version of Guidelines for Good TPA Practice agreed by the Madrid Gas Forum. They also contain provisions that substantively limit the scope of member states' freedom over the form and methods of the directives on access. If the TSOs were to insist on differing interpretations of the guidelines, the commission could, using the so-called comitology procedure,[14] amend the text of those guidelines that contains the disputed interpretation so that the obligations that the commission wishes to impose on the TSOs are created. Under Article 8(1) of the Electricity Regulation, the commission has the power to amend guidelines, enabling it to compel TSOs to comply with the texts of guidelines that are determined by the commission, following the comitology procedure.

In other words, the guidelines do not *in the last resort* rely for their effectiveness on the willingness to cooperate by the parties most affected. In that sense, they are not 'soft law' in the usual sense of being difficult or impossible to enforce, and they do not rely entirely on the cooperation of the parties most affected for their implementation. It may be noted that the wording in the Gas Regulation has been drawn more tightly over the issue of making further guidelines by this procedure, suggesting that the member states are wary of the transfer of power to the commission that is implicit in the approach of the Electricity Regulation, concluded two years earlier.

The establishment of a new European regulators' body, the ERGEG, in 2003 raised a question about the continued need for the forum process.[15] It was specifically established by law to advise the commission and consult with industry and other parties on matters relating to the achievement of the internal energy market, including legislative proposals, on the basis of a clear set of rules. It has actively sought comments on draft guidelines from industry and other stakeholders in its formal consultation process.

Historically, the forum process has been extremely useful and has constituted an important initiative of the commission immediately after the first liberalization directives. However, the decline in the number of meetings of both forums in the past couple of years (and subtle shifts in their operating procedures) also suggest that their relevance has already been undermined by this further development of the NRAs' network. This should not suggest a corresponding decline in the role of guidelines and codes of practice but rather that the leading role may have shifted towards the ERGEG as coordinator of the process of making them. The above analysis of the guidelines annexed to the Electricity Regulation 2004 suggests a fairly positive interpretation of the instruments agreed upon through the forum processes so far.

The Potential for Instability

The network of governance mechanisms described in the previous sections is still one *in statu nascendi*. The large number of government agencies in the twenty-seven member states with competence in energy matters,[16] and the diverse formal structures chosen by member states for their NRAs, means that there is a complex array of (largely untested) enforcement mechanisms in the EU. In each of the two main networks (the NRAs and the competition authorities) the European Commission plays a key role, although it shares this with the ERGEG among the NRAs. For the consumers of regulation, the energy companies and the judiciary, this regulatory regime presents an important – and still quite new – challenge. For the regulatory authorities themselves, it presents a challenge of coordination and cooperation.

As the new kids on the block, the NRAs and their role requires some comment. Compared with the national competition authorities, they are almost all of very recent origin and are developing their rules and practices for the first time. As noted by Froschauer in chapter 6, in Germany's case, the energy regulator became operational only in 2005.

The 2003 directives have significantly enhanced the legal status of the NRAs in two ways.[17]

First, there is an obligation on member states to charge one or more competent bodies with the function of regulatory authorities. The requirement is more precise than in the previous directives.[18] However, the regulatory functions may be spread over several authorities if that is deemed appropriate by the member state, permitting, say, local or regional regulatory bodies, but also a combination of NRA, ministry, and, say, a competition authority.

The independence of the regulatory authority (or authorities) is obligatory but is defined in relation to the interests of the electricity and gas *industries* rather than in relation to existing government structures. The risk of regulatory capture appears to have been uppermost in the drafters' minds. Nonetheless, those member states with state-owned utilities may have to develop mechanisms to separate the regulatory authority from the ministerial body that supervises the state-owned energy utility. In addition, member states are required to take measures to ensure that the NRAs are able to carry out their duties efficiently and expeditiously.[19]

A second change in the NRAs' roles is that, while member states continue to set out the functions, competences, and administrative powers of the regulatory authorities, a minimum set of functions and competences is set out in the directives in the interests of harmonization.[20] In particular, their supervisory role over network access and the setting or approval of network tariffs (or at least the methodologies underlying the calculation of the tariffs), prior to their entry into force (*ex ante*), has been given a basis in European law. These tariffs, or methodologies, are to allow the necessary investments in the networks to be carried out in a manner that allows these investments to ensure the viability of the networks.[21]

While both of these developments enhance the potential impact of the NRAs on the liberalization – nationally and potentially on a European scale – they also increase the risk of failure in coordination and cooperation. In many cases, the NRAs sprang up in response to specific national circumstances. The resulting diversity created a patchwork of regulatory entities with widely differing powers. It is hardly surprising, then, to note that the directives and regulations seek to avert this.[22] As a result, some member states such as Finland, Greece, Germany, and Sweden have been required to abandon their preference for *ex post* regulation.

Pressure on the design and operation of regulatory regimes can also be expected to come from the enhanced cooperation between NRAs and the commission through the ERGEG. This will be in the direction not only of harmonization but also of strengthening the NRAs' role vis-à-vis member state governments. At the same time, the relationship between the NRAs and the ministries in their respective countries that have competence for energy matters can be expected to produce some frictions. A 'regulatory culture' is still a recent phenomenon in most member states, so it is unlikely that the interrelationship between these two partners will be smooth at all times.

Indeed, if a regulatory culture is to take root, there are at least five key relationships that will have to be managed so as to encourage coordination or at least a peaceful coexistence. They are the relationships between (1) the NRAs and the national competition authorities within each member state; (2) the NRAs themselves, to ensure that their actions are not contradictory from one member state to the next; (3) the NRAs and the judiciary, more relevant in some member states than others; (4) the NRAs and the entities they regulate, and (5) the NRAs and the commission.

The NRAs and the Competition Authorities

A measure of overlap between competition law and sector regulation is in several respects inevitable. The owners of networks have a natural monopoly and therefore a dominant position in the market. A refusal to grant access may be seen as a regulatory matter but it can also be viewed as an abuse of a dominant position on the market and therefore a matter best left to the competition authorities. There are many other areas in which competence may overlap. The question arises as to how best to deal with this. Several member states have already taken steps to demarcate the competence of the various authorities and to require them to consult with each other in specified areas. Under the new German legislation, the regulator for energy will have a strong position vis-à-vis the competition authorities.[23] However, there is an argument in favour of flexibility rather than the demarcation of competence according to strict rules, which may slow down regulation and make it more complex.

Since much of competition law has an *ex post* character in contrast to sector regulation, it may seem that avoidance of overlapping competence is primarily a matter of setting out procedural guidelines and requiring consultation among the relevant authorities. But in issues concerning merger control, this does not apply. In Spain this is exactly the field in which the lack of harmony between the two sets of authorities has been most pronounced (Garayar 2005).

In Portugal procedural requirements have been introduced to address this issue. In a large number of situations, both ERSE and the competition authority can claim jurisdiction over the same facts. A typical example is a refusal to grant access where access is required by sector-specific legislation. The competition law regime established in 2003 took this into account and adopted specific rules on coordination between the two bodies. With respect to anti-competitive agreements or practices, in cases where there are facts subject to specific regulation and may be categorized as restrictive practices, the competition law requires the competition authority to immediately inform the sector authority and give the latter time to consider the issue prior to delivering its own opinion. This applies mutatis mutandis, with the sector regulator giving the competition authority an opportunity to have a prior hearing on an issue that has a restriction of competition as one of its elements. In spite of this, potential conflict cannot be ruled out over jurisdiction, and indeed such conflict has been a feature of other sectors, such as telecommunications, where liberalization has proceeded further (Protasio and Correia 2005).

In the United Kingdom an attempt to demarcate the competence of the NRA, Ofgem, from the competition authority has been made by giving Ofgem concurrent power with the director general of fair trading to apply the *Competition Act* and *Enterprise Act* prohibitions in the gas and electricity sectors. These concurrent powers also apply to the application and enforcement of Arts 81 and 82 EC (UK Office of Fair Trading 2005). However, some areas such as exploration and production of gas and matters related to offshore waters remain the exclusive preserve of the competition body.

Coordination among NRAs

Under the Electricity and Gas Directives, the NRAs are required to contribute to the development of the internal market and a level playing field by cooperating with each other and with the commission in a transparent manner.[24] To facilitate this, the commission established the ERGEG as an independent advisory group in November

2003. Its membership comprises the heads of the competent NRAs in the member states, with the EEA countries participating as observers. Its aim is to facilitate consultation, coordination, and cooperation between the regulatory bodies in member states and between these bodies and the commission, to consolidate the internal market, and to ensure the consistent application in all the member states of the two directives and regulations.[25] It tenders advice to the commission and assists it in the preparation of draft implementing measures in electricity and gas. It acts either at its own initiative or at the request of the commission. Under Article 4 of the decision establishing it, the ERGEG is required to 'consult extensively and at an early stage with market participants, consumers and end-users.'

The establishment of this advisory body was strongly supported by the European Parliament during the debates on the directives. It mirrors the roles of similar bodies already established in the telecommunications and financial services sectors.[26] According to its Rules of Procedure, the ERGEG will submit an annual report of the commission, which will then be transmitted to the Parliament and Council.[27] The chair must report to the Parliament when requested to do so (and did so for the first time in autumn 2004). The success of this coordination mechanism is likely to be driven by the more independent NRAs and the commission, since a number of them have less secure bases of support from their respective governments.

The NRAs and the Judiciary

The role of the courts in reviewing exercises of regulatory authority should not be neglected. In some member states (the Netherlands, for example) they have already played a role in constraining the scope of the regulatory bodies. Where a written constitution provides protection for private property, there may be a basis for challenging the more ambitious attempts to tackle market structure by the introduction of ownership unbundling requirements. The European Convention on Human Rights may be noted as an influence on the administrative law framework in which regulators operate. As the powers of regulators expand further with a more vigorous implementation of the existing directives and the greater powers envisaged in the third directives and regulations, it can only be expected that their actions will become routinely subject to scrutiny by the courts with respect to their operation and scope, albeit in some member states more than in others. As they explore their new powers, the NRAs will find themselves in new territory such as this.

The NRAs and the Regulated Energy Industry

A key issue for the EU is the management of this relationship. The market structure has remained highly resistant to the introduction of competition that the legal framework is designed to promote, and new efforts are being made to address this (CEC 2005c). However, at the same time there is a new appreciation among the regulatory authorities that incentives have to be provided to investors if the large investments in new energy infrastructure are to be met. To encourage this step, the 2003 legislation allowed exemptions to be granted from the mandatory requirement for third-party access (CEC 2003c, Article 22).

Elsewhere, there is evidence that industry concerns about rates of return are being treated seriously by the commission in its internal debates on the quality of regulation ('better regulation'). Moreover, the forum process has shown that the various sides of industry are welcomed by both the commission and the NRAs to contribute to the making of the detailed rules, regulations, and guidelines for electricity and gas that are essential if the liberalized electricity and gas markets are to work well. The consultation procedures agreed upon by the ERGEG also support this conclusion that industry input is actively sought by the NRAs (ERGEG 2004).

The NRAs and the European Commission

To a large extent the new European role of the NRAs is a creation of the commission itself, through progressive support for the development of firstly, an association of NRAs (the CEER) by involving it in the forum process, and secondly, the establishment by law of the explicitly European body, the ERGEG. The relationship can be expected to remain a close one. It is however an odd one: the commission encourages and formalizes the establishment of networks but the member states establish the regulatory agencies themselves. The networks can be seen as instruments for the management of the inevitable tensions that will appear from time to time in such a relationship.

Adapting the EU Model

The approach adopted by the EU towards the creation of an internal energy market has been shaped by a dilemma. As a single market in energy begins to emerge, member states are under pressure to cede more powers to a central body to avoid instability, as cross-border transactions and flows need to be coordinated, both physically and commercially. Apart from a new agency or the commission itself, the only body eligible for this role would be an enhanced regulators' entity such as the ERGEG. By early 2007 it had become clear that the current model of regulatory governance was unsatisfactory in key respects. In some countries, NRAs lack discretionary *ex ante* powers, such as those establishing rules for functional unbundling or non-tariff access conditions, or their powers are shared with a ministry or competition authority. Inconsistent decision-making and inadequate compliance is the result.

Greater integration of transmission and pipeline networks also require further powers to be given to a European network of NRAs to ensure cooperation and coordination in cross-border areas (sometimes called 'ERGEG+'). Moreover, a strengthening of the independence of NRAs from national governments is thought by many to be essential.[28] While the commission has taken the lead in making proposals for change (and the discussion is ongoing), there is general agreement that a strengthening of NRA powers along the above lines is now required.

Yet for a long time it has been clear that the establishment of a single energy market is not to entail the creation of a single, centralized regulatory authority for the sector. The choice of instruments and the way they have been used – with a heavy emphasis upon consensus-building and avoidance of the blunter legal instruments available in the treaty – illustrate vividly the extent to which member states have had to be persuaded of the lack of governance implications of the single market program so far. A slow, complex, and highly politicized result has followed. It has emerged as much by default as by design. Increasingly, however, national governance capacities are being seen to be inadequate to meet the challenges that EU energy markets are presenting.

In this context, the emergence of a complex multi-level structure of regulatory authorities, wearing a cloak of governance, may be an arrangement that is significantly easier for member states to accept than a centralized energy regulator. It represents a constraint on national governance in this area but not the potential challenge that the alternative implies.

However, the network of energy sector regulators has to coordinate with each other, with their respective governments, and with the commission or the EU legal regime for energy will not work. The network of competition authorities that has come into being must also, to the extent that it becomes involved in energy matters, coordinate with the NRAs and their association, with their respective governments, and with the commission itself. This complex of regulatory bodies has every incentive to cooperate, comparing notes on solutions to similar problems and discussing common approaches to cross-border issues. The manner of such cooperation and the subjects on which cooperation occurs may still be determined on a pragmatic, case-by-case basis rather than a rule-based system. The alternative is that the new regulatory 'system' will rapidly become a source of regulatory uncertainty on an unprecedented scale. Thus far, it appears that the member states are prepared to consider a grant of further powers to the new system in order to avoid failure. In terms of institutional design, this is a high-risk model of regulation. It contains few clear divisions of competence among the players, it is complex and untested, and it relies upon voluntary mechanisms to succeed. But it is a basis on which further expansion will take place.

This is not the only liberalizing sector of the EU economy in which these trends can be observed. Others have commented on trends of 'new governance.'[29] However, the evidence from the energy sector suggests that the EU remains a very long way from becoming a full-blown 'regulatory state.' Indeed, the multi-level form of governance outlined here may prove attractive to other parts of the world with federal structures such as Canada or have strong incentives to engage in energy cooperation (northeast Asian states, for example).

If optimism about a positive outcome in the EU is justified, that a 'regulatory culture' may indeed develop, and that member states may let it grow, this is perhaps more soundly based on the parties' awareness that energy interdependence is increasingly a fact of life in the EU as elsewhere, and that investment in the EU's ageing and increasingly inadequate energy infrastructure will not be forthcoming if the issue of regulatory risk is not squarely addressed. This – and the growing concerns about energy security for an energy importing bloc – should provide a momentum for the cooperation and coordination among the regulatory actors that this model of governance implicitly supports.

NOTES

1 Commission of the European Communities (CEC) (2003b), Article 28; (2003c), Article 31; (2003d), Article 14; (2005b), Article 15; the 2006 country reviews are contained in 2007.

2 For example, the approach adopted vis-à-vis a proposed merger in Denmark: see Commission of the European Communities (2006a), Press Release IP/06/313: 'Mergers: Commission approves acquisition by DONG of Danish electricity generators and suppliers, subject to conditions,' and the remedies agreed upon for a merger between Gaz de France and Suez in November 2006: see the comprehensive discussion by Bachour et al. (2007).

3 The Sector Inquiry into the gas and electricity markets was based on Article 17 of Regulation 1/2003: European Commission (2006b).

4 Respectively, the texts are to be found at http://www.efta.int and Commission of the European Communities (2005), COM 435 final.

5 By 2002 they were present in all member states, except one (Germany), and in almost all of the then candidate countries from central and eastern Europe: see CEC (2003).

6 There are no specific provisions against interference by government, but the EC Treaty requires member states to abstain from any measure that could jeopardize attainment of the objectives of the treaty (Article 10): in this case, this would be the creation of the internal market in energy.

7 An example is the United Kingdom: see the *Competition Act* 1998 Concurrency Regulations (2004) (London, SI 2004 No 1077) and the Competition Law Guideline for the Concurrent Application to Regulated Industries (Office of Fair Trading, London, 405).

8 See, for example, chapters 6, 11, 12, 14, and 15 of Cameron (2005).

9 For example, see the case referred by a Dutch court to the European Court of Justice, which resulted in a defeat by the Dutch government, analysed in detail in Cameron (2006).

10 The idea that a European energy regulator could be established to regulate cross-border issues is being examined by the commission, but it is doubtful whether the new concern about energy security is yet strong enough to mobilize support for such a major policy departure: see CEC (2006c, 6).

11 For a detailed assessment of the Florence Electricity Regulatory Forum, see chapter 4 of Cameron (2005), and Eberlein (2005); the origins and early meetings of both gas and electricity regulatory forums are examined in Cameron (2002, 283–311).

12 A second attempt at a regional approach was announced by the ERGEG on 27 February 2006. The Electricity Regional Initiative will be managed by the regulators and will set up seven distinct regional energy market projects. A similar initiative was commenced for regional gas markets in April 2006.

13 See Conclusions from the Florence Regulatory Forum meetings, 2002: http://ec.europa.eu/energy/electricity/florence/doc/florence-8/final-concl.pdf.

14 There are three distinct comitology procedures, using an advisory, management, or regulatory committee, with varying degrees of control over the commission's power to adopt new rules: Council of the European Union (1999).

15 But see CEC (2003a, 32): the forums 'will remain important as comprehensive discussion platforms involving all players from government, regulators, and industry.'

16 Of course, environmental authorities have a role in many energy issues; this is likely to increase with the impact of the EU Emissions Trading Scheme and legislation on renewable energy. This is treated at some length in Cameron (2007).

17 CEC (2003b), Article 23, and (2003c), Article 25.

18 Compare the wording in Article 22 of the first Electricity and Gas Directives (see n7): 'Member States shall create appropriate and efficient mechanisms for regulation, control and transparency so as to avoid any abuse of a dominant position.' In practice, however, the regulatory competences of national authorities have usually gone far beyond this. This wording reappears in the 2003 directives as Article 23(8) in Directive 2003/54/EC (CEC 2003b) and Article 25(8) in Directive 2003/55/EC (CEC 2003c).

19 Article 23(7).

20 CEC (2003b), Recital; (2003c), Recital 13. There are also some requirements imposed by the directives on member states that they may elect to devolve to NRAs, such as those on providing tendering procedures for additional capacity in the interest of security of supply and ensuring that reliable information is provided to customers about the energy sources for the electricity supplied.

21 See generally, in this context, the Interpretation Note: CEC (2004b).

22 CEC (2003b) Recital 16; (2003c) Recital 14; (2003d) (Decision on establishing Regulators Group).

23 For a detailed discussion of this issue, see Pritzsche and Klauer (2005).
24 CEC (2003b), Article 23(12); (2003c), Article 25(12); (2003d), Article 9.
25 CEC (2003a).
26 CEC (2001, 2002). The ERGEG is in practice, if not formally, an offshoot of the Council of European Energy Regulators (CEER). It shares a common chairperson and members, and ERGEG relies on the CEER for funding and expertise. The CEER is a voluntary association that includes most of the EU energy regulators, and has been highly active in the Electricity and Gas Forums since its establishment in March 2000. It has a number of working groups.
27 Article 9 (Accountability), Rules of Procedure, ERGEG: http://www.ergeg.org.
28 Conclusions of the EU Presidency, 8/9 March 2007, in which an energy policy for Europe was agreed upon by the member states.
29 Of course, the use of the forum process and indeed the way in which the energy regulators' network has been developed provide some evidence for 'new governance' arguments, even if this is not explicit. However, they coexist with more traditional instruments of law and regulation. For an interesting discussion of this combination of new and traditional instruments (but not in energy), see de Burca (2003).

REFERENCES

Bachour, K., G. Conte, P. Eberl, C. Martini, A. Paolicchi, P. Redondo, A. Van Haasteren, and G. Wils. 2007. Gaz de France/Suez: Keeping energy markets in Belgium and France open and contestable through far-reaching remedies. *Competition Policy Newsletter* (Competition Directorate, European Commission) Spring: 83–91.
de Burca, Grainne. 2003. The constitutional challenge of new governance in the European Union. *European Law Review* 28:814–39.
Cameron, Peter. 2002. *Competition in energy markets: Law and integration in the European Union.* Oxford: Oxford University Press.
– ed. 2005. *Legal aspects of EU energy regulation: Implementing the new directives on electricity and gas across Europe.* Oxford: Oxford University Press.
– 2006. The consumer and the internal market in energy: Who benefits? *European Law Review* 31:114–24.
– 2007. *Competition in energy markets: Law and integration in the European Union.* 2nd ed. Oxford: Oxford University Press.
CEC. *See* Commission of the European Communities.
Commission of the European Communities. 1996. Directive 96/92/EC of the

European Parliament and of the Council of 19 December 1996 concerning common rules for the internal market in electricity. Brussels, OJ L 27, p. 20.

– 1998. Directive 98/30/EC of the European Parliament and of the Council of 22 June 1998 concerning common rules for the internal market in natural gas. Brussels, OJ L 204, 1.

– 2001. COM 1501 (CESR – financial services).

– 2002. Brussels, OJ L 200/38 (ERG-telecommunications).

– 2003a. Commission Decision of 11 November 2003 on establishing the European Regulators Group for Electricity and Gas (2003/796/EC). Brussels, OJ L 296/34.

– 2003b. Directive 2003/54/EC of the European Parliament and of the Council of 26 June 2003 concerning common rules for the internal market in electricity and repealing Directive 96/92/EC. Brussels, OJ L 176/37.

– 2003c. Directive 2003/55/EC of the European Parliament and of the Council of 26 June 2003 concerning common rules for the internal market in natural gas and repealing Directive 98/30/EC. Brussels, OJ L 176/57.

– 2003d. Regulation (EC) No 1228/2003 of the European Parliament and of the Council of 26 June 2003 on conditions for access to the network for cross-border exchanges in electricity. Brussels, OJ L 176/1.

– 2003e. Second commission benchmarking report. Brussels, SEC 448.

– 2004a. Mergers: Commission prohibits acquisition of GDP by EDP and ENI. Press release IP/04/1455.

– 2004b. The role of the regulatory authorities. Brussels, 14.1.2004.

– 2005a. COM 435 final, 14.9.2005.

– 2005b. Regulation (EC) No 1775/2005 of the European Parliament and of the Council on conditions for access to the natural gas transmission networks. Brussels, L 289/1.

– 2005c. Report on progress in creating the internal gas and electricity market. Communication from the Commission to the Council and the European Parliament. Brussels, COM 568 final.

– 2006a. The commission takes action against member states which have not opened up their energy markets properly. Press release IP/06/430.

– 2006b. Green paper: A European strategy for sustainable, competitive and secure Energy. Brussels, COM (2006) 105 final.

– 2006c. Inquiry pursuant to Article 17 of Regulation (EC) No 1/2003 into the European gas and electricity sectors (final report). Brussels, COM (2006) 851 final.

– 2006d. Prospects for the internal gas and electricity market. Brussels, COM (2006) 841 final, 10.1.2007.

Council of the European Union. 1999. Decision of 28 June 1999 laying down the procedures for the exercise of implementing powers conferred on the commission. Brussels, OJ L 184/23.

– 2003. Regulation 1/2003 on the implementation of the rules on competition laid down in Articles 81 and 82 of the Treaty (as amended by Regulation 411/2004 (2004). Brussels, OJ L 68/1.

– 2004. Regulation 139/2004 on the control of concentrations between undertakings (the EC Merger Regulation). Brussels, OJ L 024.

Eberlein, B. 2005. Regulation by cooperation: The 'third way' in making rules for the internal energy market. In *Legal aspects of EU energy regulation: Implementing the new directives on electricity and gas across Europe*, ed. Peter Cameron, 59–88. Oxford: Oxford University Press.

ERGEG. *See* European Regulators' Group for Electricity and Gas.

Eurelectric. 2004. *Regulatory models in a liberalised European electricity market*. Brussels: Eurelectric.

European Regulators' Group for Electricity and Gas. 2004. Public guidelines on ERGEG's consultation practices. http://www.ergeg.org.

Garayar, Emiliano. 2005. Spain. In Cameron 2005, 315–44.

Pritzsche, Kai, and Stefan Klauer. 2005. Germany. In Cameron 2005, 145–71.

Protasio, Manuel, and Catarina Pinto Correia. 2005. Portugal. In Cameron 2005, 287–313.

UK Office of Fair Trading. 2005. *Application in the energy sector: Understanding competition law*. London: OFT/Ofgem.

Vasconcelos, J. 2001. Co-operation between energy regulators in the European Union. In *Regulation of Network Utilities*, ed. C. Henry, M. Mathieu, and A. Jeunemaitre, 284–9. Oxford: Oxford University Press.

PART TWO

Domestic Patterns of Governance: Canada and Germany

8 Multi-level Energy Regulatory Governance in the Canadian Federation: Institutions, Regimes, and Coordination

MONICA GATTINGER[1]

Energy regulatory governance in the Canadian federation is inherently multi-level.[2] Given the highly decentralized division of powers over energy in the Canadian Constitution, energy policymaking has long been a process of federal-provincial bargaining (Doern and Gattinger 2003). Canadian energy regulatory governance is also multi-level in that it is embedded within a complex of relations at other vertical levels – international, regional, local, etc. In addition, energy regulatory governance in Canada involves a horizontal layering of governance processes across key regulatory regimes: energy regulatory governance comprises not only the sectoral regime for energy, but also horizontal regimes, including those for the environment and competition (ibid.). Given these characteristics, exploring energy regulatory processes and outcomes in the Canadian federation requires both a vertical and horizontal analysis.

This chapter develops a framework to undertake this analysis utilizing the concepts of multi-level governance and regulatory regimes. These are closely tied to the regime features of complexity, coordination, and capacity that informs the book as a whole and also key features of the Dewees analysis in chapter 3 and some aspects of the Pineau analysis in chapter 9. The framework also incorporates structural factors (population distribution, energy resource endowments, energy market integration, etc.) that shape energy regulatory governance in Canada. The chapter utilizes this framework to explore regulatory coordination and regulatory outcomes in the energy sector, and makes three main arguments. First, I argue that enduring institutional, structural, and politico-historical characteristics in the energy domain produce configurations of domestic energy interests that militate against high levels of domestic policy and regulatory coordination. The constitutional division of powers in the energy and environmental sectors, the distribution of energy resource endowments, population and economic activity across the country, and enduring provincial memories of unwanted federal incursions in the energy sphere combine to produce patterns of federal and provincial energy interests that come into conflict more often than not and that challenge effective coordination.

Second, I argue that energy regulatory governance and domestic energy policy and regulatory outcomes in Canada are increasingly influenced by other vertical and horizontal governance levels and forums, notably international governance processes between Canada and the United States, and the horizontal regulatory regime for the environment. As continental energy market integration intensifies and, as the environmental regulatory regime expands, both provincial and federal interests in the energy sector are increasingly shaped by these vertical and horizontal governance processes. Third, I maintain that these horizontal and vertical influences can both exacerbate and ease existing coordination challenges at the domestic level. On the one hand, they may ease the political challenges of interprovincial and federal-provincial coordination in the energy sectoral regime. The growth in political interest in national or interprovincial approaches for a number of energy issues suggests there will be greater effort to coordinate regulation. On the other hand, the technical and therefore capacity challenges of energy regulatory coordination are likely to intensify in the context of electricity sector restructuring and growing Canada-U.S. electricity market integration. Similarly, in the environmental framework regime, differences between Canadian and American approaches on climate change (until recently), combined with the enduring domestic structural realities of energy, suggest that federal-provincial relations and regulatory coordination on energy-environment issues are likely to remain contentious. The election in 2006 of a Conservative government to the federal level in Canada – a government that has adopted a 'made-in-Canada' approach to climate change – may reduce some federal-provincial tensions in the energy-environment domain, although it may generate others, as chapters 1 and 2 have shown.

The chapter proceeds in two parts. The first lays out the analytical framework. The second draws on the framework to explore the three main arguments sketched out above.

Multi-Level Energy Regulatory Governance in Canada

Institutions and Regimes

This chapter focuses on energy regulation and on energy regulatory governance.[3] Regulation, as a policy instrument, is taken to mean 'rules of behavior backed up by sanctions of the state' (Doern, Hill, Prince, and Schultz 1999, 2). These rules can be expressed in a variety of forms – constitutions, statutes, delegated legislation, guidelines, standards, codes, etc. – to which varying degrees of state sanction are attached (Doern and Gattinger 2003). Regulatory governance, a broader concept than regulation, moves beyond a strict focus on the policy instrument of regulation to encompass the organizations, processes, and ideas underpinning regulatory development and implementation.

To explore energy regulatory governance in Canada, the chapter adopts a multi-level approach. As discussed in chapter 1, multi-level governance (MLG) analysis was developed in the European context primarily in response to the reconfiguration of political authority in Western Europe (Peters and Pierre 2002). While the vast majority of this literature is empirically grounded in studies of the European Union, MLG analysis is increasingly being applied to the case of North America (see, for example, Brown 2002; Clarkson 2001; Doern and Johnson 2006). Indeed, many of the theoretical objects of MLG analysis are issues central to the examination of policy and regulatory processes in Canada. MLG literature is concerned with coordination and the means of achieving coordination in situations of dispersed authority (Hooghe and Marks 2003). Dispersion of authority typifies energy policymaking in Canada, a country that probably has the most divided and decentralized jurisdictional arrangements for energy policymaking among Western federal countries (Doern and Gattinger 2003). MLG research suggests that coordination between governments is achieved primarily through negotiation (Benz 2003). In federal-provincial energy relations, negotiation has historically been an important means of achieving coordination: given the highly decentralized constitutional arrangements for energy, policymaking has always been a process of federal-provincial bargaining (Doern and Gattinger 2003).

But beyond these general characteristics, how can one characterize multi-level governance in energy regulation? Peters and Pierre offer the following 'baseline definition' of multi-level governance: 'negotiated, non-hierarchical exchanges between institutions at the transnational, national, regional and local levels' (2001, 131). These characteristics can certainly be seen in energy regulatory governance in Canada, where one finds a multiplicity of such exchanges between the federal and provincial governments and among the provinces.[4] The need for negotiation owes largely to constitutional arrangements in Canada. Provincial governments have substantial control in the energy sector, with lands, mines, minerals, and royalties conferred to them in the Canadian Constitution. Federal power in the energy sector, meanwhile, derives from the federal government's jurisdiction over offshore and northern resources, interprovincial and international trade, taxation, and treatymaking. Given these jurisdictional arrangements, energy regulatory development – particularly as it relates to interprovincial or international trade – generates strong incentives and pressures for negotiation. The constitutional sources of federal and provincial authority for the environment also give rise to pressures and requirements for negotiation. Provincial authority in the environmental domain derives from provincial jurisdiction over natural resources and legislative authority within provincial borders, while federal authority derives from federal jurisdiction over offshore and northern resources; fisheries, navigation and agriculture; trade and commerce; criminal law; the power to legislate for peace, order, and good government, and the federal government's legislative authority (Harrison 2003b).

Peters and Pierre (2001) expand on their baseline definition of multilevel governance to include the relationships between governance activities at these various levels – the vertical 'layering' of governance processes. Vertical layering also characterizes energy regulatory governance in Canada. Above and below the domestic federal-provincial and interprovincial governance processes, one finds governance processes at the local level (e.g., exchanges between provincial and local entities involved in electricity supply, or exchanges between the federal and municipal levels over gasoline tax revenues) and governance processes at the international level, notably exchanges between Canada and the United States, but also the involvement of the federal and provincial governments in multilateral processes such as those on climate change. As examined further on in this chapter, energy regulatory governance in Canada both shapes and is increasingly shaped by governance processes at these various vertical levels.

In addition to this vertical layering of governance processes, there is also a horizontal layering across key regulatory regimes. Regulatory regimes are the complex of organizations, laws, processes, ideas, and

Figure 8.1 Multi-level energy regulatory governance in the Canadian federation: A vertical and horizontal analysis

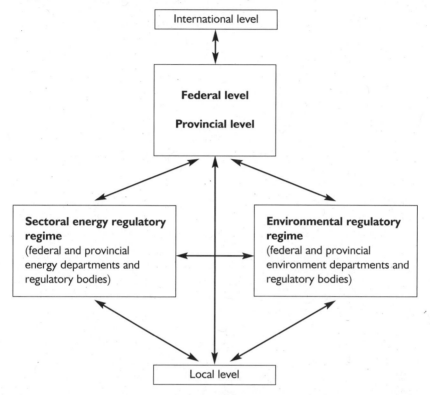

interests that interact in regulatory development and implementation (Doern and Gattinger 2003). In energy regulation, there are two key regimes layered horizontally: the sectoral energy regulatory regime and the horizontal energy regulatory regime. The sectoral regime governs energy as a discrete industrial sector, while the horizontal regime regulates for broad-based issues such as the environment, marketplace competition, and health and safety, where the energy sector is but one industry among many under the purview of general rules (ibid.). This chapter focuses on the environmental regulatory regime, given its growth and the considerable interaction between energy and environmental regulation, notably in the area of climate change.[5] Figure 8.1 illustrates the vertical and horizontal layering of governance processes in multi-level energy regulatory governance.

The energy sectoral regime institutionally comprises energy regulatory boards and energy departments at the federal and provincial levels underpinned by the constitutional division of powers in the energy sector, and energy legislation and regulation at the federal and provincial levels. There is a complex of interrelated ideas, ideals, and interests in the energy sectoral regime that vary both over time and across energy sub-sectors: balancing producer and consumer interests, ensuring workable competition, pursuing energy security, affordability, and reliability, and the like. The environmental regulatory regime, meanwhile, is characterized by its own set of institutions (largely environment departments and regulatory agencies at the federal and provincial levels), and jurisdictional, legislative, and regulatory arrangements

For example, institutionally, the sectoral energy regulatory regime mainly comprises the National Energy Board (NEB) at the federal level and provincial regulators such as the British Columbia Oil and Gas Commission (OGC), the British Columbia Utilities Commission (BCUC), the Alberta Energy and Utilities Board (EUB), and the Ontario Energy Board (OEB). The NEB, an independent federal regulatory agency, regulates the energy industry in the public interest. The board regulates offshore areas and frontier lands not covered by federal-provincial agreements; the construction of interprovincial and international energy infrastructure (oil and gas pipelines and electric power lines); tolls and tariffs for oil and gas pipelines under its jurisdiction; international exports and imports of natural gas; and international exports of oil and electricity. The board also conducts environmental assessments under the Canadian Environmental Assessment Act for projects under its jurisdiction.[6]

Provincial regulators have jurisdiction over non-renewable resource exploration, development, conservation, and management within their borders as well as over siting of and facilities for electricity generation and production. For example, energy regulation in British Columbia is assured mainly by the BC Oil and Gas Commission and the BC Utilities Commission. The OCG is a Crown corporation with statutory authority over most aspects of the upstream oil and gas sector in BC and is intended 'to provide for effective and efficient processes for the review of applications related to oil and gas activities or pipelines, and to ensure that applications are in the public interest having regard to environmental, economic and social effects.'[7] The BCUC, an independent regulatory agency, regulates electricity and natural gas utilities and intra-provincial pipelines to ensure that rates charged are 'fair, just and reasonable, and that utilities provide safe, adequate and secure service.'[8] The EUB, an independent, quasi-judicial agency of the government of Alberta, is responsible for the 'safe, responsible, and efficient development of Alberta's energy resources' (oil, natural gas, oil sands, coal and electrical energy) as well as energy pipelines and transmission lines within the province.[9] The board also regulates rates and terms of service of investor-owned gas and electric utility services and the intra-provincial natural gas transmission system with a view to safe and reliable service at just and reasonable rates.[10] The Ontario Energy Board (OEB) is a Crown corporation that regulates the electricity and natural gas sectors in the public interest. In the electricity sector, the OEB aims to protect consumer interests with regard to electricity service prices, adequacy, reliability, and quality, and to promote efficiency, effectiveness, and viability of the electricity industry. In natural gas, the board's aims include promoting competition in end-user sales, protecting consumer interests with regard to natural gas prices, reliability, and quality, and supporting opportunities for energy efficiency.[11]

These regimes also have their own politico-historical trajectories that inform and influence ideas and interests within them. In the case of the energy sectoral regime, the federal-provincial conflict provoked by the Trudeau Liberals' National Energy Program (NEP) of 1980 continues to exert significant influence over both federal and provincial interests, positions, and decision-making in the energy sector. Developed in the wake of the oil crises of 1974 and 1979, the NEP sought to achieve energy self-sufficiency in the coming decade through a range of measures, including shielding Canadian consumers from high energy prices by establishing a two-price policy for oil. The program also curtailed oil exports and froze gas exports to the United States, sought to increase Canadian ownership and exploration in the oil and gas industry, and aimed to increase federal revenues from the energy sector. The NEP was developed with virtually no provincial or industry input. Western producers, who felt entitled to receive the world price for oil, were enraged, and western provinces, notably Alberta, saw this as the height of federal arrogance and interventionism in an area of provincial jurisdiction.[12]

The National Energy Program marked not only an apogee in federal-provincial conflict in the energy sector, but in federal-provincial relations in toto. Analyses of Canadian federalism point to the

NEP as a prime example of a 'nationalizing vision' of federalism, a program that sought to Canadianize the economy and centralize power in the federal government's hands (Rocher and Smith 2003). Struggles between the federal government and energy resource–rich western provinces are also associated with the period of 'confrontational federalism' from the mid-1960s to mid-1980s (Stevenson 2003). While a revenue-sharing agreement with Alberta in the years following the NEP assuaged provincial interests, and the election of the pro-market Mulroney Conservative government in 1984 ultimately led to the demise of the program, the NEP is never far from provincial or federal memory. Indeed, it would be difficult to overstate the extent to which this program continues to influence federal and provincial interests in the energy domain: provincial governments jealously guard their constitutional authority over energy resources and the federal government is ever-careful to tread softly in the energy sector.

The vertical and horizontal analysis portrayed in figure 8.1 provides a framework to explore energy regulatory governance in Canada, but it does not tell the full story of these governance processes. Exploring energy policy and regulatory processes and outcomes requires an appreciation of a number of core structural characteristics that shape energy processes and outcomes (some of these structural characteristics are also *shaped by* energy policy and regulation, as described below). These include the distribution of energy resource endowments, economic activity and population centres across the country, the relatively small size of the Canadian marketplace, and the extent of energy market integration between Canada and the United States.

The distribution of energy resources in Canada shapes governance processes, as well as policy and regulatory outcomes, at and between the federal and provincial levels. Table 8.1 shows the distribution of population, economic activity, energy reserves, and energy production across the country. As the table reveals, in the oil and gas sector, reserves tend to be located at a distance from major population centres. The vast majority of oil and gas reserves and production are located in Western Canada (particularly in the province of Alberta), in the northern part of the country, and offshore in Atlantic Canada. A similar pattern can be found in the electricity sector, where much hydroelectricity is generated in remote areas of the provinces. Meanwhile, the vast majority of the Canadian population lives within 150 kilometres of the Canada-U.S. border, with strong population concentrations in central Canada, particularly in the Montreal to Windsor corridor. As table 8.1 shows, over 60 per cent of Canada's population lives in Ontario and Quebec. Economic activity is also concentrated in central Canada, with these same two provinces comprising close to 60 per cent of Canadian gross domestic product (GDP) in 2005. These energy resource, economic, and population characteristics can combine to generate significant producer-consumer tensions in the energy policy and regulatory domains, with the interests of oil and gas–rich regions – mostly in Western Canada but also increasingly in the East and North with the development of energy resources in these areas – coming into conflict with the interests of industrial and residential consumers in the major population and GDP-producing areas.

The table also reveals the extent to which structural geo-economic characteristics in Canada influence politics, and policy and regulatory outcomes in the environmental domain. The final column in the table shows the distribution of greenhouse gas (GHG) emissions across the country. In 2003, Alberta was the single largest emitter of greenhouse gases, owing largely to emissions associated with the energy industry. The Kyoto Protocol has been likened to 'another National Energy Program' by Alberta, given perceptions that the province will be disproportionately burdened by federal intervention to achieve Canada's Kyoto targets. These concerns have lessened, however, with the election of the Harper Conservative government in January 2006, a government that has significantly toned down Canada's commitment to the Kyoto Protocol – going so far as to announce at the May 2006 Conference of Parties to the United Nations Framework Convention on Climate Change (UNFCCC) in Bonn that Canada would not meet its targets under the protocol.

In addition to the distribution of energy reserves and production vis-à-vis population and economic activity, a second important and related structural characteristic shaping energy regulatory governance in Canada is the relatively small size of the domestic marketplace. Canada has a small population and economy relative to its energy reserves and production. Given that the majority of the Canadian population is situated at a distance from energy resources and that a sizable marketplace – the United States – is geographically contiguous to the country, Canadian energy development has been inextricably linked to the United States. The economic viability of constructing a pipeline from one part of Canada to another, for example, often depends on its passing through the United States to serve American markets along the way. As a consequence, many major energy deci-

Table 8.1 Population, economic activity, energy resources and production, and greenhouse gas emissions in Canada

Province/ territory	Population (thousands 2005)	GDP ($ billions 2005)	Oil (gas) reserves (MMbl 2004) (Tcf 2004)	Oil (gas) production (MMbl 2005) (Tcf 2004)	Generating capacity (MW 2003)	Electricity generation (GWh 2005)	GHG emissions (kt CO$_2$ equivalent 2003)
British Columbia	4,254.5	168.0	180.1 (10.2)	15.4 (1.1)	14,233	67,627	63,400
Alberta	3,256.8	215.9	175,600.0 (41.5)	623.3 (5.9)	10,797	56,758	224,000
Saskatchewan	994.1	42.5	1,181.7 (3.0)	153.0 (0.3)	3,786	19,023	65,200
Manitoba	1,177.6	41.9	24.3 (–)	5.0 (–)	5,407	37,001	21,300
Ontario	12,541.4	537.6	12.2 (0.4)	0.9 (0.001)	30,457	158,514	206,000
Quebec	7,598.1	274.9	– (0.004)	– (–)	37,637	179,820	91,500
New Brunswick	752.0	23.7		– (–)	4,470	20,281	21,000
Nova Scotia	937.9	31.5	Atlantic offshore	4.7 (0.2)	2,321	12,372	21,200
Prince Edward Island	138.1	4.1	915.0 (0.68)	– (–)	118	38	2,090
Newfoundland and Labrador	516.0	21.5	111.1 (0.1)		7,462	42,147	10,900

Table 8.1 (continued)

Province/ territory	Population (thousands 2005)	GDP ($ billions 2005)	Oil (gas) reserves (MMbl 2004) (Tcf 2004)	Oil (gas) production (MMbl 2005) (Tcf 2004)	Generating capacity (MW 2003)	Electricity generation (GWh 2005)	GHG emissions (kt CO_2 equivalent 2003)
Yukon	31.0	1.5	– (–)	– (0.007)		344	470
Northwest Territories	43.0	4.1	399.2 (0.4)	7.4 (0.03)	304	640	1,760
Nunavut	30.0	1.1	– (–)	–		142	
Total	32,270.5	1,368.7	178,312.5 (56.3)	940.2 (7.7)	116,992	594,707	740,000

Notes: GDP by income and market prices. Oil = crude oil and equivalent. Reserves = remaining established reserves. Northwest Territories excludes Nunavut. Remaining established oil reserves for Alberta drawn from Alberta Energy and Utilities Board (2005).
Sources: Alberta Energy and Utilities Board (2005); Canada, Environment Canada (2005); National Energy Board (2005); and Statistics Canada (2006).

212   Monica Gattinger

Table 8.2 Canada-U.S. energy trade, selected years, 1980–2004

	Imports to U.S. from Canada				U.S. exports to Canada			
	1980	1990	2000	2004	1980	1990	2000	2004
Petroleum (thousand barrels per day)	455	934	1,807	2,118	108	91	110	158
Natural gas (billion cubic feet)	797	1,448	3,544	3,607	0.1	17	73	395
Electricity (terawatthours)	NA	16	49	33	NA	16	13	22

Sources: United States Energy Information Administration (2005); U.S. Energy Information Administration Natural Gas Navigator.

sions in Canada necessarily involve American influence and require decisions by U.S. authorities and regulators. This complex of demographic, geological, economic, and geographic factors generates considerable interdependence between the Canadian and American energy markets.

As Clarkson's analysis in chapter 4 clearly shows, the extent of energy market integration between Canada and the United States is crucial. For our purposes, it is a third core structural characteristic that in part results from the second characteristic noted above, but also has been shaped by policy and regulatory decision-making in Canada and the United States. Trade agreements and deregulation in the oil, natural gas, and electricity sectors have resulted in rapid increases in Canada-U.S. energy trade over the last decade (Bradley and Watkins 2003). Table 8.2 shows the growth in Canada-U.S. energy trade over the last two and a half decades. Petroleum imports to the United States from Canada have grown significantly, almost quintupling from 455,000 barrels per day in 1980 to over two million barrels per day in 2004. Natural gas imports grew more than four and half times between 1980 and 2004, from 797 billion cubic feet to more than 3.6 trillion cubic feet. The table also shows considerable growth in electricity trade over the last decade and a half. In 2004, Canada exported more than 60 per cent of the oil it produced, and virtually all of this was destined for the United States (Statistics Canada 2006). In the natural gas sector, Canada exported roughly half of the gas it produced in 2004 to the United States (ibid.).

Table 8.3 Energy exports to the United States by province

Province/territory	Exports to the United States		
	Oil (MMbl 2005)	Natural gas (billions cubic feet 2004)	Electricity (GWh 2005)
British Columbia	1.2	1,032.2*	8,258.7
Alberta	398.6	17.6	–
Saskatchewan	119.5	1,331.5	691.4
Manitoba	1.6	421.6	12,140.6
Ontario	–	722.9	8,816.2
Quebec	–	62.0	10,565.1
Nova Scotia	0.4	–	–
New Brunswick	–	123.4	2,961.7
Prince Edward Island	–	–	–
Newfoundland and Labrador	54.4	–	–
Yukon	–	*	–
Northwest Territories	–	*	–
Nunavut	–	–	–
Total	575.6	3,717.3	43,623.9

* Oil = crude oil and equivalent. Oil exports are total provincial/territorial exports.(99.1 per cent of Canadian oil exports in 2005 were destined for the United States). Natural gas exports are exports by pipeline and as such do not necessarily reflect the origin of the province of production. Gas exports for British Columbia include exports from the Yukon and Northwest Territories.
Source: Statistics Canada (2006).

The regional characteristics of this growth in bilateral energy trade also shape governance processes and policy and regulatory interests and outcomes in Canada. Table 8.3 shows energy exports to the United States by province. Exports to the United States represent significant proportions of provincial energy production for some provinces. In oil, this is most notable for the western provinces of Alberta and Saskatchewan, as well as in the East for Newfoundland and Labrador. In the natural gas sector, the western provinces again emerge as significant exporters to the United States, as does New Brunswick.[13] In the electricity sector, five provinces account for virtually all of Canada's power exports to the United States: British Columbia, Manitoba, Ontario, Quebec, and New Brunswick. In contrast to oil and gas, where central Canada is a very small player in the export market, in electricity, Ontario and Quebec are major exporters to the United States.

The Challenges of and Prospects for Effective Coordination

Figure 8.2 shows a spectrum of policy and regulatory coordination,[14] with conflict at one end and harmonization at the other.[15] A move from left to right along the spectrum involves increasing levels of coordination. Beginning from the left, coordination can be characterized by open *conflict,* where divergent interests lead to a lack of coordination. *Independence* is positioned in the middle of the spectrum, and refers to situations where governments regard the policies and regulations of their counterparts as given and do not attempt to influence other governments' decisions or adapt their policy and regulatory frameworks in response. *Coordination* as developed in chapters 1 and 15 is a broader concept but in this chapter it appears between independence and harmonization, and refers to jurisdictions mutually adapting their policy and regulatory frameworks vis-à-vis one another. With coordination, governments recognize one another's distinct policy and regulatory frameworks, but consider the implications of policy and regulatory changes underway for other jurisdictions.[16] *Collaboration,* which lies between independence and coordination, involves exchanging data, expertise, or knowledge between parties, and pursuing common objectives together.[17] *Harmonization,* at the far right of the spectrum, is the strongest form of coordination: developing common policy or regulatory frameworks.

In Canadian energy regulatory governance, the institutions, regimes, and structural underpinnings of multi-level governance militate against high levels of coordination. The constitutional division of powers over energy and the environment, the distribution of energy reserves, population, and economic activity across the country, and enduring federal and provincial memories of the National Energy Program generate constellations of federal and provincial energy interests that come into conflict more often than not and that challenge effective coordination. The NEP, discussed earlier, was in part a product of the producer-consumer tensions generated by the demographic–economic–energy-resource realities in Canada. It left in its wake enduring and bitter memories of energy-producing provinces over federal intervention in the energy sector. The federal government has been gingerly engaged in the energy sectoral regulatory regime, and energy-producing provinces have often opted for means of coordination that bypass the federal government or constrain it from future intervention.

Figure 8.2 A spectrum of policy and regulatory coordination

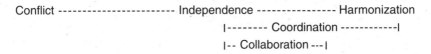

Conflict ----------------------- Independence ---------------- Harmonization
|-------- Coordination ------------|
|-- Collaboration --- |

The Alberta government, for example, has often looked to the market for coordination as a means of insulating the province from federal intervention. The Canada-U.S Free Trade Agreement (CUSFTA) was seen by the provincial government as a means of entrenching energy market liberalization and restricting the federal government from intervening as it had with the NEP. The provincial government was not concerned about American protectionism – one of the main drivers behind the federal government's interest in a bilateral Canada-U.S. free trade agreement. As Gibbons notes, 'The province was prepared to surrender control to the marketplace, but not to Ottawa ... Alberta was more concerned about protecting itself from Ottawa than it was about protecting the province's economic interests from the United States' (Gibbons 1992, 254). A similar perspective underpinned the Alberta government's approach to the internal trade agreement, when it felt strongly that the provinces should strike a deal amongst themselves as a means of protecting against federal intervention: 'Alberta was concerned that if the provincial governments could not act in concert to promote internal free trade, their failure to do so might provide an excuse for unilateral action by the federal government' (ibid., 254).

Canada's experiences with Kyoto implementation also exemplify the challenges to coordination produced by the institutions, regimes, and structural realities in the country's energy sector (see chapter 11 by Rivers and Jaccard). Under the Kyoto Protocol, which Canada ratified in December 2002, the country committed to reducing greenhouse gas emissions by 6 per cent below 1990 levels by 2008–12. Kyoto analysts remain sceptical, though, of Canada's capacity to implement and achieve its Kyoto targets. Not only do these targets constitute a virtually unattainable goal without fundamental changes to the Canadian economy (Schwanen 2000), but they are also unlikely to be met because of the domestic political-economic realities of Kyoto implementation. For reasons of national unity, the federal government, under Liberal leadership, committed to regional equity in measures to meet its Kyoto commitments, that is, not imposing an unreasonable burden on any region of the country. As shown in table 8.1, however, most of the emissions-intensive sectors are located in the western provinces, notably Alberta. The Liberal government adopted a largely voluntary approach to Kyoto implementation as a result of these politico-historical and structural realities – an implementation plan unlikely to achieve Canada's policy objectives under the protocol (Weibust 2003). The current Conservative government has significantly scaled back Canadian commitment to the protocol. Former environment minister Rona Ambrose, while presiding over the Conference of Parties of the UNFCCC, announced Canada would not meet its Kyoto targets. The Conservative government has adopted a 'made-in-Canada' approach to climate change; however, it is not clear what the overall policy framework for this approach might involve, as the government has announced only that 'first steps' on this approach involve winding down or altering fifteen federal climate change programs (Canada 2006).

In instances where one does find federal-provincial coordination, it has largely been at the level of *implementation* as opposed to policy-making or regulatory development, and there has been careful attention paid to ensuring that provincial governments are left with ample room to tailor approaches to local circumstances. In other words, one tends not to find harmonization, but rather approaches approximating coordination, as defined in the spectrum above. For example, the Canada-Wide Accord on Environmental Harmonization (signed in January 1998 by all governments save Quebec) operates on a principle of equality rather than a nationalizing vision, establishing a single window for environmental assessments, with provinces as key actors in service delivery, and putting in place a collaborative development of Canada-wide standards, with provinces having significant flexibility in means of achieving the standards (Harrison 2003a, 2003b). This sort of arrangement may well be the overall approach emerging under the Conservative government, which seeks a more decentralized model of federalism. The Conservative government repealed or cancelled key environmental programs and climate change commitments made by the previous government (e.g., announcing Canada would not meet its Kyoto target as noted above; the new government also cancelled the Energuide program, which included subsidies to Canadians undertaking renovations to improve their homes' energy efficiency). While this appears to have drawn support from the western provinces (the western premiers endorsed the 'made-in-Canada' approach to climate change at their annual meeting in May 2006), it has drawn fire from other provinces – notably Quebec, which has seen a weakening of a major expenditure commitment made by the previous government to fund provincial climate change initiatives. If the Conservative federal government leaves the brunt of responsibility for addressing climate change to the provinces, it may assuage major GHG-producing provinces, but in the absence of a clear statement of the new government's climate-change policy objectives, instruments, and programs, it is not clear what this will mean for the fate of climate-change policy in Canada.

In addition to the coordination challenges characteristic of Canadian multi-level energy regulatory governance, energy regulatory governance and domestic energy policy outcomes in Canada are also coming to be characterized by the growing influence of governance at other levels. Both vertical and horizontal governance illustrated in figure 8.1 – specifically international governance processes between Canada and the United States and the horizontal regulatory regime for the environment – are exerting a growing influence on energy sectoral regulatory governance in Canada. The growth in continental energy-market integration ties many provincial governments' interests increasingly to the American marketplace. Indeed, the government of Alberta has recently established a mission in the United States (co-located in the Canadian embassy in Washington) and has had direct interactions with key members of the Bush and Obama administrations to increase its awareness of the vast potential of the province's oil sands.[18] The growth and expansion of the horizontal environmental regulatory regime also increasingly influence provincial and federal interests in the energy sector. The energy-environment interface has grown in scope and complexity over the last number of decades – addressing such issues as climate change, species at risk, and air quality increasingly impinge on energy development, production, distribution, and consumption. Struggles at and between the federal and provincial levels over energy-environment issues are not uncommon, as environment and energy departments and federal and provincial governments often hold differing views of appropriate balance-points between environmental and economic objectives.[19] As suggested above, however, the Conservative government's approach to climate change appears to be more in line with the interests of major energy-producing and GHG-emitting provinces, attenuating, notably, Ottawa-

Alberta tensions, which were ever-present under the previous Liberal regime.

The growing influence of vertical international and horizontal environmental governance processes can exacerbate and ease coordination challenges at the domestic level. On the one hand, they may alleviate the political challenges of interprovincial and federal-provincial coordination in the energy sectoral regime. There is growing political interest in national and interprovincial approaches for energy issues such as internal energy trade. Some of this interest is propelled by growing international energy trade of the provinces; in the electricity sector, for example, reciprocity requirements of the U.S. Federal Energy Regulatory Commission (FERC) and the development of Regional Transmission Organizations can produce strong incentives for provinces to reduce barriers to internal electricity trade. Likewise, increased focus on electricity reliability and national energy security in the wake of the August 2003 blackout, as well as interest in achieving Kyoto targets, have generated strong provincial interest in the development of increased interprovincial electricity transmission ties (Government of Manitoba and Government of Ontario 2004).

On the other hand, over much of the last decade, in the environmental framework regime, differences between Canadian and American approaches on climate change have combined with the domestic structural realities of energy to generate significant tension in federal-provincial energy-environment relations. At a general level, federal initiatives to protect the environment can conflict with provincial moves to develop natural resources (Harrison 2003b). In the area of climate change, this general characteristic of federal-provincial energy-environment relations has been amplified by developments in governance processes at the international level. As chapters 1 and 2 have already shown, the Bush administration did not ratify the Kyoto Protocol, while Canada ratified the agreement in late 2002. These contrasting approaches hardened domestic opposition in Canada to ratification, and generated concerns in the energy sector that Canada's Kyoto commitments would place firms operating in Canada at a competitive disadvantage to their counterparts in the United States (Toulin 2002). Kyoto Protocol ratification also saw a resurfacing of provincial wariness of the federal government: the Alberta government has likened federal intervention for the Kyoto Protocol to 'another NEP' (Doern and Gattinger 2002). Vertical governance processes at the international level also played into the federal government's actions on climate change. As Harrison (2003b) notes, since the late 1980s, Ottawa has taken the lead on climate change and generally has not come into conflict with the provinces, with the notable exception of former prime minister Jean Chrétien committing internationally to a 6 per cent reduction in emissions – after prior agreement with the provinces to stabilize emissions at 1990 levels – a move that many have attributed to Canada's wish to retain its international reputation and Chrétien's aim to 'meet or beat' the United States on climate change. As noted earlier, however, under the current government, the tenor of federal-provincial relations over climate change is changing: as the Harper Conservatives opt for a 'made-in-Canada' approach to climate change, relations with large GHG-producing provinces are likely to ameliorate, while those with provinces looking to pursue Kyoto targets – notably Quebec – may deteriorate (also see chapter 11 Rivers and Jaccard).

A final challenging area for coordination relates to electricity. The technical capacity challenges of energy regulatory coordination are likely to intensify in the context of electricity sector restructuring and growing Canada-U.S. electricity market integration. Electricity market restructuring transforms the level and nature of government interven-tion, reducing barriers to entry of new market players and allocating a greater role for the market in the development, transmission, and sale of power. As a result, there is much greater complexity in energy market interactions and operating protocols and standards. Privatization, the introduction of competition into segments of the electricity-supply industry, and separation of the different elements of the market (gener-ation, transmission, distribution, retail supply) have transformed the electricity sector's corporate landscape. In this context, there are a far greater number and diversity of private and public sector energy players relating to one another through complex patterns of competi-tion, collaboration, and interdependence. This amplifies the technical complexity of pursuing coordination in the electricity sector. Whether it be in relation to electricity reliability standards, open access transmis-sion, pursuing workable competition, or developing an East-West power grid, electricity sector restructuring magnifies considerably the technical capacity and complexity aspects of overall policy coordination.

Conclusions

Analysing energy regulatory governance in Canada requires both a vertical and a horizontal dimension – vertical, to capture the embeddedness of federal-provincial and interprovincial regulatory arrangements in governance at the international and the local levels, and horizontal, to capture the presence of horizontal regulatory processes, such as those for the environment, that are coming to exert increasing influence on sectoral energy regulatory governance. Exploring energy policy and regulatory outcomes necessitates an appreciation of these institutional arrangements and regulatory regimes, as well as core structural characteristics – the distribution of energy reserves, population, and economic activity, the size of the Canadian marketplace, and the extent of market integration with the United States – shaping energy regulatory governance in Canada.

This chapter has argued that, in Canada, the institutional, politico-historical, and structural characteristics of energy often generate federal-provincial and interprovincial conflict, and militate against high levels of policy and regulatory coordination. Broad federal concerns over national unity and provincial concerns over federal interventionism in areas of provincial jurisdiction can produce strong disincentives to high levels of policy coordination in energy regulation. Moreover, the constitutional division of powers in the energy sector combine with the distribution of energy reserves, population, and economic activity to produce patterns of federal and provincial energy interests that challenge intense coordination.

As this chapter seeks to establish, these challenges to coordination may be both exacerbated and alleviated by two contemporary developments shaping energy regulatory governance in Canada: the growth in influence of vertical (Canada-U.S.) and horizontal (environment) governance processes. Deepening continental energy market integration and the expansion of the environmental regulatory regime are increasingly shaping energy regulatory governance in Canada. These horizontal and vertical influences may ease the political challenges of interprovincial and federal-provincial coordination in the energy sectoral regime where national or interprovincial approaches to energy issues such as internal energy trade come to be more politically salient. Meanwhile, growing Canada-U.S. electricity market integration may amplify the technical challenges of energy regulatory coordination, particularly in the context of electricity sector restructuring. In the environmental framework regime, while the Harper government's 'made-in-Canada' approach to climate change may alleviate longstanding Alberta-Ottawa tensions, it may generate new tensions with other provinces supportive of a stronger Canadian commitment to the Kyoto Protocol.

As this analysis of the institutions and regimes characterizing energy regulation in Canada has sought to reveal, energy regulatory governance in the Canadian federation is inherently and increasingly multi-level and complex, and given the institutional, politico-historical, and structural characteristics of energy, tends to militate against high levels of domestic coordination.

ACKNOWLEDGMENT

I would like to thank Bruce Doern, Burkard Eberlein, Pierre-Olivier Pineau, and Peer Zumbansen for their useful comments on an earlier draft of this text. I would also like to thank participants who commented on my paper presentation at the Energy, Sustainability and Integration: The CCGES Transatlantic Energy Conference, organized by the Canadian Centre for German and European Studies (York University, 9 and 10 September 2005, Toronto, Ontario). Any errors and omissions remain the sole responsibility of the author.

NOTES

1 This chapter examines the electricity, oil, and natural gas sectors. Given this book's special focus on the electricity sector, the chapter concentrates mainly on electricity, although key structural, institutional, political, economic, and regulatory aspects of the oil and gas sectors are also discussed where relevant.

2 The main focus of this chapter is on governance processes between public sector actors. For examination of private sector and civil society actors in the energy domain, see Gattinger (2005a, 2005b).

3 The chapter considers energy policy to the extent that it shapes regulation and regulatory development.

4 Federal-provincial and interprovincial exchanges in energy regulation may be better termed 'heterarchical' than 'non-hierarchical,' but the basic point applies.

5 For an examination of the horizontal regime for competition, see Doern and Gattinger (2003).

6 For a full treatment of the National Energy Board, see Doern and Gattinger (2003), chapter 4.

7 OGC website, www.ogc.gov.gc.ca

8 BCUC website, www.bcuc.com. The commission is also responsible for
   rate regulation of the provincial compulsory automobile insurance ·
   system.

9 EUB website, www.eub.ca.

10 The board is also responsible for regulating water utility services and
   fluid milk rates within the province. For a full treatment of the OEB, see
   Doern and Gattinger (2003), chapter 6.

11 For a full treatment of the OEB, see Doern and Gattinger (2003), chapter 5.

12 For a full discussion of the NEP, see Doern and Toner (1985).

13 The figures in table 8.3 are for pipeline shipments, and as such do not
   necessarily reflect the origin of the province of production. For example,
   while table 8.3 suggests that Alberta exported only a small natural gas
   volume to the United States relative to its production, in 2004, the
   province exported 2.52 trillion cubic feet of natural gas to the American
   marketplace (Government of Alberta 2006).

14 This discussion of coordination draws on Gattinger (2005a).

15 The spectrum is adapted from Dobson (1991, 2–3). I prefer the word *harmonization* to Dobson's use of the term *integration*, given that *integration* is
   frequently used to denote processes expanding economic, cultural, and
   political ties in North America (see Hoberg 2002).

16 While this is a somewhat weaker definition of coordination than Dobson
   proposes, it is more closely aligned with the meaning public officials
   interviewed in the context of my energy research associate with the term.

17 The word *collaboration* is used here, rather than Dobson's use of the term
   cooperation, given that the latter is used in international relations literature to denote coordination and even harmonization (see Milner 1997,
   7–9).

18 On the latter point, see Doern and Gattinger (2002).

19 For a comprehensive examination of the energy-environment interface,
   see Doern (2005).

REFERENCES

Benz, Arthur. 2003. Mehrebenenverflechtung in der Europäischen Union
   [Multilevel governance in the European Union]. In *Europäische Integration*,
   ed. Markus Jachtenfuchs and Beate Kohler-Koch, 317–51. 2nd ed. Berlin:
   Leske & Budrich.

Bradley, Paul G., and G. Campbell Watkins. 2003. Canada and the U.S.: A
   seamless energy border? *C.D. Howe Institute Commentary* 178.

Brown, Douglas. 2002. Aspects of multilevel governance in Australia and
    Canada. Paper prepared for Conference on 'Globalization, Multilevel Gov-
    ernance and Democracy: Continental, Comparative and Global Perspec-
    tives,' Kingston, Queen's University, 3–4 May.
Canada. Environment Canada. 2005. *Canada's greenhouse gas inventory:
    Overview 1990–2003*. Ottawa: Environment Canada.
Canada. Natural Resources Canada. 2006. First steps taken towards made-in-
    Canada approach. News release, 13 April.
Clarkson, Stephen. 2001. The multi-level state: Canada in the semi-periphery
    of both continentalism and globalization. *Review of International Political
    Economy* 8 (3): 501–27.
Dobson, Wendy. 1991. *Economic policy coordination: Requiem or prologue?* Wash-
    ington: Institute for International Economics.
Doern, G. Bruce, ed. 2005. *Canadian energy policy and the struggle for sustainable
    development*. Toronto: University of Toronto Press.
Doern, G. Bruce, and Monica Gattinger. 2002. Another 'NEP': The Bush
    energy plan and Canada's political and policy responses. In *Canada among
    nations 2002: A fading power*, ed. Norman Hillmer and Maureen Appel
    Molot, 74–96. Toronto: Oxford University Press.
– 2003. *Power switch: Energy regulatory governance in the 21st century*. Toronto:
    University of Toronto Press.
Doern, G. Bruce, Margaret M. Hill, Michael J. Prince, and Richard J. Schultz,
    eds. 1999. *Changing the rules: Canadian regulatory regimes and institutions*.
    Toronto: University of Toronto Press.
Doern, G. Bruce, and Robert Johnson, eds. 2006. *Rules, rules, rules, rules:
    Multi-level regulatory governance*. Toronto: University of Toronto Press.
Doern, G. Bruce, and Glen Toner. 1985. *The politics of energy: The development
    and implementation of the NEP*. Toronto: Methuen.
Gattinger, Monica. 2005a. Canada–United States electricity relations: Policy
    coordination and multi-level associative governance. In *How Ottawa spends
    2005–2006*, ed. G. Bruce Doern, 143–62. Toronto: Oxford University Press.
– 2005b. From government to governance in the energy sector: The states of
    the Canada–US energy relationship. *American Review of Canadian Studies*
    (Summer): 321–52.
Gibbins, Roger. 1992. Constitutional politics, the West, and the new political
    agenda. In *Canada: The state of the federation 1992*, ed. Douglas Brown and
    Robert Young, 133–47. Kingston: Institute of Intergovernmental Relations,
    Queen's University.
Government of Alberta. 2006. Natural gas statistics.
    http://www.energy.gov.ab.ca/1656.asp.

Government of Manitoba and Government of Ontario. 2004. The clean
energy transfer: Preliminary assessment of the potential for a clean energy
transfer between Manitoba and Ontario. Joint Manitoba/Ontario study
team. http://www.gov.mb.ca/est/pdfs/clean_energy_transfer.pdf

Harrison, Kathryn. 2003a. The evolution of environmental governance. In
Reinventing Canada: Politics of the 21st century, ed. Janine Brodie and Linda
Trimble, 55–68. Toronto: Pearson Education Canada.

– 2003b. Passing the environmental buck. In *New trends in Canadian
federalism*, ed. Francois Rocher and Miriam Smith, 98–114. 2nd ed. Peterborough: Broadview.

Hoberg, George. 2002. Introduction: Economic, cultural and political dimen-
sions of North American integration. In *Capacity for choice: Canada in a new
North America*, ed. George Hoberg, 3–13. Toronto: University of Toronto
Press.

Hooghe, Liesbet, and Gary Marks. 2003. Unraveling the central state, but
how? Types of multi-level governance. *American Political Science Review* 97
(2): 233–43.

Milner, Helen V. (1997). *Interests, institutions, and information: Domestic politics
and international relations*. Princeton: Princeton University Press.

Peters, B. Guy, and Jon Pierre. 2001. Developments in intergovernmental relations: Towards multi-level governance. *Policy & Politics* 29 (2): 131–5.

– 2002. Multi-level governance: A view from the garbage can. *Manchester
Papers in Politics*. EPRU series 1/2002. Manchester: European Policy and
Research Unit.

Rocher, François, and Miriam Smith. 2003. The four dimensions of Canadian
federalism. In *New trends in Canadian federalism*, ed. Francois Rocher and
Miriam Smith, 5–21. 2nd ed. Peterborough: Broadview.

Schwanen, Daniel. 2000. *A cooler approach: Tackling Canada's commitments on
greenhouse gas emissions*. Toronto: C.D. Howe Institute.

Statistics Canada. 2006. *Energy statistics handbook, fourth quarter 2005*. Catalogue no. 57-601-XIE. Ottawa: Minister of Industry.

Stevenson, Garth. 2003. Canadian federalism: The myth of the status quo. In
Reinventing Canada: Politics of the 21st century, ed. Janine Brodie and Linda
Trimble, 204–16. Toronto: PrenticeHall.

Toulin, Alan. 2002. Kyoto costs must be clear, Dhaliwal says: Raises competitive issue; New conditions to ratification of emissions treaty. *National Post*,
17 June.

U.S. Energy Information Administration Natural Gas Navigator.
http://tonto.eia.doe.gov/dnav/ng/ng_sum_top.asp.

Weibust, Inger. 2003. Implementing the Kyoto protocol: Will Canada make it? In *Canada among nations 2003: Coping with the colossus*, ed. David Carment, Fen Hampson, and Norman Hillmer, 77–90. Toronto: Oxford University Press.

9 An Integrated Canadian Electricity Market? The Potential for Further Integration

PIERRE-OLIVIER PINEAU

Both chapter 2 and Dewees' analysis in chapter 3 show that Canada overall lacks a national integrated electricity market. However, Dewees' account of electricity restructuring in the provinces also shows the importance of neighbours and starting points as factors in successful restructuring. In this chapter, I extend this key point further and argue that many economic and environmental reasons justify more integration among provincial electricity markets in Canada. Although the current political situation, as both the Gattinger and Metz and Doern chapters show, prevents or severely limits such an institutional change from happening, in part due to both coordination and complexity problems, I argue in this chapter that growing economic and environmental pressures can change this context. Once this is done, I then ask how can the bargaining of new institutions unfold?

This chapter analyses the electricity markets in Canada to answer this question, by looking at them through the institutional change framework developed by Aggarwal (1998). In a different way, the Aggarwal framework raises some of the same concerns inherent in the complexity, coordination, and capacity framework suggested in chapter 1 and examined further in chapter 15. While some provinces have already reformed their market, I find that this may actually not help reaching a more integrated Canadian electricity market. 'Hydro' provinces, on the contrary, are currently more integrated with their neighbours on many dimensions and have a significant cost advantage. They could therefore become the strongest advocates of integration. I also conclude that the federal government could use three key powers it holds to foster integration: more interprovincial transmission through the National Energy Board (NEB), more nuclear power through Atomic Energy of Canada (AECL), and a greenhouse gas (GHG) tax for environmental protection. Such policies could lead to an acceptable equilibrium solution for all provinces.

In the first section, I present some key definitions and Aggarwal's analytical framework to study institutional change. This framework is based on rational choice institutionalism, but integrates important concepts from historical institutionalism, such as path-dependence.[1] I adopt this framework because of its encompassing characteristics and suitability to analyse electricity reforms and integration among jurisdictions. In the second section, the framework is applied to Canada. As a result, the Canadian electricity market institutional bargaining game is defined in detail, with an important focus on the comparative situation of each province and territory. Possible institutional outcomes are analysed in the third section. This analysis is based on the game specified in the section on the Aggarwal framework and on historical and current measures of the level of integration in the Canadian electricity sector. Conclusions then follow.

Definitions and Framework

Definitions

Electricity market integration involves institutional change because integration leads to new or modified institutions. To see how electricity market integration relates to institutional changes, I first define institutions. Peters (1999, 18) characterizes institutions by four elements: (1) the formal and informal structures they instil in society, (2) their sustainability over time, (3) their impact on individual behaviour, and (4) the shared value and meaning they have among members of the society. Campbell (2004, 1) offers a more operational definition:

> [Institutions] consist of formal and informal rules, monitoring and enforcement mechanisms, and systems of meaning that define the context within which individuals, corporations, labor unions, nation-states, and other organizations operate and interact with each other. Institutions are settlements born from struggle and bargaining.

Past electricity-market reforms involved modifications of rules and trade mechanisms, with new modes of interactions among market participants. Market forces replaced regulators' decisions and, from ensuring satisfaction of public needs, the goal of supplier became max-imizing their profits. As electricity-sector integration happens, inevitably there is bargaining among jurisdictions. New or modified institutions have to be created from the existing ones. Integration involves much more bargaining than a reform in a single jurisdiction and thus increases coordination and capacity problems.

Institutional change, resulting from bargaining, leads to a new governance regime that Campbell defines as follows:

> Governance regimes are combinations of specific organizational forms, including markets, corporate hierarchies, associations, and networks ... that coordinate economic activities among organizations in an industry or economic sector. (1993, 152)

For the purpose of our analysis of the electricity sector's integration, 'governance regime' and 'institutions' are considered equivalent. I aim at understanding how electricity-market integration can result from an institutional bargaining game, which could be alternatively described as a game setting up a new governance regime.

The Aggarwal Analytical Framework:
An Institutional Bargaining Game

For Aggarwal (1998, 7), institutional change is the result of a game described by three elements. The first one is the type of goods for which an institution is needed. Depending on the characteristics of goods (level of excludability and rivalry in consumption), different games are played. For instance, a bargaining game to set up institutions for the provision of a public good (no excludability and no rivalry in consumption) will be different from the game played for a private good (perfect excludability and rivalry). The second element characterizing the game is the individual situation of players (their power situation, adherence to domestic coalitions and local politicians' beliefs). Finally, the third element is the larger institutional context in which the game takes place: the *meta-regime* (informal principles and norms characterizing interactions among players) and the *regime* (formal rules and procedures), defining the context of bargaining.

If an initial impetus is powerful enough, Aggarwal argues that an institutional bargaining game will start among players. Depending on their situation, players may opt to try to alter the provision of the underlying goods, to avoid changing institutions. They may also try to alter their own individual situation or another player's situation to change the setting of the game. Finally, they might directly negotiate the new institutional setting with other players, by either creating or modifying institutions. Of particular interest in the analysis of institutional change will be how these new or modified institutions are *linked* to previous ones (or not linked at all); in other words, how the reconciliation of old and new institutions is done. Two main options are possible: new institutions can be *nested* in older ones (as in a hierarchy), or they can be *parallel* to older ones, by replicating or complementing each other. In both cases, the link can be tactical or substantive. Tactical links can arise as a way to preserve most aspects of old institutions while acknowledging other players. Substantive links may be the outcome of a greater cooperation among players, where the resulting institutions are more sustainable. The outcome of the game can be described as an equilibrium (a state of the world where no player has an individual interest in changing the negotiated institutions).

The Canadian Electricity Market Institutional Bargaining Game

This section presents the Canadian electricity market institutional bargaining game that provinces and territories may decide to play with the federal government. I characterize this game in terms of the goods involved in the game, the Canadian institutional context (regime and meta-regime), and the individual situation of players. As a backdrop, I discuss the current integration impetus that could start the game.

The Integration Impetus: Economic and Environmental

Forces pushing for more integration in the energy sector are economic and environmental. From an economic perspective, better integrated markets allows efficiency gains to be realized, as well as reliability improvements, as energy sources can more easily be substituted in order to respond to price signals or physical supply disruptions. From an environmental perspective, as a large share of natural consequences and risks of environmental disruptions are shared across the world, without considerations to jurisdictions, an integrated environmental approach is the only possibly successful avenue to build a sustainable energy sector. These forces are the same forces that are behind the *vertical* international governance process and *horizontal* environmental regulatory regimes described by Gattinger in chapter 8 of this book.

These integration forces play out in Canada in very specific ways that I review in the following initiatives from stakeholders calling for a more integrated approach in the energy and electricity sectors.

DEVELOPING A CANADIAN ENERGY POLICY

Although the 1980–4 National Energy Program leaves bitter memories in Canadian energy politics, the need to develop a more integrated Canadian approach in energy is increasingly being recognized. The most significant example of such recognition is the report released by the Energy Dialogue Group (2005), an alliance of energy industry associations. This report makes a strong call for a Canadian energy 'framework' to all provincial energy ministers, meeting in the context of the Canadian Council of Energy Ministers. They argue that strong governmental leadership should be exercised in the fields of energy efficiency, information and public understanding, technology, and smart regulation. Along these lines, provincial governments are working at integrating energy services in the 1995 Agreement on Internal Trade (ITS 2006). This could provide a first step towards a more integrated energy framework. Progress, however, is very slow, with the 'framework for negotiations for the Energy Chapter underway' since 1995 (ITS 2005).

A national environmental strategy has been developed to try to meet the GHG emission reduction targets set by the Kyoto Protocol (NRCan 2005). In particular, in the context of the electricity sector, 'strengthening the national electricity grid' (ibid., 5) and the facilitation of hydropower initiatives to replace high-emissions coal power plants are directly discussed.

More concretely, Ontario is multiplying its interprovincial electricity projects. A joint Ontario–Hydro-Québec–SNC Lavalin bid for a hydropower project in Labrador was submitted in 2005 (Ontario Ministry of Energy 2005b). This would be the first electricity initiative in Canada involving three different provinces. Another project with Manitoba could lead to an additional 5,000 MW of generation capacity, with an increased transfer capacity of 1,500 MW to Ontario (Joint Manitoba/Ontario Study Team 2004). However, environmental and energy planning remains under provincial jurisdictions, and little coordination among provinces exists.

CONTINUING NORTH AMERICAN INTEGRATION

If electricity was mostly left out of NAFTA (Pineau 2004; Plourde 1993), there are continuous talks to promote energy and electricity integration at the North American level. A particular working group was established in spring of 2001 by Canada, Mexico, and the United States (NAEWG 2002a), with a particular focus on electricity trade (NAEWG 2002b, 2005).

Furthermore, some Canadian provinces have already started to comply with regulatory requirements made by the U.S. Federal Energy Regulatory Commission (FERC) to allow provincial companies to market wholesale energy products and services in the United States. These regulatory requirements certainly extend the regulatory integration between these provinces and the United States.

Finally, as energy services are included in WTO service negotiations, with the goal of progressively opening the electricity sector to international competition and investment, integration will have to be enhanced, even if only to harmonize the regulatory framework of member countries. The negotiation of the Free-Trade Area of the Americas (FTAA) may also promote more advanced integration of energy services, as the FTAA, unlike NAFTA, may fully include these services (Pineau 2004).

STRENGTH OF IMPETUS

Interprovincial and national electricity initiatives are being developed, and integration discussions are taking place at the national and international levels. However, forces behind these developments are still too small to change Canadian electricity institutions. Indeed, when the Canadian context is taken into account (see more below), it becomes clear that the involved changes would discourage players to start an institutional bargaining game.

However, because the economic and environmental impetus will only increase over time, and because the need for a more coherent national electricity institution will only grow stronger, understanding the main elements of the game is both important and interesting. This exercise can help prepare for negotiations, and could eventually lead to faster policy changes.

Goods and Externalities in the Electricity Sector

Understanding goods and their externalities, for which institutions provide rules, monitoring, and enforcement mechanisms, is an important step of the game specification. It is the first element of the game description proposed by Aggarwal.

The complexity of defining goods involved in the electricity sector stems from the complexity of the sector itself. This difficulty is reflected by the way international classification systems such as the Harmonized Commodity Description and Coding System (HS) or the Central Product Classification (CPC) consider electricity. These classification systems are used in trade agreements to define which goods and services are subject to trade rules. They have treated electricity in many different ways, all of them unsatisfactory. WTO negotiations are being held to better classify 'electricity' (Pineau 2004). For the purpose of this chapter, however, a general classification of the goods involved in the electricity sector is sufficient.

When the electricity sector is considered as a supply chain, the good delivered is energy (quantified in kilo or megawatt hours – kWh or MWh). Generation capacity is required to produce it, and transmission and distribution capacity are needed to deliver it. Simply having the possibility to use generation capacity is a service in itself, and transmission and distribution services are also independent products. Furthermore, 'reliability'[2] is an independent service associated with the electricity sector that is usually highly valued by consumers.

These five products are different in their level of excludability and rivalry in consumption. This defines if they are public goods, private goods, 'common pool resources,' or 'inclusive club goods' (Cornes and Sandler 1996). Energy is probably the easiest to classify, as a private good, because it is easy to exclude someone from energy consumption, and once someone has a kWh, someone else cannot have it (hence its rival consumption nature). At the other extreme, reliability is a public good, because its provision is global to the entire electricity system, and it is impossible to exclude someone from a reliable system (if connected to the system). Also, one's enjoyment of reliability is not in competition with another's.

Generation, transmission, and distribution capacities are more difficult to characterize. Until full capacity is reached, and if network technical constraints and interactions (e.g., loop flows) are ignored, there is no rival consumption. Exclusion is usually ruled out by regulation in the case of transmission and distribution, and this makes them public goods. For generation capacity, unless a plant can be ordered to be run by a system operator (as in many jurisdictions), exclusion is possible. When this is the case, generation capacity can be considered as an inclusive club good. Table 9.1 summarizes the classification of these five electricity market products.

As free markets are sub-optimal for the provision of public goods,

Table 9.1 Types of good involved in the electricity sector

		Rival consumption	
		Yes	No
Possibility of exclusion	Yes	Private good: Energy	Inclusive club good: Generation capacity*
	No		Public good: Transmission capacity* Distribution capacity* Reliability

*Non-rival consumption until capacity is exhausted.

regulation is necessary. In the case of generation capacity, as its nature is debatable, the type of institutions guiding its provision is likely to vary. In Canada, provinces have opted for very different institutions to regulate generation-capacity provisions. It is only for energy that a market institution can clearly be relied on in the electricity sector.

However, even energy markets can be unsatisfactory because of negative externalities. In particular, GHG emissions are associated with electricity production when fossil fuels are used. When a nuclear technology is used, nuclear wastes pose a hazard for a long period of time. With other technologies (hydro, wind), negative externalities are not associated with energy production per se, but with generation capacity. Among possible negative externalities for these technologies are flooding, social impacts of population displacements, and visual pollution. Transmission and distribution capacities also share some of these negative externalities.

The Canadian Institutional Context

The institutional context of the Canadian electricity market can be described by its regime and meta-regime.[3] The regime includes the formal rules under which players have to act (provinces, territories, and federal government). The meta-regime consists of the informal norms of interactions. I limit the presentation here to the regime, as the Canadian meta-regime would involve too much speculation. I can mention, however, that it is usually characterized by respect and collaboration, by an overstatement of players' own needs, and by a tendency to complain. Constitutional fights and, more recently, credibility crises linked to financial scandals, also dominate the meta-regime. They tint many political interactions and play an important role on setting priorities.

The main institutional component framing the electricity sector in Canada is the *Constitution Act* (1867), where federal and provincial powers over various sectors are defined. In particular, section VI, Distribution of Legislative Powers, and its article 92A Laws respecting non-renewable natural resources, forestry resources, and electrical energy define the jurisdictional division of responsibilities between federal and provincial governments. Provinces are responsible for resource management within provincial boundaries, intra-provincial trade, commerce, and environmental impacts. The federal government is responsible for resource management on frontier lands, uranium and nuclear power, interprovincial and/or international trade and commerce, trans-boundary environmental impacts, and policies of national interest (economic development, energy security, and federal energy science and technology [NRCan 2002]). Under 'policies for national interest' rests some ambiguity that may lead the federal government to interfere with provincial responsibilities.

Federal policy in energy is made in Natural Resources Canada (NRCan), while federal regulation on interprovincial and international trade and commerce of electricity is made at the NEB. The Canadian Nuclear Safety Commission regulates uranium and nuclear power.

Other important institutions are the North American Electricity Reliability Corporation (NERC) and the U.S. FERC. The NERC is a non-profit voluntary organization in charge of the technical regulation of reliability. Cooperation in the NERC is ensured by the recognition that reliability is a public good. FERC dictates some open access rules in transmission for provinces with companies trading energy in the United States. It is therefore part of the Canadian institutional context, by the influencing provincial transmission and commercial regulations.

Individual Situations: Electricity Markets in Canada

All provinces and territories, with the federal government, are players in the electricity institutional bargaining game. Apart from the federal government, which has been described above, the description of individual situations proceeds by groups, defined as follows:

- **Reformed provinces**: Alberta, New Brunswick, and Ontario. They reformed their electricity sector by breaking its vertical integration and creating an independent system operator. Wholesale electricity prices are not regulated.
- **Hydro provinces**: British Columbia, Manitoba, Newfoundland and Labrador, and Quebec. Their electricity system is based on hydropower and they are very active in energy trade. They have not significantly reformed their electricity sector and there is little wholesale price fluctuation. Except for Newfoundland and Labrador (with no border with the United States), they comply with FERC regulatory requirements.
- **Traditional provinces**: Saskatchewan, Nova Scotia, and Prince Edward Island. Their electricity sector is vertically integrated and regulated. They rely almost exclusively on fossil fuel (coal) for generation.
- **Territories**: Northwest Territories, Nunavut, and Yukon. They have very small electricity sectors with no integrated trans-mission system. Size and remoteness marginalize these players.

In the following sub-sections, I present the provincial situations group by group, focusing on generation and ownership, infrastruc-tural integration, regulatory integration, and commercial integration (Pineau, Hira, and Froschauer 2004). The choice of these three dimen-sions of integration facilitates analysis of the bargaining game: as provinces decide to negotiate new institutions in the electricity sector, their level of integration shapes negotiations. Indeed, as path-depend-ence plays an important role in institutional change, some provinces may reach equilibrium more quickly.

GENERATION TECHNOLOGIES AND OWNERSHIP

Generation technologies and ownership are important when assessing the respective power of provinces and possible internal coalitions among them. Indeed, provinces gain strength with generation tech-nologies less constrained by GHG emissions, and with less vulnerabil-ity to fossil fuel prices. Furthermore, with a concentrated ownership, internal coalitions will be easier to achieve, making their position stronger in the bargaining game. Figure 9.1 serves the dual purpose of showing fuels used in each province and electricity outputs.

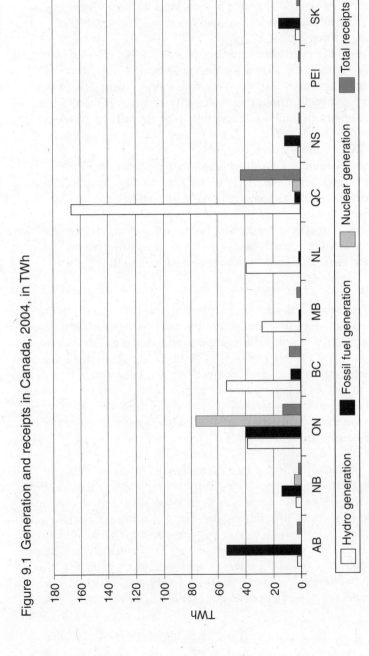

Figure 9.1 Generation and receipts in Canada, 2004, in TWh

Source: Statistics Canada (2005).

From figure 9.1, fossil fuel reliance in reformed and traditional provinces is made obvious. It constrains them in GHG emissions and price fluctuations of coal and natural gas. Hydro provinces are exempt from such constraints and are larger producers.

Table 9.2 presents the main Canadian utilities.[4] Hydro and traditional provinces have a concentrated ownership: Crown corporations dominate (all hydro provinces, Saskatchewan, and territories), or a single private investor owns the integrated utility (Nova Scotia and PEI). Public ownership also dominates in reformed provinces, although in Alberta it is through municipalities. Alberta and Ontario have a more partitioned ownership, which was necessary for their reform. In New Brunswick, the strong functional separation of Crown corporations could also make internal coalitions more difficult to reach, weakening their overall strength in the game.

Non-utility (industrial) electricity producers also play a role in the bargaining game, as the prevailing institutions influence their fate. It is mostly in the hydro provinces that industrial generators are active, with BC and Quebec having respectively 22 per cent and 11 per cent of their total production generated by the industry (table 9.3). All other provinces have high percentages of utility-generated electricity, much higher than the Canadian average of 92 per cent, indicating that industries saw little incentives in self-generation, even with open wholesale markets (Alberta and Ontario).

INFRASTRUCTURAL INTEGRATION

Infrastructural integration is the first of the three dimensions to measure how electricity markets are integrated with their neighbouring jurisdictions. One measure of infrastructural integration is the percentage of interconnection capacity one jurisdiction has relative to its generation capacity. The higher this percentage, the more integrated the jurisdiction, as a greater share of capacity can be used elsewhere. Table 9.4 presents generation capacities, interconnections with other Canadian provinces and U.S. states, and the percentage of generation capacity these interconnections represent.

There is little surprise in the finding that hydro provinces have their infrastructure much more integrated with their neighbours (30 per cent to almost 70 per cent of their generation capacity can be exported). The New Brunswick and PEI exceptions are explained by one fact: PEI receives almost all its energy from New Brunswick. This explains the higher interconnection percentages.

Table 9.2 Ownership of main utilities in Canada, 2005

	Crown corporation (or owned by provincial government)	Municipal	Investor-owned utility
Alberta		Epcor^{G,T,D} Enmax^D	TransAlta^G ATCO Group^G Altalink^T Fortis (Fortis Alberta)^D Centrica (Direct Energy)^R
New Brunswick	NB Power Generation NB Power Nuclear^G NB Power Transmission NB Power Distribution	Saint John Energy^D	
Ontario	Ontario Power Generation^G Hydro One^{T,D}	Toronto Hydro^D Hydro Ottawa^{G,D} Local distribution companies (LDCs)	LDCs Licensed retailers^R
BC	BC Hydro Generation BC Transmission Corporation BC Hydro Distribution		
Manitoba	Manitoba Hydro^{G,T,D}		
NL	NL Hydro^{G,T,D}	Fortis (Newfoundland Power)^{G,T,D}	
Quebec	Hydro-Québec Generation Hydro-Québec TransÉnergie^T Hydro-Québec Distribution		

Table 9.2 (*continued*)

	Crown corporation (or owned by provincial government)	Municipal	Investor-owned utility
Nova Scotia			Emera (Nova Scotia Power) [G,T,D]
PEI			Fortis (Maritime Electric) [G,T,D]
Saskatchewan	SaskPower[G,T,D]		
NW	Northwest Territories Power Corporation[G,T,D]		ATCO Group (Northland Utilities)[G,T,D]
Nunavut	Nunavut Power Corporation[G,D]		
Yukon	Yukon Energy Corporation[G,T,D]	ATCO Group (Yukon Electrical) [G,D]	

[G]Generation   [T]Transmission   [D]Distribution and retail sales   [R]Retail sales only

Table 9.3 Percentage of utility and industrial generation, 2005

	Reformed			Hydro				Traditional			Territories			Canada
	AB	NB	ON	BC	MB	NL	QC	NS	PEI	SK	YT	NT	NU	
Total utility generation	92	96	97	78	100	98	89	98	100	97	100	53	100	**92**
Total industrial generation	8	4	3	22	0	2	11	2	0	3	0	47	0	**8**

Source: Statistics Canada (2007).

Table 9.4 Provincial generation capacities, Canadian and U.S. interconnections in MW

		Interconnections				
	Generation capacity	Canadian	U.S.	Total	% of capacity	Difference from Canadian total (%)
Alberta	9,738	1,250	0	1,250	**12.84**	-57.30
New Brunswick	4,398	1,650	487	2,137	**48.59**	+61.62
Ontario	24,840	1,435	3,215	4,650	**18.72**	-37.74
BC	12,091	1,100	2,575	3,675	**30.39**	+1.10
Manitoba	5,333	838	1,538	2,375	**44.53**	+48.13
NL	7,437	5,200	0	5,200	**69.92**	+132.57
Quebec	34,344	7,175	3,515	10,690	**31.13**	+3.53
Nova Scotia	2,298	325	0	325	**14.14**	-52.96
PEI	109	200	0	200	**183.49**	+510.30
Saskatchewan	3,417	688	190	878	**25.68**	-14.58
NW	157	0	0	0	**0**	
Nunavut	79	0	0	0	**0**	
Yukon	130	0	0	0	**0**	
Total	104,371	19,860	11,520	31,379	30.06	

Sources: Hydro-Québec TransÉnergie (2004); IESO (2005); NEB (2004); Statistics Canada (2004).

The most interesting finding is that two reformed provinces, Alberta and Ontario, are the least integrated with their neighbours (along with Nova Scotia), hence Dewees' key point in chapter 3 about the importance of neighbours and starting points for institutional change. Interconnections of Alberta and Ontario are less than 13 per cent and 19 per cent of their capacity, almost 60 per cent and 40 per cent less than the Canadian average. These figures are surprising, as electricity sector reforms usually aim at reducing prices, which could have been done by increasing access to cheap hydropower from direct neighbours. Arguably, especially if path-dependence plays a role, their tradition of isolation will make Alberta and Ontario more reluctant than other provinces to integrate a Canadian system.

REGULATORY INTEGRATION

Tables 9.5 to 9.8 present regulatory organizations of each province and territory. All (except the Northwest Territories) have a provincial ministry or department in charge of energy and a regulator dealing at the

Table 9.5 Regulatory structure: Reformed provinces

	Alberta	New Brunswick	Ontario
Provincial ministry	Alberta Energy	Department of Energy	Ministry of Energy
Long-term planning	Long-term adequacy monitoring (AESO)	Adequacy of the integrated electricity system (10-year capacity assessment made by NBSO)	Ontario Power Authority
Regulator	Alberta Energy and Utilities Board	NB Board of Commissioners of Public Utilities	Ontario Energy Board
System operations	Alberta Electric System Operator (AESO)	New Brunswick System Operator (NBSO)	Independent electricity system operator (IESO)
Wholesale market	AESO	Free bilateral contracts	IESO

minimum with retail price monitoring. Major differences arise at three levels: long-term planning, system operations, and wholesale market.

In most traditional and hydro provinces, long-term planning is still under the responsibility of the utility, with approval of investment plans made by the regulator or the provincial energy ministry. In the case of BC and Quebec, it is up to the distribution company (in both cases a division of the main Crown corporation) to provide a long-term 'integrated electricity plan' (BC) or 'supply plan' (Quebec). The regulator approves this plan, and generation capacity requirements are planned according to forecasts. In Alberta and Ontario, after an initial period without long-term planning, new mechanisms have been introduced. In Alberta, capacity is under 'long-term adequacy monitoring' by the system operator (Alberta Department of Energy 2005a), with the system operator sending warning to generation companies if capacity margins are too thin. In Ontario, planning is under the supervision of a new independent body facilitating cooperation among market players (Ontario Ministry of Energy 2005b). New Brunswick has a structure similar to Alberta's. A striking feature of all these long-term planning mechanisms is the exclusion of other jurisdictions, despite the benefits of pooling resources and trade.

Systems operations vary between reformed and other provinces. In

Table 9.6 Regulatory structure: Hydro provinces

	BC	Manitoba	NL	Quebec
Provincial ministry	Ministry of Energy and Mines	Manitoba Energy, Science, and Technology	Department of Natural Resources	Ministry of Natural Resources and Wildlife
Long-term planning	Integrated Electricity Plan (BCHydro)	Utility	Utility	Supply Plan 2005–2014 (from HQ Distribution)
Regulator	BC Utility Commission	Public Utilities Board of Manitoba	Board of Commissioners of Public Utilities	Régie de l'énergie
System operations	BC Transmission Corporation	Manitoba Hydro	Newfoundland and Labrador Hydro	Hydro-Québec TransÉnergie
Wholesale market	Bilateral contracts	Bilateral contracts	Bilateral contracts	Bilateral contracts

reformed provinces, an independent body was created, while in all other provinces and territories this role remains either with the transmission company or with the integrated utility. Reformed provinces could more easily move towards an integrated Canadian system, as their regional system would already have an independent operator. However, creating such an organization has never been a concern in integration reforms.

A more important concern is to define how the wholesale electricity market functions. In Alberta and Ontario, system operators operate hourly wholesale markets. In New Brunswick, no such spot market exists, with only freely negotiated bilateral contracts in operation. In other provinces, wholesale markets also rely on bilateral contracts, but regulators approve retail prices. Large consumers in BC and Quebec can freely negotiate prices without the regulator's involvement.

Consequently, regulatory structures differ critically among reformed and other provinces in planning, system operations, and wholesale markets. Integration is therefore low, with many bargaining challenges ahead.

COMMERCIAL INTEGRATION

The last dimension of electricity market integration is assessed through two measures: level of trade with other jurisdictions, and differences in price levels. Level of trade is a common measure of commercial inte-

Table 9.7 Regulatory structure: Traditional provinces

	Nova Scotia	PEI	Saskatchewan
Provincial ministry	Department of Energy	Department of Environment, Energy, and Forestry	Provincial Cabinet and Crown Investments Corporation
Long-term planning	Utility and NS Utility and Review Board	Department of Environment, Energy, and Forestry (Prince Edward Island Energy Framework)	Utility
Regulator	Nova Scotia Utility and Review Board	Island Regulatory and Appeals Commission	Saskatchewan Rate Review Panel and Open Access Transmission Tariff customer dialogue group
System operations	Nova Scotia Power	Maritime Electric	SaskPower
Wholesale market	Bilateral contracts	Bilateral contracts	Bilateral contracts

gration. It can be quantified by two percentages: (1) production exported to other provinces and to the United States; and (2) available electricity imported from other provinces or the United States. High percentages indicate a high level of commercial integration. Figures 9.2 and 9.3 and table 9.9 provide data for these percentages.

Price levels are the second measure of commercial integration: uniform price levels are an indication of high commercial integration, as trade tends – in the long run and in the absence of congestions – to flatten price differences. Table 9.10 provides a picture of retail electricity prices across Canada, with their variation compared to the national average.

Figures 9.2 and 9.3 show that commercial integration is low in Canada. Once extreme values are taken out of consideration, even provinces with more integrated infrastructures prove to be poorly commercially integrated with their neighbours. Indeed, while provinces have interconnections representing 30 per cent of their generation capacity (table 9.4), less than 15 per cent of production is exported and about 13 per cent of electricity is imported (2004 data, Statistics Canada 2005).

Table 9.8 Regulatory structure: Territories

	Northwest Territories	Nunavut	Yukon
Provincial ministry		Ministry of Energy	Department of Energy, Mines and Resources
Long-term planning	Utility	Utility	Utility
Regulator	Public Utilities Board of the NWT	Utility Rates Review Council	Yukon Utilities Board
System operations	NTPC	Nunavut Power Corporation	Yukon Energy
Wholesale market	Bilateral contracts	Bilateral contracts	Bilateral contracts

Starting with figure 9.2, the extreme value of NL is explained by long-term contracts this province has with Quebec. No active spot trading takes place. The high import figure of Québec is therefore explained by the NL exports. Low hydraulicity in 2003 and 2004 cut exports by almost half, compared to the period 1999–2001 (from 22 twh on average during 1999–2001 to about 13 TWh in 2003 and 2004 [Statistics Canada 2005]). This explains the relatively low Quebec exports. The last 'anomaly' to mention is that half of the high Canadian exports from New Brunswick (figure 9.2) are explained by PEI imports (figure 9.3). This is due to PEI's structural dependency on New Brunswick for electricity. For these reasons, I leave out NL, Quebec, and PEI from the analysis of table 9.9.

In relative terms, once anomalies are taken out, Manitoba is the most commercially active province in Canada, with 32 per cent of its production exported and 14 per cent of its electricity imported (table 9.9). BC, Ontario, and Saskatchewan follow, with between 8 per cent and 13 per cent of exports and imports. Finally, other provinces (New Brunswick, Nova Scotia, and Alberta) follow, with levels of exports and imports close to 2–3 per cent.

Looking at residential prices (table 9.10), a very large gap is observed between hydro provinces and all others (commercial and industrial prices would lead to similar findings). With monthly fixed fees four dollars below the national average and cost of energy per kwh almost two cents below the national average, hydro province cus-

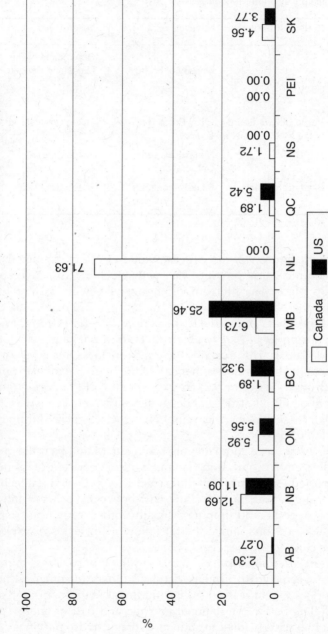

Figure 9.2 Percentage of production exported to other provinces and the United States, 2004

Source: Statistics Canada (2005).

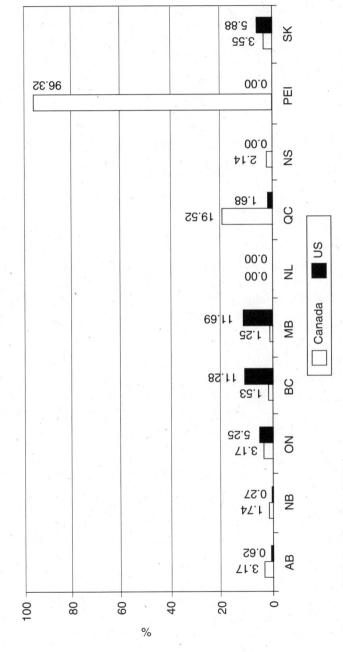

Figure 9.3 Percentage of available electricity imported from other provinces or the United States, 2004

Source: Statistics Canada (2005).

Table 9.9 Ranks of electricity exporters and importers, 2004

Rank	Total production exported	(%)	Total imported available electricity	(%)
1	NL	71.63	PEI	96.32
2	MB	32.20	QC	21.20
3	NB	23.78	MB	14.07
4	ON	11.49	BC	13.31
5	BC	11.21	SK	9.42
6	SK	8.33	ON	8.46
7	QC	7.31	AB	3.79
8	NS	2.64	NS	2.46
9	AB	2.56	NB	2.02
10	PEI	0.00	NL	0.13

Source: Statistics Canada (2005)

tomers benefit from better prices. In terms of incentives for Canadian integration, there is little for these consumers to gain, from a superficial price-only analysis. However, with considerations for energy savings made possible by higher prices, GHG emission reductions induced through more trade and higher revenues (and profits) for Crown corporations, hydro province citizens may be convinced of the benefit of increased commercial integration.

Conversely, all other consumers would benefit from a greater commercial integration, with retail prices converging towards a national average. Two findings would require further investigation: first, the high level of fixed charges in some provinces; and second, the high cost of energy in NL, a hydro province. In the case of Alberta, the high cost of fixed charges is of particular concern, as this cost is independent of energy production (based on coal). High operating costs of the market may explain their top position in fixed charge prices.

Institutional Outcomes: What Level of Integration?

Institutional Bargaining Game Analysis

The impetus to negotiate appears weak and, as argued by Gattinger in chapter 8 of this book, Canadian institutions seem almost designed for confrontation rather than for coordination and integration. This impetus will nevertheless grow as energy issues become more important. With escalating fossil fuel prices, integrated institutions could

Table 9.10 Provincial residential electricity rates (2005, per month)

	Fixed charge $	Difference from national average (%)	$ per kWh	Difference from national average (%)	First block max (kWh)	Beyond, $ per kWh	Source
Alberta (Edmonton)	14.94	+13.61	0.1061	+30.48	1,300	0.0663	EPCOR (2006)
New Brunswick	17.74	+34.90	0.0837	+2.94	750	0.0991	NB Power (2005)
Ontario	12.07	-8.21	0.0911	+12.04			Hydro One (2005)
Average reformed	**14.92**		**0.0936**				
BC	3.63	-72.40	0.0605	-25.59	175	0.0565	BCHydro (2005)
Manitota	6.25	-52.47	0.0578	-28.91			Manitoba Hydro (2005)
NL	15.69	+19.32	0.0846	+4.03			NLH (2005)
Quebec	12.36	-6.01	0.0502	-38.26	912	0.0633	Hydro-Québec (2005)
Average hydro	**9.48**		**0.0633**				
Nova Scotia	10.83	-17.64	0.0922	+13.40			NS Power (2005)
PEI	23.60	+79.47	0.1033	+27.05	1,200	0.0801	Maritime Electric (2005)
Saskatchewan	14.39	+9.43	0.0836	+2.82			SaskPower (2005)
Average traditional	**16.27**		**0.0930**				
National average*	13.15		0.0813				
Network (average)	18.00	+36.88	0.0000	-100.00	700	0.6786	NTPC (2005)
Nunavut	18.00	+36.88	0.3346	+311.53			Nunavut Power (2005)
Yukon	11.90	-9.51	0.1001	+23.17			Yukon Energy (2005)
Average Territories	**15.97**		**0.1449**				

* The 'national' average is the provincial average, as territories have different market conditions.
Note: The city/urban standard residential rate was selected. In the case of Alberta and Ontario, the residential regulated energy rate was selected and additional delivery (distribution and transmission) and other charges were added. Prices are shown before taxes and special rebates (except for the Northwest Territories, where the subsidy for the first monthly 700 kWh is shown).

generate efficiency gains balancing economic losses. Furthermore, from a Canadian perspective, reactions to U.S.-made regulations (FERC) or to WTO/FTAA-induced regulation might provide enough incentives to make electricity integration an item on the political agenda. Environmental issues will also require integration, especially if the federal government starts to assume its GHG control responsibilities. As the Rivers and Jaccard analysis in chapter 11 of this book shows, such responsibilities are at best only beginning to be recognized. As the climate change challenge is increasingly recognized and the need for action acknowledged by all political forces, coherent, integrated solutions will have to be explored. The energy industry already advocates more integration, through the already mentioned Energy Dialogue group or the National Electricity Round Table. When (or if) the game is played, our description can be useful to better understand the bargaining situation.

TYPE OF GOODS

From the type of goods discussion, an agreement on common regulation for reliability, transmission, and distribution could be made. Especially on reliability, an extension of the NERC to give it a greater Canadian orientation and more power in transmission could help in making progress. More debate can be expected on how to handle generation capacity and on how to price energy, especially with GHG emissions. Given regulatory institution differences amongst players, disagreements will be hard to ease. Furthermore, GHG emission externalities will be a major issue between fossil-fuel (reformed and traditional) provinces and hydro provinces.

INSTITUTIONAL CONTEXT

The current institutional context presents some challenges for the federal government. Many obstacles have to disappear before change can happen. Other policy issues such as health care or provincial autonomy have to become less dominant. But these issues will lose some of their importance in the future, at least relatively (compared to emerging energy and environmental issues) and a new momentum could be created.

Nevertheless, despite provincial jurisdiction in electricity and U.S. influence, the federal government has institutional responsibilities on which it could capitalize: nuclear power, interprovincial trade, and environmental policy. With this institutional context, under a more favourable political conjuncture, a possible institutional outcome is attainable (see more below).

INDIVIDUAL SITUATIONS

An assessment of the players' situation in terms of their power, domestic coalition potential, and politicians' beliefs (an aspect of Aggarwal's framework not yet covered) is now possible.

Reformed provinces. Despite a possible impression that these provinces could be strong bargaining players because of their reforms, many elements weaken their position. First, as illustrated both in the presentation of infrastructural and commercial integration, Alberta and Ontario do not have a tradition of electricity integration. If path-dependence is a factor in institutional change, then some internal forces will make them resist the creation of Canadian institutions. Second, their reliance on fossil fuel will likely be a disadvantage in an integrated market, making it harder for generators from these provinces to compete. As ownership is also more fragmented, counteracting the unwilling provincial companies to open the market might prove to be difficult.

Political beliefs might play in different directions. If a more integrated Canadian electricity sector relies on market principles more than on regulation, then there might be support for integration. However, few politicians usually push for pan-Canadian solutions.

On the strength side for these provinces, their importance in terms of population and economic size (Ontario) and financial situation (Alberta) gives them a lot of influence. If, furthermore, residential and industrial consumers realize the gains they could make from a Canadian integration, and give it an equivalent political weight, then Ontario, Alberta, and New Brunswick could become leaders in the integration game.

Hydro provinces. Because of their important, emission-free electricity production, of the possible hydro developments in Manitoba, Quebec, and Labrador, and of their tradition of infrastructural and commercial integration, these players are in a powerful situation in the electricity sector. Their internal potential for coalition is also great from a utility point of view. However, from a consumer point of view, strong resistance will arise because of integration's price impacts. Furthermore, they would have their own weaknesses in this game. BC, under its current provincial government, has more interest in fossil fuel developments than in improving its electricity sector (and even less the Canadian one). Quebec, a very large player, will reluctantly lose its independence under Canadian institutions. Both political and commercial issues could play out in this respect. Manitoba and Newfoundland and Labrador, being small provinces, are less significant players and could not play a major role in this Canadian game.

Traditional provinces and territories. Both these groups are too small to really make a difference. Territories, because of their location, cannot realistically be integrated in the electricity institutions. Traditional provinces can gain only from a more integrated electricity market, through increased access to cheaper and cleaner electricity sources.

Possible Integration Outcomes

Given the above analysis, status quo is likely to be the short-term outcome. However, a possible new equilibrium outcome could be reached if the informal context discussed above evolves. Three major, but realistic, institutional changes, in the direction of greater Canadian electricity market integration, could result from future negotiations:

- **Overhaul of the NEB to give it more power in interprovincial trade.** This aspect is already under its responsibility and could be presented as a change to develop a stronger Canadian equivalent to the FERC. Federal programs in transmission could create more interconnections. Benefits would be distributed over (1) to sellers of electricity, getting higher prices than in their province; (2) to buyers, getting lower prices; and (3) to society in general, through reduced GHG emissions coming from less fossil fuel–electricity production.
- **Greater role of Atomic Energy of Canada Limited** (AECL), by replacing coal power plants by new nuclear plants. This strategic move from the federal government would have the benefits of (1) making Kyoto targets achievable; (2) balancing the power of hydro provinces by developing a low-cost electricity source; (3) fostering competition with hydro provinces by developing this alternative; and (4) reducing fossil fuel dependence in a period of increasing prices, with the related benefit of reducing exposure to volatile price. Negative public reactions can be answered by adequate com-

municatións to explain energy challenges and nuclear power safety issues. Also, simultaneous efficiency programs should be integrated, including strong price signals.

- **Introduction of a GHG tax** as an essential price signal accounting for the negative externality associated with GHG emissions. Proceeds of this tax could be earmarked to renewable energy, such as wind and solar, to demonstrate commitments to sustainability.

These three institutional changes have the potential to rally everyone because they address issues they face, without creating conflicts that are not appeased by parallel measures. These changes create new linkages between current institutions: federal institutions develop new partnerships with nested provincial institutions, such as long-term planning agencies, transmission companies, and system operators.

Institutional Barriers

If the impetus for negotiating integration never becomes stronger than the institutional barriers inherited from the past (such as the confrontational federal-provincial history described in chapter 8 or the policy inertia described in chapter 11), then little further integration will take place. Predicting how political will and forces will develop in the future, given the changing environment, is beyond the scope of this chapter. Institutional barriers are great, but the economic and environmental risks of not integrating are critical. This chapter explored one possible outcome of negotiations for integration, without addressing the distinct issue of whether or not political and institutional actors will be motivated enough to reach an acceptable equilibrium.

Conclusions

This analysis of the institutional bargaining game in the Canadian electricity market has used Aggarwal's analytical framework both to examine current electricity institutional features and to suggest possible pathways through which institutions might be changed to develop a more integrated electricity system in Canada.

The game's characterization first allowed many aspects of the Canadian electricity market to be revealed, such as the levels of integration in infrastructure, regulation, and commercial activity. The relative position of each province and provincial group was assessed. Territories have also been covered, but they remain marginal players as a result of their size. In this game, reformed provinces suffer from a technological disadvantage (fossil fuel generation), low level of integration, and a fragmented sector. Hydro provinces, on the contrary, benefit from their clean and low-cost technology, a tradition of integration, and a strong and dominating company. Finally, traditional provinces, with their small size, are also marginal players. They would, however, significantly benefit from Canadian integration.

The chapter, in concert with previous chapters, has shown that the current institutional context prevents a different bargaining game from starting, because the status quo is still acceptable for provinces and because the federal government has other political priorities. However, energy and environmental challenges will call for new solutions, and integration offers significant gains that could benefit all players. In particular, three institutional changes could represent a negotiated equilibrium, as all players would be better off under the new context. They consist in (1) overhauling the NEB with new interprovincial transmission objectives; (2) giving a greater role to AECL, to lead nuclear power developments in hydro-poor provinces; and finally (3) introduce a GHG tax with revenues earmarked to renewable generation.

These changes are complex but they would benefit hydro provinces through increased revenues in the short run. They would answer energy needs of other provinces and promote long-term solutions adequate from economic and environmental points of view. They could therefore be accepted as a bargained solution. This chapter thus hopefully contributes to a better understanding of the current Canadian electricity market and in its future integration in a complex multi-level policy and regulatory context where coordination and capacity problems can be identified and then gradually overcome.

NOTES

1 For other institutional theories, see Peters (1999). Campbell (2004) and Sjöstrand (1993) present alternative political science approaches to institutional change. North (1993) and Williamson (1993) offer economic approaches.
2 Reliability is 'the degree of performance of the elements of the bulk electricity system that results in electricity being delivered to customers

within accepted standards and in the amounts desired. Reliability can be addressed by two basic and functional aspects of the electric system: adequacy and operating reliability' (NEB 2005, 89).

3 Chapters 8 and 11 of this book provide some additional background on the Canadian regime and meta-regime. Chapter 8 describes the inherently multi-level energy governance structure in Canada, while chapter 11 provides some specific background on GHG regulation in Canada.

4 A utility is 'an entity owning and operating an electric system and having the obligation to provide electricity to all end users upon their request' (NEB 2005, 90).

REFERENCES

Aggarwal, V.K. 1998. Reconciling multiple institutions: Bargaining, linkages, and nesting. In *Institutional design for a complex world: Bargaining, linkages, and nesting*, ed. V.K. Aggarwal, 1–31. Ithaca, NY: Cornell University Press.

Alberta Department of Energy. 2005. *Alberta's electricity policy framework: Competitive, reliable, sustainable*. Edmonton: Alberta Department of Energy.

Alberta Energy and Utilities Board. 2005. *Alberta's reserves 2004 and supply/demand outlook 2005–2014* Calgary: Alberta Energy and Utilities Board.

BC Hydro. Electricity rates: Residential rates. http://www.bchydro.com/policies/rates/rates757.html (accessed 21 August 2005).

Campbell, J.L. 1993. Property rights and governance transformation in Eastern Europe and the United States. In *Institutional change: Theory and empirical findings*, ed. S.-E. Sjöstrand, 151–70. London: Sharpe.

– 2004. *Institutional change and globalization*. Princeton: Princeton University Press.

Canada. Natural Resources Canada. 2002. Energy in Canada 2000. http://www2.nrcan.gc.ca/es/ener2000/online/html/toc_e.cfm (accessed 23 August 2005).

– 2005. *Moving forward on climate change: A plan for honouring our Kyoto commitment*. Ottawa: Natural Resources Canada.

Cornes, R., and T. Sandler. 1996. *The theory of externalities, public goods, and club goods*. 2nd ed. Cambridge: Cambridge University Press.

Energy Dialogue Group. 2005. Investing in Canada's energy future: Getting the framework right. Submission to the Council of Energy Ministers, St Andrews, NB, 20 September.

EPCOR. 2006. *2006 regulated rate tariff: Price schedule applicable to RRT cus-*

tomers in the EPCOR Distribution Inc. service area effective January 1, 2006. Edmonton: EPCOR Energy.

Hydro One. 2005. Residential customers: Rates and pricing. http://www.hydroonenetworks.com/en/customers/residential/rates_pricing (accessed 21 August 2005).

Hydro-Québec. 2005. Tarif D: Structure du tarif domestique. http://www.hydroquebec.com/residentiel/facture/tarif_d.html (accessed 21 August 2005).

Hydro-Québec TransÉnergie. 2004. The long and short of our power transmission system. http://www.hydroquebec.com/transenergie/en/reseau/bref.html (accessed 16 August 2005).

IESO. See Independent Electricity System Operator.

Independent Electricity System Operator. 2005. Ontario transmission system. Toronto: Independent Electricity System Operator.

Internal Trade Secretariat. 2005. Status of obligations by chapter as of December 31, 2005. Winnipeg: Internal Trade Secretariat.

– 2006. Agreement on internal trade: Consolidated version. Winnipeg: Internal Trade Secretariat.

ITS. See Internal Trade Secretariat.

Joint Manitoba/Ontario Study Team. 2004. Preliminary assessment of the potential for a clean energy transfer between Manitoba and Ontario. Winnipeg: Joint Manitoba/Ontario Study Team.

Manitoba Hydro. 2005. Customer service & rates: Energy rates. http://www.hydro.mb.ca/your_service/er_monthly_rates.shtml (accessed 21 August 2005).

Maritime Electric. 2005. Rate schedules and policies base rate. http://www.maritimeelectric.com/16policies.html#n1 (accessed 21 August 2005).

NAEWG. See North American Energy Working Group.

National Energy Board. 2004. A compendium of electric reliability frameworks across Canada. Calgary: National Energy Board.

– 2005. Outlook for electricity markets 2005–2006: An energy market assessment. Calgary: National Energy Board.

NB Power. 2005. Rates and policies: Residential rates. http://www.nbpower.com/en/customers/residential/rates/rates.aspx (accessed 21 August 2005).

NEB. See National Energy Board.

Newfoundland and Labrador Hydro. 2005. Complete schedule of rates. St John's: Newfoundland and Labrador Hydro.

NLH. *See* Newfoundland and Labrador Hydro.

North, D.C. 1993. Institutional change: A framework of analysis. In *Institutional change: Theory and empirical findings*, ed. S.-E. Sjöstrand, 35–46. Armonk: Sharpe.

North American Energy Working Group. 2002a. *North America: The energy picture*. Ottawa: North American Energy Working Group.

– 2002b. *North America: Regulation of international electricity trade*. Ottawa: North American Energy Working Group.

– 2005. *Guide to federal regulation of sales of imported electricity in Canada, Mexico, and the United States*. Ottawa: North American Energy Working Group.

Northwest Territories Power Corporation. 2005. Residential account power rates. http://www.ntpc.com/grey/haccount (accessed 21 August 2005).

Nova Scotia Power. 2005. Domestic service tariff. http://www.nspower.ca/AboutUs/RatesRegulations/Residential/DomesticService.html (accessed 21 August 2005).

NRCan. *See* Canada. Natural Resources Canada.

NTPC. *See* Northwest Territories Power Corporation.

Nunavut Power. 2005. Sample invoice. http://www.nunavutpower.com/Pages/Sample%20Invoice.html (accessed 21 August 2005).

Ontario Ministry of Energy. 2005a. Highlights of the McGuinty government's new vision for Ontario's electricity sector. Backgrounder, 15 April.

– 2005b. Ontario and Quebec partner to propose major hydroelectric project in Labrador. News release, 30 March.

Peters G. 1999. *Institutional theory in political science: The 'new institutionalism.'* London: Pinter.

Pineau P.-O. 2004. Electricity services in the GATS and the FTAA. *Energy Studies Review* 12 (2): 258–83.

Pineau P.-O., A. Hira, and K. Froschauer K. 2004. Measuring international electricity integration: A comparative study of the power systems under the Nordic Council, MERCOSUR, and NAFTA. *Energy Policy* 32 (13): 1457–75.

Plourde A. 1993. Energy and the NAFTA. *C.D. Howe Institute Commentary* 46.

SaskPower. 2005. Residential rates. http://www.saskpower.com/services/rates/residential.shtml (accessed 21 August 2005).

Sjöstrand S.-E., ed. 1993. *Institutional change: Theory and empirical findings*. Armonk: Sharpe.

Statistics Canada. 2004. *Electric power capability and load: 2001*. Catalogue 57-204-XIB. Ottawa: Statistics Canada.

– 2005. *Energy statistics handbook, first quarter.* Catalogue no. 56-500-XIE. Ottawa: Minister of Industry.
– 2006. *Energy statistics handbook, fourth quarter 2005.* Catalogue no. 57-601-XIE. Ottawa: Minister of Industry.
– 2007. *Electric power statistics.* Table 127-0001. Ottawa: Statistics Canada.
United States Energy Information Administration. 2005. *Annual energy review 2004.* Washington: U.S. Government Printing Office.
U.S. Energy Information Administration Natural Gas Navigator. http://tonto.eia.doe.gov/dnav/ng/ng_sum_top.asp.
Williamson O.E. 1993. Comparative economic organization: The analysis of discrete structural alternatives. In *Institutional change: Theory and empirical findings*, ed. S.-E. Sjöstrand, 75–108. Armonk: Sharpe.
Yukon Energy. 2005. Reading your bill. http://www.yukonenergy.ca/customer/residential/reading/ (accessed 21 August 2005).

10 The Transformation of German Energy Regulation: Struggling with Policy Legacy

CHRISTIAN THEOBALD

This chapter investigates the evolution of the complex and multi-layered system of German energy market regulation since markets were opened to competition. As such, it complements the comparative Canadian-German analysis in chapter 6 by Froschauer, by providing important background and details on regulatory issues, actors, processes, and outcomes in the German case. The chapter speaks in particular to the theme of technical and political *complexity*, as developed in the analytical framework in chapters 1 and 15. It shows, similar to Dewees' analysis in chapter 3 on electricity restructuring in Alberta and Ontario, that successful market creation is extremely demanding, prone to design flaws, and easily derailed by coordination problems and politics. For the German case, this chapter highlights how most regulatory effort has been invested in improving third-party access to the grid, while market concentration in generation accelerated unchecked, not least for political reasons, and now constitutes the Achilles heel of German market reform.

Furthermore, the German case as presented here illustrates how (externally driven) adaptations of regulatory systems both modify and incorporate traditional features of the institutional environment. Thus, under EU pressure, Germany adopted a new agency-model, yet traditional elements of regulation by the federal states and cartel authorities persist, raising new challenges of *multi-layered coordination* of energy regulatory governance.

The energy market in Germany – as in most other states – has not been an open market for a long time as power, and gas supply were regarded as a natural monopoly. The liberalization of the German energy market started only very recently and was carried out in two steps. The first liberalization move took place in 1998 when the German energy market was opened for competition for the very first time. The second step was the enactment of the new Energy Industry Act in 2005, which generally extended the scope of regulation, and created the new federal energy authority, the Bundesnetzagentur. Both reforms were the reaction to European framework legislation, which had to be implemented by the German legislature, as detailed by Froschauer and Cameron, in chapters 6 and 7 respectively. While the European directives were taken as a starting point for generally reforming the domestic law, the reforms of German law were to a large extent also the mere implementation of European directives. Thus, the influence of the EU on the development of the German energy market must not be underestimated. This also holds true for the future: the March 2008 EU Summit has agreed to adopt an ambitious energy and climate package by the end of 2008, and the third energy liberalization package, tabled by the European Commission in September 2007, is set to obtain legislative approval in the second half of 2008 as well (for details on the evolving EU framework, see Cameron, chapter 7 of this volume.)

The transition from a monopolistic market structure to a liberalized energy market causes a number of problems, since it is impossible to instantly create a functioning market with fair competition between competing companies. The German case illustrates these problems very well. Almost a decade after the launch of competition, the results of liberalisation are still not satisfactory. While there are certainly a number of reasons for this problem, it will be argued in this chapter that one of the main obstacles for competition is the high degree of market concentration, which has to a large extent developed only after the liberalization.

This chapter provides an overview of the energy market in Germany and analyses the regulative framework in the light of European directives. The chapter starts with a brief overview over the current structure of the German energy market. It then describes the different phases of liberalization in the German energy market, focusing on the legal reforms in 1998 and 2005. As the concentration on the access to grids is a particular feature of the German energy regulation, I pay special attention to the different models of access to the grids and the transition from the negotiated to the regulated access. Moreover, I deal with the specific multi-level structure of the energy authorities, consisting of energy and cartel authorities both on the national and the federal state level. Finally, the results of the market liberalization are

Figure 10.1 Sources of electricity production in Germany, 2005

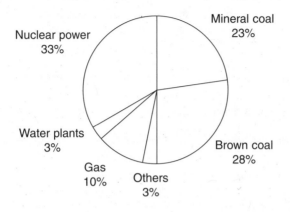

Source: Federal Ministry of Economy (2005).

critically assessed with the focus on the particular problem of market concentration in the German energy market and its repercussions on the regulation of the energy market.

The Structure of the German Energy Market

Being the country with the largest population and the strongest economy in Europe, Germany has also the most important energy market in the European Union. Thus, both the German electricity market with a total consumption of approx. 616 TWh, and the gas market with a total consumption of approximately 1.016 TWh are the biggest European market segments (Schiffer 2007, 36).[1]

In 2006 Germany generated about 636 TWh of electricity. The German electricity production is based on three main sources: mineral coal, brown coal, and nuclear power (see figure 10.1). The proportion of nuclear power will, however, decrease in the following years as the former German government has decided – in cooperation with the nuclear industry in the 'nuclear consensus' – to close down all nuclear energy plants by 2021 (for details, see the analysis in chapter 5 by Mez and Doern). The recent incidents at German nuclear power plants started a controversial debate on turning off at least the old production sites well before 2021.

As the analysis by Mez in chapter 14 shows, one primary objective of the former as well as the current government is the advancement of renewable energies in the generation and production of electricity. This is mainly ensured by two instruments: firstly, the Renewable Energy Act of 2000 and the revised version of 2004 guarantee the producers of renewable energies a certain remuneration from the network operators that exceeds the general price for electricity; secondly, renewable energies are exempted from the newly introduced ecological tax, which is generally imposed on the use of all other forms of energy.

Apart from its leading role in electricity production, Germany leads Europe in trade in electricity as the largest importer and exporter of electricity. The importance of Germany as an energy trader is based mainly on its geographical situation in the heart of Europe as well as its high-performance transmission networks.

With a consumption of about 1.016 TWh, gas plays a prominent role in the German energy supply. This importance of gas results mainly from the disappearance of oil from the heating market, which started in the 1980s. One of the most remarkable features of the German gas market is its high dependence on imports. Only about 15 per cent of the German gas consumption originates from domestic extraction. Amongst the remaining 85 per cent, the largest proportion is imported from Russia (35 per cent), Norway (26 per cent), and the Netherlands (20 per cent) (Schiffer 2007, 36). It is obvious that the large import dependence has a heavy impact on the structure of the German gas markets.

Both the electricity market and the gas market are characterized by a high number of companies in the production sector as well as in the transmission sector. There exist more than three thousand energy supply companies, including more than 1,700 network operators acting on the value chain of the energy industry. A particular feature of the German energy market is the prominent role of small and medium-sized companies on the regional and particularly the municipal level (Stadtwerke). Legally these enterprises are corporations under private law, but their shares are by the majority held by municipalities and thus indirectly under public control.

While the great number of companies suggests a pluralistic structure of the markets, a huge segment of the German energy market is in fact dominated by only a few large companies. Thus, in the gas industry the most important long-distance pipelines are owned by only six

Figure 10.2 Traditional supply chain (gas)

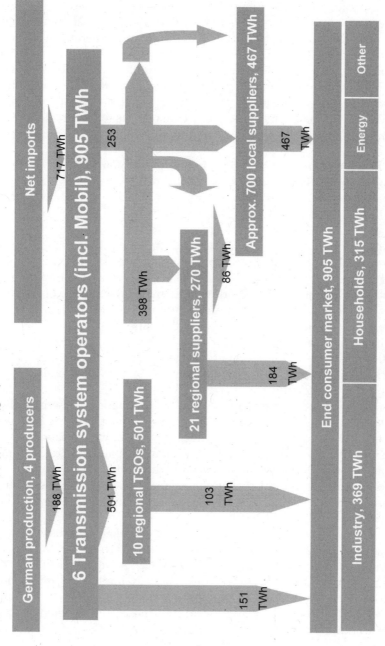

Source: Federal Association of German Gas and Water Industries, Statistics (2001)

companies. In the electricity industry there are four so-called interconnection companies (transmission system operators) that own the high-
voltage grids. At the same time these companies operate on all stages
of the value chain and are shareholders of a multitude of especially
local network operators. In the energy industry, these four interconnection companies unify about 80 per cent of the energy generation
market. This structure is a challenge for the German regulatory
system. We shall come back later to the reasons for these oligopolistic
structures and the prospects for future development.

The Transition from a Monopoly Energy Economy
to a Competitive Energy Economy

The First Step: The Energy Reform Law of 1998

The German energy market was traditionally characterized by the
monopoly of local energy suppliers. The energy market was – in line
with the economic theory at the time – regarded as a natural monopoly where competition would result in the ineffective use of resources
as well as a ruinous competition between different companies – both
of which would be detrimental for the national economy. Therefore,
according to Sections 103 and 103a of the *Gesetz gegen Wettbewerbsbeschränkungen* (GWB, German Act against Restraints on Competition),
the energy market was exempted from the general rules of the competition and cartel law.

The monopolistic structure of the energy market in Germany was
practically implemented by two instruments. First, licence agreements
between the local energy companies and the municipalities gave one
company exclusive rights for the use of municipal rights of way for the
operation of grids in their streets and other traffic areas. Second, territorial agreements between supply companies demarcated the different
areas where a company had exclusive rights to provide energy to customers (see Theobald 2003b, 18).

The liberalization of the German energy market started in 1998 with
the first major reform of the *Energiewirtschaftsgesetz* (EnWG, Energy
Industry Act), which came into force on 29 April 1998.[2] In 2003, the
provisions of this act, which were originally limited to the electricity
market, were extended to the supply of natural gas.

This reform was to a large extent influenced and triggered by European framework legislation: the EC directive of 1996 on electricity and

the EC directive of 1998 on gas.[3] As further explained by Froschauer and Cameron in chapters 6 and 7 and in this volume, these directives aimed at the opening of European energy markets by means of unbundling the transmission and production of energy as well as the competition around networks. The directives provided that energy companies are to be vertically separated. In the area of electricity, however, only a limited organizational unbundling of the transmission network operator from other business sectors has to be done. In addition, network access had to be granted on a non-discriminatory basis, but the kind of access could be either regulated by the state directly (regulated grid access) or negotiated by the companies (negotiated grid access).

The implementation of the EC framework legislation by the amendment of the Energy Industry Act meant a complete conceptual change for the German energy market. It eliminated the existing monopolies in the production as well as distribution of energy by abolishing the exemption of energy producers from the general competition law. Moreover, it resulted in the inadmissibility of exclusive concessions and territorial demarcation agreements and thus meant the end of closed supply areas for the energy companies.

The Different Forms of Competition in a Network-Based Industry

One of the main instruments for the liberalization of the energy market was the launch of the competition around grids. Grids are the central element in any network-based industry since they form the basis for the transmission and thus the trade of the relevant good. The competition in network-based industries can generally occur in three different forms: competition between grids, competition for grids, and competition within grids (Theobald 2003a).

Competition between grids means the competition between functionally equivalent grids. This type of competition is the exception in Germany and may be found only in the area of gas supply. Since the market entry of Wingas in the 1990s, there exist some parallel gas pipelines (Held 2003, 162), but no parallel electricity grids. The German legislator did not explicitly rule out the putting up of parallel networks, nor does German law encourage this aspect of competition. The main reason for this is the idea that the doubling of a network as a basically natural monopoly is economically inefficient. So the competition between grids has not become practically relevant yet and will probably not play a major role in future.

Competition for grids is the competition for the licence to operate a grid. It has been established only in the realm of local distribution grids used for the supply of end consumers. According to the Energy Industry Act, municipalities may grant exclusive licences to utilities or other business entities to use public land for the construction and operation of local supply networks. This includes the right to deliver energy to all general customers, which is the vast majority, namely those which have not expressly opted for another supplier.

As a matter of law, these licences have a maximum duration of twenty years. After their expiry, the right to run the local distribution network and the general supply business must basically be put out to tender. This is where 'competition for the market' takes place. On more advantageous conditions to the local community, a different operator may very well be awarded the supply licence and would then be entitled to take over the local grid as well as the appertaining end customers. But these situations are not the major area of competition for the German energy supply industry either.

Instead, the most important aspect affecting the energy industry is the competition within existing grids. *Competition within grids* means the competition between suppliers of energy using the same transmission and distribution grid. If the network operator was independent from the producers of energy, competition within grids would not be problematic, since the owner of the grid had an interest in opening the grid for as many producers as possible.

However, for historic reasons, electricity and gas grids in Germany have been built and are operated by companies that are also heavily present in the energy supply market. Thus, all grids in Germany are owned by 'vertically integrated' companies – companies that both supply and distribute energy through their grids. Therefore, the market entry for competing suppliers is particularly difficult, since the operators do not have an interest that other suppliers deliver electricity through their grids.

A theoretical alternative for resolving this conflict and ensuring the start of a 'competition within grids' would have been to expropriate the energy suppliers of their grids or – conversely – the network operators of their energy production facilities (ownership unbundling). Although being proposed by the European Commission as an effective mean to ensure and foster competition, ownership unbundling has not been considered a real option in Germany, not only due to possible political trouble but mainly because of the constitutional rights of the companies, in particular their right to property as guaranteed in Article 14 of the German Grundgesetz (constitution). The constitutional rights also bind the legislator and cannot be superseded by legislation.

The Negotiated Access to Grids

Under the Energy Industry Act from 1998, Germany was, together with Luxemburg, the only country in the European community to follow the alternative of negotiated third-party access. *Negotiated access* means that the conditions of grid access are only roughly defined by legislation, whereas most of the relevant topics must be negotiated and contractually agreed upon by the interested parties in every single case. The only legislative guidance in Germany had been a general claim by any business entity for access to any electricity or gas grid on fair and non-discriminatory terms under sections 6 and 6a of the Energy Industry Act 1998. These provisions, however, did not define the concrete terms and conditions for the access to networks, for electricity grids or for gas pipeline systems. Instead, these questions had been intentionally left to the market participants. The different companies in the market, however, were in a very uneven situation – new market entrants and small start-up companies as suppliers were claiming access to the grids of long-standing, well-established, and mostly large companies. This situation was even aggravated by strong cartelization efforts among the grid operators (see below).

Very soon after the liberalization enactment of the new Energy Industry Act 1998, the access conditions, including the calculation of access fees, were uniformly defined in the Verbändevereinbarung (VV, the so-called Associations' Agreement). This was a comprehensive contract between the industrial associations of the German grid operators, the large electricity producers, and the large industrial customers. The agreement laid down detailed parameters for the conditions and prices of grid access. It was amended twice, the last version (so-called VV II plus) is dated January 2002 (for details, see de Wyl and Müller-Kirchbauer 2003, 782).

Although the Associations' Agreements were a form of regulative framework for the access to grids, they did not have binding legal authority. They received, however, some form of – at least temporary – legislative recognition after the amendment of Section 6 of the Energy Industry Act. Section 6 required that the conditions for the access to grids must be not only fair and non-discriminatory but also be in line with 'good professional practice' (*gute fachliche Praxis*).[4] After the amendment it contained the assumption – which could be rebutted in special cases – that the conditions of the Associations' Agreement reflected 'good professional practice.'

However, the provision that was planned to be a legal experiment from the beginning expired at the end of 2003. After that, the Associations' Agreements were merely a substitute for individual contractual agreements on the terms and conditions of access to the energy grids in Germany. In practice, the Associations' Agreements kept an important function, since the courts used them as a reference point in interpreting the concept of good professional practice and fair conditions for the access to grids.[5]

Although the Associations' Agreements had only limited legal force for a limited period, they can be considered a first step away from a negotiated to a regulated access to grids. The function of shaping the actual conditions of grid access by way of the Associations' Agreements has been practised mainly in the electricity sector; in the gas sector the agreements did not receive such high importance.

The Role of Courts and Cartel Authorities

The development of the regulation of grid access after the liberalization of the energy markets can be subdivided in three different phases. In the beginning, the question of the 'if' of the grid access – the reasons for the denial of third-party access – were the main concern. In a second phase, the activities of the courts and authorities focused on the modalities of grid access. Only in a last step has the focus of the regulation shifted from the question of 'how' to the question of 'how much': the prices of the network access fees.

The cartel authorities and the civil courts played a major role in implementing and supervising the negotiated grid access as a pillar of liberalization. This was not expected, since the authorities actually responsible for implementation of the Energy Act were the energy authorities of the federal states, which had been rather passive, as the result of a long-standing tradition of collaboration with and leniency towards their regional energy companies.

The legal bases for the strong role of the cartel authorities were provisions in the Act against Restraints on Competition, according to which the denial of non-discriminatory access to grids was a violation of the antitrust laws. In applying these provisions, the Federal Cartel Office in several decisions laid down detailed directions for the permissible costs of grid access and thereby attempted to 'simulate' the fee regulation. It also expressed certain objections against the cost approaches in the Associations' Agreement. In a landmark decision, the Oberlandesgericht (Higher Regional Court) Düsseldorf ruled in 2004, however, that federal antitrust law does not provide for a preventative price control and that the Associations' Agreements are the sole criterion for the assessment whether the prices for the utilization of the grids are abusive.[6]

Another area where court decisions had a major impact on energy law was the question of the validity of long-term supply contracts. Different courts declared these contracts invalid,[7] because they were an obstacle for establishing competition in the energy market. The courts left open, however, whether the complete supply contract was invalid and which obligations for renegotiation existed.

As a result, the new energy law took a somewhat unexpected development in its first years. Firstly, the most effective legal instrument for enforcing fair grid access conditions became the antitrust and not the Energy Industry Act. Secondly, and more importantly, the negotiated grid access had – almost unnoticed – in practice taken many facets of a regulated grid access. The transition to a regulated grid access had firstly been caused by the conclusion of the Associations' Agreements, which functioned as guidelines for the interpretation of fair and reasonable access. Secondly, the active role of the Cartel Authority and the courts limited the scope of negotiated agreements.

The New Energy Act 2005

The first liberalization movement through the reform of the Energy Industry Act in 1998 had generally not resulted in the desired opening of the market and competition between energy suppliers in Germany. Instead, during the first years of the new act, one could observe even a backward movement in many respects. Thus, the decrease of energy prices, which had been one of the main objectives of the liberalization of the market, had not taken place. Instead, the prices rose constantly during recent years. This resulted in a strong cost pressure in the heavy-industry sector in Germany as well as strong demands from the consumer protection associations. The attempts of the Federal Cartel Office to bring down the level of prices by challenging the excessive fees for the access to the grids were mostly unsuccessful. The negative development of liberalization was also reflected by the fact that most of the foreign energy traders had left the German market.

The New Directives of the European Community

The EC Commission observed this development very critically and saw its first liberalization initiative largely undermined. Consequently, the commission started a new initiative to further advance the liberalization of the gas and electricity market. These endeavours resulted in the two 'Acceleration directives.'[8] They were enacted on 26 June 2003 and had to be implemented into national law by 1 July 2004.

The requirements of the new directives were much higher, compared to the previous directives from 1996 and 1998 that had initiated the first movement of liberalization (for details, see Cameron's analysis in chapter 7). The first major change was the obligatory introduction of regulated grid access, thereby banning the negotiated grid access that had been practised in Germany so far. The second important change was that the member states had to establish a regulatory authority with considerable powers. The main task of the regulatory authority should be ensuring the efficient functioning of the market by supervising the energy companies and implementing the principle of non-discrimination. The main instrument for the authority should be the permission of fees, or at least the control of the methods for the calculation of fees for the access to the grids, as well as particular powers to intervene into the price policies subsequently (ex post). A third central element of the new directives was the extensive provision on the so-called unbundling, that is, the separation of the production of energy and the operation of the grids. The directives required functional and legal unbundling as well as unbundling of accounting and confidentiality. The regulatory authority should also have substantive powers in monitoring the unbundling.

The new EC directives from 2003 required a major shift for the German energy law, particularly in the model for the grid access and the role for the regulatory authority. The German legislature took the directives from Brussels as a starting point for the complete revision of the German energy law. The initiative for legal reform was started by government already in 2003, but the legislative debate was rather complicated as a result of the strong demands of different lobbying groups whose interests were often in conflict. Thus, the process of leg-

Table 10.1 Overview of key provisions of the New Energy Industry Act of 2005

Key provisions	Related aspects
Unbundling	Legal and operational unbundling Confidentiality Accounting unbundling Monitoring tasks of the regulatory authority
Energy supply to consumers	Obligation of general supply (under free choice of suppliers) Compensatory supply Misuse of surveillance by state authorities Electricity labelling
Siting permission of energy facilities	Standardized procedure Local concession contracts and fees Use of roads
Security, energy supply	Supply inventory Monitoring Call for new production capacities
Regulatory authorities	Responsibility for network access Cooperation of authorities (cartel, state, and federal) General instructions
Procedure	Procedures before regulation authorities: Investigation rights Legal means Sanctions/fines

islation took until 2005 and the new Energy Industry Act was finally enacted in July 2005.

The Different Models for the Regulation of Network Access Fees

The EC directive prescribed that the 'regulatory authorities shall have the authority to require transmission and distribution system operators, if necessary, to modify the terms and conditions, tariffs, rules, mechanisms and methodologies … , to ensure that they are proportionate and applied in a non-discriminatory manner.' This provision could be implemented into national law in different ways (Hummel and Theobald 2003, 178). Firstly, the system of the negotiated access and the Associations' Agreement could be continued, whereby the methods in the agreements would then have to be approved by the authority. The advantage of this system is that the market participants can negotiate prices in line with their preferences, whereas the role of the regulatory authority, which might find it difficult to ascertain the fair fees in every case, is limited. Secondly, the state could establish conditions for access to the grids, either by parliamentary regulation or by government regulation, and the authority would supervise the compliance with these legal requirements subsequently (ex post). Thirdly, the authority could have the function to approve the compliance of network access fees with the legal requirements in advance (ex ante). This means that the authority has to control the fees in each single case.

The different models for the regulation of network access fees were a central point in the discussion of the new energy law in Germany. The German legislature eventually opted for the ex ante control and thus gave the regulatory authority a stronger role. This must be seen not only in connection with the political pressure for lower energy prices and the expectation that a stronger control would guarantee a higher drop of the network access fees and, as a result, of the energy prices in general. It is also in line with the existing German model for the control of energy prices for the end customers and the system of price control in the telecommunications sector. As the questions of 'if' and 'how' of the access to grids have generally become a regulated grid access already under the former Energy Industry Act by means of antitrust law and court rulings (see above), the new legal situation does not mean such a major change as it might appear at first.

The Regulated Access to Grids under Current Law

The general rule for access to grids is that any network operator must provide access to its grid for an energy producer on a non-discriminatory basis; the network operator may deny access only if it is impossible or unreasonable. Moreover, conditions and fees for access to the grid must be reasonable, non-discriminatory, and transparent. The Energy Industry Act provides that the details for the conditions for access to grids and the calculation of fees are to be regulated in government regulations. These regulations, which were enacted separately for the gas and the electricity sectors, came into force shortly after the Energy Industry Act at the end of July 2005.[9]

According to the Energy Industry Act 2005 and the regulations, the fees must be calculated on the basis of the real costs of the particular network operator. These costs must be ascertained on the basis of an efficient and structurally comparable network operator and must exclude costs that would not arise in a competitive situation (see Section 21, Energy Industry Act). Procedurally, the network operators must file an application proposing a certain fee, which must be ascertained by a calculation in accordance with the legal requirements and the relevant data of the company. The deadlines for the first applications for network fees were the end of October 2005 for electricity and the end of January for gas network operators. The first permissions were granted in 2006 (also see Becker and Boos 2006, 297). With regard to Section 21a of the Energy Industry Act 2005 and the ongoing legislative work, the cost-based system of network fees described above will soon be replaced by a so-called incentive-based regulation.

The regulated access to grids under the new law does not mean that all details of the grid access are directly prescribed by the regulatory authority. Instead, the modalities of the network access can still be regulated on a contractual basis between the user and the owner of the grid. Especially in the gas sector, this has caused a lot of controversy. Although Section 20 (1b) of the Energy Industry Act 2005 clearly obliges gas network operators to apply an entry-exit model, it took over eighteen months to put it into practice. In any case, the relevant contracts have to be cleared by the regulatory authority, and the authority is even entitled to interfere in the contractual relations and to change provisions of a contract. Thus, it can be expected that the energy companies will develop such agreements and to put them forward to their partners, and that these agreements will become more standardized over the next few years.

The Provisions on Unbundling

It was said before that in the German energy market the production of energy and the operation of the grids are traditionally in the hand of the same companies, which is an obstacle for a functioning competition on the energy market. Therefore, in addition to the elaborate network regulation regime, the provisions on unbundling – the separation of network operation and energy supply – are another central part of the new energy law. At the same time it must also be emphasized that the regulation of network access and unbundling are two sides of the same coin, since the objective of both instruments is fair grid access without discrimination. The particular role of unbundling lies in creating the general circumstances for fair network access.

The provisions of the German law in relation to unbundling are very closely related to the European directives. Accordingly, they do not provide for ownership unbundling, meaning the obligation that the different branches of energy supply and production must be owned by different companies. However, any so-called vertically integrated company has to implement four other forms of unbundling. Firstly, operational unbundling must be implemented, which means that the management of the network operator must be separated from other branches of the company. Secondly, legal unbundling requires that the network operator is legally independent from the other branches and activities of the company. Thirdly, a vertically integrated company must keep separate accounts and establish a separate profit and loss statement for every area of operation (unbundling of accounts). Finally, informational unbundling requires that the company must treat economically sensitive information confidentially and must disclose economically advantageous information in a non-discriminatory manner so that competing network operators do not have disadvantages.

The provisions on legal and operational unbundling do not apply to companies that have fewer than 100,000 customers directly or indirectly connected to their grid. This means that at least very small enterprises do not have to comply with the extensive provisions on unbundling. But for a great number of small and medium-sized electricity and gas suppliers in Germany with more than 100,000 customers, the unbundling provisions apply without exception. For these companies, the extensive legal obligations of the unbundling provisions can mean high additional transaction costs due to the excessive administrative requirements of the law. As a consequence, the weakening of the smaller companies by the unbundling provisions possibly have the opposite outcome and will result in an increasing vertical forward integration. Whereas the general aim of unbundling must be appreciated, the dangers of the current regulation must not be underestimated.

The Authorities

The Situation before 2005

Under the former Energy Industry Act, the regulation of the energy market was mainly in the hands of the energy authorities of the federal states. The cartel authorities played an important role in the regulation of the energy market due to the important provisions in the cartel laws on the access to grids. Cartel authorities exist both on the national level and in the federal states, but in practice, in most cases, only the federal authority – whose responsibility grew with the size of the energy companies – was relevant.

The responsibility of both the energy and the cartel authorities meant an extraordinary doubling of authorities without a clear demarcation of the competences for the different authorities. In practice, as stated above, the cartel authorities played a much more prominent role in the regulation of the energy market, whereas the energy authorities of the federal states made only very limited use of their competences.

The Competences of the Bundesnetzagentur
(National Regulatory Authority)

Under the new Energy Industry Act 2005, a new central regulative authority was created. It emerged from the former regulatory authority for the post and telecommunications market (Regulierungsbehörde für Post und Telekommunikation). The new Energy Industry Act assigned this authority the additional task of regulating electricity and gas networks and was renamed Bundesnetzagentur (Federal Network Agency). Its seat is in the former German capital, Bonn. In the regulation of the energy grids it has extensive power. Its main task is regulation of access to grids and particularly the permission of network access fees. Moreover, it has to control implementation of the unbundling provisions. A new central function of the authority is the comprehensive control over operators of energy networks with regard to the abuse of their market power and the non-discrimination of network users. This includes wide procedural rights to enforce the operators' compliance with the legal provisions, such as the right to require information from the companies, including sensitive information and the right to enter and to search the business premises under certain conditions. The regulatory authorities may also enforce damages and impose fines.

The Structure of Energy Authorities under the
New Energy Industry Act 2005

It is one of the remarkable features of the new act that the legislator decided for a federal structure of regulatory authorities – that all sixteen federal states have the option of creating their own regulatory authority. This decision was taken particularly in response to political pressure by the German federal states, which had to consent to the new Energy Industry Act and whose interests had to be taken into account during the legislative process in the Bundesrat (for details on the effects of federalism on energy governance, see chapter 1 of this volume). For the smaller German federal states, however, the establishment of their own energy authorities may be a relatively high burden due to limited financial and staff capacities. It has therefore been decided that the competences of the authorities in these federal states can be performed by the Federal Network Agency. German administrative law provides for these cases the instrument of the so-called *Organleihe* (lending of organs of state). It gives one state the right to make use of the administrative capacity of another state authority. While the state confers the responsibility of one of its authorities to another authority, it keeps the responsibility and the right to give directions to the other authority. If responsibilities are conferred to the Federal Network Agency in this way, it is consequently – in this limited area – under the control of the federal states. Although this procedure is not provided in the new Energy Industry Act, it has been approved in the legislative process for the energy authorities. Amongst others, the federal states of Bremen, Schleswig-Holstein, Berlin, and Mecklenburg-Vorpommern decided not to establish their own energy authorities and to confer their rights to the Federal Network Agency.

Section 54 (2) of the Energy Industry Act lists the competences of the energy authorities in the states. Its responsibilities are generally limited to energy companies with up to 100,000 customers connected to their grid and whose network is situated in only one federal state. For these companies the authorities in the federal states do not have all of the competences, but most of the important responsibilities – such as the permission of network access fees – are included. In cases where no competence is legally established, the federal Bundesnetzagentur is, according to Section 54 (3), the competent authority, thereby constituting the leading role of the federal agency.

The Remaining Role of the Cartel Authorities

The new act now provides for the primary responsibility of the energy authorities in all matters that are completely regulated in the new Energy Industry Act. This mainly refers to the above-mentioned issues of the regulation of grid access and the general control of the network operators' behaviour in the market. The Energy Industry Act, however, does not regulate the German energy law comprehensively. Consequently, it does not give the energy authorities, in particular the Federal Network Agency, a comprehensive responsibility for all issues in relation to energy law and energy companies.

Although the act means a substantive extension of responsibilities for the energy authorities, the cartel authorities will keep important areas of competence under the new law (Büdenbender and Rosin 2005, 221, 289). Thus, cartel authorities will remain competent for the cartel contracts and in particular for the control of mergers. Cartel authorities will also be responsible for cases of the abuse of a dominant position in the market if it is not related to the area of grid access and grid connection. For example, energy prices can be subject to investigation by the cartel authorities. This is particularly important, due to the fact that the federal control for electricity prices (Bundestarifordnung Elektrizität) expired on 1 July 2007, leaving companies relatively free to set prices. In that respect, the federal government has taken initiatives to strengthen the power of the cartel authorities by introducing a shift in the burden of proof, meaning that energy companies have to give legitimate reasons for demanding high energy prices. Otherwise, it is supposed by law that energy companies are abusing the dominant market position. Consequently, the cartel authorities can take appropriate actions.

In order to achieve an effective functioning of both authorities and to prevent contradictory decisions, the new Energy Industry Act 2005 establishes certain duties of cooperation. Apart from a general obligation for mutual support and rights to exchange information, it is also provided that in certain matters the authorities may take their decisions with the consent of the other.

The Current Energy Market in the Wake of Liberalization

Monopolization and Regulation

Since the first major reform of energy regulation in German in 1998, the German energy market has undergone major changes. It must, however, be stated that the objectives of the liberalization have not been completely achieved. Hence, the public's and also the legislator's perception that the first liberalization move did not lead to the expected results the act had been aimed at, were – besides the directives from the European level – the main reason for the second reform of energy law in 2005.

A major problem – and probably the main reason for the unexpected shortages of the liberalization in the German energy market in many respects – was the enormous market concentration that had taken place after the first liberalization move. The high level of market concentration has also been highlighted by the Monopolkommission (German Monopoly Commission, 2004, IV. 2). The commission concluded that the market structures are very similar to the closed monopolies before liberalization. It observed that a great number of mergers resulted in an oligopoly without a real competition. Moreover – according to the Monopoly Commission – shares of the big companies in the small regional companies prevented new competing companies' access to the markets. Similarly, the Federal Cartel Office revised its positive forecast from 2000 (Vieth 2003, 90). The critical evaluation of the German energy market is reinforced by the sector inquiry of the European Commission of 2005, which critically assesses the German energy market.

Market Concentration in the German Energy Market

The market concentration was the result of a number of mergers in the energy market after the first liberalization move (Zenke, Neveling, and Lokau 2005, 32). Hence, there were mergers between VEBA and VIAG, becoming the new company E.ON, which thereby became the biggest electricity supplier in the German market. Moreover, RWE merged with VEW and now constitutes the second-biggest German electricity supplier. Another significant electricity company, EnBW, got a new shareholder EdF, being the only major foreign market participant. Finally, Vattenfall took over a number of smaller companies – many of these takeovers were the result of duties to sell participations in the course of the mergers of VEBA and VIAG as well as RWE and VEW – and thereby became the fourth force amongst the big market participants on the German energy market.

As a result, in the field of electricity there now exists an oligopoly of E.ON, RWE, EnBW, and Vattenfall, which altogether control more than 80 per cent of the domestic capacities of energy production and at the same time own major parts of the grids. Moreover, these companies hold several shares in smaller companies on the regional and municipal level. Amongst the four big companies in the German energy

Figure 10.3. Market concentration in German energy market

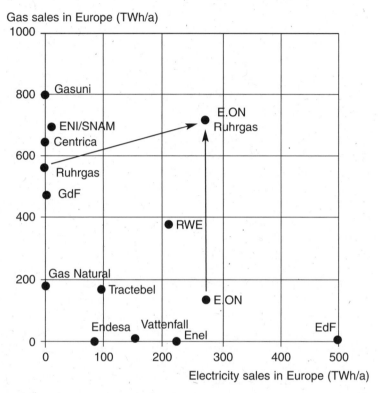

Source: Enervis Energy Advisors GmbH (0000).

market, E.ON and RWE are by far the two leading forces in the market, so that one can even speak of a duopoly on the energy market.

The Merger of E.ON and Ruhrgas

The market concentration in the German energy market culminated in the integration of the biggest German gas supplier, Ruhrgas, into the E.ON corporate group to the new company of E.ON Ruhrgas in 2003 (for details, see Zenke, Neveling and Lokau 2005, chap. 4). This company is now the biggest supplier of gas and electricity within the European Union.

The Federal Cartel Office had initially rejected the merger between the two companies because it regarded it as an impediment for a functioning competition in the energy market.[10] According to German competition law, the rejection of a merger by the cartel authority can, however, be overruled by the minister of economics, who can grant a *Ministererlaubnis* (ministerial permission) on the grounds of a special interest for the national economy or an outstanding interest for the general public. In July 2002, the minister of economy acceded to the application of the two companies by granting a ministerial permission. One of the major arguments for the permission was the idea of a 'national champion' – the argument that Germany needed a company that was able to compete with the other big companies in Europe. This was considered an important tool for ensuring the secure supply of the German energy market with gas on reasonable conditions. Besides, job security and the more effective protection of the environment were brought forward in favour of the merger.

After a multitude of plaintiffs had taken legal action against the ministerial permission, it was declared unlawful and thus invalid by the Higher Regional Court in Düsseldorf.[11] The minister reacted to the defeat in court by granting a new permission only three months later in September 2002 on changed conditions, which supposedly were in line with the ruling of the court. These conditions included the obligation to sell certain shares in other companies as well as special contractual rights of termination and a gas release program. The following spectacular court proceedings against this second permission, which involved a multitude of plaintiffs, were eventually settled out of court. The merger could then be completed in February 2003.

In view of the structure of the German energy market, the permission of the merger between E.ON and Ruhrgas must be criticized. Considering the existing market concentration, the national economy and the interests of the German energy consumers would have rather required a segmentation of the market, not an even stronger concentration. The interest for a domestic company that can compete on the international markets cannot compensate for the negative effects on the German market.

Conclusions

The analysis has shown the complexity and multi-level nature of Germany's system for regulating energy and its difficult coordination problems as market liberalization was sought in Germany and through EU regulatory change. The chapter has shown how the legal framework for the regulation of the German energy market has undergone enormous changes in the last decade. Whereas the first Energy Industry Act dating back to 1935 was in force with minor modifications until 1998 and thus for over sixty years, the second act lasted only seven years until 2005. Concurrent with the acceleration of the development of the law, the extent of the legal provisions has grown enormously. Hence, the current Energy Industry Act comprises 126 sections, whereas the former consisted of only 24.

While the German energy market is still characterized by a high number of energy companies in particular on the municipal level, competition has not developed satisfactorily. The concentration in the energy supply market must be considered the main obstacle for a functioning competition in the energy market. The problem is aggravated by the fact that the big companies own a substantive part of the relevant networks. Generally, one can observe that pressure groups try to protect the closed market in an extremely hard-fought energy market.

The relevance of market concentration on the energy supply market has often been underestimated in the debate on the regulation of the energy market. Instead, the discussion has focused mainly on the regulated grid access in Germany and thus overshadowed the problematic development of market concentration. Although fair and reasonable access to grids is an important tool for opening the market to new competing companies, it is questionable whether it will fully challenge the predominance of the currently existing oligopoly. A reasonable access to grids might be of limited value for new or existing competing companies only if they suffer from other general disadvantages in the market. Moreover, it must be realized that the current regulation might also mean a way of raising transaction costs in particular for smaller companies. This might then even jeopardize the actual objective of the European directives to lead to competition and a greater number of competitors.

The new Energy Industry Act from 2005 and the European directives have been enacted in part as a reaction to the disappointing results of the liberalization. The central modifications of the new regulative framework are the new provisions on unbundling, as well as the introduction of regulated access to grids with an ex-ante control of the network tariffs. While the former model of negotiated access had taken a number of features of a regulated grid access due to the importance of the Associations' Agreements, the ex-ante control is a completely new feature in the German energy market. By implementing the European directive and creating a regulated grid access, Germany now leaves its special path. Moreover, by extending the provisions on unbundling, Germany also changes the focus of its energy regulation, which had so far concentrated on the competition around energy networks and the network tariffs for third parties.

The effects of the new energy law cannot be fully assessed yet. Apart from the normative content of the new law, the role of the new regulatory authority as well as the courts and their application of the legal provisions will be of central importance. The first indications by the Federal Network Agency on its view on the application of certain provisions under the new Energy Industry Act appear, however, to be disappointing. Thus, the regulative authority prefers interpretations that result in discrimination for smaller companies, particularly the municipal companies, in comparison to the companies of the oligopoly. Thus, the application of provisions on the consideration of business taxes and capital resources in the calculation of network fees are more unfavourable for the municipal companies than for the 'big players' (Theobald and Böck 2006, 1). As a consequence, there is a danger that the regulative authority, which intends to create better conditions for competition on the German energy market, in fact achieves the opposite by weakening the municipal companies and thereby destroying the basis for competition – the multitude of competitive companies (danger of 'concentration by regulation').

There can be no doubt that the main challenges for both the energy and the cartel authorities in the future will remain the problems resulting from the market concentration. In view of the disappointing results so far, the prominent role of Europe as a promoter of effective liberalization in the energy market will remain of crucial importance.

ACKNOWLEDGMENT

The author would like to thank Sven Fischerauer for his contribution to the revision of this chapter.

NOTES

1   Comprehensive statistics on the German energy market are also provided by the German Ministry of Economics and can be found at http://www.bmwi.de/BMWi/Navigation/Energie/Energiestatistiken/energiedaten.html.

2 BGBl. (Federal Law Gazette) 1998 I, 730 ff.

3 Directive 96/92/EC, OJ L27, 20 ff. (30.1.1997); Directive 98/30/EC, OJ L204, 1 ff. (22.6.1998).

4 Good professional practice is a legal construct that allows for some degree of industry self-regulation, provided that industry practice complies with the basic goals of legislation. This includes, for example, rules on how information on available network capacity needs to be made available.

5 See, for example, Higher Regional Court Karlsruhe, *Recht der Energiewirtschaft* (Law of the Energy Industry) 2005, 51; Higher Regional Court Düsseldorf, *Recht der Energiewirtschaft* (Law of the Energy Industry) 2004, 118.

6 Higher Regional Court Düsseldorf, *Recht der Energiewirtschaft* (Law of the Energy Industry) 2004, 118 ff.

7 Higher Regional Court Düsseldorf, *Wirtschaft und Wettbewerb* (*Journal of German and European Competition Law*) 2002 494 ff.; Higher Regional Court Stuttgart, *Zeitschrift für Neues Energierecht* (*Journal of New Energy Law*) 2002, 232 ff.

8 Directive 2003/55/EC, OJ L176, 37 ff.; Directive 2003/55/EC, OJ L176, 57 ff.

9 *Verordnung über den Zugang zu Elektrizitätsversorgungsnetzen* (Electricity Network Access Regulation), BGBl. 2005 I, 2243 ff.; *Verordnung über die Entgelte für den Zugang zu Elektrizitätsversorgungsnetzen* (Electricity Network Tariff Regulation), BGBl. 2005 I, 2225 ff.; *Verordnung über den Zugang zu Gasversorgungsnetzen* (Gas Network Access Regulation), BGBl. 2005 I, 2210 ff.; *Verordnung über die Entgelte für den Zugang zu Gasversorgungsnetzen* (Gas Network Tariff Regulation), BGBl. 2005 I, 2197 ff.

10 Bundeskartellamt (Federal Cartel Office) (17.1.2002), *Wirtschaft und Wettbewerb*/E DE-V (Journal of German and European Competition Law – Germany / Public Administration) 2002, 511 ff., 533 ff.

11 *Wirtschaft und Wettbewerb* / E DE-V (*Journal of German and European Competition Law – Germany / Public Administration*) 2002, 885 ff.

REFERENCES

Becker, Peter, and Philipp Boos. 2006. Stromnetzentgeltprüfungen durch die Regulierungsbehörden: Genehmigungsbescheide und erste Gerichtsentscheidungen [Control of electricity network access fees by the regulatory authorities: Permissions and first judgments]. *Zeitschrift für Neues Energierecht* [*Journal of New Energy Law*] 12 (2): 297–303.

Büdenbender, Ulrich, and Peter Rosin. 2005. *Energierechtsreform 2005* [Reform of Energy Law 2005], vol. 1. Essen: Energie and Technik (ETV).

De Wyl, Christian, and Joachim Müller-Kirchbauer. 2003. Vertragliche Ausgestaltung der Netznutzung bei Strom und Gas [Contractual embodiment of network usage in electricity and gas]. In *Handbuch zum Recht der Energiewirtschaft* [Handbook on the law of the energy industry], ed. Jens-Peter Schneider and Christian Theobald, 762–75. Munich: Beck.

Held, Christian. 2003. *Structural and legal requirements of the energy market in Germany*. Frankfurt/Main: Associated European Energy Consultants (AEEC).

Hummel, Konrad, and Christian Theobald. 2003. Entgeltregulierung im künftigen Energiewirtschaftsrecht [Tariff regulation in the future law of the energy industry]. *Zeitschrift für Neues Energierecht* [Journal of New Energy Law] 7 (3): 176–84.

Monopolkommission, ed. 2004. Wettbewerbspolitik im Schatten 'Nationaler Champions' 15. Hauptgutachten [Competition policy in the shadow of 'national champions,'15th Main Report] 2002/2003. Baden-Baden.

Nill-Theobald, Christiane, and Christian Theobald. 2008. *Grundzüge des Energiewirtschaftsrechts* [Main features of the law of the energy industry]. 2nd ed. Munich: Beck.

Schiffer, Hans-Wilhelm. 2007. Deutscher Energiemarkt 2006 [German energy market 2006]. *Energiewirtschaftliche Tagesfragen* [Daily issues of the energy industry] 7 (3): 32–6.

Theobald, Christian. 2003a. *Competition in the German electricity and gas industries*. Frankfurt/Main: Associated European Energy Consultants.

– 2003b. Grundlagen des deutschen Rechts der Energiewirtschaft [Basics of the German law of the energy industry]. In *Handbuch zum Recht der Energiewirtschaft* [*Handbook on the law of the energy industry*], ed. Jens-Peter Schneider and Christian Theobald, 4–10. Munich: Beck.

Theobald, Christian, and Rudolf Böck. 2006. Werden Städte sturmreif geschossen? [Are cities subject to a softening-up barrage?]. *Zeitung für kommunale Wirtschaft* [*Journal of Municipal Industry*] (February) 4:1–12.

Vieth, Reinhard. 2003. Die Entwicklung der Fusionskontrolle im Energiewirtschaftsbereich in den letzten zwei Jahren [The development of energy industry merger control in the past two years]. *Zeitschrift für Neues Energierecht* [Journal of New Energy Law] 7 (2): 90–102.

Zenke, Ines, Stefanie Neveling, and Bernhard Lokau. 2005. *Konzentration in der Energiewirtschaft* [Concentration in the energy industry]. Munich: Beck.

11 Talking without Walking: Canada's Ineffective Climate Effort

NIC RIVERS AND MARK JACCARD

Since the late 1980s, Canada has been an active participant in international negotiations to limit emissions of greenhouse gases (GHG) in order to reduce the risk of human-induced climate change. In these processes it has made several commitments to decrease its domestic GHG emissions. To meet these commitments, the government's dominant policy approach has been to provide information and subsidies to encourage Canadian businesses and consumers to voluntarily shift to technologies and lifestyles that reduce GHG emissions.

As chapters 1 and 2 have shown, however, during this period domestic GHG emissions have continued to rise and the country's GHG trajectory shows no signs of deflecting downward. In fact, domestic emissions have risen more rapidly in the past fifteen years than in the preceding decade of 1980 to 1990 when government had no GHG policy.

In this chapter, we attempt to explain the reasons why Canada has done a lot of talking but not walking when it comes to GHG emissions reduction. Some of the reasons relate to complex forces of growth that governments are usually unable or unwilling to control in pursuit of environmental objectives: population growth, economic growth, and growth in the exploitation of valuable natural resources such as the oil sands of Alberta. Some of the reasons relate to reliance on ineffective policies, such as information and subsidies, to induce wide-scale voluntary actions by firms and households. These ineffective policies are explained in part by a poor understanding of the full costs of technological change. They are also explained by jurisdictional and regional divisions in Canada and, as Clarkson's analysis in chapter 4 has shown, by the country's close trading ties to the United States – a country that has refused to make a national commitment to reduce GHGs.

Finally, it is important to recognize that Canada's Kyoto target is much more challenging that almost any other Kyoto signatory, presumably the consequence of poor preparation and lack of coordination or unrealistic optimism during the international negotiation of national commitments. This does not justify Canada's continued emissions growth, but it helps explain why Canada's gap between commitment and reality is extreme, relative to other signatories of the Kyoto Protocol, including that of Germany, as examined by Weidner and Eberlein in chapter 12.

Government Commitments versus Actual Emissions

In 1988, Canada hosted the World Conference on the Changing Atmosphere, the first scientific conference on climate change. During these talks, Canada developed a target of reducing its output of GHG by 20 per cent from 1988 levels by 2005. Later that year, Canada pushed to have climate change included on the agenda for G7 talks. During these discussions, Canada's prime minister made an international commitment to stabilize national GHG emissions at 1990 levels by 2000.

These commitments were echoed in national policy documents in 1990, and again committed to internationally at the 1992 Earth Summit in Rio de Janeiro, when Canada ratified the United Nations Framework Convention on Climate Change (UNFCCC), which came into effect in 1994. This latter agreement was superseded by the Kyoto Protocol to the UNFCCC, under which Canada committed to a 6 per cent reduction from 1990 GHG emissions levels during the period 2008–2012. Canada signed the Kyoto Protocol in 1997 and ratified it in 2002. In 2005, Canada hosted the first Meeting of the Parties to the Kyoto Protocol, the largest intergovernmental climate conference since the Kyoto Protocol was adopted in 1997. More recently, mounting public pressure and increasing scientific confidence has spurred the Canadian government to make new longer-term emissions-reductions commitments. As chapter 1 has shown, in 2007 the Conservative federal government promised to reduce emissions by 20 per cent by 2020 and by 65 per cent by 2050, compared to 2006 levels.

While Canada has been an engaged participant in the negotiation of international agreements to abate climate change, the evolution of its GHG emissions stands in sharp contrast to the domestic commitments

Figure 11.1 GHG emissions in Canada, 1990–2003, and international commitments to reduce GHG emissions

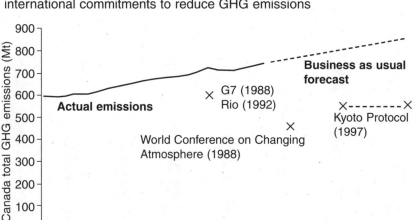

Source: Canada's Greenhouse Gas Inventory 2005 (Environment Canada 2006).

it has agreed to. Figure 11.1 compares Canada's international commitments to reduce GHG emissions with its actual emissions record from 1990 to 2003. Canada's emissions had risen to 24 per cent above 1990 levels by 2003, meaning that it has missed targets agreed to at the 1988 G7 meeting, the 1992 Earth Summit in Rio, and the 1988 World Conference on the Changing Atmosphere. In addition, Canada's domestic emissions will greatly exceed its Kyoto commitment in the 2008–2012 target period. Current estimates are that, in spite of domestic commitments and apparent policy efforts, Canada's emissions are on a path to exceed its Kyoto target to a very significant extent in 2010 (Government of Canada 2005).

Canada's record on GHG emission reduction appears to be more ineffective than that of other G7 countries, including the United States, even though the latter has refused to ratify the Kyoto Protocol. Figure 11.2 shows that Canada's high level of GHG emissions per capita in 1990 had increased by 2002, while that of the United States and most other countries declined. Japan and Italy saw some increase in per capita emissions, but their levels remain less than half that of Canada. At an aggregate level, Canada's increase of over 20 per cent

Figure 11.2 GHG intensity per capita in G7 countries, 1990 and 2002

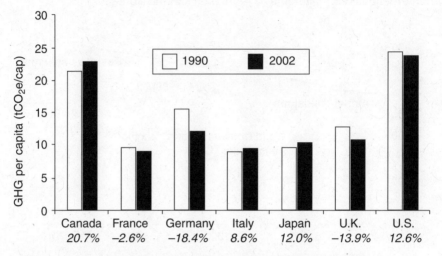

Source: United Nations Framework Convention on Climate Change.
Note: Values below columns show total 1990–2002 growth in GHG
emissions (not per capita).

in its total emissions during this period far exceeds that of any other
G7 country.

To understand why Canada's GHG emission abatement effort has
been so ineffective in achieving, or even progressing toward, its international commitments, it can be helpful to distinguish between the different drivers of GHG emissions. The Kaya Identity (Kaya 1990)
decomposes total GHG emissions into a series of explanatory factors:

$$GHG = \sum_{ij} Pop \cdot \frac{GDP}{Pop} \cdot \frac{GDP_i}{GDP} \cdot \frac{E_i}{GDP_i} \cdot \frac{E_{ij}}{E_i} \cdot \frac{GHG_{ij}}{E_{ij}}$$

Pop is population, *GDP* is gross domestic product, and *E* is energy,
and where the subscript *i* indexes subsectors of the economy and *j*
indexes fuel types. The Kaya Identity shows that total GHG emissions
in a country result from the size of the population, per capita income
(GDP per capita), economic structure (relative size of different sectors

of the economy), energy intensity (the amount of energy consumed per unit of GDP produced in each sector of the economy), fuel mix, and GHG per unit of fuel (a result of fuel type and/or the existence of GHG emission-capture technologies). A change in any of these factors, everything else held constant, changes the overall GHG emissions of a country.

Typically, governments consider the first three factors in the equation – population, per capita income, and economic structure – to be drivers of GHG emissions that are unavailable as levers for emissions policy. No government yet has tried to slow population or economic growth, or to redirect economic activity, as part of its climate policy. These are therefore even further broader aspects of both complexity and coordination, as suggested in the framework introduced in chapter 1 and examined further in chapter 15.

Instead, government GHG control policies focus on changing the evolution of the last three factors in the equation – reducing the amount of energy consumed to produce a unit of output in the economy (energy efficiency), lowering the relative share of high GHG emission fuels (fuel substitution away from high-emission fossil fuels like coal), and GHG emissions controls. In the following section we focus on the uncontrolled drivers of GHG emissions and show that at least part of Canada's fast growth in emissions is due to demographic and economic factors that are generally considered outside the scope of climate change policy.

Uncontrolled Drivers of GHG Emissions

Population Growth

Compared to most other developed countries, Canada has a very high rate of population growth. As shown in figure 11.3, Canada's population increased by 1.05 per cent annually between 1990 and 2002. Of the G7 countries, only the United States had a faster population growth rate during this period, and population growth in the other five G7 countries was much slower.

Canada's population growth rate results from the combination of two factors: a natural increase (birth rate – death rate) of about 0.4 per cent per year, and a net immigration of about 0.65 per cent per year. Although Canada's natural rate of increase during this period is

Figure 11.3 Population growth in G7 countries, 1990–2002

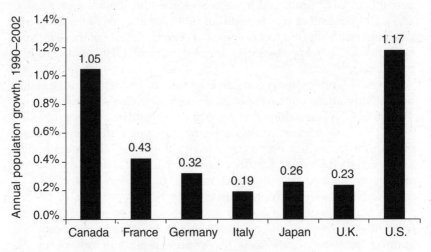

Source: Energy Information Administration 2003.

second only to that of the United States, it is Canada's high immigration rate that has contributed most to the relatively high population growth from 1990 to 2002. Canada had the highest immigration rate of the G7 countries during the period, about 17 per cent higher than the United States, and far higher still than European countries and Japan (Statistics Canada 2005).

Canada's relatively fast growing population has been an important contributor to its increasing GHG emissions. Had its growth rate been 0.3 per cent per year, similar to that of the European countries and Japan, Canada's GHG emissions would have grown only by 10.6 per cent from 1990 to 2003, instead of 24 per cent.

Canada's population growth rate is likely to remain high, relative to that of other developed countries, for several decades to come. Because it has a higher birth rate and somewhat younger population than European countries, Canada's death rate is not expected to exceed its birth rate until about 2025 (Statistics Canada 2005). Further, there is no indication that Canada will attempt to lower its immigration rate in the near future. As a result, population growth will continue to exert a strong upward influence on overall GHG emissions in Canada for the foreseeable future.

Figure 11.4 Trends in economic growth in G7 countries, 1990–2002

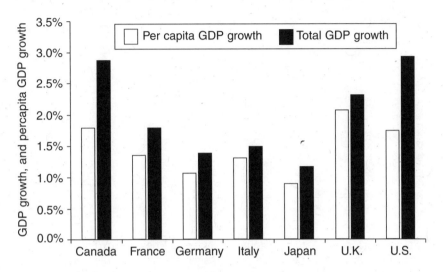

Source: Energy Information Administration 2003.

Economic Growth

Canada's annual GDP growth (US$2000) from 1990 to 2002 was 2.9 per cent, equal to that of the United States and significantly greater than that of all other G7 countries (Energy Information Administration 2003). Economic growth in Canada surpassed that of Europe and Japan in part because of much faster population growth, but also because Canada's per capita GDP grew much faster than that of all other G7 countries except the United Kingdom. Trends in both total GDP growth and per capita GDP growth are shown in figure 11.4.

This trend is important because in the absence of energy efficiency, fuel switching, or emission controls, economic growth will cause rising GHG emissions in the country's fossil fuel–based energy system. If Canada's per capita GDP had grown at 1.1 per cent annually as in most of Europe and Japan, emissions would have grown by only 12.1 per cent from 1990 to 2003, instead of 24 per cent.

Canada's GDP is expected to continue its rapid growth rate. A projection by the Conference Board of Canada (2004) suggests that

Figure 11.5 Canadian oil sands output and forecast, 1975–2015

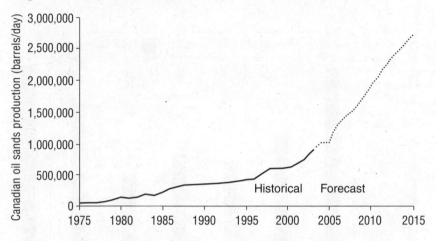

Source: Historical oil sands output from National Energy Board (2004). Forecasted oil sands output from Canadian Association of Petroleum Producers (2005).

Canada's GDP will grow at an average rate of 2.6 per cent through 2025.

Oil Sands Growth

With 174 billion barrels of proven oil reserves, Alberta's oil sands make Canada the country with the second-largest oil reserves in the world after Saudi Arabia (*Oil and Gas Journal* 2002). Limited commercial development of the oil sands started in 1967, but engineering challenges and high extraction costs constrained output for several decades. However, since the mid-1990s, technological advances, and more recently higher world crude oil prices, have stimulated significant expansion of oil sands operations. Daily oil sands production has tripled in volume since 1990, and is projected by the National Energy Board to continue its rapid growth (figure 11.5).

Oil sands are extracted either by surface mining (and then washed to remove bitumen from sand, silt, and clay) or by injecting steam into deeper deposits, which frees oil from the sand and drives it to the surface. The resulting heavy oil must be upgraded through the addition of hydrogen. Each of these steps requires a significant amount of energy and, as a result, extracting oil from oil sands is more GHG- and energy-intensive than extracting it from conventional oil fields.[1]

Canada's surging oil sands production is an important reason for its increasing GHG emissions. We estimate that increases in oil sands production between 1990 and 2003 have increased Canada's GHG emissions by about 15–20 megatonnes (Mt). Without growth in oil sands since 1990, Canada's emissions would have increased by only 21 per cent instead of 24 per cent. The forecasted rapid expansion of oil sands production will continue to exert strong upward pressure on Canada's GHG emissions in the foreseeable future.

Ineffective Policies

As noted, governments have been unwilling or unable to restrain population growth, per capita income increases, or economic structural change (such as increasing oil sands production) using climate change policy. In fact, the Canadian government has aggressively pursued increases in population (through a high immigration rate), per capita income growth (through economic development and taxation policies), and oil sands production (through tax exemptions and research assistance for oil sands developers). Growth in all of these factors has significantly increased GHG emissions in Canada since 1990.

In this section, we assess the policies that the Canadian government has applied to influence those GHG emissions factors that it perceives to be within its domain: energy efficiency, fuel switching, and emissions control. We present reasons why its policies have been ineffective. These include underestimation of the full cost of GHG emissions reduction, and the choice of non-compulsory policies that are ineffective at changing technology choices by firms and households when GHG emissions reduction is costly. We conclude the section by explaining Canadian-specific obstacles in achieving effective policies in Canada.

Underestimating the Full Cost of Reducing GHG Emissions

Since climate change has been recognized as a serious environmental problem, researchers have attempted to understand the costs associated with greenhouse gas abatement, especially from the energy sector (Jaccard, Nyboer, Bataille, and Sadownik 2003). Researchers have historically fallen into two groups. Environmentalists and engineers have a good understanding of technologies, but a limited understanding of economics and human behaviour. They tend to see myriad technological opportunities throughout the economy for cost-effective reductions of greenhouse gas emissions. For example, their typical analysis of the transportation system shows simultaneous GHG benefits and financial cost savings for individuals that would accompany a wholesale switch from private automobiles to public transit. They call such examples no regrets opportunities for GHG reductions. Because they identify many no regrets opportunities, they conclude that the cost of major GHG reductions is small or even negative. Given this low cost, they often recommend that government use information and subsidies to convince households and firms to act on these GHG reduction opportunities for financial gain or for moral reasons.

The second group consists primarily of economists, who have a less developed understanding of technologies, but a more complex understanding of costs and economic feedback effects. Economists argue that market evidence shows that the financial cost identified by the engineers/environmentalists is only one factor that determines the full costs of adopting a particular technology or lifestyle. For various reasons, competing technologies may differ such that some are seen as more valuable to consumers and firms than others. In the example above, where the engineer/environmentalist sees large cost savings from a switch to public transit from private automobiles, the economist sees substantial intangible costs, related to convenience, status, and comfort associated with such a switch. As a result of these high intangible costs, economists predict that consumers would not make a wholesale switch from private automobiles to public transit without extremely aggressive policies.

As experience is gained with estimating costs of reducing GHG emissions, and as strengths and weaknesses of both approaches are recognized, estimates of the cost of GHG emissions reduction are converging towards an estimate between the two groups. Jaccard et al. (2003) report that reductions of GHG emissions of about 25 per cent over ten years would reduce Canada's GDP by about 3 per cent, roughly equivalent to a one-year recession. These estimates are similar to cost estimates produced for the U.S. government using the National Energy Modeling System, and fall between estimates of abatement cost produced by a conventional engineering costing approach and a conventional economics costing approach (Rivers and Jaccard forthcoming). They imply that a GHG tax of about \$150/t CO_2e (1995 \$CDN) would need to be applied to generate a 25 per cent reduction of GHGs over a short timeframe of less than a decade. Such a policy is far more aggressive than anything the government has attempted, as is explained below, and would likely generate significant financial and competitiveness impacts on specific sectors of the economy.

In other words, reducing GHG emissions by a significant amount over a short time is likely to be expensive. This has important implications for policy design.

Choosing Ineffective Policies

Many different GHG emission reduction policies have been pursued around the world and studied by academics and governments. Most of these policies can be arranged along a spectrum that portrays their degree of compulsoriness (Jaccard, Rivers, and Horne 2004). A strict government regulation that dictates the types of technologies that can be purchased would be at the compulsory end of the spectrum, while a government program that focused on education and moral suasion would be at the non-compulsory end. Instruments like taxes and subsidies, which offer some flexibility of response, but still produce an impact on prices and government spending, would be somewhere between the two extremes, with subsidies closer to the non-compulsory end of the spectrum, and taxes closer to the compulsory end.

Canadian policies to address climate change have been developed over the course of a decade, in several distinct initiatives. The government included GHG initiatives in its omnibus Green Plan of 1990. This plan, which involved over two hundred environmental policy initiatives and a budget of \$3 billion over five years, included \$175 million for twenty-four GHG reduction policies, focused mostly on energy-efficiency and alternative energy programs. In 1995, Canada issued a major policy document on mitigating climate change, the *National Action Program on Climate Change* (NAPCC), which encouraged voluntary actions through information programs and some modest subsidies (Environment Canada 1995). The primary policy instrument for addressing GHG emissions under the NAPCC was the Voluntary Challenge and Registry (VCR), under which companies submitted an action plan for GHG reduction and provided regular progress reports,

Table 11.1 Primary policies for GHG reduction under Action Plan 2000

Sector	Initiative	Policy type
Transportation	Partnerships with automotive manufacturers and ethanol producers	N/A
	Information provision through *EnerGuide for Vehicles*	Information
	Demonstration projects for hydrogen distribution infrastructure and efficient urban transportation	Information
Energy sector	Demonstration project for carbon sequestration	Information
	Information provision and moral suasion through the Canadian Industry Program for Energy Conservation	Information
	Voluntary agreements with industry	Voluntary
	Financial incentive for renewable energy	Subsidy
	Purchase of green power by government	N/A
Industry	Information gathering and benchmarking	Information
	Energy-efficiency audits for small and medium enterprises	Subsidy
Buildings	Information provision to encourage retrofits in commercial sector	Information
	Information provision through *EnerGuide for Houses*	Information

Source: Adapted from Action Plan 2000 on Climate Change.

all on a voluntary basis. The NAPCC also included other policy measures at the non-compulsory end of the policy evaluation spectrum, including the Federal Buildings Initiative, whereby federal government buildings would be retrofitted for energy efficiency, and the National Communication Program would educate Canadians about climate change.

After signing the Kyoto Protocol in 1998, the federal government launched Action Plan 2000 on Climate Change, a set of initiatives designed to reduce annual domestic emissions of GHGs by 49 Mt CO_2e by 2010 (Government of Canada 1998). As table 11.1 shows, most of these initiatives continued the non-compulsory approach, including some limited subsidies for renewable energy and some financial assistance for energy audits in small businesses.

Prior to ratifying the Kyoto Protocol in 2002, the federal government released the Climate Change Plan for Canada, which outlined policies for reducing emissions by a further 100 Mt CO_2e by 2010 (Government of Canada 2002). The primary program proposed in the Climate

Change Plan, responsible for 55 Mt of emissions reductions, was a system of negotiated covenants with large industrial emitters (including electricity generators), including an emissions intensity cap for key sectors and a tradable permit system. If implemented, this policy would have deviated somewhat from the non-compulsory approach that had characterized the government's policy direction. However, the extent to which the proposed emissions cap-and-tradable permit system should be considered a compulsory policy depends on whether government negotiators had a political mandate for firm reductions, even were these to cause some costs to industry, or were instead constrained to negotiate only what industry was willing to accept.

Other policies in the Climate Change Plan continue the focus on voluntary action complemented with modest government subsidies. These programs include some financial support for public transit coupled with a voluntary target for increased transit use; encouraging high-efficiency insulation standards by commercial building developers; a voluntary target of 10 per cent renewables for new electricity generation; and a voluntary target for improved vehicle efficiency. Through a combination of these programs in concert with broader information programs, government expected that each Canadian would reduce average annual GHG emissions by one ton. It counts for 24 Mt of these reductions (assuming that over 75 per cent of Canada's 31 million citizens reduce GHG emissions by one ton) in forecasting the impact of its approach on emissions.

In early 2005, the government released Project Green: A Plan for Honouring Our Kyoto Commitment (Government of Canada 2005). While much of this new plan continues previous programs, there are some differences. The system of negotiated covenants with the large final emitters was eliminated, and the proposed target for the sector was adjusted from 55 down to 45 Mt. In addition, Project Green proposed that large final emitters be allowed to contribute to a government-administered research and development fund for greenhouse gas reduction technologies instead of reducing emissions or purchasing offset credits (contributions to this fund can count for only a maximum of 9 Mt of the large final emitter goal), effectively further reducing the large final emitter target to 36 Mt.

Other major thrusts in Project Green include expanded support for renewable energy through continued funding of the Wind Power Production Incentive and the start of the Renewable Power Production

Incentive, which both provide about \$0.01/kWh for qualifying power generation projects; a Climate Fund, with initial funding of \$1 billion, that aims to purchase domestic and international offset credits; a Partnership Fund to encourage provincial participation in climate change mitigation; and the One-Tonne Challenge to encourage voluntary action by Canadians.

Finally, in 2006 and 2007, the newly elected Conservative government launched a series of initiatives under its 'ecoACTION' banner, culminating in the release in April 2007 of its 'regulatory framework for air emissions.' Although billed as a new policy effort, many of the elements of the new Conservative policies are nearly identical to those of the previous Liberal government. Economic analysis of the ecoACTION policies revealed that the policies would be insufficient to counter the rising GHG emissions in Canada (Jaccard and Rivers 2007).

In summary, the past fifteen years of Canadian climate policy development can be summarized as follows:

- Early policies focused almost entirely on educating individual Canadians and businesses about climate change and opportunities to reduce greenhouse gas emissions, and on attempting to convince Canadians to take voluntary action on climate change.
- In subsequent policy development, some modest financial incentives (subsidies) were included, but the overall focus was still on information provision, education, and moral suasion.
- More recently, government has increased its reliance on subsidy mechanisms.
- In 2002, government first presented a plan for a regulated emission cap for large industrial emitters, although it is uncertain if this policy would lead to significant reductions by industry.
- The Conservative government elected in 2006 has generally continued the policy approach of the previous Liberal government, with a few small changes.

In stark contrast to Germany (see chapter 12 by Weidner and Eberlein), Canada relies primarily on non-compulsory policy measures. This evaluation of policy compulsoriness is significant, given that mounting research puts into question the effectiveness of non-compulsory policies. They do not, in relation to this book's focus, supply the capacity to act effectively and in a coordinated way (see chapters 1 and 2). Harrison and Antweiler (2003) find that voluntary policies have had limited success in controlling pollutants released by firms in Canada, and Harrison (1999) shows that the aggregate effect of voluntary policies is questionable. In a survey of voluntary approaches to environmental protection, Khanna (2001) noted that only a few empirical studies have tried to estimate the actual environmental impact of such programs, and found that these have not had much effect. Similarly, the OECD recently concluded that the 'environmental effectiveness of voluntary approaches is still questionable.' It added, 'The economic efficiency of voluntary approaches is generally low' (OECD 2003, 14). Studies have also specifically addressed the voluntary nature of Canada's GHG reduction program, and found them almost entirely ineffective (Bramley 2002; Takahashi, Nakamura, van Kooten, and Vertinsky 2001).

Similar criticism has been made of subsidy programs to encourage energy efficiency and reduced GHG emissions. It is difficult to design subsidy programs to exclude free-riders – participants who qualify for the subsidy even though they would have undertaken the action anyway. Presence of such participants significantly reduces the cost-effectiveness of a subsidy program. Sutherland (2000) conducted a simple analysis of subsidy programs, using comparative statistics, and found that most benefits of subsidy programs accrue to free-riders. He concluded, 'The simple, but unfortunate principle is that rebates (subsidies) have their greatest appeal to exactly the wrong participants. An implication of this principle is that rebates (subsidies) are unlikely to be cost-effective' (Sutherland, 2000, 91). There is empirical evidence to support this claim. Loughran and Kulick (2004) showed, in a survey of demand side management programs in the United States, that the cost of subsidy programs is often higher than expected. By comparing relative changes in electricity consumption over a decade in jurisdictions with demand side management (usually subsidy) programs to those without, they found that the benefits are systematically overestimated, often because the electric utilities ignore the effects of free-riders.

Subsidy programs also suffer from the unintended problem of encouraging a rebound effect in the demand for energy services. By subsidizing efficient technologies, government is effectively making the service provided by the technology less expensive. As a service become less expensive, consumers demand more of it, reducing the impact of the government subsidy program. The magnitude of this rebound effect is disputed, but most studies suggest that the rebound effect reduces the effectiveness of energy efficiency programs by about 10–35 per cent (Greening, Greene, and Difiglio 2000).

Together, the rebound effect and the presence of free-ridership significantly weaken the environmental effectiveness of subsidy programs and render them much less economically efficient. The non-compulsory nature of voluntary GHG reduction programs likewise renders them ineffective.

More generally, the government's application of non-compulsory policies has been ineffective because the overall cost of GHG abatement is higher than the engineering/environmentalist perspective suggests, as we discussed in the preceding section. In order to generate large reductions of GHG emissions in a short time, government needs to apply and have the capacity to implement compulsory policies. So far it has been unwilling to do that.

Canadian-Specific Obstacles to Effective Policy

The policy shortcomings we describe above are not unique to Canada. In fact, our criticisms can be levelled at other industrialized countries that have ratified the Kyoto Protocol: most started by applying non-compulsory policies for GHG reduction. However, as evidence of the ineffectiveness of the information and subsidy approach has become apparent, other countries, especially in Europe, have shifted toward more compulsory policies, in particular Germany (see chapter 12 by Weidner and Eberlein). There are a couple of reasons why Canada has lagged behind.

First, Canada's continued focus on non-compulsory policies is partly explained, as Gattinger's analysis in chapter 8 has shown, by the allocation of powers within its federal system of government. While the federal government has the sole authority to sign international treaties, like the Kyoto Protocol, the provinces have control over natural resources, the electricity sector, and municipal government – all critical areas for reducing GHG emissions. Thus, efforts by the federal government to reduce GHG emissions from fossil fuel exploitation and use require cooperation from the provinces, little of which has been forthcoming. Alberta in particular has been vocal in suggesting that federal policies to reduce GHG emissions will constrain its economic growth or divert some of its growing fossil fuel income to the federal government. More recently, the federal government has redefined CO_2 as a pollutant under the *Canadian Environmental Protection*

Act, giving itself greater jurisdictional authority to take actions under its environmental protection mandate. This will improve its ability to pursue compulsory policies.

Second, Canada's status as one of the most open economies in the world (it derives almost half of its GDP from trade) has also hindered its inherent capacity and ability to implement stringent GHG reduction policies, especially after its U.S. trading partner withdrew from the Kyoto Protocol in 2001. Industry and labour groups in Canada are concerned that implementation of policies that would reduce emissions substantially in Canada would slow economic growth and cause job losses. This opposition has constrained the ability of the federal government to pursue more stringent climate change abatement policies.

Canada's Exceptionally Unrealistic Kyoto Commitment

Even if Canada had applied effective, compulsory policies within two years of signing the Kyoto Protocol in 1997, it would have been extremely difficult to have achieved its Kyoto commitment in 2010. Its commitment is exceptionally aggressive, compared to the Kyoto commitments of other countries.

Canada has significantly missed past GHG emission targets, and with 2003 GHG emissions 24 per cent above the 1990 level, appears on track to dramatically exceed its Kyoto Protocol target. Canada's Kyoto Protocol target is shown in table 11.2 relative to all other Annex B signatories of the Kyoto Protocol.[2]

Increasingly, Canada's GHG commitments, particularly its Kyoto Protocol target, are recognized as the most challenging in the world. Canada's Kyoto Protocol target to reduce emissions to 6 per cent below the 1990 level by 2008–12 is at the more aggressive end of the range of targets negotiated by Annex B countries, although somewhat less aggressive than that of most European countries. However, even in the absence of climate change policies, GHG emissions in European countries would have decreased after 1990 as a result of two major economic changes. First, the dissolution of the Soviet Union caused a major economic downturn in countries that formerly comprised it, including, as the Weidner and Eberlein analysis of German climate change in chapter 12 shows, East Germany. This economic downturn was accompanied by a large decrease in GHG emissions in these countries throughout the 1990s. Second, Britain closed most of its coal mines in the 1980s and 1990s, and made a major switch from coal to

Table 11.2 Countries included in Annex B to the Kyoto Protocol, their emissions targets, and their change in emissions

Country	Target (1990[b]–) 2008/2012)	Change in emissions (1990–2003)[d]
EU-15,[a] Bulgaria, Czech Republic, Estonia, Latvia, Liechtenstein, Lithuania, Monaco, Romania, Slovakia, Slovenia, Switzerland	-8%	EU-15 = -1.4% FSY countries = -25% to -60% except Liechtenstein = +5%
U.S.[c]	-7%	+13.3%
Canada, Hungary, Japan, Poland	-6%	Canada = +24.2%, Japan = +12.8%
Croatia	-5%	-6.0%
New Zealand, Russian Federation, Ukraine	0	Russian Federation = -38.5%
Norway	+1%	+9.3%
Australia[c]	+8%	+23.3%
Iceland	+10%	-8.2%

[a]The EU-15 members have agreed to redistribute their targets amongst themselves.
[b]Some economies-in-transition have a baseline other than 1990.
[c]The United States and Australia have indicated that they will not ratify the Kyoto Protocol.
[d]Excluding land-use, land-use change, and forestry.
Source: United Nations Framework Convention on Climate Change, Key GHG Data, 2005.

natural gas for power generation, primarily for economic reasons. This change reduced methane emissions from coal mining and GHG emissions from power generation significantly. Because of these changes, the Kyoto targets agreed to by European nations do not represent a large departure from business as usual trends. In contrast, because of a fast-growing economy and population, as well as rising oil sands output, GHG emissions have increased quickly in Canada since 1990. In other words, the factors beyond government control acted to reduce GHG emissions in the European countries, while they exerted the opposite pressure in Canada.

Table 11.2 shows that the United States negotiated a -7 per cent Kyoto Protocol target, which is more aggressive than Canada's.

However, the United States has indicated its intention not to ratify the protocol, effectively negating its target. Norway negotiated a +1 per cent target, with the less aggressive target reflecting limited opportunities for GHG reductions from Norway's predominantly hydroelectric power generation system, as well as its forecasted growth in crude oil output for export throughout the 1990s. Australia (which did not ratify the Kyoto Protocol) negotiated a +8 per cent target, which still represents an aggressive target in the face of Australia's fast-growing population and economy. Canada, with a predominantly hydroelectric power generating system and rising crude oil production, like Norway, and with a fast-growing population and economy, like Australia, still negotiated a large reduction in GHG emissions under the Kyoto Protocol. Taking into account the trends discussed throughout this chapter, Canada's GHG reduction targets are probably the most aggressive of all countries bound by the Kyoto Protocol.

Conclusions

Since 1988, Canada has committed internationally to several GHG reduction targets, with the most recent being a 6 per cent reduction of GHG emissions below the 1990 level between 2008 and 2012, under the legally binding Kyoto Protocol. Canada's GHG emissions since 1990 have risen by 24 per cent (through 2003), and appear on track to continue this fast-paced growth. As a result, Canada has missed several historic GHG reduction targets, and domestic emissions appear likely to substantially exceed the Kyoto Protocol target. Canada's record on GHG emissions growth is amongst the worst in the developed countries. As we have seen, there are several reasons why Canada's emissions have increased so quickly since 1990.

First, Canada's population is growing quickly, partly as a result of natural increase (births and deaths), but more importantly as a result of Canada's high immigration rate. Canada's fast population growth, which is somewhat unusual amongst developed countries, is the largest contributor to the fast growth in GHG emissions. Second, Canada's growth in per capita economic activity, which is also somewhat unusual amongst developed countries, has been an important factor. Third, Canada has aggressively developed its oil sands since 1990. Since production of oil sands is energy- and GHG-intensive, this has been an important factor. All of these factors are generally considered beyond the scope and capacity of governments in addressing climate change.

Also, Canada has been ineffective in influencing those factors generally considered to be within the scope of climate policy. In stark contrast to Germany (see chapter 12 by Weidner and Eberlein), Canada's federal government has relied almost completely on non-compulsory policies to encourage GHG reduction, even though increasing evidence suggests that this approach is ineffective and hard to coordinate. Canada negotiated perhaps the most aggressive GHG target in the world under the Kyoto Protocol, and its main trading partners are not faced with similar targets. As a result, Canada's government has been constrained in its lack of capacity to enact policies because of complex arguments by industry, labour, and regional interests that this will have negative impacts on economic competitiveness and employment. It seems likely that Canada will fail its Kyoto Protocol targets more dramatically than any other country.

Most of these trends are not likely to change over the next two decades. Canada's population is projected to continue growing, as a result of natural increases and immigration, which will increase GHG emissions. Canada's economy is also projected to continue its fast pace of growth over the coming two decades. Forecasts have been developed for oil sands production in Canada over the coming two decades, and show continued rapid expansion for the foreseeable future. In the absence of dramatically different processing technologies (such as carbon capture and sequestration) this trend will also increase GHG emissions. In terms of policy, although Canada has tentatively begun to explore more compulsory GHG reduction policies, it continues to concentrate mostly on less effective non-compulsory policies in order to minimize political resistance.

Postscript May 2008

In the period between the writing of our chapter and the final editing of this collective manuscript, there have been several climate policy developments in Canada, at the provincial and federal levels. In presenting these, we focus on the policy initiatives in Alberta and BC. at the provincial level, before turning to review the most recent incarnation of the federal government's approach. The movement toward compulsory policies in BC has been remarkable. In contrast, while the federal government and Alberta have tightened somewhat their regulations on some industrial emissions, these provisions have retained mechanisms by which industrial emissions might not even decline over the next two decades.

Alberta

In 2007, after a decade of unfulfilled negotiations with industry by the federal government, Alberta introduced the country's first cap-and-trade regulatory system on the major industrial GHG emitters within the province. The policy covers only large industrial emitters – oil and gas extraction and processing, refineries, electricity generators, petrochemicals, and others – but these represent a significant share of Alberta's total emissions. The cap is intensity based. By July 2008, each industrial emitter must have reduced its emissions per dollar of production by 12 per cent from its 2006 levels. Any emitter failing to reach this target must either purchase excess permits from emitters who have exceeded their 12 per cent reduction target (tradable permits), purchase 'offsets' from unregulated businesses, consumers, or farmers 'only within Alberta' who have apparently reduced their emissions, or pay fifteen dollars per ton to a 'technology fund' administered by the provincial government. Because the emitter must pay only for its emissions in excess of its intensity target, the fifteen dollars per ton represents only its incremental cost of emissions. With the 12 per cent reduction requirement, this $15 leads to an average emission cost closer to three dollars / tCO_2 for some of the large industrial emitters. To the extent that an emitter can purchase lower-cost excess permits from other industries or lower-cost offsets from unregulated emitters in Alberta, the average cost of emissions could be even lower than three dollars for an industrial emitter.

This policy is attractive for several reasons. With the exception of the technology fund, it exempts government from the politically challenging task of collecting and redistributing revenues, which it would have to do with a carbon tax. The policy also has a minimal impact on the production costs of large emitters (the three dollars / tCO_2), yet it creates an incentive for emitters to reduce emissions where they can do so for less than fifteen dollars / tCO_2 (unless the cost of offsets or tradable industry permits are lower than this, which they could well be). Finally, the Alberta policy levies a lower financial hit on rapidly growing sectors, like the oil sands, since it focuses on emissions intensity rather than absolute emissions levels. This is desirable to the Alberta government, although it may not be desirable to anyone hoping to substantially reduce Canadian emissions as cost-effectively as possible.

The criticisms of the policy are predictable. First, intensity targets do not guarantee that emissions will fall. If, over the next few years, the high-intensity sectors like oil sands grow much faster than the 12 per cent intensity reduction required by the regulation, then emissions could actually rise. Indeed, the Alberta policy is conspicuously silent on future rates of intensity reduction. (This is in contrast with the proposed federal policy that starts with an 18 per cent requirement by 2010 and then an annual 2 per cent intensity reduction in future periods.) Second, the policy does not provide a carbon price signal across the entire Alberta economy. The offset provision for unregulated sectors is supposed to take care of this job, but we have already shown the overwhelming evidence from international research and past Canadian policy that subsidies to emission reduction, whether from government or other private entities, are likely to be highly ineffective because of the impossibility of preventing free-ridership – offset payments to farmers, foresters, small businesses, and consumers for reductions they were going to make anyway, and therefore have no downward effect on the GHG trajectory. Third, the value of emissions reductions tend to be more uncertain in a cap-and-trade system in comparison to a carbon tax. But this critique is only partial in that the technology fund provides a sort of price cap for industry, at least for the next while.

In January 2008, in anticipation of the March provincial election, the Alberta government released a climate policy update that included some additional policies and set a long-run target for GHG reduction. The major policies included an offer to subsidize carbon capture and storage by industry, support for renewable energy, tighter energy efficiency standards for buildings, assistance to municipalities to plan low-emission urban development, and assistance for sequestration and emissions reductions in the forestry and agricultural sectors.

According to the government, the net effect of its policies over several decades will be to reduce Alberta emissions about 50 per cent from their projected levels in 2050. However, because these emissions were expected to grow rapidly with the growth of the oil sands, this represents only a 14 per cent reduction from current levels – after more than forty years. Yet research by the National Roundtable on the Environment and the Economy has shown that Alberta's emissions need to fall by about 40 per cent from current levels for Canada to achieve an aggregate 50 per cent reduction by 2050. In other words, if the federal government fails to implement more stringent policies that override these of the Alberta government, Canada will not reach its emissions target of a 50 per cent reduction from current levels by 2050.

Of course, this situation is not unique to the province of Alberta. With the exception of perhaps British Columbia, none of the other provinces have enacted policies that could collectively achieve the federal target of a 50 per cent reduction from current levels by 2050.

Over the past year, some people – notably Peter Lougheed, Alberta's former premier and elder statesman – have suggested that climate policy will lead to a major constitutional crisis in Canada. This may be true. But we must be careful not to see the present through the prisms of the past. The issue is different in that the climate risk is a global problem in which all countries are grappling with the design and implementation of effective policies, and one of the objectives is to make sure that other jurisdictions are also contributing and not free-riding on the efforts of others. This explains why proposed U.S. state and federal legislation increasingly focuses on how policies that incur obligations and costs on U.S. domestic industry will also impose similar costs on their external competitors.

The state of California and even the U.S. federal government have pursued legislation that mandates a maximum level of emissions from a given quantity of commercial fuel, including emissions associated with the production of that fuel. This means that gasoline produced from the oil sands must not produce more emissions throughout its production than gasoline produced from a conventional oil well. In effect, Alberta would be barred from selling oil from the oil sands into the U.S. market.

British Columbia

The British Columbian government, under the premiership of Gordon Campbell, has quickly distinguished itself as a government that is truly serious about reducing emissions. Ironically, in the Campbell government's first term in office, from 2001 to 2005, it showed little interest in climate policies, focusing on economic performance. But starting in 2006, Campbell has demonstrated a keen understanding of the need for compulsory policies if GHG emissions are truly to fall. A key first step was to restructure responsibilities within government. Campbell created a powerful climate change secretariat with a deputy minister reporting directly to the premier. The secretariat's mandate is to focus all aspects of government on the achievement of the emissions target, and to this end the quick implementation of strong climate policies has become a clear priority for the government.

Already in 2007, while the secretariat worked away at drafting a slate of new legislation, the government took its first major initiative, the announcement of a new electricity policy. This could be achieved without legislation because of the government's control of BCHydro, the large Crown corporation that dominates the BC electricity sector. According to the new electricity policy, BCHydro is required to ensure that at least 90 per cent of new electricity generation in the province comes from clean sources, meaning zero emission. The remaining 10 per cent simply allows for unique locations or circumstances where diesel or natural gas generation might be required or where co-generation projects are desirable. The new policy also stated that coal plants would not be allowed unless they included carbon capture and storage technology that cut emissions almost to zero.

With its electricity policy alone, the BC government had already distinguished itself as a leader in Canada, North America, and even globally. In effect, virtually all new electricity would be zero emission. Then, the provincial budget of February 2008 introduced North America's first substantial carbon tax. While it should be recognized that Quebec had already introduced a carbon tax in 2007, with the tiny tax of three dollars / tCO_2, the Quebec government acknowledged that it did not expect increases in the prices of gasoline or other fuels, arguing that fuel producers should somehow swallow the increase.

In contrast, the BC carbon tax was set at ten dollars / tCO_2 in 2008, with a schedule setting out annual increases of five dollars / tCO_2 until the price reached thirty dollars / tCO_2 by 2012. This would be a 2.4 cents per litre increase of the price of gasoline in 2008, rising to 7.5 cents per litre by 2012.

A key component of the BC carbon tax is that it is revenue neutral. The government has tabled legislation that requires all revenues from the carbon tax to be returned to British Columbian businesses and households in the form of corporate and income tax reductions, as well as some provincial sales tax reductions on 'low-emission' technologies. The personal income tax cuts are especially targeted at families earning less than $70,000 per year in order to offset any regressive aspects of the carbon tax.

With the carbon tax as centrepiece, the Campbell government has also pushed ahead with a flurry of other regulations, many requiring new legislation. To date, these include a low carbon fuel standard, requiring that all gasoline and diesel sold in the province by 2010 have at least 5 per cent biofuel content, legislation to allow BC to participate in the industrial emissions cap-and-trade system being developed by states in the western United States, with the potential participation of some Canadian provinces, and potential changes to vehicle emissions standards and building codes.

It is too early to say if the BC government's policies will be sustained. But for the moment, they represent a radical departure from two decades of ineffectual policies.

Canada

In reports for the C.D. Howe Institute, we have assessed the Canadian government's recent climate policies. In 2007, we estimated that while the policy package developed in 2006–7 by the federal Conservative government would significantly slow the growth of Canadian emissions over the next decades, these policies would not achieve the government's commitment of a 20 per cent reduction from 2006 levels by 2020. We estimated that Canadian emissions in 2020 would be close to today's levels rather than 20 per cent below them.

The main reason that the government's claims are once again likely to be an exaggeration are because of its substantial reliance on the ineffective subsidy approach – this time in the form of the offset loophole that allows large industrial emitters to subsidize apparent reductions in the uncapped and untaxed emissions of all the other sectors of the economy. We were not alone in predicting that the government's policies would not put the country on a path to achieve either its 2020 and 2050 emissions targets. Similar conclusions were drawn by the Conference Board, the Toronto Dominion Bank, the Pembina Institute, and the National Roundtable on the Environment and the Economy.

After a year of in-depth consultations with the industries to be regulated, the Conservative government released a refinement of its industrial policy in March 2008. While this updated policy is not significantly different in design, it incorporates detailed refinements and more aggressive technology requirements. The updated policy retains the same requirement for an 18 per cent reduction in emission intensity by 2010, followed by annual 2 per cent reductions thereafter. It retains the technology fund at fifteen dollars / tCO_2, with this option for industry declining to zero by 2017. It also retains other 'flexibility provisions,' including limited recourse to credits for early actions, limited international offsets in developing countries through the Clean Development Mechanism of the Kyoto Protocol, and unlimited offsets in the unregulated sectors of the Canadian economy – just like the Alberta industrial policy with its unlimited Alberta-specific offsets.

Implicitly acknowledging the critiques from various parties (including us) that the government's 2007 policy package would not achieve its 2020 emissions target, the government also set facility-specific, technology-based emission intensity requirements on future investments in oil sands production and coal-fired electricity generation. Specifically, oil sands processing plants and coal-fired electricity generation facilities completed after 2017 will have their intensity target based on the assumed incorporation of carbon capture and storage technologies. In the interim, facilities completed between 2004 and 2017 would be required to meet the emissions intensity levels equivalent to the best conventional technologies available today in oil sands production and electricity generation. This would be oil sands production using natural gas for upgrading and coal-fired generation using 'supercritical' steam.

These are not technology requirements. They are facility-specific emission intensity requirements based on low-emission technologies expected to be commercially ready over the next decade. Estimating the effect of these policies on future industrial emissions is complicated. It depends on the definition and relative costs of the flexibility provisions. If offsets are of relatively low cost, large industrial emitters may reduce their emissions very little, instead purchasing offsets from the unregulated sectors of the economy. If these offsets are not real emissions reductions from a business-as-usual forecast, which they are likely to be, then total Canadian emissions will not fall and Canada will not hit the Conservative government's 2020 emissions reduction target.

In modelling the policy, however, government assumes that industry will acquire no offsets from the unregulated sector other than a limited number of projects that capture methane emissions from agriculture and urban landfills. Because of this assumption of a restrictive market, the government forecasts an offset and permit trading price that rises already to sixty-five dollars / tCO_2 by 2018.

However, we find no basis for this assumption. It is more likely that the market price for carbon will remain very low, reflecting the fact that many different kinds of offset projects will be eligible for funding from industrial emitters. And, based on past experience, a large percentage of these projects are likely to cause much less emissions reduction than advertised. For the government to be credible in this area, it should put a tight cap on the allowance for offsets. Better still, it should disallow them all together and extend the cap-and-trade system to the entire economy or use a carbon tax to cover all remaining unregulated emissions.

A key benefit of a uniform economy-wide price on greenhouse gas emissions is that it ensures that society does not pursue high cost emissions reductions in one sector while ignoring low cost actions in another. Such an approach is a more costly way to achieve a given level of emissions reduction. Yet the government's policy is headed in just this direction. Large industrial emissions face a price different from that for consumer emissions. In fact, the emissions from using a backyard patio heater, and thousands of other such devices, are free under the Conservative government's approach. Even within the industrial sector, the 'refined' policy has many similar conditions. Emissions from new facilities face a emissions price different from that for old facilities. Process emissions, which are not covered by the regulation, face in effect a price of zero dollars / tCO_2. This is likewise the case for emissions from small industrial facilities that are exempt from the federal policy. With these and other provisions, the federal policy will be much more costly than need be.

Another cost associated with the federal climate policy approach, which stands in sharp contrast to a carbon tax, is all of the extra bureaucratic and transaction costs it causes. Conservative governments promote themselves as being especially keen to reduce the burden of government on society. Yet the offset system and other technology-specific provisions in the policy require multiple regulatory procedures and will require a large staff to administer them properly. The offset system alone has a great potential for fraud, as investigators are already finding out with companies providing offset services to the airline industry. Administrative costs are likely to be substantial.

At the same time, a cap-and-trade system requires many brokers and traders for permit exchanges – costs to society that are not required by a simple carbon tax, which relies on existing taxation systems. It is again ironic that a Conservative government should be responsible for taking such a costly approach to achieving society's climate policy objectives.

Finally, another concern is how the federal government's climate policy approach will mesh with the policies of provincial governments and Canada's major trading partners. This is a difficult question. Europe has an absolute cap-and-trade system, while Canada's is intensity based. The United States may implement a policy similar to that of Europe. Within Canada, the new carbon taxes in Quebec and BC create a challenge for attaining national policy cohesion.

The latest developments in federal climate policy in Canada do, indeed, represent an improvement over the largely non-compulsory policies of the past. But with the exception of the policies of the government of British Columbia, Canada has a long way to go before closing the climate policy gap with many European countries such as Germany.

NOTES

1 Extracting synthetic crude from oil sands produces about 100 kg carbon dioxide equivalent (CO_2e) per barrel, while extracting conventional light crude oil in Canada produces only about 50 kg CO_2e per barrel. In countries where the majority of conventional light crude oil is extracted offshore, like Norway and the United Kingdom, GHG emissions are only about 20 kg CO_2e per barrel.
2 Annex B countries are the thirty-nine emissions-capped industrialized countries and economies-in-transition listed in Annex B of the Kyoto Protocol.

REFERENCES

Bramley, M. 2002. *The case for Kyoto: The failure of voluntary corporate action.* Calgary: Pembina Institute.

Conference Board of Canada. 2004. *Canadian long-term economic forecast 2004.* Ottawa: Conference Board of Canada.

Energy Information Administration. 2003. *International energy annual 2003.* Washington, DC: Government Printing Office.

Environment Canada. 1995. *National action program on climate change.* Ottawa: Environment Canada.

Government of Canada. 1998. *Action plan 2000 on climate change.* Ottawa: Environment Canada.

– 2002. *Climate change plan for Canada.* Ottawa: Environment Canada.

– 2005. *Project green: Moving forward on climate; A plan for honouring our Kyoto commitment.* Ottawa: Environment Canada.

Greening, L., D. Greene, and C. Difiglio. 2000. Energy efficiency and consumption: The rebound effect; A survey. *Energy Policy* 28:389–401.

Harrison, K. 1999. Talking to the donkey: Cooperative approaches to environmental protection. *Journal of Industrial Ecology* 2 (3): 51–72.

Harrison, K., and W. Antweiler. 2003. Incentives for pollution abatement: Regulation, regulatory threats, and non-governmental pressures. *Journal of Policy Analysis and Management* 22 (3): 361–82.

Jaccard, M., J. Nyboer, C. Bataille, and B. Sadownik. 2003. Modeling the cost of climate policy: Distinguishing between alternative cost definitions and long-run cost dynamics. *Energy Journal* 24 (1): 49–73.

Jaccard, M., and N. Rivers. 2007. Estimating the effect of the Canadian government's 2006–2007 greenhouse gas policies. *C.D. Howe Institute e-brief*, 12 June.

Jaccard, M., N. Rivers, and M. Horne. 2004. The morning after: Optimal greenhouse gas policies for Canada's Kyoto obligations and beyond. *C.D. Howe Institute Commentary* 197.

Kaya, Y. 1990. Impact of carbon dioxide emission control on GNP growth: Interpretation of proposed scenarios. Paper presented to the IPCC Energy and Industry Subgroup, Response Strategies Working Group, Paris.

Khanna, M. 2001. Non-mandatory approaches to environmental protection. *Journal of Economic Surveys* 15 (3): 291–324.

Loughran, D., and J. Kulick. 2004. Demand side management and energy efficiency in the United States. *Energy Journal* 24 (1): 19–43.

Oil and Gas Journal. 2002. Worldwide Report.

Organisation for Economic Co-operation and Development. 2003. *Voluntary approaches for environmental policy: Effectiveness, efficiency, and usage in the policy mixes.* Paris: Organization of Economic Cooperation and Development.

Rivers, N., and M. Jaccard. Forthcoming. Useful models for simulating policies to induce technological change. *Energy Policy.*

Statistics Canada. 2005. The daily: Demographic statistics. 28 September. Statistics Canada.

Sutherland, R. 2000. No-cost efforts to reduce carbon emissions in the US: An economic perspective. *Energy Journal* 21 (3): 89–112.

Takahashi, T., N. Nakamura, G. van Kooten, and I. Vertinsky. 2001. Rising to the Kyoto challenge: Is the response of Canadian industry adequate? *Journal of Environmental Management* 63:149–61.

United Nations Framework Convention on Climate Change. 2005. Key GHG data. Bonn.

12 Still Walking the Talk? German Climate Change Policy and Performance

HELMUT WEIDNER AND BURKARD EBERLEIN

Few countries seem to be further apart on the scoreboard of climate protection than Canada and Germany. As the previous chapter by Rivers and Jaccard has shown, Canada is a 'leading laggard' in the reduction of greenhouse gases (GHG). Germany, by contrast, has been, since the mid-1980s, at the forefront of domestic and international efforts to combat climate change by limiting GHG emissions. As early as June 1990, the federal (West German) government adopted a reduction target for energy-related carbon dioxide (CO_2) emissions of 25–30 per cent until 2005, compared to 1987 levels. And under the 1997 Kyoto Protocol, Germany voluntarily took the largest share (almost 75 per cent) of the EU-15 reduction burden, by committing to a 21 per cent reduction, compared to 1990 levels, by the 2008–12 period. Furthermore, Germany has played a key role on the international stage, helping to secure the passage of progressive climate protection regimes and declarations (Weidner 2005, 2007).

In marked contrast to Canada, Germany has also been walking the talk: it has been the leader among OECD countries in the reduction of GHG, with a cut of 17.4 per cent by 2004, an achievement unrivalled by any other industrial nation. Germany is basically on track to meet its Kyoto obligation, although emissions have been on the rise again since 2000 and additional efforts are required (IEA 2007, 43).

In this chapter, we investigate the background of what is often portrayed as the German success story. We will attempt to identify the reasons for Germany's pioneer role and impressive track record by looking into the specific conditions and determinants of Germany's climate policy path.

Borrowing from the analytical framework used by Rivers and

Jaccard in the previous chapter, we distinguish between three sets of factors that affect the capacity of a jurisdiction to formulate and implement GHG emission reduction commitments: *structural factors and sector properties, policy measures and instruments,* and *formal and informal institutional environment.* While Rivers and Jaccard look at direct drivers of GHG emission, our focus is on the institutional *capacity* of public policy to address climate change. In line with the three-part analytical framework of complexity, coordination, and capacity, presented in chapters 1 and 15, we conceptualize the climate policy capacity of a jurisdiction as the result of the interaction between substantive and structural properties on the one hand, and the institutional environment on the other hand. The choice of policy measures and instruments is closely linked to the institutional environment but merits separate analysis because of its crucial independent impact on the success of GHG emission reduction and avoidance.

Our key argument is that Germany's success and leadership is the result of positive 'path dependence' (Pierson 2004). Thus, a mutually reinforcing set of technological and economic, institutional, and ideational capacities and capabilities, built over many years, helped Germany to pursue a progressive climate policy path, and, crucially, to employ strong policy measures and instruments with a comparatively high degree of compulsoriness. However, there are certain deficits and gaps in Germany's climate policy, especially in relation to the utility sector. Germany has also benefited significantly from favourable structural conditions, especially from the 'wall-fall' effect of economic restructuring and deindustrialization in former East Germany. Paradoxically, the very success of Germany's policy so far now raises questions about the sustainability of the path as the country moves toward ever more ambitious goals. Taking Germany to the next level or threshold of emission abatement (while phasing out nuclear power) will raise thorny distributive issues, especially with regard to the energy industry and in the new context of global recession – issues that will put the current consensus on climate protection to a severe test.

We first trace the origin and development of German climate policy, with a special focus on the progressive entrenchment of strong policy commitments in governmental policy and process, and on the close relationship between international leadership and domestic commitments. In a second step, we compare commitments with actual achievements in emission reductions and energy efficiency. In a third part, we investigate the key factors that account for the relative success of Germany's policy: structural determinants, the choice of policy measures and instruments, and the broader institutional environment that has facilitated strong commitments and policy measures. In a fourth and concluding section, we briefly sketch current and emerging challenges for Germany's climate protection policy in the post-Kyoto period.

Path Origins and Entrenchment of Climate Protection Commitments

Climate change emerged as an issue on Germany's political agenda in the mid-1980s (Beuermann and Jäger 1996; Cavender and Jäger 1993; Watanabe and Mez 2004). Prior to that, problems caused by conventional air pollutants (acid rain, smog, forest dieback) had dominated the public discussion. The long-standing tradition of West German systematic clean-air policy, going back to the 1970s, was important in that it contributed to public awareness of long-range trans-boundary pollution and the need for international cooperation. It had also generated administrative and policy experience that would prove valuable in the domain of climate protection.

The prestigious German Physics Society captured public attention around climate change in 1986 when its Energy Study Group released a report on the anthropogenic greenhouse effect, and warned in a statement addressed to the public of an 'imminent climate catastrophe.'[1] Soon after, the leading weekly magazine *Der Spiegel* carried a widely debated series, 'Die Klima-Katastrophe' (The Climate Catastrophe) on the potential effects of global warming, featuring a flooded Cologne Cathedral on the front page (*Der Spiegel*, 11 August 1986). The climate issue rose to federal political prominence in March 1987 when Conservative Chancellor Kohl declared that the climate issue represented the most important environmental problem. His 1987 government declaration was themed 'Conserving the Creation,' and emphasized the importance of national and international environmental protection. This was shortly after the creation of the Federal Ministry for the Environment, Nature Conservation, and Nuclear Safety (BMU) in 1986, in the wake of the Chernobyl nuclear accident that had galvanized environmental concerns (see Mez and Doern, chapter 5). This new institutional basis strengthened governmental capacity in environmental policy and bolstered the position of environmental advocates within the government. The German government also placed the ozone layer protection on top of the European Community agenda under the 1987 German presidency.

Domestically, a step of great importance for the political and scientific debate was the decision, by the German Bundestag, to establish, in 1987, the Enquête Commission on Preventive Measures to Protect the Earth's Atmosphere – a parliamentary study commission composed of both policy experts and members of parliament. The commission enjoyed high esteem, and its work helped to forge a consensus on the climate challenge and to generate policy strategies. A follow-up parliamentary committee (Protection of the Atmosphere) was set up for the 1990–4 period. It is remarkable that the federal government adopted the central recommendations of both committees.

Unlike in the earlier case of forest dieback (*Waldsterben*), there was no competition between different camps of experts, but a broad, bipartisan consensus. Experts and political actors alike agreed on the seriousness of the climate change challenge and on the notion that the burning of fossil fuels was the main source of the greenhouse effect – even though there were, of course, differences on which approaches and instruments would be most appropriate to address the challenge.

In its third and final report of 1990 (*Protecting the Earth*), the parliamentary Study Commission called for a 30 per cent reduction of 1987 levels of CO_2 (and methane) emissions by 2005 and recommended an 80 per cent reduction by 2050. It also emphasized the need for fundamental reforms of energy policy (German Bundestag 1991). In June 1990, the (West German) federal government adopted a reduction target for energy-related CO_2 emissions of 25–30 per cent of 1987 levels by 2005.

At the same time, an inter-ministerial working group (IMA) on 'CO_2 reduction' was established under the chairmanship of the Federal Ministry for Environment, with a mandate to develop proposals for achieving the 25 per cent reduction target. The group proposed a broad range of measures to reach the reduction goal (Beuermann 2000; Beuermann and Jäger 1996). This program resulted in a variety of energy- and technology-related legislation, such as the Electricity Feed-In Law of 1990 (for details, see below and Mez, chapter 14 of this volume).

Organized in five sub-groups (energy supply, transport, buildings, new technologies, and agriculture), and involving several ministerial portfolios, the Inter-Ministerial Group emerged as a major instrument for the cross-sector formulation and coordination of climate change policy, and ultimately, for the entrenchment of the climate agenda in the governmental process. This is of particular significance in the German political-administrative context, where there is a high degree of ministerial independence and segmentation, especially under coalition governments (see Eberlein and Doern, chapter 1, this volume).

Path Dependence and Two-Level Dynamics of International Leadership

German unification in October 1990, and the economic downturn and unemployment crisis that was to follow on the heels of rapid restructuring in East Germany, meant a setback for environmental policy priorities, generally. However, while climate policy lost some of its momentum in the 1990s, it never suffered as much from economic recession as other environmental policy areas. Climate policy was protected by its strong institutionalization (by way of the Inter-Ministerial Group) in the governmental process. Perhaps it also benefited from the perception that the highly inefficient energy structure of former East Germany provided favourable conditions for climate-focused transformations.

In any case, after some modification (but no softening) of the reduction targets to take account of the new situation of a reunified Germany, the federal government announced, in 1995, a CO_2 reduction target of 25 per cent, based on 1990 levels. The new reference year 1990 (instead of 1987), now applicable to both West and East Germany, had the effect of making the target stricter than ever. The fact that the government committed to such a bold target, which was certain to require deep structural adjustments and to lead to conflicts with the powerful utility and energy industry, has to be understood in the broader political context.

The pledge was made by Chancellor Kohl during the first Conference of the Parties (COP 1) to the UN Framework Convention on Climate Change (FCCC), hosted by the German government in Berlin in 1995. This was a unique opportunity to receive worldwide acknowledgement as climate protection champion and leader. However, in fairness, it has to be noted, that Germany's diplomatic leadership, with Angela Merkel, the current chancellor, acting then as environment minister, was crucial in injecting new momentum into stagnating international negotiations, and it arguably paved the way for the successful passage of the Kyoto Protocol in 1997.

The mutually reinforcing relationship between international leadership and domestic commitments is a consistent feature of German climate policy, independent of political orientation. Since the mid 1980s, Chancellor Kohl and various federal environmental ministers (of different political background) played an active and, at times, decisive role in keeping progressive international climate protection agreements and policies on track (Weidner 1999, 2007). A good case in point is the crucial contribution that Kohl and his Environment Minister Klaus Töpfer made to the 1992 Rio Conference, which allowed it to achieve a breakthrough on the UN FCCC.

Social-Democrat Gerhard Schröder, who succeeded Kohl in the chancellor's office in 1998 at the helm of a Red-Green coalition government, continued the tradition of German leadership in international climate policy (for example, at the World Summit on Sustainable Development in Johannesburg in 2002), although in other environmental policy areas he was clearly leaning towards industry interests, for instance on the EU automobile scrap directive. Given the political complexion of the coalition, climate protection policy enjoyed high priority from the very beginning in the fall of 1998 (Mez 2003). In the coalition agreement, the parties agreed on a 25 per cent reduction target for CO_2 emissions, and in October 2000, a comprehensive National Climate Protection Programme was launched, envisaging, among a total of sixty-four measures, a sharp increase in renewable energy, combined heat and power (CHP), and a significant increase in energy productivity. The program was based on the fifth report of the aforementioned Inter-Ministerial Working Group on CO_2 reduction. In contrast to climate change programs of the former Conservative government, the 2000 program listed specific CO_2 reduction targets for seven sectors (households, transport, industry, energy, renewables, waste management, and agriculture). It was accompanied or followed by a number of specific and controversial energy policy measures (see more below).

However, also during the tenure of the Red-Green coalition, the federal government silently retreated from one of Germany's strongest commitments: when it became obvious that Germany would not be able to meet the 25 per cent CO_2 reduction target by 2005, the government simply dropped this goal from public statements. Instead, it now referred to the less demanding commitment made under the EU-15 burden-sharing system to a 21 per cent GHG emission reduction by 2008–12. However, this has so far been the only incidence of lowering an internationally pledged commitment.

Finally, the current grand coalition between Conservatives and Social-Democrats, under the leadership of Chancellor Angela Merkel, has continued most of the environmental policy agenda of previous governments, including the nuclear phase-out (Mez and Doern, chapter 5). In the area of climate policy, there has actually been further progress towards more aggressive goals and targets. The coalition agreement stipulated that Germany should aim to exceed a 30 per cent reduction in emissions (1990 base year) by 2020, provided that the EU would commit itself, in the context of a new international agreement, to a 30 per cent target.

Policy continuity is partly, of course, a result of the recent spectacular rise of the climate change issue on the international stage over the last couple of years. At their March 2007 Brussels Summit, EU leaders endorsed ambitious emission reduction targets, as part of a push towards an integrated energy and climate strategy, and also with a view to solidify the EU position at the forefront of international efforts to combat climate change. The EU committed itself to cut GHG emissions unilaterally – not conditional on an international agreement – by at least 20 per cent by 2020, and suggested that a post-Kyoto (post-2012) framework should aim for a 30 per cent cut in emissions from developed countries by 2020. That means that the EU is prepared to cut its GHG emissions by 30 per cent (to the 1990 baseline), provided that other industrialized countries commit to comparable reductions (EU Council / German Presidency 2007).

At the same time, Germany continues to be the driving force on the climate issue, within the EU and on the international stage of negotiations on a post-Kyoto framework. In the EU context, it was primarily due to the persistent lobbying of the German government that the so-called 3 x 20 per cent target was approved as part of the 2007 energy and climate package: by 2020, EU GHG emissions shall be reduced by 20 per cent, energy efficiency increased by 20 per cent, and the share of renewables in energy production raised by 20 per cent. At the G8 Summit in June 2007 in Heiligendamm (Germany) host Angela Merkel went into the talks backed by the EU unilateral commitment. She skilfully exploited Germany's parallel EU and G8 presidency to extract a joint climate policy declaration from G8 leaders that they 'will seriously consider' at least a halving of global emissions by 2050 (G8 2007). Furthermore, all parties, including the Kyoto non-signatory United States, agreed to pursue negotiations on post-Kyoto emission reductions within the UN framework process. The UN Climate Change Conference in Bali in December 2007 did not yield agreement on specific emission reduction targets but it delivered a road map for future negotiations.

Domestically, the federal government has set even higher targets, even though the reduction rate of GHG emissions (especially CO_2) slowed significantly over the past few years (see below). Nevertheless, in a government declaration of policy in April 2007, Federal Environment Minister Gabriel increased the GHG emission reduction target to 40 per cent (compared to 1990) by 2020, provided that the EU and other industrial countries agree to reduce GHG by 30 per cent, as part of a new international agreement. Gabriel proposed a set of measures in eight key areas, to cut emissions by 270 million tons, compared to 2006, which is the quantity required to meet the 40 per cent target (BMU 2007a). However, the decision by the federal cabinet (23/24 August 2007) on a twenty-nine-Measures Package for Climate Policy will obviously allow for no more than a 36 per cent reduction (BMU 2008).

To summarize, a review of climate protection commitments over the last twenty years shows remarkable continuity and positive path dependency. If anything, Germany's commitment to lead in combating climate change has intensified. In sharp contrast to other industrial countries and to Canada in particular, there was no fundamental opposition to the *principle* of climate policy, by influential interest groups, political parties, or certain regional governments or regionally based producer groups. This consensus on the need for strict and internationally coordinated policy commitments is, for example, reflected in the unanimous ratification vote on the Kyoto Protocol by the two houses of the German parliament in March and April 2002.

However, conflicts and arguments surrounding the *implementation* of climate protection commitments do obviously exist: they mostly centre on the nuclear phase-out policy, questions of suitability, rationality and feasibility of instruments, reasonable time frames for implementation, and distortion of competition between energy sources.

The argument that climate protection measures impose an unfair burden on German industry in international competition is of increasing importance, as Germany prepares to adopt more substantial policy measures for the post-Kyoto period (see concluding section).

Figure 12.1 Reduction of climate gases: Kyoto target and actual
reduction as of 2004

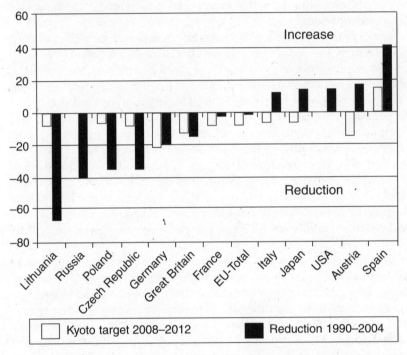

| | Kyoto target 2008–2012 | ■ | Reduction 1990–2004 |

Source: Green Budget Germany (GBG) – Fördeverein Ökologische Steuerreform e.V. (FÖS).

Achievements: Really Walking the Talk?

Overall, Germany made remarkable progress in the reduction of greenhouse gases, especially in comparison to other industrialized nations. To
be sure, the initial target, that was later shelved, of a 25 per cent reduction by 2005 was, as Ziesing notes in chapter 13, missed by almost 100
million tons. But Germany is basically on track to meet its Kyoto target
of a 21 per cent reduction in GHG emissions by 2008–12, compared to
1990 levels. In 2003, a reduction peak of 18.5 per cent was reached. The
latest National Inventory Report on German GHG (UBA 2006) shows a
reduction value of 17.4 per cent for 2004 (1990 base level). As figure 12.1
illustrates, this puts Germany in clear leadership in the Western world.

A provisional estimate by the German government Institute for Economic expects a GHG reduction level of 18 per cent for 2006 (BMU 2008, III).

The reduction of CO_2 emissions (which account for almost 88 per cent of all six greenhouse gases) stands at 16 per cent in 2005, from 1990 levels (with a significant reduction of 2 per cent from 2004 to 2005). Germany is thus one of the few industrialized countries that significantly reduced its CO_2 emissions since the early 1990s (Ziesing 2005, 2006), whereas in the United States, for example, emissions rose by more than 16 per cent, or in Japan by more than 14 per cent by 2005.

This positive assessment holds true even when taking the 'wall-fall' effect into account. Economic restructuring in East Germany after reunification, especially the closure of emission-intensive (coal-fired) generation and other industrial plants, led to a dramatic drop of CO_2 emissions in the Eastern Länder by 43 per cent between 1990 and 1995 (Schleich et al. 2001, 367). This resulted in an overall decline of energy-related CO_2 emissions in united Germany by 12.2 per cent between 1990 and 2004 (IEA 2007, 43). 'Wall-fall profits are estimated to have contributed almost 50% of the reduction of all greenhouse gases. This share increases to 60% if only energy-related CO_2 emissions are considered' (Schleich et al. 2001, 378). At the same time, this was not a 'free lunch' for climate protection. A comprehensive assessment would have to consider the enormous costs incurred by unification (financial transfers to the East, high unemployment and welfare expenses). Some of these amounts could, theoretically, have been spent on emission abatement measures.

It is true, however, that the bulk of emission reduction occurred in the early 1990s, with the strongest decrease in non-CO_2 emissions (figure 12.2). Since the turn of the century, emission reduction stalled. Between 2000 and 2004, energy-related CO_2 emissions have increased slightly, at an average annual growth rate of 0.6 per cent (IEA 2007, 44), before the recent 2 per cent drop in 2005, as noted above.

As figure 12.3 documents, sector contributions and developments diverge quite considerably.[2] In 2004, the energy sector remains with 43 per cent the single biggest source of CO_2 emissions, 37 per cent alone emitted by generating plants. Over the 1990 to 2004 period, the energy sector reduced emissions by 12.5 per cent, or 55 million tons (while global CO_2 emissions caused by power generation increased by 19 per cent between 1999 and 2003) (BMU 2006a). However, since 2000, emissions have increased again by about 18 million tons, pri-

Figure 12.2 Emissions of greenhouse gases in Germany 1990/base year to 2003

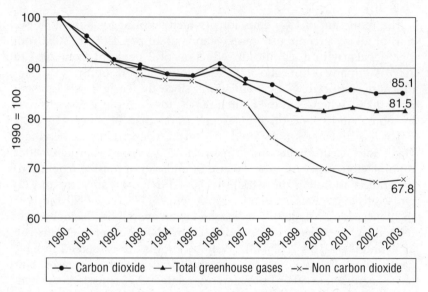

Sources: National Emissions Inventory (2003), calculations by DIW Berlin.

marily due to an increase in the burning of brown hard coal (lignite). In the broader industrial sector, there has been a consistent and strong reduction trend, with cuts worth 50 million tons or 38.3 per cent. The transport sector, the second-most important emitter, by contrast, has increased emissions by 15 per cent between 1990 and 1999. This was because of consistent volume growth in road transport that cancelled out efficiency improvements and stricter emission norms. A drop of 8.5 per cent occurred between 2000 and 2003, due to reduced (domestic) gas consumption, in reaction mainly to the introduction of the eco-tax. But by 2004, transport still emitted 5.7 per cent more than in 1990. Private households have reduced emissions by 10.7 per cent in 2004, compared to 1990, but they account for only 14 per cent of CO_2 emissions.

An important indicator of success is improvement in energy efficiency, which reflects the relation between energy use and economic output. On this front, significant progress can be noted as well.

Figure 12.3 Development of greenhouse gas emissions by sector, 1990–2004 (in mio. t CO_-eq)

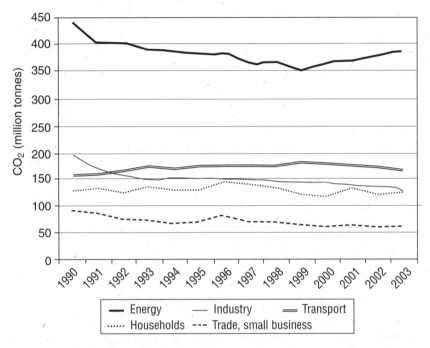

Source: Federal Ministry for the Environment, Nature Conservation, and Nuclear Safety, Germany (BMU) 2006.

Primary energy consumption (PEC) in Germany decreased from 15,345 petajoules (1990) to 14,364 petajoules in 2005, and the consumption of fossil-based primary energy reserves was reduced by over 10 per cent. More importantly, the PEC value per inhabitant, in spite of rising prosperity, was reduced by almost 10 per cent as well. More specifically, CO_2 emissions per capita declined by almost 20 per cent, from 13.2 tons in 1990 to 10.6 tons in 2005. Energy efficiency of economic output, in relation to CO_2, was improved dramatically: in 2005, a third less of CO_2 was emitted per GDP unit than in 1990, a dramatic decline in energy intensity for the German economy (Wittke and Ziesing 2006, 156). Germany's energy intensity improved, declining by an annual 1.8 per cent from 1990 to 2005, which 'places Germany among the leading group of industrial nations' (IEA 2007, 53).

Yet the annual rise of energy productivity (economic output per unit of energy) has slowed considerably. In the early 1990s, the annual rate of energy productivity increase was more than 2 per cent, mainly as a result of investments in former East Germany. Annual energy productivity improvements declined to about 1 per cent per year between 2000 and 2002, because of the high base level of productivity that had already been achieved.

Studies that seek to assess the broader environmental efficiency of economic production and consumption lend support to the notion of Germany as leader in the efficient use of natural resources, including water, air, and energy (Bardt 2006). By 2005, Germany reduced the consumption of energy (PEC) per GNP unit to 80.6 per cent of 1991 (= 100) levels; GHG emission-intensity was reduced to 71.7 per cent per GNP unit in the same period. The environmental efficiency indicator developed by the Institute of the German Economy Cologne (IW) accords Germany a score of 85.2 out of 100 on energy efficiency specifically (rank eleven out of thirty countries), whereas Canada scores only 41.2 out of 100, at the bottom of the league table (Bardt 2006, 11).

In sum, the data show considerable evidence of success in emission reduction and increased energy efficiency. How can we account for these considerable achievements? Let us first turn to structural factors and sector properties.

Supportive Structural Determinants of GHG Reductions

Economic and population growth as well as structural features of the economy (relative size of sectors) are important determinants of GHG emissions developments. As Rivers and Jaccard show in chapter 11, all these factors essentially work as strong drivers of emission growth in Canada. Germany, by contrast, has so far benefited from most structural elements. First of all, as noted earlier, about half of the emission reductions can be attributed to the economic collapse in East Germany after unification. This climate protection 'benefit,' however, resulted in huge costs to the German economy and society, and made much less money available for climate protection measures.

Second, sluggish demographic and economic growth over most of the period has helped Germany to contain energy use and reduce overall emissions. As figure 11.3 in chapter 11 by Rivers and Jaccard indicates, Germany's annual population growth was stuck at about 0.3 per cent over the 1990s, and then was practically zero from 2000 to 2005. In terms of economic growth, only Japan had lower annual growth rates in the G7 Group than Germany between 1990 and 2002 (see figure 11.4, in the Rivers and Jaccard chapter). Between 2000 and 2005, average annual economic growth stood at only 0.7 per cent.

However, while these numbers might explain a stagnation or slight decrease of emissions, they are not sufficient (in combination with the wall-fall effect) to explain the extent of emission reduction, and even less the decline in energy and CO_2 intensity and the impressive improvement in energy efficiency. Furthermore, it should be noted that Germany's fuel mix constitutes a significant structural burden for emission reduction: the share of coal in total primary energy supply is still at almost one quarter in 2005 (although down from 40 per cent in 1985), and the share of (emission-intensive) bituminous coal and lignite in electricity generation capacity is 36 per cent (IEA 2007, 18, 119).

Hence, overall, we need to look at the impact of policy measures to account for significant emission reduction and improvements in energy efficiency.

Strong Policy Measures for Climate Protection

In order to achieve its ambitious targets for GHG emission reduction, Germany introduced a variety of public policies that used all three levers of climate protection policy (identified by Rivers and Jaccard): the shift to low-emission fuels (renewables), the improvement of energy efficiency (inter alia, efficiency gains in housing and transport, expansion of CHP), and the control of emissions (emission cap-and-trading). In contrast to Canada, Germany has not shied away from strong, regulatory and tax policies with a high degree of 'compulsoriness' (Jaccard, Rivers, and Horne 2004) that impose significant costs on industry and the general population. However, the utility companies in the energy sector, as well as the automotive industry in transport, were given preferential treatment, which reduced policy effectiveness. Germany has also frequently used voluntary industry agreements, but results have been less impressive.

The most significant programs and policy measures were introduced on the watch of the Red-Green coalition (1998–2005). The abovementioned National Climate Protection Programme of 2000, updated in 2005, served as a broad cross-sector umbrella for a variety of measures. We sketch below the most significant and representative set of measures. Further details can be found in chapter 14 by Mez and in chapter 13 (on emission trading) by Ziesing.

The most controversial instrument, the so-called eco-tax, was first enacted in 1999 and combined 'green' policy targets with social-democratic concerns about job creation. The idea was to encourage energy savings and the development of energy-saving technologies, while at the same time making employment cheaper. It introduced a levy on electricity consumption (at a reduced rate for industry) and raised existing mineral oil taxes (gasoline, diesel, natural gas, and mineral oils). Tax levels for gasoline, diesel, and electricity increased in five steps until 2003.[3] The bulk of the revenue – rising from 4.3 billion in 1999 to 18.1 billion in 2004 (BMF 2005) – is earmarked to lower the social security contributions paid by employers and employees, thus encouraging job creation. A small amount per year (102 million) was reserved for renewable energy subsidies. The German Institute for Economic Research (DIW) estimated that the eco-tax reform would reduce CO_2 emissions by 2 to 3 per cent (or 10 Mt) by 2005 (Ziesing 2006).

The eco-tax met massive opposition from the business sector, and it was largely unpopular with the public. A number of exemptions were granted, so that the eco-tax lost much in policy consistency in terms of incentives and fairness. For example, the tax rates for industries are much lower than for the residential sector, and the tax is not based on the carbon content of fuels.[4] As a result of nationwide protests against (supposedly socially unfair effects of) high fuel prices in 2000, the government was forced to introduce one-time compensation mechanisms for those hit hardest by the eco-tax (commuters and low-income households.) While the government has ruled out further tax increases because of rising energy prices, the increased tax rates (2003 level) remain in place, and thus constitute evidence of government determination to see this policy through.[5]

The aggressive promotion of renewable energy sources is probably the most significant and successful policy measure in the fight against climate change. Between 2000 and 2005 alone, Germany's total renewables supply increased by 70 per cent, and Germany surpassed its 2010 target to have renewables provide 4.2 per cent of primary energy supply by 2006 already (IEA 2007, 11, 65).

Lutz Mez in chapter 14 gives a detailed account of how Germany achieved world leadership in renewable sources for electricity generation, where the most spectacular expansion of renewables, especially of wind power, has taken place. Hence, suffice to emphasize here that the primary tool to enhance the share of renewables has been a strong feed-in tariff system in electricity generation, that provides renewables producers a guaranteed, attractive rate for electricity production and ensures access to the power grid. This system has received much praise but also attracted some criticism. The argument is that guaranteed rates (while declining over time according to a fixed degression rate) have been too generous (especially for solar power that contributes relatively little capacity) and that the continuation of long-term subsidies does not put enough pressure on prices. There is the issue of cost to costumers, who are expected to pay about 10 eurocents per kwh for the feed-in tariff by 2012 (for details, see IEA 2007, 68–70). Yet, notwithstanding concerns about the cost-effectiveness of this program, it can hardly be denied, as Mez demonstrates, that this strong policy instrument has had high output success and is a cornerstone in Germany's climate protection strategy. It was also adopted by many other countries.

Today's single-most important energy-related climate policy instrument, however, is the EU Emission Trading System (EU-ETS), that, initially, Germany was very sceptical about. When in 1996 the United States started to push for the introduction of emissions trading into the negotiation of the Kyoto Protocol, opposition was voiced not only by Germany but also at the EU level. There was concern that this instrument might be abused as a right to pollute and would therefore not be as effective as regulatory policy. In the end, the EU countries agreed to emissions trading, however only as a complementary instrument to keep the United States on board (Oberthür and Ott 1999). Germany remained sceptical about potential pitfalls of emissions trading also during the negotiations of an EU system that followed the Kyoto conference. This was also due to pressure from the energy sector and other GHG-intensive industries that preferred voluntary agreements (Schafhausen 2007).

Hans-Joachim Ziesing in his chapter examines the ETS in detail. In Germany, it covers about 55 per cent of total CO_2 emissions and includes most industrial installations and larger power plants (but excludes transport, households, and services). The basic idea of the system is that individual countries, subject to EU approval, allocate emission permits to energy and industrial installations. The EU trading system allows companies that exceed their quota to buy certificates from companies with excess permits. However, as described in detail in Ziesing's analysis (see chapter 13), the German National Allocation Plan for the first ETS period (2005–7) was far too generous to coal-fired power plants in particular.[6] As a result of lobbying and bargaining with the federal government, energy and industry companies were granted an annual reduction target for their sector of only 2 million tons CO_2 for 2005–7. Curiously, the total allowance of CO_2 emissions (about 500 million tons per year for 2005–7) set a much less strict target than the one fixed in the voluntary industry commitment (see below).

As a consequence, the reduction burden was shifted to transport and households, hence to individual consumers, to the benefit of large industry emitters. The second National Allocation Plan (2008–12), enacted in June 2007, brings a tightening of the cap. Originally set at 482 and later 462 million tons per year by the federal government, the European Commission insisted on a cap at 453 million tons per year, a reduction of over 10 per cent, compared to the first period. This will require an 8 per cent cut in reduction for industry and energy (compared to current emissions). Further improvements for the second period include that 10 per cent of all permits in Germany are no longer grandfathered for free to installations but sold by auction (BMU 2007b). Most of the auction proceeds are administered by the Ministry of the Environment. It is estimated that the sale of permits might generate up to 800 million in 2008.

In addition to these key tax and regulatory policies, Germany has implemented a wide variety of further programs and measures that provide mainly monetary incentives (subsidies, loans) but that have regulatory elements as well (also see Mez, chapter 14).

In the area of promotion of renewables, the 100,000 Roofs Program, a market creation program for photovoltaics, was adopted in January 1999. It provided (till 2003) reduced loans for PV roof installation through the federally owned KfW bank group. Combined with the feed-in tariff system, it resulted in solar power installations of 350 MW. The Market Incentives Program for Renewables launched in 1999 is designed to promote the use of biomass, solar energy, and geothermal energy in heat generation through grants and loans. Until the end of

2005, funding was provided for more than 421,500 solar collector system and 60,000 small-scale biomass boilers (IEA 2007, 71). The promotion of combined heat and power (CHP law 2002, see Watanabe and Mez 2004, 11) has been another, more recent priority area for active policy measures. In transportation, tax breaks on biofuels were granted, and, more recently, a biofuel mixing obligations for diesel and gasoline was introduced.

In the area of energy efficiency, the 2002 Energy Savings Ordinance set higher standards for new and old buildings in an integrated approach covering heating supply and demand including warm water. Efficiency requirements for new buildings were introduced that exceed current levels by 30 per cent. It also prescribed insulation levels and exchange of heating system for older buildings (UBA 2007). A recent revision of this ordinance (June 2007) made an energy passport (certificate) for buildings mandatory, designed to serve as an incentive to upgrade. The relaunched CO_2 Building Rehabilitation Program has received increased funding of 1.5 billion (compared to 360 million previously) per year (investment grants and tax relief) beginning in 2007.

Finally, Germany has drawn on its long-standing tradition of industrial self-regulation to experiment with voluntary industry commitments to reduce CO_2 emissions and to expand the share of combined heat and power (CHP) installations. For industry, the conclusion of voluntary agreements has traditionally been an important tool to avoid environmental regulatory measures (Wurzel et al. 2003). In 1995, the German Industry Federation (BDI) signed a first commitment declaration, after the government agreed not to introduce a carbon tax. It was revised in 1996, and then updated again in 2000 and amended in 2002. The 2000 agreement pledges to achieve a 28 per cent reduction of specific CO_2 emissions compared to 1990 levels, by 2005. Furthermore, for all six greenhouse gases listed in the Kyoto Protocol, specific emissions are to be reduced by 35 per cent until 2012 (1990 levels). In 2002, an amendment to CHP promotion stipulated that measures in this area were to reduce the six 'Kyoto' gases by 45 million tons of CO_2 equivalents from 1998 to 2010/12. Achievements are monitored by independent institutes.

However, the success of these agreements has been mixed at best. German industry, for example, did not comply with the specific combined heat and power commitments (of 2001 and 2004) to reduce CO_2 emissions by 20 million tons by 2005. Instead, energy industry emissions rose by 30 million tons. Furthermore, the German automobile

Table 12.1 Primary policies for GHG reduction 1995–2007

Sector	Initiative	Policy type
Energy	Eco-Tax	Tax/regulatory
	Renewable Energy Sources Act – feed-in tariff	Subsidy/regulatory
	Emission Cap and Trade – EU-ETS	Regulatory/auctioning (2008)
	Market Incentive Programs for Renewable Energy	Subsidy
	Combined Heat and Power Act	Regulatory/subsidy
	Two voluntary agreements with industry (automobile industry, high-emission industries, and power plants)	Voluntary
	Information Program for Households	Information
	Federal Energy Research Program	Subsidy
Transportation	Eco-Tax	Regulatory
	Biofuel tax breaks and mixing obligation	Subsidy/regulatory
	Exhaust Emission Standards	Regulatory/tax
Buildings	Energy Saving Ordinance for New Buildings	Regulatory
	Energy Passport	Information
	100,000 Roofs Program (solar power)	Subsidy
	Financial Incentive Program for Buildings	Subsidy

industry did not comply with its (EU-level) voluntary commitment to reduction of exhaust gases. The German car industry and the government, in particular Chancellor Merkel, lobbied hard in Brussels to arrive at a new EU target that would be favourable for German car manufacturers.

This underscores the observation by Rivers and Jaccard in relation to Canadian policies, as well as findings in the broader literature, that voluntary agreements are of limited effectiveness (OECD 2003, 14). There has been certain disenchantment with this instrument in the German case as well, and recent initiatives, both domestic and international, indicate that voluntary agreements will not play a significant role in German climate protection policy in the future.

As the overview in table 12.1 shows, Germany has drawn on a wide variety of policy measures in the implementation of climate protection commitments.

Quite clearly, and in stark contrast to Canada (see table 11.1 in Rivers and Jaccard) compulsory, regulatory measures feature prominently in

Germany's toolbox. Subsidies have also taken on an important role. While their effects are difficult to quantify, these strong measures have arguably been effective in reducing emission levels, notwithstanding open questions about the cost-effectiveness of some measures (promotion of renewables in particular). This raises the question why German governments have been able to implement such strong policies that impose significant costs on industry and the general population. The answer lies in an extremely favourable institutional environment.

A Favourable Institutional Framework

Our account of development of German climate change policy in the first part of this chapter has already hinted at key institutional elements facilitating progressive climate protection commitments and policies. We can also draw on the presentation of the German multi-level energy regulatory regime provided by Eberlein and Doern in chapter 1, and on elements contained in the three chapters by Mez, Ziesing, and by Mez and Doern on nuclear policy.

Firstly, and more generally, it should be noted that Germany, over the last thirty years, has progressively developed a broad and solid foundation of *environmental governance capacities and capabilities* (Jänicke and Weidner 1997; Weidner 2002; Weidner and Mez 2005). These include administrative and policy capacities but also ideational-cognitive and technological and economic capabilities.

Early experience with and conflicts about air pollution control beginning in the 1970s established a strong focus on the airborne environmental effects of energy production and related industries. During the 1980s, West Germany became the pacesetter in air pollution control policy and technologies. After unification in 1990, the legacy of heavy air pollution and massive waste of energy resources in East Germany helped to reinforce this focus and to further strengthen different kinds of capacities for environmental management and control. These include the establishment of highly specialized institutions with expertise in research, implementation, or monitoring, the development of an 'abatement industry,' a broad monitoring network, and the enactment of laws and regulations that encouraged pollution-control technologies and markets. It also helped to develop capabilities of NGOs to exert influence in this policy arena.

On the level of policy ideas and principles, the *Vorsorgeprinzip* (precautionary principle) not only gained in legal strength (through court rulings and legislation), but also as a broader principle guiding environmental discourse and policy. Experiences made with air pollution control underscored the position of environmental advocates that a risk-averse strategy is the best course to deal with situations of uncertainty that may lead to disastrous environmental consequences.

Furthermore, the concept of 'ecological modernization' as an environmental win-win strategy has gained wide acceptance. It builds on the recognition (and empirical evidence) that environmental regulations such as strict air pollution control do not only impose costs but enhance technological innovation and employment opportunities, and, more generally, encourage the modernization of industrial sectors involved (Weidner 2005).

In terms of governmental-administrative capacities, we noted earlier that the creation of the Federal Environment Ministry in 1986 established an important administrative resource and sponsor of environmental policies in the federal Cabinet. The new ministry later acquired more competences and emerged as important counterweight to the Ministry of Economics, in charge of the energy portfolio, that traditionally defends the interests of the utilities and the energy industry. The Inter-Ministerial Working Group on CO_2 Reduction was crucial in providing cross-sector focus and continuity on the climate change issue in a governmental process that normally suffers from poor coordination between sectors and portfolios.

German federalism was not a barrier to federal leadership in climate policy, as most policy areas relevant for climate protection fall under federal jurisdiction insofar as the federal level chooses to legislate (concurrent jurisdiction – konkurrierende Gesetzgebung). Moreover, Länder and local authorities (with the exception of coal advocates in the Ruhr region, see below) have been very supportive of the climate policy agenda and launched their own emission reduction programs, as well as a variety of other initiatives, inter alia under the Local Agenda 21.

Turning more directly to the politics and political economy of German climate policy, the most striking favourable element is the high degree of broad political support for the climate policy agenda. As noted earlier, there was no fundamental opposition to the principle of climate protection among political parties or major interest groups. The fact that Germany has had no major producer industries or regions in oil and natural gas certainly helped to forge a consensus.

However, the major energy utilities have an important stake in carbon-intensive brown coal (lignite) use that accounts for a large share of GHG emissions. The utilities have used their strong power base in the German political economy to oppose and to water down specific policy measures, sometimes successfully, as, for example, Ziesing shows in the first-period allocation of emission permits under the EU cap-and-trade system. The effectiveness of the eco-tax was diluted by concessions to industry interests. And in transportation, automobile industry lobbying has had similar effects. Yet, overall, there has been no change in direction of climate policy.

While there has been broad bipartisan continuity on climate change over more than twenty years, it is important to acknowledge that some key policies and measures were implemented under the Red-Green coalition (1998–2005), when the German Green Party was in charge of the Ministry of the Environment. Strong policies such as the eco-tax reflect the environmental and regulatory preferences of the Green coalition partner. The presence of a strong Green Party was also important in that it put competitive-electoral pressure on the other parties to adopt environmental policies.

However, it is also important to understand that the green agenda, beyond the party-political arena, draws significant social support from a broadly based environmental movement, with a healthy network of influential environmental NGOs, whose origin can be traced back to the social movements of the 1970s, as also seen in the analysis by Mez and Doern (chapter 5), who stress that environmental concerns are much more deeply embedded in German society and politics than in most countries. The structural factor of Germany's poor natural resource base also plays an important role in this context: during the energy crises of the 1970s, the government nursed nuclear and coal to impressive dimension, which, as Mez explains in his chapter 14, gave rise to a strong anti-nuclear and environmental movement.

Furthermore, there is broad media and public awareness of environmental challenges and issues, and large support for active environmental policies. As surveys show, a majority of the population considers global warming as the most pressing environmental issue (BMU 2006b). Since early 2007, in the wake of the latest IPCC Panel and the Stern report, there has been a true 'climate-hype' in the German media, putting climate change front and centre in public debate.

Finally, and also in contrast to Canada, Germany's international environment provided incentives and opportunities for progressive climate protection policies. On the one hand, the EU framework allowed Germany to project the climate agenda onto the European and international stage and to exercise international leadership. On the other hand, the EU is an important actor and level of climate policy-making in its own right that has initiated (sometimes against member state resistance) key regulatory policy measures such as the emission trading system. Quite obviously, the EU itself has recently entered a long-term path toward progressive climate protection policy.[7]

In short, a confluence of supportive institutional conditions and capacities has put and sustained Germany on a track of progressive climate protection commitments and active policies. But how sustainable is this path?

Conclusions: Path Sustainability and Future Challenges

Our key argument in this chapter has been that Germany's success and leadership in climate protection is the result of 'positive path dependence': progressive capacity-building and a supportive institutional and political (domestic and international) environment have allowed Germany to pursue comparatively strong and often effective public policies to reduce GHG emissions and increase energy efficiency. However, as Germany now prepares to tackle even more ambitious emission reduction targets, the question arises if this path is sustainable.

First, one has to consider that certain structural factors that have worked in Germany's favour so far will be less important or favourable in the future. For one, the wall-fall effect has now been consumed, as it were. Moreover, while population growth is very unlikely to pick up (unless dramatic changes to immigration policies are made), higher economic growth, 2.9 per cent in 2006 and 2 per cent in 2007, may result in a rise in emissions – although the onset of the global recession in 2008 has made substantial growth an unlikely scenario in the near future. While energy efficiency has improved considerably, this might still negatively affect emission reductions.

Second, Germany will have to confront ever more ambitious reduction goals while at the same time phasing out nuclear power, a key source of largely carbon-free – if highly controversial – energy supply. As discussed by Mez and Doern in chapter 5, Germany's phase-out decision is likely to hold, albeit over an extended deadline date, and that presents energy policy with a conundrum. One curious outcome could be the revival of (cleaner) coal. The utility industry has already announced that it plans to build up to thirty new coal-fired power plants with more than 25,000 MW capacity to replace aging electricity generation capacity.[8] It is far from clear how far clean-coal technologies (especially CO_2 capture and storage technology) will be available and commercially viable to allow keeping emission levels down while burning coal for electricity generation.

Third, the very success of emission reduction so far makes it more difficult to make further, relative progress. To continue to improve its record, Germany has to take emission reduction to a new level or threshold that poses not only quantitatively but also *qualitatively* different challenges. A good example is the case of biofuel. There is a growing consensus among experts that the current and prospective biofuel policy is not sustainable and may contribute to price increases for staple foods – a development already severely affecting poor countries. Furthermore, the envisaged mandating of a 10 per cent share of bio-ethanol in gasoline (a measure to help German car makers reach the CO_2 emission standard of the EU) had to be abandoned because of the risk of engine damage. Both 'failures' must now be compensated by measures in other areas, probably in the consumer sector, if ambitious GHG goals are to be met.

Another good example is improvement in energy productivity. As noted earlier, after energy productivity improved at an annual rate of over 2 per cent through the 1990s, the rates of improvement have slowed to about 1 per cent in the early 2000s, due in part to the higher base level. To still reach the coalition agreement target of doubling energy productivity from 1990 to 2020, Environment Minister Gabriel now aims for an annual 3 per cent increase in energy productivity – however, this target (which is still unparalleled) will be impossible to achieve without taking emission reduction policies to a new level, which will meet stiff resistance by the utility and energy lobby.[9]

In August 2007, the federal Cabinet endorsed an 'integrated climate and energy package' of twenty-nine measures to meet the 40 per cent reduction target by 2020. It includes very ambitious measures, such as significantly increased spending on the promotion of CHP and renewables, tougher standards for the energy efficiency of buildings, and setting the vehicle tax according to CO_2 emissions. The package of eleven key measures tabled by the environment minister in April 2007 (BMU 2007a), in a drive to cut 270 million tons by 2020 (to meet the 40 per cent reduction) included very ambitious measures, such as an 11 per cent reduction in electricity consumption through massive increase in energy efficiency, or an increase in the share of renewables in electricity generation (from less than 12 per cent) to more than 27 per cent. In August 2007 the federal Cabinet endorsed an 'integrated climate and energy package' of thirty measures that was submitted to parliamentary debate in the fall of 2007. It includes significantly increased spending on the promotion of CHP and renewables, tougher standards for the energy efficiency of buildings, and setting the vehicle tax according to CO_2 emissions.[10] On 5 December 2007 the federal Cabinet passed a comprehensive 'action package,' including fourteen laws and ordinances as a first step to implement this program, with a second step to follow in 2008. The unusual speed at which the twenty-nine-measures package was translated into concrete policies was largely due to the government's determination to demonstrate its commitment to an ambitious climate policy in the run-up to the UN Climate Change Conference in Bali in December 2007.

Among the main measures in the action package are subsidies for the promotion of CHP to increase its share from a current 12 to 25 per cent by 2020; reduction of energy consumption of buildings (primarily heating energy) by 30 per cent from 2009 on; systematic and strong emphasis on energy efficiency of products and services in public procurement; amendment of the Renewables Law (EEG) to massively promote offshore wind power; obligatory standards for the use of renewable energy for heating in private houses to increase its share from 6 per cent to 14 per cent in 2020 (the government will support this with 500 million per year from 2009 on); and strong increase of obligatory admixing of biofuel in gasoline and diesel. Mainly due to a sharp increase in financial incentive programs for the reduction of GHG emissions, the 2008 federal budget for climate policy rose to about 3.3 billion – an increase of 1.8 billion compared to 2005. The government also put itself under pressure to continuously implement the program by public transparency rules: all federal ministries involved are required to publish every two years (beginning in 2010) a progress report, supervised by independent experts (see BMU 2007c).

It is clear that more aggressive measures will raise thorny distributive issues. Will the government be able to impose a higher share of the adjustment burden on the utility and energy-intensive industry that has so far successfully lobbied for preferential treatment? And will the German citizens' willingness to pay decrease with rising costs, especially if the socially regressive distributive effects of climate policies become more transparent? Finally, will the global recession curb support for costly climate policies and instead put economic recovery front and centre? In any case, it seems safe to assume that emerging challenges and developments will put the current consensus on the direction of German climate policy to a severe test, even if the majority continues to agree that climate change is the 'biggest challenge of the 21st century.'[11]

NOTES

1 This statement was meant primarily to garner support for nuclear power compared to fossil fuels. However, shortly after the publication, the Chernobyl nuclear disaster occurred and undercut the attempt to raise public acceptance of nuclear power (Cavender and Jäger 1993).
2 In 2000, energy industries accounted for 42 per cent of total CO_2 emissions, followed by transport (20.9 per cent), other industry (16.4 per cent), residential (14.3 per cent), and other sectors (6.4 per cent) (IEA 2002, 35).
3 Coal and nuclear fuels were not affected. The tax is not levied on fuels used in CHP and decentralized production (up to five MW), nor for natural gas–fired power plants with an efficiency of 57.5 per cent or more.
4 Sectors exposed to international competition (manufacturing, agriculture, forestry) were entitled to eco-tax rebates of up to 80 per cent (although rebates were gradually reduced after 2003).
5 Due to further sharp increases in gasoline prices at the pump, pressure on the government to withdraw or reduce the eco-tax has intensified since early 2008.
6 More generally, the over-allocation of free permits resulted in windfall profits for the utilities that priced the trading value of permits into the electricity tariffs charged to consumers. Allocations were so generous that the German companies actually emitted less than they had been allocated and could sell the excess permits on the market! However, the inflationary effects of general over-allocation in most countries has meanwhile reduced the price of allowances to very low levels, from initially sixteen euros per tonne to, at one point, less than one euro per tonne.
7 See, for instance, EU Commission (2007). This initiative owes much to the strong influence of the German government.
8 In order to help investors, new generating plants are exempted from the emission requirements under the EU cap-and-trade system until 2012. Originally, the government had planned to grant new plants fourteen years of free emission allocation, but had to revise this under EU pres-

sure (Krägenow and Ruch 2007). Environment Minister Gabriel supports new coal-fired plants, as part of a fuel mix of renewables, coal (and CHP), (less) gas, and energy efficiency but without nuclear power.

9 The CEO of BASF, Jürgen Hambrecht, denounced this 3 per cent target as 'completely unrealistic.' He called for international efforts to reduce climate change, as opposed to Germany pressing ahead by itself, to the detriment of the international competitiveness of German industry (Spiegel Online International 2007). However, steeply increasing energy prices since the fall of 2007 make the government's efficiency target seem more attractive and sensible, even from an industry perspective.

10 See BMU (2008). The package of measures agreed on between the Ministries of the Environment and Economics will allow for a reduction of up to 36 per cent by (220 million tons CO_2 by 2020). Nevertheless, Minister Gabriel called the '29-Measure Package' a 'quantum leap in climate policy' (*Frankfurter Rundschau*, 24 August 2007). At least, the climate policy targets of this grand coalition government are significantly more demanding than those of the previous Red-Green governments.

11 On the occasion of the Energy Summit held on 3 July 2007, Chancellor Angela Merkel declared climate protection to be the 'biggest challenge of the 21st century' (*Frankfurter Allgemeine Zeitung*, 4 July 2007) – almost twenty years after former chancellor Helmut Kohl had declared the climate the most pressing environmental problem. This demonstrates how long the German government has been committed to climate policy.

REFERENCES

Bardt, Hubertus. 2006. Umwelteffizienz im internationalen Vergleich. IW-Trends [Environmental efficiency in international comparison]. *Vierteljahresschrift zur empirischen Wirtschaftsforschung aus dem Institut der deutschen Wirtschaft* [Quarterly Empirical Economics Research, Institute of the German Economy] 33 (4): 1–12.
Beuermann, Christiane. 2000. Germany: Regulation and the precautionary principle. In *Implementing sustainable development: Strategies and initiatives in high consumption societies*, ed. William M. Lafferty and James Meadowcroft, 85–111. Oxford: Oxford University Press.
Beuermann, Christiane and Jill Jäger. 1996. Climate change policy in Germany: How long will any double dividend last? In *Politics of climate change: A European perspective*, ed. Timothy O'Riordan and Jill Jäger, 186–227. London: Routledge.

BMF. *See* Bundesministerium der Finanzen [Federal Ministry of Finance].

BMU [Federal Environment Ministry]. 2006a. *Environmental policy: Demonstrable progress report; 2006 Report under the UN Framework Convention on Climate Change.* Berlin: BMU.

– 2006b. *Umweltbewusstsein in Deutschland 2006* [Environmental awareness in Germany 2006]. Berlin: BMU.

– 2007a. The federal government's climate policy in the wake of the European Council. Policy statement by Minister Gabriel, 26 April, Bundestag. http://www.bmu.de/english/speeches/doc/pdf/39349.pdf.

– 2007b. *Germany moving forward in EU-wide auctioning of emissions allowances.* Press release, 22 June.
http://www.bmu.de/english/current_press_releases/pm/39746.php.

– 2007c. Das Integrierte Energie – und Klimaprogramm der Bundesregierung [Integrated Energy and Climate Program of the Federal Government]. http://www.bmu.de/klimaschutz/downloads/doc/40515.php.

– 2008. Bundesregierung startet Integriertes Energie -und Klimaprogramm [Federal government launches integrated energy and climate program]. *Umwelt* 1.

Bundesministerium der Finanzen. 2005. *Bilanz der ökologischen Steuerreform* [Balance sheet of the Ecological Tax Reform]. Berlin, August.

Cavender, Jeannine, and Jill Jäger. 1993. The history of Germany's response to climate change. *International Environmental Affairs* 3 (1): 3–18.

EU Council / German Presidency. 2007. Historical agreement on climate protection. Press release, Brussels. http://www.eu2007.de/en/News/Press_Releases/March/0309BKBruessel.html.

EU Commission. 2007. *Green book: Adaptation to climate change in Europe.* Brussels, COM 2007/354.

G8. 2007. Growth and responsibility in the world economy. Summit declaration, 7 June. http://www.g-8.de/Content/EN/Artikel/_g8-summit/anlagen/2007-6-07-gipfeldokument-wirtschaft-eng,templateId=raw,property=publicationFile.pdf/2007-06-07-gipfeldokument-wirtschaft-eng.

German Bundestag, ed. 1991. *Protecting the earth: A status report with recommendations for a new energy policy.* Third report of the Enquête Commission of the 11th German Bundestag, preventive measures to protect the earth's atmosphere. Vol. 2. Bonn: Deutscher Bundestag.

IEA. *See* International Energy Agency.

International Energy Agency. 2002. *Energy policies of IEA countries: Germany 2002 review.* Paris: International Energy Agency.

– 2007. *Energy policies of IEA countries: Germany 2007 review.* Paris: International Energy Agency.

342   Helmut Weidner and Burkard Eberlein

Jaccard, Mark, Nic Rivers, and M. Horne. 2004. The morning after: Optimal greenhouse gas policies for Canada's Kyoto obligations and beyond. CD Howe Institute Commentary 197.

Jänicke, Martin, and Helmut Weidner, eds. 1997. National environmental policies: A comparative study of capacity-building. Berlin: Springer.

Krägenow, Timm, and Matthias Ruch. 2007. Gloomy future for coal-fired power plants. Financial Times Germany. 18 April.

Mez, Lutz. 2003. Ökologische Modernisierung und Vorreiterrolle in der Energie- und Umweltpolitik? Eine vorläufige Bilanz [Ecological modernization and pioneer role in energy and environment policy? A preliminary balance sheet]. In Das rot-grüne Projekt. Eine Bilanz der Regierung Schröder 1998–2002 [The Red-Green Project: A review of the Schröder government 1998–2002], ed. C. Egle, T. Ostheim, and R. Zohlnhöfer, 329–50. Wiesbaden: Westdeutscher Verlag.

Oberthür, Sebastian, and Hermann Ott. 1999. The Kyoto protocol: International climate policy for the 21st century. Berlin: Springer.

OECD. See Organisation for Economic Co-operation and Development.

Organisation for Economic Co-operation and Development. 2003. Voluntary approaches for environmental policy: Effectiveness, efficiency, and usage in the policy mixes. Paris: Organisation for Economic Co-operation and Development.

Pierson, Paul. 2004. Politics in time: History, institutions, and social analysis. Princeton: Princeton University Press.

Schafhausen, Franzjosef. 2007. Perspektiven des Emissionshandelns aus deutscher Sicht [Perspectives of emissions trading from a German viewpoint]. Vierteljahresschrift zur Wirtschaftsforschung [Quarterly Economics Research] 76 (1): 99–117.

Schleich, Joachim, W. Eichhammer, U. Boede, F. Gagelmann, E. Jochem, B. Schlomann, and H-J. Ziesing. 2001. Greenhouse gas reductions in Germany: Lucky strike or hard work? Climate Policy 1:363–80.

Spiegel Online International. 2007. I have a problem with the term climate change. Spiegel interview with BASF CEO Juergen Hambrecht. 27 June. http://www.spiegel.de/international/business/0,1518,491075,00.html.

UBA. See Umweltbundesamt [Federal Environment Agency].

Umweltbundesamt. 2006. Nationaler Inventarbericht zum deutschen Treibhausgasinventar 1990–2004 [National inventory report, German GHG 1990–2004]. Dessau: Umweltbundesamt. http://unfccc.int/national_reports/annex_i_ghg_inventories/national_inventories_submissions/items/3734.p hp.

– 2007. Klimaschutz in Deutschland: 40%-Senkung der CO_2-Emissionen bis 2020 gegenüber 1990 [Climate protection in Germany: 40 per cent reduction of CO_2 emissions by 2020 compared to 1990]. Dessau: Umweltbundesamt.

Watanabe, Rie, and Lutz Mez. 2004. The development of climate change policy in Germany. *International Review for Environmental Strategies* 5 (1): 1–17.

Weidner, Helmut. 1999. Umweltpolitik: Entwicklungslinien, Kapazitäten und Effekte [Environmental policy: Trajectories, capacities and effects]. In *Eine lernende Demokratie – 50 Jahre Bundesrepublik Deutschland* [A learning democracy, 50 years of the Federal Republic of Germany], ed. Max Kaase and Günter Schmid, 425–60. Berlin: WZB-Jahrbuch.

– 2002. Environmental policy and politics in Germany. In *Environmental politics and policy in industrialized countries*, ed. U. Desai, 149–201. Cambridge, MA: MIT Press.

– 2005. Global equity versus public interest? The case of climate change policy in Germany. Discussion paper SP IV 2005-102. Berlin: WZB [Social Science Research Centre Berlin]. http://bibliothek.wzb.eu/pdf/2005/iv05-102.pdf.

– 2007. Climate change policy in Germany: An analysis of moral and other capacities. Paper prepared for the Climate and Renewable Energy Section, ECPR Conference, Pisa, 6–9 September.

Weidner, Helmut, and Lutz Mez. 2005. Climate change and renewable energy policy in Germany: The driving forces and conflicts. Paper prepared for the Environmental Politics Section, 'The Politics of Renewables,' ECPR Conference, Budapest, 8–10 September.

Wittke, Franz, and Hans-Joachim Ziesing. 2006. Hohe Energiepreise dämpfen Primärenergieverbrauch in Deutschland [High energy prices depress primary energy consumption in Germany]. *DIW Wochenbericht* [DIW Weekly Reports] 73 (10): 117–31.

Wurzel, Rüdiger K.W., A. Jordan, A. Zito, and L. Brückner. 2003. From high regulatory state to social and ecological market economy? New environmental policy instruments in Germany. *Environmental Politics* 12 (1): 115–36.

Ziesing, Hans-Joachim. 2005. Stagnation der Kohlendioxidemissionen in Deutschland im Jahr 2004 [Stagnation of CO_2 emissions in Germany in 2004]. *DIW-Wochenbericht* [DIW Weekly Report] 9:163–72.

– 2006. Kohlendioxidemissionen in Deutschland im Jahr 2005 deutlich gesunken [CO_2 emissions decreased significantly in 2005 in Germany]. *DIW-Wochenbericht* [DIW Weekly Report] 12:153–62.

13 EU Emission Trading and National Allocations Plans 2005–2007: The Case of Germany

HANS-JOACHIM ZIESING

While the previous two chapters by Rivers and Jaccard and Weidner and Eberlein contrast Canadian and German approaches and achievements in overall climate protection policies, this chapter probes one of the key instruments in the European toolbox to reduce greenhouse gas (GHG) emissions, the EU cap-and-trade emissions system. Based on a detailed analysis of the first implementation phase in Germany, the chapter reveals the technical and political complexity of introducing new approaches and instruments in a policy domain where vested economic interests are exceptionally strong.

The outcomes have been sobering and disappointing. As result of a highly political process with heavy utility and industry lobbying, German implementation produced a bureaucratic system of emissions permit allocation that was heavily biased in favour of specific utility and other industry interests and required only marginal emission reduction rates. Notable improvements have been introduced for the second phase (2008 to 2012), but the EU emissions trading system and national implementation in particular still have to improve significantly to fully nurse the potentially enormous benefits of a new instrument in climate protection policy.

On 1 January 2005 the EU Emission Trading Scheme (EU-ETS) was launched. With this, the early attempts of the European Union to reduce GHG emissions made an important step forward. All member countries agreed to implement a common and, in principle, effective instrument to fight against global warming. The introduction of an emission trading scheme adopted one of the three market-based 'flexible mechanisms' of the Kyoto Protocol: emission trading, Joint Implementation (JI) and the Clean Development Mechanism (CDM). The EU decided not to wait for the Kyoto Protocol to come into force. Instead, in anticipation of the Kyoto commitment period 2008 to 2112, it started with its emission trading scheme in the period 2005 to 2007.

This chapter concentrates on the implementation of the EU-ETS in Germany by means of the 'National Allocation Plan' (NAP). In the first section, the chapter gives a short overview of the policy background of the EU-ETS. Then we describe the specific requirements of the relevant EU directive that all member states have to take into account. The third and main part of the chapter, however, focuses on the preparation and implementation of the NAP in Germany. It highlights the main features of this plan and then analyses the implementation procedure, with a special focus on the political process that underpins decision-making. It will become clear that Germany's implementation was far from the faithful execution of a theoretically sound emission trading system. Rather, it was the result of hard-nosed bargaining between the federal government and industry interests, as well as between different political forces within the government.

EU Emission Trading

The Background: EU-15 Not on the Right Emission Reduction Track

In 1992 the United Nations Framework Convention on Climate Change (UNFCCC) was adopted and came into force in 1994. One of the main purposes of this convention is the 'stabilization of greenhouse gas concentrations in the atmosphere at a level that would prevent dangerous anthropogenic interference with the climate system' (UNFCCC 1992). But this declaration was without any obligation. It took five years before the Kyoto Protocol to the UNFCCC was adopted in December 1997. The agreement stipulated, 'Parties included in Annex I shall, individually or jointly, ensure that their aggregate anthropogenic carbon dioxide equivalent emissions of the greenhouse gases ... do not exceed their assigned amounts, calculated pursuant to their quantified emission limitation and reduction commitments inscribed in Annex B' (Kyoto Protocol 1997). With the ratification by the Russian Federation, the Kyoto Protocol came into force on 16 February 2005. It should be mentioned that the EU played a major role in bringing the negotiations on the Kyoto Protocol to a successful conclusion, in particular after the U.S. withdrawal.

The reduction commitments according to the Kyoto Protocol range between a minus of 8 per cent in most of the Annex B countries and a plus of 10 per cent from 1990 GHG emissions level during the period 2008 to 2012. The EU-15 in total committed to an 8 per cent reduction. To comply with this target the member states agreed at the meeting of the EU Environment Council of 16–17 June 1998 to follow different targets within the so-called European burden sharing with a range of commitments from -28 per cent in Luxembourg to +27 per cent in Portugal.

As discussed in greater detail in chapter 12 by Weidner and Eberlein, Germany committed itself to a 21 per cent reduction of greenhouse gas emissions. This decision has to be seen against the background of the strong emissions decrease in the 1990s, mainly as a result of the economic crash in East Germany after unification. In 1998 the emissions were already 14 per cent below the level of 1990, and there was a hope of an ongoing trend.

Soon it became obvious that the empirical trend of GHG emissions in the EU-15 deviated from the Kyoto reduction requirements. By comparing the assigned amounts in the commitment period with past trends, some European countries showed substantial differences. At least eleven out of the fifteen member states appeared set to fall far short of their agreed share of the stabilization target for greenhouse gases in the EU (see figure 13.1).

Against this background, it was clear that significant further efforts would be required by the EU and its member states to meet their obligations under the Kyoto Protocol. At a very early stage, the EU Commission was convinced that emission trading should play an important role, particularly in bringing the less well performing EU member states back on track.

Apart from advocating emission trading, the EU was taking serious steps to address its own greenhouse gas emissions. The backbone of the commission's effort to implement the Kyoto Protocol is the European Climate Change Programme (EECP), which was launched in March 2000 (EU Commission 2001). The ECCP's goal is to identify and develop, jointly with all relevant stakeholders, cost-effective measures that will help the EU meet its 8 per cent Kyoto target, complementing the efforts of the member states. Since the ECCP was launched, more than two hundred stakeholders have been involved in eleven different working groups.

While the ETS is the most significant and strongest policy, the council and the European Parliament have adopted several other ini-

Figure 13.1 Quantified emission limitation or reduction commitment from 1990 GHG emissions level until the commitment period 2008 to 2012 under the European 'burden sharing' and the changes of GHG emissions from base year to 2004

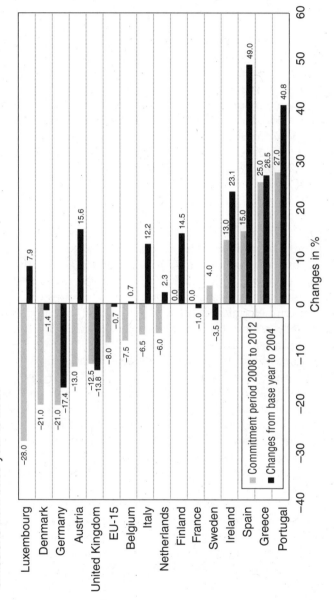

Source: National Greenhouse Gas Inventories (2006).

tiatives, such as legislation to promote renewable energies in electricity production and biofuels in road transport, and legislation on the energy efficiency of buildings. Other measures have been proposed by the commission, such as a directive to promote combined heat and power.

The European Commission also negotiated an agreement with all European, Japanese, and Korean car makers to cut average CO_2 emissions of new cars in the order of 25 per cent below 1995 levels by 2008/2009 (EU Commission 2003c). More recently, the March 2007 European Council Summit endorsed an integrated energy and climate package, that includes ambitious CO_2 emission reduction commitments (20 per cent by 2020, compared to 1990 levels) and related programs (for EU developments, see also chapter 7 by Cameron and chapter 12 by Weidner and Eberlein).

The EU Directive on Emission Trading

With the 'Directive 2003/87/EC' (EU Commission 2003a) the preconditions for the beginning of emission trading in 2005 had been created. This directive was supplemented in October 2004 by the so-called linking directive, which opens the opportunity to use emission credits generated through project activities in third countries outside the EU trading system, eligible pursuant to Articles 6 (Joint Implementation JI) and 12 (Clean Development Mechanism CDM) of the Kyoto Protocol (EU Commission 2004c).

The passage of these directives had been preceded by a long legislative history (for details, see EU Commission 2006). An intensive discussion already started in 2000 with the 'Green Paper on Greenhouse Gas Emissions Trading within the European Union' (EU Commission 2000). It might be worth mentioning that the discussion on emission trading in the 1990s within the OECD was dominated mainly by the United States, and not at all by the EU.

In fact, in the Kyoto Protocol negotiations, the majority of the EU member states argued against the inclusion of emission trading in the protocol. One reason was that most European countries traditionally preferred administrative regulations instead of market based instruments. Another argument was the risk that Russia could make use of the 'hot air,' resulting from the radical fall of emissions due to the economic slump after the collapse of the Soviet Union.

Europe did not agree until it was clear that the United States would not ratify the protocol without including emission trading and the other Kyoto mechanisms. In 1998 the EU Commission published a communication in which for the first time emission trading was mentioned as an important instrument for climate protection. From that time on, the commission was the driving force in favour of emission trading supported especially by the United Kingdom, the Netherlands, and Scandinavian countries.

As also discussed by Weidner and Eberlein in chapter 12, Germany was actually one of the countries that blocked or at least delayed the introduction of the ET directive for a long time (Bundesregierung 2001a). There were concerns about the compulsory character of an emission trading system and about the potentially high costs of this system. There was also limited trust in the functioning of emission trading. And many felt that Germany would not need emission trading because the reduction targets could be met with less compulsory measures.

However, at the end a compromise was found to accommodate Germany's concerns. After all, it was imperative that Germany as the most important emitter of GHG emissions in Europe was included in the trading system. The compromise included an opt-out option for specific installations as well as the option to form a pool of installations with the same type of activity. However, quite remarkably, no company in Germany made use of these options – probably because the National Allocation Plan proved to be comfortable enough for the companies involved.

Essentials of the ET Directive on Emissions Trading

The directive was based on the understanding that the crucial promise of emissions trading is to reduce GHG emissions in the most cost-efficient way. Given defined targets, emissions trading would bring advantages in comparison to other economic instruments. Emissions trading systems can and will not be without costs, but they will be much less costly than other instruments to meet given emission limitations. However, emissions trading will work only on the basis of a *cap-and-trade* system. If there are no caps, there will be no trade! This requires price signals for business decisions made at a decentralized level. The required price signal is a function of the reduction target and of the nature of the individual structural elements.

The main purpose of the directive on emission trading is defined in Article 1: the 'Directive establishes a scheme for greenhouse gas emission allowance trading within the Community ... in order to promote reductions of greenhouse gas emissions in a cost-effective and economically efficient manner' (EU Commission 2003a).

Any assessment of the directive has to take into account its specific rules.

1 The directive applied only to emissions from activities listed in Annex I. Essentially it applied to energy activities, the production and processing of ferrous metals, parts of the mineral industry, and some other activities. The transport sector as well as the residential and service sectors are not included. Therefore, coverage of the existing emissions trading system is limited by design.

2 The directive at this stage referred only to the period 2005 to 2007 with some notes about the second period 2008 to 2012. Therefore, long-term planning for those activities that are subject to the emissions trading was not possible.

3 In principle the directive applies to all greenhouse gases, defined in the Kyoto Protocol, but within the period 2005 to 2007 it applied to CO_2 only.

4 Although, theoretically, the most efficient method of allocation would be based on auctioning or at least on a gradual transition to the auctioning option, the ET Directive imposed tight limits on auctioning. It stipulated that 'for the three-year period beginning 1 January 2005 Member States shall allocate at least 95% of the allowances free of charge. For the five-year period beginning 1 January 2008, Member States shall allocate at least 90% of the allowances free of charge' (EU Commission 2003a). Therefore, auctioning could play only a very limited role.

5 There are some more specific rules; for example, concerning the possibility to form a pool of installations, to allow a temporary exclusion of certain installations of pooling, the inclusion of so-called early actions, or the designation of a 'competent authority' within the emission trading scheme.

Most important for all the member states is Article 9 of the ET Directive that asks them to develop a national allocation plan 'stating the total quantity of allowances that it intends to allocate for that period and how it proposes to allocate them. The plan shall be based on objective and transparent criteria, including those listed in Annex

III, taking due account of comments from the public' (EU Commission 2003a).

The eleven criteria listed in Annex III not only are essential for the development and the design of the respective allocation plans but also form the basis for the commission's assessment and decision upon these plans. According to these criteria, the total quantity of allowances to be allocated for the relevant period shall be consistent with the member state's obligation to limit its emissions pursuant to the Kyoto Protocol.

It also means that the total quantity of allowances to be allocated shall not be more than is likely to be needed. Prior to 2008, the quantity shall be consistent with a path towards achieving each member state's target under the Kyoto Protocol. It is interesting that the plan also shall include provisions for comments to be expressed by the public, and contain information on the arrangements by which due account will be taken of these comments before a decision on the allocation of allowances is taken.

Emission trading systems can be efficient only if there is a clear monitoring and reporting system attached to it. Annex IV of the ET Directive erects principles for that purpose. On 29 January 2004 the commission published appropriate guidelines for the monitoring and reporting of greenhouse gas emissions (EU Commission 2004a). Member states are required to ensure that emissions are monitored in accordance with these guidelines, which are legally binding.

Each emission trading system needs to impose financial sanctions for non-compliance. According to Article 16 ET Directive, the excess emissions penalty shall be 100 for each ton of CO_2 equivalent emitted by that installation for which the operator has not surrendered allowances. In the first period from 2005 to 2007, however, the member states shall apply a lower excess emissions penalty of 40 for each ton of CO_2 equivalent. As important as the amount of the penalty is, the payment of the excess emissions penalty shall not release the operator from the obligation to surrender an amount of allowances equal to those excess emissions in the following calendar year. This regulation guarantees that the operators will not be able to buy their way out of the obligation to comply.

The EU Trading System: Lacking in Compulsoriness?

The ET Directive comprises a mixture of 'shall' and 'may' provisions for the member states. However, member states were required to transpose the directive, to establish a permitting process, to assign the competent national authorities, and, finally, to prepare and notify the national allocation plan (EU Commission 2003b). They also needed to establish an allowance registry (ibid.). In addition, there are some specific rules to be observed, such as the limits for auctioning, or the definition of activities that are subject of the directive.

However – and this is of utmost importance for the process – the directive leaves a wide margin of discretion for member states. This is true even in the nucleus of the emissions trading system: how the member state proposes to allocate the total quantity of allowances. This means that it is up to the member state to decide which caps should be directed towards which activities, out of those subject to the directive.

Hence, the implementation design, especially the discretion granted to member states, does not match the eco-economic ideal of what an emissions trading system should look like. Rather, the ET Directive is the result of a complex political compromise between supranational and national interests.

At least, however, the European Commission had the right of the final decision on the national allocation plan of each member state. This includes the right to require certain corrections within the individual allocation plans. The commission's first decisions on national allocation plans were made on 7 July 2004. The last national allocation plan, the Greek plan, was not approved until 20 June 2005.

In total, the commission approved the allocation of about 6.57 billion allowances to more than 11,400 installations for the trading period 2005 to 2007. It demanded cuts in the number of allowances to be allocated in fourteen out of the twenty-five plans. These cuts total over 290 million allowances, or about 4 per cent of the notified number of allowances. In addition, the commission disallowed intended ex-post adjustments in thirteen plans.

The National Allocation Plan of Germany[1]

To understand the specifics and the debate around the German National Allocation Plan (NAP), it might be helpful to first have a look at Germany's GHG emissions profile. Also, it is important get a general idea of the process of NAP preparation, in particular of the formal and informal political process. After this, we will describe the basic structure of the NAP and give some more detailed information on the so-called Macro-and Micro-Plan. We address the issue of industry influence on specific regulations. We will then describe the final result allowance allocation for the first commitment period 2005 to 2007, before ending the chapter with some conclusions.

Greenhouse Gas Emissions in Germany

According to the Kyoto Protocol and the European burden sharing agreement, Germany is committed to achieving a 21 per cent reduction in GHG emissions by 2008 to 2012 compared to 1990 levels. Germany's achievements are presented in detail in chapter 12 by Weidner and Eberlein. Suffice here to note that an 18.5 per cent reduction was realized by 2003 already; and the GHG inventory 2006 noted a reduction by 17.4 per cent from 1990 to 2004. As detailed in the preceding chapter by Weidner and Eberlein, the bulk of the emissions reduction happened in the early 1990s, mainly because of the economic collapse in East Germany following German unification.

Under the ET Directive, emission trading will initially be confined to CO_2 and specified installations. Table 13.1 shows how CO_2 emissions developed from 1990 to 2002 in different sectors. Based on an average for 2000 to 2002, total CO_2 emissions had fallen by about 152 Mt or 14.9 per cent since 1990.

The biggest contributions were made by the energy sector (72 Mt) and by other industry (59 Mt). CO_2 emissions also declined in the trade, commerce, and service sectors (30 Mt) and in the residential sector (7 Mt), while emissions from transport were 16 Mt higher in 2002 than in 1990. There has, however, been a slight reduction in emissions in this sector every year since 1999, likely as a result of the eco-tax (see chapter 12 by Weidner and Eberlein, and chapter 14 by Mez for details).

Table 13.1 also provides some preliminary indications of the level of CO_2 emissions in the sectors covered by emission trading. These are mainly the emissions caused by the energy sector and the industry. Average annual CO_2 emissions from both sectors in 2000 to 2002 amounted to some 505 Mt. Compared with 1990, this is a decline of almost 131 million tons (-20.6 per cent). CO_2 emissions from all other sectors fell by almost 21 Mt (5.5 per cent) only. The sharp decrease of emissions in the sectors that are subject to the emissions trading system was one of the arguments used by the companies and associations against further obligations to reduce CO_2 emissions.

Table 13.1 CO$_2$ emissions in Germany 1990–2002 by sectors

Sectors	Mt CO$_2$					Average 2000–2	Change 1990 to 2002 %
	1990	1995	2000[a]	2001[a]	2002		
Energy production/conversion	439.2	377.7	361.1	369.1	373.0	367.7	-16.3
Power plants	353.8	319.7	309.5	316.9	322.0	316.1	-10.7
CHP plants, heating plants, and other conversion activities	85.4	58.0	51.6	52.2	51.0	51.6	-39.6
Industry							
Industry (energy-related)	169.3	126.3	116.0	112.6	109.1	112.5	-33.5
Industry processes[b]	27.6	26.3	26.1	24.4	24.4	25.0	-9.5
Subtotal	196.9	152.6	142.1	137.0	133.5	137.5	-30.2
Energy and industry	636.1	530.3	503.2	506.1	506.5	505.2	-20.6
Other sectors							
Trade, commerce, services[c]	90.5	68.1	59.2	63.0	59.0	60.4	-33.3
Transport[d]	158.8	171.9	178.4	174.6	172.6	175.2	10.3
Residentials	129.0	128.4	116.0	129.9	119.9	121.9	-5.5
Subtotal	378.4	368.5	353.6	367.5	351.5	357.5	-5.5
Total emissions[b]	1104.4	898.8	856.8	873.54	858.0	862.8	-14.9

[a]Provisional
[b]2002 estimated
[c]Including military services
[d]Excluding international air traffic and marine bunkers
Sources: Umweltbundesamt; Arbeitsgemeinschaft Energiebilanze. Calculations by DIW Berlin.

*The Formal Regulatory and Consultation Structure
and the Informal Process*

As discussed more widely in the chapters by Mez and Weidner and Eberlein, the responsibility for climate change policy within the federal government lies with the Federal Ministry of the Environment, Nature Conservation, and Nuclear Safety (BMU). BMU is also the lead body for drawing up the National Allocation Plan and the laws and regulations required for implementation. In addition, the BMU provides the technical and legal oversight for the national Emissions Trading Authority (Bundesregierung 2005).

The 'competent authority,' according to the ET Directive, is the Deutsche Emissionshandelsstelle (DEHSt, German Emissions Trading Authority), which was set up within the Federal Environmental Agency. The federal law implementing Directive 2003/87/EC (*Greenhouse Gas Emissions Trading Act*, TEHG) defines the tasks of the DEHSt as the allocation and issuance of emission allowances, supervision and oversight, maintaining the National Register as well as national and international reporting.

Independent of the responsibility of the BMU as the lead body, final decisions on the National Allocation Plan had to be made by the German government. Within the government, the Federal Chancellery as well as the Federal Ministry of Economics (BMWi) played an important role in the decisions on the NAP.

A predictable yet important line of conflict, regarding the design of the NAP, separated the BMU on the one hand from the Chancellery and the BMWi on the other hand. While the BMU was concerned mainly about an effective trading system that would set strong incentives to reduce CO_2 emissions, the BMWi and the Chancellery sought to lower the reduction burden, especially for the energy and industry sector, guided by concerns about the competitiveness of the German industry. Another reason for conflict was the fact that the different portfolios were held by different political parties: under the Red-Green Coalition, the Environment Ministry was held by the Green Party, whereas the traditionally industry-friendly Ministry of Economics was led by a Social-Democrat (also see chapter 1, Eberlein and Doern, for a more detailed discussion of the political process in energy regulatory governance).

In spite of its earlier opposition to the emissions trading system, Germany was early off the mark in preparations for the introduction of an emissions trading system. As early as 18 October 2002 – the EU Green Paper on greenhouse gas emissions trading within the EU had just been published – the federal Cabinet established, under the chairmanship of the BMU, the Working Group on Emissions Trading as a Means to Combat Climate Change (AGE). Members of this working group included eighty representatives of the federal government, of the Länder governments, of business (associations as well as companies, mainly from the energy and industrial sectors), and of environmental NGOs and trade unions.

Then, immediately after the Common Position of the European Council in December 2002 had cleared the way, the BMU implemented the first concrete steps towards emission trading. As a part of these activities the BMU commissioned a consortium of research institutes to assist the ministry with the preparation and implementation of the National Allocation Plan. Members of this consortium are the German Institute for Economic Research (DIW Berlin); the Fraunhofer Institute for Systems and Innovation Research (ISI), Karlsruhe; and the Öko-Institut (Institute for Applied Ecology), Freiburg and Berlin.

In mid-2003 the consortium presented the report National Allocation Plan (NAP), which gave a first systematic overview of the different options of allocations that were conceivable for Germany. The plan's priority was to take account of the interplay and the consistency of different rules (DIW Berlin et al. 2003).

The consortium had been strongly involved in the discussion with working papers, consultations with decision-makers, and innumerable discussions with representatives of industrial associations and companies – which all argued that their installations were unique and needed the full amount of emission certificates that they were asking for. However, it should be pointed out that the members of the advisory consortium (including the author of this chapter) are not in any way responsible for the final version of the German NAP.

In mid-October 2003 negotiations between the federal government and the industry started in a new format. In relatively short intervals high-ranking representatives of the federal government (state secretaries of BMU and BMWi) and the CEOs of the most important energy and industry companies met, in order to reach an agreement on the central points of the NAP for the first period 2005 to 2007. However, this attempt failed because a draft (about eighty pages strong) which had been finalized by the BMU in early January 2004 was presented to the high-level group on 29 January 2004 as a handout. The representatives of the industry (assisted by the BMWi state secretary) used this surprise presentation of a very complex paper as an opportunity to drop out of this high-level negotiation.

The collapse of this process was followed by extremely complicated negotiations between the federal Chancellery, the BMU, and the BMWi. Negotiations were all the more difficult as they took place in the shadow of heavy industry lobbying. The simple goal of the companies and associations involved was to avoid any obligations to significantly reduce CO_2 emissions. A number of different arguments were put forward, such as the impossibility of cutting emissions for technical and economic reasons, or the dangers that these obligations would pose to economic growth and employment. A very popular argument was that new investment, such as new power stations, would migrate to foreign locations. In this context, a highly political compromise was finally reached on 30 March 2004, so that the Cabinet could vote on the NAP for Germany on 31 March 2004 (BMU 2004).

The Basic Structure of the National Allocation Plan

The National Allocation Plan of Germany consists of a Macro-Plan and a Micro-Plan.

- The *Macro-Plan* defines the national emissions budget and determines the total quantity of allowances to be allocated. This figure must be consistent with national climate protection targets and the climate protection program. The overall budget of greenhouse gas emissions available to Germany in Kyoto period 2008–2112 is derived from the EU burden sharing agreement (reduction by 21 per cent compared to 1990 levels). The budget for greenhouse gas emissions in the period 2005 to 2007 must be consistent with this target. The Macro-Plan spells out these requirements in some detail, breaking the emissions budget down by greenhouse gas and sector.
- The *Micro-Plan* for the intended allocation of allowances to operators of individual installations defines the methods, rules, and criteria that determine allocation decisions and the question of what quantity of allowances will be granted to installations on the basis of the available data. The principles applied include grandfathering (allocation based on an installation's historical emissions in a reference period) and benchmarking (allocation based on the

average specific emissions of a product category). The Micro-Plan, which determines the allocation to an individual installation, is calculated using CO_2 emissions from the individual installations in the reference period 2000 to 2002 and the compliance factor. Quantities must be consistent with the Macro-Plan to ensure that the overall quantity of allowances actually allocated does not exceed or fall short of the quantity envisaged in the Macro-Plan.

THE ALLOCATION ON THE MACRO LEVEL

The Macro-Plan as part of the National Allocation Plan establishes how the national emissions budget is shared between the greenhouse gases and what proportion will be allocated to the emissions trading segment or to other sources. It determines the total quantity of allowances to be allocated to the emissions trading sectors.

The two parameters that serve as a starting point are greenhouse gas emissions in the baseline year 1990 and the target pledged by the German government as part of the European burden sharing agreement for the period 2008 to 2012 (minus 21 per cent). First, however, the NAP had to be established for the period 2005 to 2007. According to Annex III of ET Directive, the emission budgets to be set for this period are determined in a manner that ensures that the total quantity of allowances allocated is consistent with the reduction pledge for 2008 to 2012.

Table 13.2 sums up the decision on the structure of the national emissions budgets in period 2005 to 2007 and period 2008 to 2012.

The key element to note is that the required CO_2 emissions reduction target for the 2005 to 2007 period is in effect almost marginal, being set at 0.4 per cent (in comparison to the average in the period 2000 to 2012). In comparison with the CO_2 emissions in 2002 there is even a slight increase. Hence, it was no major challenge for the industry to comply with this target.

The reduction rate up to the second period 2008 to 2112 is a little more ambitious: emitters need to reduce CO_2 emissions (compared to the average 2000 to 2002) by 2.2 per cent; in comparison with the first period 2005 to 2007 the reduction rate will be 1.7 per cent. This means that the activities to reduce CO_2 emission have to be reinforced in the transition from the first to the second period.

The emissions budget defined above is distributed to the macro sectors in line with the breakdown by sectors used in the system of the German energy balances (energy conversion, industry; trade/com-

Table 13.2 Greenhouse gas emissions (excl. sinks) in Germany from base year to 2001/2002 and targets for 2005–7 and 2008–12

EU Emission Trading and National Allocations Plans   359

| | Mt CO$_2$ equivalent per year | | | | | | | |
	CO$_2$	CH$_4$	N$_2$O	HFCs	PFCs	SF$_6$	Total non-CO$_2$ emissions	Total
Base year	1014.4	101.1	87.9	6.4	1.8	6.6	203.7	1218.2
1990	1014.4	101.1	87.9	3.5	2.7	3.9	199.1	1213.5
1995	898.8	69.8	78.6	6.4	1.8	6.6	163.1	1061.8
1998	881.4	60.9	62.3	7.0	1.5	6.0	137.7	1019.1
1999	854.7	59.3	59.0	7.3	1.2	4.4	131.3	986.0
2000 (prov.)	856.8	54.5	59.4	6.6	0.8	4.0	125.3	982.1
2001 (prov.)	873.5	52.2	60.2	8.1	0.7	3.3	124.6	998.1
2002 (prov.)	858.0				No data yet			
Average 2000–2 (non-CO$_2$: 1999–2001)	863.0	55.0	60.0	7.0	1.0	4.0	127.0	990.0
Target 2005–7	859.0						123.0	982.0
Target 2008–12	844.0						118.0	962.0
				Changes in %				
2002/2001 (CO$_2$/non-CO$_2$) vs. base year	-15.4	-48.4	-31.5	27.8	-58.9	-49.9	-38.9	-18.1
2005–7 vs. average 2000–2/1999–2001	-0.4						-3.2	-18.1
2008–12 vs. average 2000–2/1999–2001	-2.2						-7.1	-2.8

Sources: National Allocation Plan for the Republic of Germany, 31 March 2004; Act on Allocation 2007 (Zuteilungsgesetz 2007), 26 August 2004.

merce/services, residential, transport). Non-energy-related CO_2 emissions (industrial processes) also are taken into account. On the macro level, the CO_2 budget of 859 Mt per year in the period 2005 to 2007 and of 844 Mt per year in the period 2008 to 2012 must be allocated between these sectors.

The goal of the BMU was that the overall reduction in the emissions trading sectors (ET sectors) should reflect the targets of the Voluntary Agreement between the German Federal Government and the German Industry to Reduce CO_2 Emissions and the Promotion of Combined Heat and Power Generation (Bundesregierung 2001b). This would entail that by 2010 the energy and other industry sectors achieve an emissions reduction of up to 45 million tons (Mt) CO_2, compared with 1998. Taking in account the emissions from sectors not participating in the emissions trading, and the compensation for the agreed phasing out of nuclear power plants, the voluntary agreement would have left 28 Mt CO_2 per year in 2008 to 2012 and around 20 Mt CO_2 per year in 2005 to 2007 for participating industries to absorb. According to this scenario, the CO_2 emissions budget for the trading sectors would amount to 488 Mt CO_2 or -3.3 per cent in the first period and 480 Mt CO_2 or -4.9 per cent in the second period. From the very beginning and for a long time, the BMU clearly preferred this scenario.

Soon it became clear that neither the energy nor the other industry companies would ever agree simply to apply the amounts committed to under the 'voluntary agreement approach' to the compulsory ETS. Their main argument was that a strict emissions cap would hurt the competitiveness of their companies, and would pose a general threat to the health of the German economy.

At the end of a long and controversial discussion within the German government itself – especially between the BMU and the BMWi (assisted by the Chancellery) – and after difficult negotiations between the government and the business associations and companies, an agreement was found that is actually very close to the position of the industry (see table 13.3). Thus, industry pressure, with the help of the BMWi, prevailed over the initial BMU plan.

According to this plan, the energy and other industries together had to reduce their CO_2 emissions by only 2 Mt or 0.4 per cent up to 2005 to 2007 and by 10 Mt or 2 per cent up to 2008 to 2012. This was even less than recent forecasts expected in a business-as-usual scenario of emissions development! This was a disappointing outcome that was going to be only somewhat corrected with the second National Allocation Plan, enacted in June 2007 (see conclusions).

Table 13.3 CO$_2$ emissions in Germany 1990 to 2002 and emissions budget 2005–7 and 2008–12 by sector

	Energy sector (E)	Industry[a] (I)	**Emissions budgets E+I**	Other sectors				
				Trade, commerce, services	Transport	Residential	Total other sectors	Total
Base year 1990	439	197	**636**	91	159	129	378	1014
1998	365	143	**508**	66	176	131	373	881
2000 (prov.)	361	142	**503**	59	178	116	354	857
2001 (prov.)	369	137	**506**	63	175	130	367	874
2002 (prov.)	373	132	**505**	59	173	120	352	857
Average 2000–2	368	137	**505**	61	175	122	358	863
Target 2005–7	*No further differentiation*		**503**	58	298		349	844
Target 2008–12			**495**	58	291		349	844
Structure by sector in %								
Average 2000–2	43	16	**59**	7	20	14	41	100
Target 2005–7	*No further differentiation*		**59**	7	35		41	100
Target 2008–12			**59**	7	34		41	100

[a]Including industrial processes
Sources: National Allocation Plan for the Republic of Germany (2004): Act on Allocation (2007).

In distributing the emissions budget among the sectors not covered by emissions trading (see table 13.3), the German government is guided by the need to contain the rise in transport-related greenhouse gas emissions with the aid of appropriate measures and to initiate a moderate decline in the trade/commerce/service sectors and a slightly greater decline among private households. Although household emissions have increased since the reference period, there is a noticeable reduction if temperature-adjusted figures are compared.

MICRO-PLAN: A BUNDLE OF SPECIFIC AND SPECIAL INTEREST RULES

Very early on the government decided that allowances allocated to existing and new installations would be *free of charge* in both periods on the basis of historical emissions for *existing* installations and on the basis of emissions calculated on the basis of benchmarks for *new entrants*. To permit the allocation of allowances to new entrants free of charge, a proportion of the total budget for installations participating in emissions trading is set aside as the *new entrant reserve*. Against the recommendation of the advisory group the possibility given by the ET Directive to *auction* at least 5 per cent (first period) or 10 per cent (second period) of the allowances was not used in the first period (but will be introduced for the second period). This decision was made mainly in response to the arguments of the manufacturing industry that auctioning would cause competitive disadvantages compared to industries in countries without an emissions trading system.

In addition to this general rule there are some specific rules that are, not surprisingly, often the result of individual claims and lobbying by some companies or business associations. Some of the most important rules of this kind are listed as follows:

- Allowances from installations that have been decommissioned can be transferred for four years to installations or extensions to installations commissioned from 1 January 2005 (*transfer rule*). Following this transfer period, allocations to the new installation will be based on a compliance factor of one for the next fourteen years. This rule especially serves those electricity companies with a high share of old capacities that will be substituted by new power plants within the following trading periods. This refers especially to RWE, one of the biggest electricity companies.

- Existing installations can be qualified as *early action* installations if they can demonstrate a predefined reduction in specific CO_2 emissions, provided that these reductions were not achieved simply by decommissioning plants and/or a decline in productive output. A compliance factor of one can then be applied to existing installations that have been modernized between 1 January 1996 and 31 December 2002. This rule particularly serves companies active in East Germany, like Vattenfall, which invested a lot of money in new and efficient lignite power plants in the 1990s, with the consequence that the potential of further modernizations of the power plants (and that means a further reduction of emissions) is restricted (in contrast to the situation of RWE). The amount of emissions due to the early action rule adds up to 22 per cent of the total CO_2 emissions in the trading sector.
- From the very beginning it was clear that a compliance factor of one (no reduction needed!) will apply to *process-related emissions* (which are defined as the atmospheric release of CO_2 resulting from a chemical reaction other than combustion). But, in the course of discussion and independent of a strict interpretation of its definition, especially the iron and steel industry succeeded in including most of their emissions as 'process-related.' Other industrial branches followed, with the result that the former amount of process-related emissions, calculated to be 21 to 23 Mt CO_2, now reached a high of 72 Mt CO_2.
- The support of *combined heat and power generation* (CHP) is traditionally an important field of climate protection policy in Germany (see chapters 12 and 14, by Weidner and Eberlein, and Mez respectively). There is a specific problem caused by the emission trading system: CO_2 emissions are higher when power and heat are generated together, compared to exclusive power-generation. This raised the question of how to protect otherwise desirable CHP installations. Disadvantages for *existing CHP* installations are offset by granting the operators of CHP installations additional allowances tied to CHP implementation. For the period 2005 to 2007 the special allocation for CHP installations was set at 27 t CO_2 per GWh. The allocation for *new* CHP installations will be based on a dual benchmark: the power benchmark will determine the allocation for power output, and the heat benchmark will determine the allowance for heat output. Apart from this, new entrants in CHP are subject to the same rules as other new entrants. This rule is not

only in the interest of climate protection policy but even more so in the interest of those companies (mainly municipal utilities) that are already running CHP plants.

• Against the advice of the scientific advisory group, which proposed a *specific benchmark system* for electricity generation in new power plants, *independent of the fuel burned*, the decision was made to use benchmarks *according to the individual fuel basis*. This decision meant that the originally intended incentives for fuel switch (such as gas instead of coal), which contributes to emissions reduction (switch to more efficiently burning fuels), were deliberately not set. This was to protect electricity companies with a high share of coal-fired power plants.

To complete the story of special rules in favour of industry, it should be added that the compliance factor was accorded not only for the period 2005 to 2007 but for many years to come (process-related emissions without a time limit, installations with 'early actions' for twelve years, new entrants for fourteen years, installations installed in 2003 and 2004 for twelve years).

THE DECISION OF THE EU COMMISSION

On 7 July 2004, the European Commission decided upon the NAP of Germany for the period 2005 to 2007. In its decision the commission stated that some aspects of the German NAP were incompatible with criteria 5 and 10 of Annex III to the ET Directive respectively. This refers to the intended *ex-post adjustments* of the allocation of allowances to new entrants. In the commission's view, this is not compatible with the ex ante principle, and, therefore, the commission did not accept the German allocation plan. The German government went to the European Court of Justice to seek clarification on this specific issue.

This conflict, however, did not impede the implementation of the German NAP. Article 3 of the commission's decision stated, 'Germany may issue allowances in advance of the implementation of the amendments referred to in Article 2' (EU Commission 2004b).

Allocation of Allowances for the Period 2005 to 2007

In total, 1,849 installations of the energy sector and emissions-intensive industry sector in Germany participated in the EU emission trading

Table 13.4 Number of installations by size of compliance factor

Compliance factor including proportional adjustment ... %	Installations	
	Number	%
0	378	20.4
0–2	112	6.1
2–4	150	8.1
4–6	387	20.9
6–7.4	259	14.0
7.4	563	30.4
Total	1849	100.0

Source: Deutsche Emissionshandelsstelle (2005).

scheme in the first period 2005 to 2007 (Deutsche Emissionshandelsstelle 2005). The amount of allowances applied for exceeded the maximum budget set by the legislators of 1,485 million allowances for the years 2005 to 2007 (495 million allowances per year) by 2.8 per cent. In order to meet the budget restrictions, certain allocations were subject to a proportionate adjustment.

At the end, about one-fifth of all installations had no compliance factor (table 13.4), but almost one-third of all installations received the highest reduction of 7.4 per cent. This wide variety is the result mainly of the special rules mentioned before. The consequence is quite clear: in comparison with the overall compliance factor of 0.4 per cent, the bulk of reduction activities refer to distributional effects within the emission trading sectors. Insofar as emissions had to be reduced in any installation by more than 0.4 per cent, this was caused only by the successful interventions of other powerful companies.

By far the highest number of installations and of allowances allocated under the ET Directive belongs to the energy sector (table 13.5). The 1,234 installations (two-thirds of the total) received allowances for 1170 million tons in the first period or 390 million tons per year (almost 80 per cent of the total amount of allowances).

There are 574, or almost one-third of all installations, that received fewer than 30,000 allowances; their share of the total allowances is even less than 1 per cent. In contrast, only 16 installations with more than 15 million allowances received almost 40 per cent of all allowances (table 13.6). This shows the high concentration in this field.

Table 13.5 Number of installations and allocations according to activities

| | Installations | | Allowances allocated 2005–7 | | | Average 2005–7 |
	Number	%	Mt	Mt/a	%	Mt/install
Energy	1234	66.7	1170.3	390.1	78.8	0.948
Iron & steel	39	2.1	101.6	33.9	6.8	2.605
Refinerie	37	2.0	73.3	24.4	4.9	1.981
Cement	48	2.6	71.2	23.7	4.8	1.483
Lime	68	3.7	28.0	9.3	1.9	0.412
Paper	123	6.7	15.0	5.0	1.0	0.122
Glass	89	4.8	14.0	4.7	0.9	0.157
Ceramics	207	11.2	7.5	2.5	0.5	0.036
Pulp	4	0.2	4.3	1.4	0.3	1.075
Total	1849	100.0	1485.2	495.1	100.0	0.803

Source: Deutsche Emissionshandelsstelle (2005).

Table 13.6 Installations and allowances allocated related to the size of allowances

| Size of allowances allocated | Installations | | Allowances allocated | | Average million per installation |
	Number	%	Million	%	
> 15 million allowances	16	0.9	585.4	39.4	36.588
1.5–15 million allowances	147	8.0	643.4	43.3	4.377
150,000–1,500,00 allowances	407	22.0	196.8	13.3	0.484
30,000–150,000 allowances	705	38.1	51.3	3.5	0.073
< 30,000 allowances	574	31.0	8.1	0.5	0.014
Total	1849	100.0	1485.0	100.0	0.803

Source: Deutsche Emissionshandelsstelle (2005).

Hence, only eleven operators received almost 60 per cent of the total allowances; nine of them are electricity companies. By far the biggest of them is the RWE Power AG, with around 110 Mt per year, followed by Vattenfall, with almost 78 Mt, and the E.ON Company, with 35 Mt (table 13.7).

One further distributional consequence of the emissions trading system has ignited some public debate, mostly fuelled by electricity

Table 13.7 Allowances allocated, ranked according to individual operators
of installations

		Period 2005 to 2007			
		Mt CO$_2$		Share in %	
Operator	Activity	Total	Per year	Single	Cumulative
RWE Power Aktiengesellschaft	Electricity	332.2	110.7	22.4	22.4
Vattenfall Europe Generation					
AG & Co. KG[a]	Electricity	233.0	77.7	15.7	38.1
E.ON Kraftwerke GmbH	Electricity	103.9	34.6	7.0	45.0
STEAG AG[b]	Electricity	40.2	13.4	2.7	47.8
EnBW Kraftwerke AG	Electricity	30.2	10.1	2.0	49.8
ThyssenKrupp Stahl AG	Steel	26.8	8.9	1.8	51.6
SaarEnergie GmbH[c]	Electricity	21.9	7.3	1.5	53.1
Großkraftwerk Mannheim					
Aktiengesellschaft	Electricity	19.8	6.6	1.3	54.4
swb Synor GmbH & Co. KG,					
Bremen	Electricity	19.6	6.5	1.3	55.7
SWM Services Energie und					
Wasser GmbH, München	Electricity	13.2	4.4	0.9	56.6
Salzgitter Flachstahl GmbH	Steel	10.1	3.4	0.7	57.3
Subtotal		850.9	283.6	57.3	
Total combustion		1169.9	390.0	78.8	
Total allocation of allowances		1485.2	495.1	100.0	

[a]Including Bewag AG & Co. KG and Hamburgische Electrcitäts-Werke AG.
[b]Including STEAG Fernwärme GmbH and STEAG and RWE Power – Gemeinschaftskraftwerk Bergkamen A oHG
[c]Including SaarEnergie AG
Source: Deutsche Emissionshandelsstelle (2005)

consumers' associations. It concerns the fact that the utilities incorporated the price of emissions certificates in their calculations of end-user electricity tariffs, although the certificates had been allocated cost-free. As noted by Weidner and Eberlein in chapter 12, there was a remarkable increase of electricity prices on the one hand and higher profits of the utilities on the other hand.

These windfall profits provoked a lot of ideas on how to deal with this perceived injustice: to impose a special tax on these windfall profits, to impose a ban on pricing in the cost-free allocated certificates, or to intensify electricity tariff regulation. However, from an economic point of view, even cost-free allocated certificates have a commercial value, and it is consistent with this theoretical approach that these 'opportunity costs' are an element of product prices – in this case, the electricity prices. The only consistent and workable alternative could be to hold an auction instead of a cost-free allocation. Unfortunately, the EU directive on emissions trading only allowed a 5 per cent share of auctioning within the first period (and not more than 10 per cent in the second period). Therefore the problem of windfall profits cannot be solved in an efficient way for the time being.

Conclusions

On 1 January 2005, the EU emission trading system, the world's first cap-and-trade system of this scale and complexity, was launched. Considering that this was new territory for all the actors involved, it should be noted that at least certain formal conditions for a potentially effective emissions trading scheme have indeed been established, and from a technical viewpoint, the system has been put into place successfully, including the platform for trading between companies.

However, the ETS suffers from certain design flaws, in particular with regard to enforceable national obligations to comply with agreed targets. The national implementation of the ETS for the first period (2005 to 2007) has been very disappointing, to the point of violating the very idea of any emissions trading system, as the German case amply illustrates. As result of a highly political process with heavy utility and industry lobbying, the German implementation for the first period produced a bureaucratic system of allowance allocation that is heavily biased in favour of specific industry interests (of coal-fired electricity generators in particular) and achieves only marginal reduction rates.

According to the Kyoto Protocol and the European burden sharing agreement, Germany is committed to achieve a 21 per cent reduction in emissions of greenhouse gases by 2008 to 2012 compared to 1990 levels. Taking into account the projected development of non-CO_2 emissions, the German government set the CO_2 target for the period 2005 to 2007 at 859 Mt – only 0.4 per cent less than the average of 2000 to 2002 (863 Mt). And within these limits the total quantity of allowances allocated to the trading sector were 499 Mt of CO_2, compared to 501 Mt in 2000 to 2002 (-0.4 per cent). In short, this is only a marginal reduction rate at best.

To make matters worse, a number of special arrangements were made in favour of specific companies and branches, which resulted in a broad spread of compliance factors between 0 per cent and 7.4 per cent. Therefore, those industries that were not in a position to obtain special rules could face a compliance factor of up to 7.4 per cent in the period 2005 to 2007. The consequence is that, in comparison with the overall compliance factor of 0.4 per cent, the bulk of reduction activities reflects distributional effects within the emission trading sectors only.

Hence, the German National Allocation Plan was, to say the least, very comfortable for most of the companies involved. This interpretation is confirmed by the first results of the monitoring of actual emissions in 2005, published in mid-May 2006. According to this monitoring report, the verified emissions of all installations under the emission trading scheme in 2005 amounted to 474 Mt only – 21 Mt, or 4 per cent *less* than allocated to these installations (Deutsche Emissionshandelsstelle 2006).

This chapter has detailed how the allocation of allowances resulted from political bargaining and coordination, not only between government and industry but also between the Federal Ministry of Environment on the one hand and the Federal Ministry of Economics, together with the Chancellery, on the other hand. Not only did this process result in marginal reduction targets, due to the political power of vested utility and energy industries. It also produced extremely complex rules for certain emitter groups, which further undermine the very foundations of an effective emissions trading system. More generally, it is fair to say that national implementation, instead of putting into place a simple market mechanism, created a complex, partly opaque, highly bureaucratic, and heavily skewed system. The fact that there are *fifty-eight* possible combinations of different rules seems to be a clear indicator of complexity.

The obvious weakness of (not only German) implementation is the over-generous allocation of allowances. An allocation of allowances according to 'industry needs,' as requested by the industrial lobbyists, undermines the basis of emissions trading, by producing an oversupply of allowances. Special rules also can undermine the effectiveness of the emissions trading system.

In the future, it would be desirable to set common standards for the initial allocation plan between all European countries, in order to avoid opportunistic behaviour and a weakening of the entire trading system.

The most important lessons learnt from this German implementation experience are to keep the emission trading system as simple as possible, to avoid special rules and exemptions that are not in line with the principles of the system, and not to give in to the pressure of lobby groups but assure the primacy of consistent political decisions.

This, however, is a tough call in a highly political environment with powerful vested interests. Yet first steps to improve the EU ETS have already been taken. The second National Allocation Plan for Germany (2008 to 2012) enacted in June 2007 brings a tightening of the cap. Originally set at 482 and later 462 Mt per year by the federal government, the European Commission insisted on a cap at 453 Mt, a reduction of over 10 per cent, compared to the first period. This will require an 8 per cent reduction for energy and other industry, compared to current emissions. Further improvements include Germany's extending the share of allowances distributed by auction to 10 per cent, the maximum allowed under the directive (BMU 2007).

The Kyoto process is only the first step of an international policy of climate protection. What we need are long-term and strong reduction targets up to the middle of this century and binding obligations not only for the industrialized countries but more and more for less developed countries as well. Emissions trading can and must play a leading role to meet the targets. The European and German experience with the ETS holds many lessons on how such a scheme could and should be improved. Then, hopefully, it will be possible to establish a truly efficient emissions trading system for 2008 to 2012 and beyond.

NOTE

1   Unless otherwise noted, the numbers used in this chapter are based on the German National Inventory Report 2003 (with data from 1990 to 2001) and CO_2 data provided by the German Institute for Economic Research, DIW (Ziesing 2003).

REFERENCES

BMU [Federal Environment Ministry]. 2004. *National allocation plan for the Federal Republic of Germany 2005–2007*. Berlin, 31 March.
– 2007. Germany moving forward in EU-wide auctioning of emissions

allowances. Press release, 22 June. http://www.bmu.de/english/
current_press_releases/pm/39746.php.

Bundesregierung. 2001a. Stellungnahme der Bundesregierung zur Ein-
führung eines EU-weiten Handels mit Treibhausgasen [Position of the
federal government towards the introduction of EU-wide trade with GHG
emissions]. Positionspapier für die Diskussion mit der Europäischen Kom-
mission [Position paper for discussion with the European Commission], 10
September.

– 2001b. *Vereinbarung zwischen der Regierung der Bundesrepublik Deutschland
und der deutschen Wirtschaft zur Minderung der CO2-Emissionen und der
Förderung der Kraft-Wärme-Kopplung in Ergänzung zur Klimavereinbarung
vom 9.11.2000* [Agreement between the government of the Federal Republic
of Germany and German industry regarding the reduction of CO_2 emissions and the promotion of CHP, complementing the climate agreement
from 9 November 2000]. Berlin, 25 June.

– 2005. *Report on the application of the EU emissions trading directive 2003/87/EC
in Germany in 2005.* 27 June.

Deutsche Emissionshandelsstelle. 2005. *Emissions trading in Germany:
Allocation of allowances for the first commitment period 2005–2007.* 2nd ed.
Berlin.

– 2006. *Emissionshandel: CO2 Emissionen des Jahres 2005.* [Emissions trading:
CO_2 emissions in 2005]. 15 May.

DIW Berlin, Öko-Institut, Fraunhofer-ISI. 2003. White paper: National allocation plan (NAP); Overall concept, criteria, guidelines and fundamental
organisational options. Berlin, 7 July.

EU Commission. 2000. Green paper on greenhouse gas emissions trading
within the European Union. COM(2000)87.

– 2001. *European climate change programme.* Long report. Brussels, June.

– 2003a. Directive 2003/87/EC of the European Parliament and of the
Council of 13 October 2003 establishing a scheme for greenhouse gas emis-
sion allowance trading within the Community and amending Council
Directive 96/61/EC.

– 2003b. The EU emissions trading scheme: How to develop a national allocation plan. Non-paper. 2nd meeting of Working 3. Monitoring Mechanism
Committee, 1 April.

– 2003c. *Kyoto Protocol.* Memo 03/154. Brussels, 23 July.

– 2004a. Commission decision of 29 January 2004 establishing guidelines for
the monitoring and reporting of greenhouse gas emissions pursuant to
Directive 2003/87/EC of the European Parliament and of the Council.

– 2004b. Commission decision of 7 July 2004 concerning the national allocation plan for the allocation of greenhouse gas emission allowances notified by Germany in accordance with Directive 2003/87/EC of the European Parliament and of the Council.

– 2004c. Commission Regulation (EC) no. 2216/2004 of 21 December 2004 for a standardised and secured system of registries pursuant to Directive 2003/87/EC of the European Parliament and of the Council and Decision no. 280/2004/EC of the European Parliament and of the Council.

– 2006. Emission trading scheme (EU ETS): Legislative history of Directive 2003/87/EC.
http://ec.europa.eu/environment/climat/emission/history_en.htm.

Kyoto Protocol to the United Nations Framework Convention on Climate Change. 1997. Kyoto.

United Nations Framework Convention on Climate Change. 1992. Rio de Janeiro.

Ziesing, Hans-Joachim. 2003. Treibhausgas-Emissionen nehmen weltweit zu – Keine Umkehr in Sicht [GHG emissions increase globally: No reversing trend in sight]. *Wochenbericht des DIW Berlin* [DIW Weekly Report] 39.

14 Renewables in Electricity Generation: Germany as Pioneer?

LUTZ MEZ

The previous three chapters have examined the performance of climate protection policies of Canada and Germany, with one chapter dedicated to the implementation of the EU cap-and trade instrument in Germany in particular. This chapter probes the most important and successful instrument in Germany's toolbox to reduce greenhouse gas (GHG) emission: the promotion of renewable energy sources for electricity generation (RES-E) through a feed-in tariff. The chapter underscores two major points that also emerged from the previous three chapters. Firstly, strong public policies with a high degree of compulsoriness (and consistency) are required to achieve significant progress, although they may come at a cost. Secondly, the necessary political support for such measures needs to be built up progressively. Thirdly, political support rests on favourable institutional conditions in the broader polity and political economy.

In the German case specifically, the evolution of renewables policy seems to indicate that a weak natural resource base actually worked as an important facilitator as it spurred the search for alternatives to the carbon fuel economy. As further developed in the next and concluding chapter 15, natural resource capacity on the one hand, and institutional capacity, especially in terms of sustainability policies, seem to pull into different directions.

Among the large industrialized countries, Germany is today preeminent in the promotion of renewable energy sources for electricity generation. The promotion policy goes back to the period after the first oil price crisis when German governments began to implement public policies to support innovation and distribution of RES-E technologies. At the end of 2006 Germany held world leadership in installed wind

Table 14.1 Installed PV and wind energy power per country, 2005 and 2006

Country	Total capacity installed end 2005 (MW)		Total capacity installed end 2006 (MW)	
	PV	Wind	PV	Wind
Germany	1,537.0	18,427.5	3,063.0	20,621.9
USA	455.2	9,149.0	475.0	11,603.0
Japan	1,412.0	1,040.0	1,712,0	1,394.0
Canada	14.9	683.0	20.5	1,451.0

Sources: EurObserv'ER (2007), IEA PVPS (2007), Photon (2007), World Wind Energy Association (2007).

power capacity and ranked first in photovoltaics (PV) too (see table 14.1).

This chapter addresses a number of key questions. How did Germany come to occupy such a special position in RES-E, and what precisely is the evolution and status of installed capacity? Is German RES-E regulation – particularly the feed-in tariff system – successful in terms of usual economic and commercial criteria? Is it of such excellence as to invite imitation by other countries, and is it likely to survive?

The chapter gives a historical account of German RES-E policy, focused in particular on the evolution of feed-in legislation since 1990. After the first oil price crisis in 1973, RES-E policy was launched with research and development programs. Market creation measures came on the agenda only in the end of the 1980s. Of these, the Feed-In Law was the most important. During the 1990s, it managed to survive, but several amendments were adopted. Significant improvement occurred after the 1998 election when the new Red-Green coalition greatly strengthened RES-E support, particularly for PV and biomass. After the 2005 parliamentary elections, which led to a coalition between the Conservatives and the Social Democrats, RES-E policy was set to continue and remained the province of the Environmental Ministry. The RES-E targets of 12.5 per cent in 2010, 20 per cent in 2020 and 50 per cent by mid-century were retained unchanged.

As table 14.1 shows, Germany is a clear leader of renewable energy use, occupying the first rank in installed wind energy capacity, and – since 2005 – in photovoltaics (PV) too. This chapter argues that this is not due to an exceptional natural resource base but rather because of consistent public policy in this area, even if this policy was conducted in a rather lukewarm fashion until 1998. In any case, it led to a remarkable expansion of this sector. The Red-Green coalition, in office from 1998 to 2005, developed the vision of achieving 50 per cent and more of electricity generated from renewable energy sources by 2050, a goal that seems well accepted by the public but not by the established energy business interests. The Conservative–Social Democratic coalition, which took office in November 2005, basically continues this course. The 'integrated climate and energy package' endorsed by the federal Cabinet in August 2007 aims for a further expansion of renewables to 25 to 30 per cent by 2030.[1]

The Beginnings

Renewable energy policy in Germany began in 1974, after the first oil crisis. For about a decade and a half, this policy consisted almost exclusively of the promotion of research activities, from training personnel to development of prototypes and laboratory production. Spending was very modest in 1974 (about €10 million). It rose gradually until 1978 (about €60 million) and reached its peak with €150 million in 1982, declining thereafter until 1986 (€82 million). Further decline was scheduled but arrested by the Chernobyl nuclear accident in 1986 (see the Mez and Doern analysis of nuclear policy in chapter 5). The main response of the German government to the oil crises consisted of the promotion of nuclear power and hard coal. Support for RES-E was chiefly then a concession to dissenters (Jacobsson and Lauber 2006).

Since 1979, there were also first efforts to stimulate demand for RES-E by use of the tariff. At that time the government relied on the national competition law to oblige electricity distributors to purchase electricity from renewable sources produced in their area of supply, based on the principle of avoided costs.

The accident in Chernobyl had a deep impact in Germany, as further detailed in chapter 5 by Mez and Doern. Public opinion had been divided about evenly on the question of nuclear power between 1976 and 1985. This changed dramatically in 1986. Within two years, opposition to nuclear power increased to over 70 per cent, while support barely exceeded 10 per cent (Jahn 1992). While the Social-Democrats committed themselves to phasing out nuclear power within ten years, the Greens demanded an immediate shutdown of all plants.

Also the career of the climate change issue and of climate policy, as presented in more detail by Weidner and Eberlein in chapter 12, affected the trajectory of RES-E policies. In 1986, reports warning of an impending climate catastrophe received much attention, and in March 1987 Chancellor Kohl declared that the climate issue represented the most important environmental problem (Huber 1997). On the national level the Committee for the Environment, Nature Conservation, and Nuclear Safety of the German Bundestag agreed to establish an Enquête Commission on Preventive Measures to Protect the Earth's Atmosphere, with the mandate to study the ozone problem as well as climate change and to make proposals for action. The Inter-Ministerial Working Group on CO_2 reduction was also established. The commission worked very effectively in a spirit of excellent cooperation between the parliamentary groups of government and opposition parties. There was general agreement that energy use had to be profoundly changed (Ganseforth 1996; Kords 1996).

The first Enquête Commission recommended a goal of 30 per cent reduction of 1987 CO_2 and methane emissions by 2005, and of 80 per cent by 2050 (German Bundestag 1991), and also advocated a fundamental reform of energy policy. A series of proposals were formulated, which included an electricity feed-in law for generation from RES (Schafhausen 1996). There was growing consensus among MPs of all party groups that it was time to create markets for renewable energy technologies (Lauber and Pesendorfer 2004).

First Steps to Market Creation

The measures adopted to create markets for RES-E technologies were in particular the 100/250 MW wind program, the 100,000 solar roof program, and the creation of a legal basis for utilities to pay higher costs for RES-E than were 'competitive' in the – quite distorted – marketplace.

When in 1988 two backbench conservative MPs in the Bundestag proposed a feed-in tariff to support wind energy, the government, to buy off the dissenters, initiated two important market creation programs for RES-E: a 100 MW wind program and 100,000 roof program for PV (Kords 1993). From 1991 to 1995, under the 100,000 roof program, applicants received 50 per cent funding of investment costs from the federal government plus 20 per cent from the Land government. Eventually 2,250 roofs were equipped with PV modules, leading to about five MW of installations (Staiss 2000,1–140). As to wind energy, a program for subsidizing 100 MW – later 250 MW – of wind turbines (by a payment of €0.04/kWh, later reduced to €0.03) was justified by the need to gain practical experience with different approaches under real-life conditions. As this program in 1991 joined forces with the Feed-in Law, installed wind capacity grew at a high rate. In subsequent years, these subsidies declined rapidly (Hirschl et al. 2002).

In this period the German Länder and some municipalities (such as Aachen and Hannover) gained an important role by creating innovative subsidy schemes and support mechanisms for renewable electricity applications (Reiche 2004, 178). This strong regional and local support continued until the end of the 1990s.

The 1990 Feed-In Law

To build support for a feed-in tariff, a political coalition of convenience was successful only for a short period of time. Soon afterwards, a new bill for such a tariff circulated among MPs, supported both by Conservative (CDU/CSU) and Green deputies who gathered support among the other parliamentary groups as well. In the Ministry of Economics and in parliament this idea met with acceptance; support came also from the ministries of Research and of the Environment. The bill secured consent from all parliamentary parties and became the Electricity Feed-in Law of 1990 (Kords 1993). The large utilities did not mobilize at that point, probably because they underestimated the importance of the law, which was expected to support mainly small hydro.

The Feed-in Law required electric utilities to connect RES-E generators to the grid and to buy the electricity at rates of 65 to 90 per cent of the average tariff for final customers. Generators were not required to negotiate contracts or otherwise engage in much bureaucratic activity. Together with the 100/250 MW program and subsidies from state programs, the Feed-In Law gave considerable financial incentives to investors, although less for solar power as a result of the high cost (Hemmelskamp 1999). One of the declared purposes of the law was to 'level the playing field' for RES-E by setting feed-in rates that took account of the external costs of conventional power generation. In parliament external costs of about €0.03 to €0.05/kWh for coal-based electricity were mentioned by Conservative MPs. Before adoption, the law was forwarded to the European Commission for approval under state aid provisions. The commission decided not to raise any objections because of its insignificant effects and because it was in line with the policy objectives of the European Community. However, it announced that it would examine the law after two years of operation.

Challenges to the Feed-In Law

These incentives greatly stimulated the formation of markets and led to expansion for wind, from about 20 MW in 1989, to over 1,100 MW in 1995. This encouraged technological and political learning in this sector, but also strengthened the resolve of the large supra-regional utilities to attempt a rollback of this law, via both politics and the judiciary. This was more than just opposition to small and decentralized generation. First, no provision had been made to spread the burden of the law evenly in geographical terms. A satisfactory solution to this problem came only in 2000. Second, the utilities were by this time marked by the experience of subsidies for hard coal used in electricity generation, which had grown from €0.4 billion in 1975, the year the *Kohlepfennig* ('penny for coal') was introduced, to more than €4 billion annually in the early 1990s. Two-thirds of this cost was covered by a special levy on electricity, one-third had to be paid by the utilities directly but was also passed on to the consumers. In 1994 the *Kohlepfennig* was ruled unconstitutional by the Constitutional Court.

In April 1998 the Energy Supply Industry Act was adopted to transpose Electricity Directive 96/92/EC and modified the Feed-in Law in several points (for further details, see chapter 10 by Theobald). In particular, it created a new compensation mechanism for distributing the supplementary cost to the utilities. The 1990 law had provided a hardship clause, which was practically never applied. Wherever RES-E exceeded 5 per cent ('first ceiling') of the total electricity supply, the upstream network operator had to compensate that undertaking for the supplementary costs caused by this excess amount. A similar rule applied in favour of the upstream network operator, who could ask for compensation from a network operator situated further upstream if the compensation that was required exceeded 5 per cent of the operator's output ('second ceiling'). As it was obvious that in some coastal areas the 10 per cent limit would be reached, wind power growth could be impaired unless an alternative solution was found. This conflict led to insecurity for investors and stagnating markets for wind turbines from 1996 to 1998.

Other Programs

A federal energy research program from 1990 to 1998 amounted to more than 1 billion for all forms of renewable energy. The Länder contributed another 0.85 billion for the period 1990 to 1997, most importantly North Rhine-Westphalia. Loan programs by the federal government's banking institutions Deutsche Ausgleichsbank and Kreditanstalt für Wiederaufbau permitted more than €3 billion in reduced interest loans for RES installations in the period 1990 to 1998. Other measures privileged wind turbines under the construction code (every local community had to present a plan with zones appropriate for wind power, which greatly facilitated permitting), reformed training programs for architects, and stressed public information (Staiss 2000, 1–140).

Makeshift Support for Solar PV

While the Feed-In Law of 1990, combined with the 250 MW wind program, led to the breakthrough for wind, solar PV did not benefit similarly. The 100,000 roof program of 1989 had been a success and led to installations of 5.3 MW by 1993, but this market volume did not justify the installation of new production facilities in the solar cell industry. The Feed-In Law provided little help, since rates did not come near PV costs, and a new demonstration program was not forthcoming.

However, help came from solar activists and municipal utilities. The 1989 modification of the federal framework regulation on electricity tariffs permitted utilities to conclude cost-covering contracts for electricity using renewable energy technologies, even if these 'full cost rates' exceeded the long-term avoided costs of the utilities concerned. While the supra-regional utilities generally rejected such an approach, local activists now petitioned local governments to impose such contracts on municipal utilities. Several dozen cities opted for this model.

Additional help came from several Länder market introduction programs, most strongly in North Rhine-Westphalia. Some states acted through their utilities, subsidizing solar installations for special purposes, such as schools. Some offered 'cost-oriented rates' somewhat below the level of full cost rates. Finally, Greenpeace gathered several thousand orders for solar cell rooftop 'Cyrus installations' (Ristau 1998). As a result of these initiatives, the market did not collapse at the end of the 100,000 roof program but continued to grow, attracting new firms and demonstrating public support for PV. Various solar energy organizations lobbied for a larger market-creation program.

Energy Reform and Liberalization

Reforming Germany's electricity sector proved to be a difficult task because of key features of the German political economy, as examined by Eberlein and Doern in chapter 1. Thus most reform attempts were doomed to failure because of the political power of the German energy supply industry (ESI). Already before unification it was partly privatized and later opened for foreign investors. The powerful ownership links between the ESI and major financial and industrial interests in Germany indicate that this industry is an integral part of what Shonfield (1968) termed German 'alliance capitalism' to describe the corporate culture of German industry, dominated by alliances with banking and insurance capital for decades.

In contrast to competitive capitalism, alliance capitalism is characterized by collaborative relationships between commercial entities, and success relies on the concerted orchestration of large resources for common goals. With its huge turnover, vast profits, and monopoly status, the ESI grew into the major cash cow of the German economy. Its political status was consolidated by links to state bodies at all levels and, through revenue sharing, to German municipalities by way of generous concession fees.

As Theobald's analysis in chapter 10 has shown, German electricity regulation traditionally relied on a mix of public and private law. Basic energy law was embodied in the *Energiewirtschaftsgesetz* (Energy Industry Act) adopted in December 1935 and laying down the framework for a cheap and secure electricity supply. It defined German state control of the sector for more than sixty years. The other important piece of legislation is the *Gesetz gegen Wettbewerbsbeschränkungen* (GWB, German Act against Restraints on Competition or Monopolies), which generally exempted electricity and gas supply. Contracts for concessions, territorial boundaries, supply to special customers, the technical conditions for feeding surplus electricity into the grid, reserve deliveries, and other arrangements are all based on private law.

There have been numerous attempts to reform the German energy sector, but both bottom-up and top-down approaches initially failed.

In the mid-1980s, after the Chernobyl disaster, a strategic about-turn in energy policy and the re-municipalization of electricity supply (Hennicke, Johnson, and Kohler 1985) were articulated and widely discussed. This has remained, as previous chapters have shown, the policy position of the SPD and the Green party, and is also supported by local activists.

The introduction of environmental concerns into the German system was more successful than initiatives towards liberalization. The Ordinance on Large Combustion Plants introduced in 1983 strict limitations on all emissions such as SO_2, NO_x, and particulate matter. With the restrictions it places on private property rights in favour of the environment, it constitutes an exemplary top-down policy tool (Mez 1995). The same applies to the Technical Guidelines on Air Quality. The Electricity Feed-In Law, enacted in 1990 on the initiative of the German parliament, provides yet another notable environmentally oriented change in the framework conditions.

In response to long-standing criticism of monopolistic practices in the electricity industry brought forward by the Monopolkommission (German Monopolies Commission, 1976), the Deregulation Commission, and international deregulation discussions, the Conservative-Liberal federal government after 1991 wanted to subject the energy sector to more competition and more effective public control. A first concrete reform proposal drafted by the Ministry of Economics in October 1993 included a partial break-up of the industry, third-party access, and stricter control of electricity prices. However, it was heavily modified subsequently and finally retracted in March 1994, because of open resistance from the municipalities and from the opposition Social-Democrats who held a Länder majority in the Bundesrat, the upper chamber of the German parliament, whose approval was essential.

In autumn 1996, the German government submitted a second draft, this time backed by the EU reform process around the directive on the internal electricity market (96/92/EC, enacted on 19 December 1996 – for further details, see the Cameron and Froschauer chapters in this volume). The reform's main goal was to reduce electricity and gas prices in order to strengthen Germany's international competitiveness. The draft included provisions to remove both the demarcation treaties and the single supplier formulae in concession treaties. Proposals for state control of investment in new power stations and transmission lines were dropped, however. More than a year later, after much controversy, the new legal framework, as set out in the analysis by Theobald in chapter 10, was approved.

Only a few days later, the utility company PreussenElektra (now E.ON) took the law to the Constitutional Court, joined shortly afterwards by the SPD federal parliamentary party group and its Land counterparts from Hesse, Saarland, and Hamburg. The energy policy spokesman for the SPD announced that a review of the new *Energy Reform Act* would enjoy priority under a newly elected, SPD-led federal government.

However, after the change of government in October 1998, the SPD lawsuits were suspended. Finally, on 28 September 1999, the government, the parliamentary parties of SPD and Greens, and leading trade unionists signed a common statement confirming the basic principles of the energy law reforms: the end of demarcation treaties, full opening of the network for all suppliers, and free choice of supplier for all customer groups (ARE 2000, 12). Liberalization made a little more headway in 2003 and 2004.

Electricity liberalization favoured the expansion strategies of the energy giants. The trend towards internationalization and globalization of German energy undertakings is evident and led to mergers and higher yields. After protected markets and guaranteed returns, the new period is characterized by risk and insecurity. Deregulation was followed by some re-regulation.

The New Energy Policy of the Red-Green Coalition

The then new Red-Green federal government emphasized ecological modernization and climate change policy as well as job creation and socio-economic development; energy policy was to be a leading example. As noted in Mez and Doern's chapter 5 analysis of nuclear policy, it included tax reform (eco-tax on energy), phasing out nuclear power, and strengthening of renewable energy sources and of combined heat and power (CHP).

Nuclear Power Phase-Out

The fundamental revision of nuclear policies examined in chapter 5 reflected the consensus among Greens and many Social-Democrats since the Chernobyl accident. The basic decision against the future construction of nuclear power plants was enshrined in the 2002 *Nuclear Energy Phase-Out Act.*

Climate Change Policy

Within the framework of the Kyoto Protocol and the European burden-sharing agreement, Germany committed to reduce GHG emissions by 21 per cent from 1990 to 2008–12. Weidner and Eberlein, in chapter 12 of this volume, provide a detailed account of climate policy commitments, policy measures, and performance. In the context of this chapter, it is important to also track certain policy measures and developments that have an impact on the trajectory of renewables.

The first element to note is that the promotion of RES-E became a key element of the government's National Climate Protection Program of October 2000. Both RESA and the CHP Act were integral parts of this program. These two areas of activity were expected to contribute reductions of 15 Mt CO_2 and 23 Mt CO_2 respectively, or about 50 per cent of the target (Bundesregierung 2000, 9, 77, 80).

The energy and industry sectors were covered by the new EU cap-and-trade instrument, examined in detail by Ziesing in chapter 13. Specific reduction targets were set for each branch of industry and the individual installations concerned. This applies to all large combustion plants (thermal output higher than 20 MW). Over 1,800 installations belonging to energy companies and the energy intensive industries participated in the first phase (2005 to 2007) of emissions trading. In total, emissions allowances for 1,485 million tons of CO_2 – 495 million per year – were available to companies for 2005 to 2007.

The National Climate Protection Program 2005, an update of the 2000 program, also focused on actions deemed necessary in the transport and private households sectors. The joint reduction objective for both sectors was set at 291 million tons per year (household sector: 120 million tons/year; transport sector: 171 million tons/year). Correspondingly, a reduction of 8 million tons in the household sector and 8 to 10 million tons in the transport sector were required. For the trade/business/service sector it was assumed that the 2008 to 2012 targets would be met without further intervention. The program provides for a continuous evaluation of whether the measures produce the projected emissions reductions and the 'IMA CO_2-Reductions' (an inter-ministerial body) submits an annual assessment report to the cabinet.

As Weidner and Eberlein (chapter 12, this volume) show, government support for these policy fields has been rather consistent and 'path-dependent,' independent of specific complexions of the government in power. First, this policy area has been given high priority by Germany as host of various climate change conferences. Second, the two action packages mentioned above are likely to achieve real reductions, which is not true for all measures. However, under the Red-Green coalition it was primarily the Green Party and the Environment Ministry, together with energy policy experts of the SPD – with a comparatively weak link to the Chancellor's Office or the Economics Ministry – that promoted an active approach to German climate change policies and showed serious commitment. In contrast, the Economics Ministry has traditionally been rather sceptical, stressing potential conflicts with German industrial competitiveness (also see chapter 1 on the political economy and politics of German energy regulatory governance).

The Eco-Tax Reform

This reform was passed as one of the first environmental initiatives of the new Red-Green government in two consecutive laws that introduced a tax on the consumption of electricity (at a reduced rate for industry) and raised existing mineral oil taxes: on petrol, diesel, natural gas, and various mineral oils. Tax levels for petrol, diesel, and electricity increased in five steps until 2003. Coal and nuclear fuels were not affected. The tax is not levied on fuels used in CHP and decentralized production (up to 5 MW), or for natural gas–fuelled power plants with an efficiency of 57.5 per cent or more. This gave these energy sources an advantage of up to 1.53 ct/kWh over others. But in a rather low-price market, this was not sufficient to bring about their expansion.

The main part of the revenue – rising from €4.3 billion in 1999 (€8.8 billion in 2000, €11.8 billion in 2001, and €14.3 billion in 2002) to €18.7 billion in 2003 (BMF 2004) – is earmarked to lower the social security contributions paid by employees as well as employers, reducing the production factor cost of labour while increasing that of energy. Yet, a small amount of about €102 million per year (1999 and 2000) was reserved for renewable energy subsidies, particularly to finance the 100,000 roof program. The promotion of renewable energy sources increased to €153 million in 2001, €190 million in 2002, and €250 million in 2003. The eco-tax reform was expected to reduce GHG emissions by about 2 to 3 per cent by 2005. For 2002, its impact on CO_2 reduction stood at 7 million tons.

Combined Heat and Power and End Use Efficiency

The efforts to increase efficiency were also reflected in support for CHP, whose share was to increase substantially from 12 per cent in 1999, substantially below that of other European countries. CHP plants have been under severe pressure since electricity liberalization. A new act for the support of CHP plants for public supply entered into force in April 2002 and was supposed to create incentives for modernization until 2010, leading to a reduction of some 11 million tons of CO_2. From the beginning, it seemed unlikely that the reduction goal would be reached (Mez 2003b). Additional support was provided for small-scale CHP and fuel cells.

As to end use efficiency, activities were initiated in line with EU policy. As a first step, the Energy Savings Ordinance entered into force in February 2002. It set the total energy requirement of new buildings at 30 per cent below current standards; for old buildings, insulation requirements and exchange of heating systems were prescribed.

Renewable Energy Targets

The Red-Green government formulated a target to increase the share of RES-E in the electricity supply to 12.5 per cent in 2010 and 50 per cent in 2050; in 2004 the goal of 20 per cent by 2020 was added. The long-term target must be viewed as a programmatic goal, which in concert with energy efficiency programs is ambitious but not unrealistic, either technically or economically.

Several measures were taken in favour of renewable energy. They included a five-year market incentive program for RES, which provided about €445 million from 1999 to 2002. A tax break on biofuels was applied in keeping with an EU directive on the subject. On the international level, the German government in 2004 hosted the international conference on renewable energy in Bonn. As to RES-E, the most important measures adopted were the 100,000 roof program for PV and above all the Renewable Energy Sources Act (RESA) adopted in 2000 and substantially amended in 2004.

The 100,000 Roof Program

As noted above, solar PV had not been able to develop much during the 1990s. The Red-Green government wanted to provide new initiatives. As the design of a new feed-in regulation was expected to take time, another market creation program along the lines of the 100 MW wind and 1,000 roof program (both 1989) was adopted in January 1999 as a stopgap measure. It provided for reduced loans for PV roof installations; the goal was to achieve an installed capacity of about 300 MW. The program was taken up slowly at first, but took off when RESA was introduced. By 2003, the two measures had led to installations of 350 MW. At that point, the 100,000 roof program was terminated and PV market development turned over to improved feed-in tariffs.

The Renewable Energy Sources Act of 2000

While the parliamentary party groups of the Red-Green majority pressed for more favourable feed-in rates for RES-E, the Economics Ministry repeatedly delayed and diluted efforts (Lauber and Pesendorfer 2004). The big utilities were of course opposed; they placed their hope on a lawsuit pending before the European Court of Justice that challenged the old Feed-In Law as state aid, an argument that could be applied also to the new act. This was also the view of the opposition. The Economic Affairs Ministry at one point even managed to persuade the government to postpone this legislation until the commission had had a chance to react to it.

However, the two parliamentary party groups of the Red-Green majority managed to find important allies, particularly with the Association of Machinery and Industrial Equipment Manufacturers (VDMA) and the metalworkers union. In April 2000, the Act on Granting Priority to Renewable Energy Sources (RESA) was adopted; its declared purpose was to double RES-E production by 2010. This act, which became one of the pivotal acts of the Red-Green coalition (Mez 2003a), repealed the Feed-In Law of 1990 but maintained the essential feature of feed-in tariffs to stimulate the development of RES-E. In many respects the law brought improvements for generators in rates and above all security. It also declared expressly that RES-E compensations should take external costs of conventional generation into account, and also support an industrial policy aiming at the long-term development of renewable energy technologies.

While under the Feed-In Law compensation rates were expressed as percentages of average end customer tariffs, the new rates were now fixed for twenty years. For wind power, they were made dependent on the quality of the location: all operators would receive a favourable rate for at least five years, thereafter the rate would decline, but later in the case of less favourable locations. Rates were particularly favourable for PV, offshore wind, and biomass. At the same time, there now was an annual decline in compensation for most sources, not for existing installations but for new installations, and determined by the year they would go on line.

A key regulatory element of the act was the distribution of costs from RES-E compensation across all power grid operators on a pro rata basis, calculated on the ratio of RES-E in nationwide electricity sales. Also, the utilities were now entitled to benefit from the special feed-in rates for their own RES-E generation facilities. This had not been the case earlier and might become lucrative for utilities, particularly in the case of highly capital-intensive investments such as those in offshore wind farms, where they might beat back the new RES-E generators that arose in recent years.

The 1997 European Commission White Book and the 2001 EC Directive (77/EC) on the promotion of electricity produced by renewable energy sources in the internal electricity market also helped as additional drivers of renewables development.

The RESA Amendment of 2004

After the re-election of the Red-Green coalition in autumn 2002, responsibility for RES changed from the Economic Ministry (headed by a Social-Democrat and always sceptical of RES-E) to the Environment Ministry (headed by a Green); the parliamentary committee in charge changed in a parallel fashion. This opened new perspectives. The first draft by the Environment Ministry led to a lively conflict with Economics Minister Clement, a well-versed politician from coal state North Rhine-Westphalia.

Clement attacked the very principle of the feed-in tariff and wanted to replace it by a tender system, arguing that rates were excessive, particularly for wind energy. His main concern seems to have been to protect coal interests. After a compromise within the government, the Red-Green majority in parliament proceeded to revise the government bill, largely against the preferences of Clement. However, Clement was

Table 14.2 Total capacity installed of wind power and PV in Germany

Year	Wind power (MW)	PV (MWp)
1990	55	1.5
1991	106	2.5
1992	174	5.6
1993	326	8.9
1994	618	12.4
1995	1,121	17.8
1996	1,546	27.9
1997	2,080	41.9
1998	2,871	53.9
1999	4,439	69.5
2000	6,104	113.8
2001	8,754	194.7
2002	11,994	278.0
2003	14,609	431.0
2004	16,629	934.0
2005	18,428	1,537.0
2006	20,622	3,063.0

Source: DEWI and BSW.

successful in obtaining reduced rates for wind and in defending coal interests.

In the Bundesrat, the Länder ruled by Conservative governments opposed the bill. The Bundestag majority could simply have insisted on its earlier version. However, the Red-Green coalition negotiated with the Conservatives in an effort to secure support for maintaining RESA beyond 2007. Some of the Länder wanted an expiry date of 2007 for the act, or a declaration reversing the nuclear energy phase-out; some criticized the 20 per cent RES-E target for 2020. But the Conciliation Committee between the two houses of parliament was content with more modest changes, and the bill was adopted in both houses.

The chief changes are a general strengthening of generators vis-à-vis the utilities; reduction of rates for onshore wind and exclusion of low-wind zones, but also improved rates for offshore wind; inclusion of hydro plants up to 150 MW, and significant new incentives for biomass (especially small plants) with additional bonuses for innovative technologies (Bechberger and Reiche 2004). Probably most important was the increase of PV rates, which made them commercially attractive without additional support. This was introduced already in late 2003 and led to a veritable solar boom in 2004, which continued in the following years and boosted Germany to first position in installed capacity of PV (see table 14.2).

RESA and the Conservative–Social Democratic Coalition: 2005 and Beyond

As the Mez and Doern analysis in chapter 5 has shown, a conservative-liberal victory at the national level was widely anticipated in 2004–5 and dramatic changes in German energy policy were expected as the consequence. The Free Democrats emphasized the need to return to nuclear power and coal and wanted to subject RES-E to market discipline. The position of the conservative CDU-CSU alliance was more complex. Angela Merkel, the Conservative leader, proposed to reverse the nuclear phase-out decision but did not say clearly how for long the lifetime of reactors should be extended. Merkel also proposed to reduce support for German hard coal.

As to RES-E, Merkel had induced practically all conservative MPs to vote against the RESA amendment in 2004; the CDU leadership had unsuccessfully demanded, as price for its consent, that the law be scheduled to expire in 2007. One of Merkel's favourite topics was the 'excessive subsidies' for RES-E.

When the close results of the 2005 parliamentary elections became evident, the RES community breathed a sigh of relief. Under the grand coalition between the Conservatives and the Social Democrats, RES was to stay with the Environment Ministry (under the Social Democratic Minister Gabriel). After some weeks of negotiation, the coalition agreement between CDU, CSU, and SPD made clear in its passage on RES-E that the policy was set to continue in the path traced by the Red-Green coalition.

The text stated that RESA would continue in its basic structure. At the same time, the economic efficiency of the individual rates would be subject to review by 2007. The share of RES-E would increase to reach at least 12.5 per cent in 2010 and 20 per cent in 2020. Framework conditions for offshore wind power and repowering onshore would be improved. The calculation of costs resulting from RESA would be made transparent, so that customers would pay only for costs really incurred. International activities to step up renewable energy would be continued, and initiatives would be taken to found an International Renewable Energy Agency. Finally, the hardship clause for energy-intensive industry would be modified to be more predictable in its effect on firms (Coalition Agreement 2005).

In April 2006, at the energy summit, the German utilities made the commitment to invest €30 billion until 2012 and the RES-E suppliers in addition €40 billion. The government announced a 30 per cent increase of research and development for new energy technologies for the legislature.

German RES-E industry is likely to prosper from the current boom in wind power and biomass power and, above all, from the incredible market expansion in PV.

At the EU level, Energy Commissioner Piebalgs no longer advocates an early introduction of quota-certificate systems, which turned out to be quite expensive and rather inefficient so far. Spain has joined Germany as an ardent defender of the feed-in model, and new feed-in laws were adopted by a range of EU member states, including Italy, the Czech Republic, and Slovenia.

Conclusions

German wind power installations represented about 30 per cent of the total stock worldwide in 2005, and for solar PV the figure is similarly impressive. Strong global growth of installed wind power capacity reduced Germany's share to about 24 per cent in 2007 but Germany remains the world leader, ahead of the United States and Spain. For the sake of perspective it must be added that all this capacity, together with hydro, supplies more than 10 per cent of electricity in Germany; in 2007, all renewables combined achieved a share of 14.2 per cent of gross electricity consumption. However, there are plans to reach 50 per cent by mid-century. At the same time, Germany developed a wind turbine industry that is second only to that of Denmark, and a PV industry second to that of Japan. These industries are expected to make key contributions to future exports.

German leadership in the area of RES-E is the result of a complex process. Weidner and Eberlein's analysis in chapter 14 attribute Germany's success in overall climate protection policy to 'positive path dependence,' facilitated by an extremely favourable institutional environment. This argument holds equally well for this specific but core element of German climate policy.

With few colonies in the nineteenth century, Germany until the late twentieth century was one of only two large industrial states without oil resources and no large oil corporation of its own (Karlsch and Stokes 2003), the other one being Japan. It came to rely with particular intensity on domestic coal, and later on nuclear energy. During the energy crises of the 1970s, coal and nuclear were nursed to impressive dimensions, politically as well as economically. But this policy also led to intense controversies and the rise of a strong anti-nuclear movement in the 1970s, a strong environmental movement in the 1980s, the spread of green ideas throughout society, and the first big Green party in Europe.

This counter-movement viewed renewable energy sources as an alternative to a nuclear plutonium economy, not merely as another additional source. Under pressure from this movement, governments reluctantly supported the development of renewable energy sources on a modest scale when compared to the funds spent on coal and nuclear energy, and not even for domestic use at first. Additional drivers could be located on the Länder level and in innovative municipalities, inventing new promotion schemes for the support of electricity generated by renewable energy sources.

When the Red-Green government came into office in 1998, its parliamentary party groups – once more in opposition to the Economics Ministry – soon took measures to improve the economics of RES-E. They also made PV attractive for the first time. For this purpose, the coalition drew new actors into the RES policy network, composed of environmental associations and the renewable energy sector – such as equipment producers, owners and operators of installations and their associations – but also 'conventional' associations such as the Association of Machinery and Industrial Equipment Manufacturers or the metalworkers union, which had joined the coalition during the preceding years. In 2003/2004, this coalition, supplemented by new allies, repeated this feat against renewed opposition from nuclear and coal interests.

In addition to these favourable social and political constellations, the more specific causal factors for the rapid expansion of renewable capacity are planning security for investors and the technology-specific remuneration for RES-E. Germany guarantees investors the feed-in tariff for a period of twenty years (and even thirty years for hydro till 5 MW). The different power production costs of RES technologies are considered in the form of varying remuneration, depending on the technology used, the size of the plant and – in the case of wind energy – also the age and generated power output of the installation.

Finally, Germany also mobilized the European level in its drive for an increased share of renewables. And the German model implementation of the Directive 2001/77/EC (on the promotion of renewable energy sources in electricity generation) has been exemplary for the large majority of EU member states.

What is the political future of the feed-in scheme? The legal challenges from the German utilities and the European Commission (DG Competition) have all been defeated so far. Energy Commissioner Piebalgs has postponed the issue of harmonization of support schemes during his term, given insufficient experience with the different schemes and given especially the poor performance of quota-certificate systems introduced since 2002 when compared to feed-in systems.

In Germany, there is a consensus among environmental groups and the general public that highly industrialized countries have a moral obligation to lead in policies coping with global climate change, to cover most of the costs of these efforts, and to support developing countries in adapting to or mitigating negative climate change consequences (also see Weidner and Eberlein, this volume). It is also widely agreed that the challenges of climate change are best tackled by a government-driven policy of promoting renewable energy sources. Only a minority perceives nuclear power as a sustainable solution to both the climate issue and potential energy shortages. With the exception of the utilities association and the Liberal party, most of the actors are generally in favour of RES-E support scheme. Also the coalition agreement (2005) of the new grand coalition government reconfirmed the use of a feed-in scheme. The amendment of RESA that is expected to be enacted later in 2008 may well bring steeper rates of digression for feed-in tariffs over time. In particular, it may not offer sufficient rates to continue the expansion of offshore wind power capacity at previous growth rates, against a backdrop of increasing manufacturing costs and of the general saturation of the domestic offshore wind market also in terms of siting options. However, offshore wind power will likely receive significant additional support, and the general direction and goal of renewable policy (25–30 per cent increase in the share of renewables by 2020 remain unchanged). In fact, the promotion of renewables is a key building block of the larger 'integrated climate and energy package' adopted by the German Cabinet in August 2007 (also see Weidner and Eberlein, chapter 11).

It also remains to be seen in which ways the coordination of the EU support system will affect further developments of RES-E in Germany (Di Nucci, Mez, and Reiche 2005). Furthermore, one will have to see how the RES market will interact with the second period of EU emission trading and the associated implementation of the Second National Allocation Plan (2008 to 2012). However, beyond that date, the career of RES-E will depend increasingly on the state of world energy markets at that time – the development of the oil and natural gas price, implementation of energy efficiency programs, and an international follow-up regime, after the Kyoto Protocol expires.

NOTE

1 *Der Spiegel*, online edition, 23 August 2007.

REFERENCES

ARE. *See* Association of Regional Energy Providers.
Association of Regional Energy Providers. 2000. *Regionale Energieversorgung 1998–1999*. Tätigkeitsbericht, Hanover (Association of Regional Energy Providers, regional energy supply, report).
Bechberger, Mischa, and Danyel Reiche. 2004. Renewable energy policy in Germany: Pioneering and exemplary regulations. *Energy for Sustainable Development* 8 (1): 25–35.
BMF. *See* Bundesministerium für Finanzen.
Bundesregierung [Federal government]. 2000. *Nationales Klimaschutzprogramm, Beschluß der Bundesregierung* [National climate protection program, government decision]. Fünfter Bericht der Interministeriellen Arbeitsgruppe „CO$_2$-Reduktion" [Fifth report of Inter-Ministerial Working Group 'CO$_2$-Reduction']. Berlin.
Bundesministerium für Finanzen [Federal Finance Ministry]. 2004. *Ökologische Steuerreform in Deutschland* [Ecological tax reform in Germany]. Berlin.
CDU, CSU, and SPD (Christlich Demokratische Union, Christlich – Soziale Union, and Sozialdemokratische Partei Deutschlands). 2005. Gemeinsam für Deutschland. Mit Mut und Menschlichkeit. Koalitionsvertrag zwischen CDU, CSU und SPD. http://koalitionsvertrag.spd.de/servlet/PB/show /1645854/111105_Koalitionsvertrag.pdf.
Di Nucci, M.R., Lutz Mez, and Danyel Reiche. 2005. *Country report: Germany,* http://www.realise-forum.net/pdf_files/060103_German_Report.pdf.

Ganseforth, Monika. 1996. Politische Umsetzung der Empfehlungen der beiden Klima –Kommissionen (1987–1994) – eine Bewertung [Political implementation of the recommendations of both climate commissions]. In *Klimapolitik*, ed. H.G. Brauch, 215–24. New York: Springer.

German Bundestag, ed. 1991. *Protecting the earth: A status report with recommendations for a new energy policy.* Third report of the Enquete Commission of the 11th German Bundestag, preventive measures to protect the earth's atmosphere. Vol. 2. Bonn: Deutscher Bundestag.

Hemmelskamp, Jens. 1999. *Umweltpolitik und technischer Fortschritt* [Environmental policy and technological progress]. Heidelberg: Physica.

Hennicke, Peter, J.P. Johnson, and S. Kohler. 1985. *Die Energiewende ist möglich* [The energy turnaround is possible]. Frankfurt/Main: Fischer.

Hirschl, Bernd. 2002. *Markt und Kostenentwicklung erneuerbarer Energien. 2 Jahre EEG – Bilanz und Ausblick* [Market and cost developments of renewable energy sources: Two years of feed-in law; Balance sheet and outlook]. Berlin: Erich Schmidt Verlag.

Huber, M. 1997. Leadership and unification: Climate change policies in Germany. In *Cases in climate change policy: Political reality in the European unity*, ed. Ute Collier and Rudolf Löfstedt, 65–86. London: Earthscan.

Jacobsson, Staffan, and Volkmar Lauber. 2006. The politics and policy of energy systems transformation: Explaining the German diffusion of renewable energy technology. *Energy Policy* 34 (3): 256–76.

Jahn, Detlef. 1992. Nuclear power, energy policy and new politics in Sweden and Germany. *Environmental Politics* 1 (3): 383–417.

Karlsch, R., and R.G. Stokes. 2003. *Faktor Öl: Die Mineralölwirtschaft in Deutschland* [Factor oil: The oil industry in Germany]. Hamburg: Hoffmann & Campe.

Kords, Udo. 1993. *Die Entstehungsgeschichte des Stromeinspeisungsgesetzes vom 5.10.1990* [The origins of the feed-in law of 5 October 1990]. MA thesis, Free University of Berlin.

– 1996. Tätigkeit und Handlungsempfehlungen der beiden Klima-Enquete – Kommissionen des Deutschen Bundestages (1987–1994) [Activities and recommendations of both climate commissions of the German Bundestag 1987–1994]. In *Klimapolitik*, ed. H.G. Brauch, 203–14. Berlin: Springer.

Lauber, Volkmar, and Dieter Pesendorfer. 2004. Success through continuity: Renewable electricity policies in Germany. In *Renewable electricity policies in Europe*, ed. Isabelle de Lovinfosse and Frédéric Varone, 121–82. Louvain: Presses de l'Université catholique de Louvain.

Mez, Lutz. 1995. Reduction of exhaust gases at large combustion plants in the Federal Republic of Germany. In *Successful environmental protection: A critical evaluation of 24 Cases*, ed. Martin Jänicke and Helmut Weidner, 173–86. Berlin: Edition Sigma.

– 2003a. New corporate strategies in the German electricity supply industry. In *Competition in European electricity markets: A cross-country comparison*, ed. Jean-Michel Glachant and Dominique Finon, 193–216. Cheltenham, UK: Elgar.

– 2003b. Ökologische Modernisierung und Vorreiterrolle in der Energie- und Umweltpolitik? Eine vorläufige Bilanz [Ecological modernization and pioneer role in energy and environmental policy? A preliminary balance sheet]. In *Das rot-grüne Projekt. Eine Bilanz der Regierung Schröder 1998–2002* [The Red-Green Project: A review of the Schröder government 1998–2002], ed. C. Egle, T. Ostheim, and S. Zohlnhöfer, 329–50. Opladen: Westdeutscher Verlag.

Monopolkommission. 1976. *Mehr Wettbewerb ist möglich. Hauptgutachten 1973/1975* [More competition is possible: Main report 1973–1975]. Baden-Baden: Nomos.

Reiche, Danyel. 2004. *Rahmenbedingungen für erneuerbare Energien in Deutschland. Möglichkeiten und Grenzen einer Vorreiterpolitik* [Context factors for renewable energy sources in Germany: Opportunities and limits]. Frankfurt am Main: Verlag Peter Lang.

Ristau, Oliver. 1998. *Die solare Standortfrage* [The solar dimension of siting industries]. Bad Oeynhausen: Solarthemen.

Schafhausen, Franzjosef. 1996. Klimavorsorgepolitik der Bundesregierung [Climate protection policy of the federal government]. In *Klimapolitik*, ed. H.G. Brauch, 237–49. Berlin: Springer.

Shonfield, Andrew. 1968. *Modern capitalism*. Oxford: Oxford University Press.

Staiss, Frithjof, ed. 2000. *Jahrbuch Erneuerbare Energien 2000* [Yearbook of renewable energy sources 2000]. Radebeul: Bieberstein.

15 Conclusions: Complexity, Coordination, and Capacity in German and Canadian Energy Regulatory Governance

BURKARD EBERLEIN AND G. BRUCE DOERN

This book has investigated and compared the dynamics of multi-level energy regulatory governance in Germany and Canada. Regulatory governance has been conceptualized as a response to energy policy challenges that include a renewed emphasis on energy security as well as on environmental sustainability in a global and competitive resource economy. We argue that today's energy policy faces unprecedented challenges that arise from mounting tensions between core policy goals in a context of increasing interdependence and rapid internationalization. The governance of these challenges increasingly involves multi-level patterns of interaction across established territorial and functional boundaries.

As set out in chapter 1, the theoretical roots of the analysis reside in conceptual work on multi-level governance and multi-level regulation, neo-institutional theory, and the nature of energy resources and policy.

On this basis, we argue that energy regulatory governance is shaped by two key factors: by the substantive structures and endowments of the energy field in the two countries and by the specific multi-level institutional settings of energy policy, in which public and private actors interact, based on their resources and interests. As we have emphasized from the outset, energy governance does not deal with institutions and processes or politics and economics somehow disembodied from the substance and content of the energy field.

We have also lodged our analysis in the larger array of macro political institutions that govern Germany and Canada. As we have seen, in the German case, these are (1) 'cooperative federalism,' including strong municipal self-government; (2) coalition governments; (3) the strong role of organized interests under sectoral corporatism; (4) the heavy reliance on competition law and courts as opposed to sector-specific economic regulation; and (5) a domestic institutional context that is being increasingly influenced and reshaped by Germany's integration in the EU policymaking framework. In the Canadian case these macro institutional realities include (1) a cooperative but more dual system of federalism; (2) Westminster parliaments and typically majority governments; (3) pluralist business lobbying; (4) more segmented sectoral regulation and competition policy; (5) regional integration under NAFTA.

Chapter 1 set the policy and historical context and introduced the analytical framework and definitional and theoretical underpinnings of our study, while also providing a comparative overview of the German and Canadian multi-level energy regulatory regimes. Chapter 2 presented and examined today's major energy policy challenges, and their impact on Germany and Canada specifically.

In this final chapter we review the major findings of this collaborative work, as they emerge from the preceding chapters, in the light of the three-part analytical framework (see table 15.1) that guides our study of multi-level energy regulatory governance in Germany and Canada. The framework themes for energy regulatory governance are *complexity, coordination,* and *capacity.* We then offer final conclusions on German versus Canadian performance in meeting the energy governance challenge and on their capacity to deal with future energy puzzles under conditions of complex multi-level regulation.

Complexity captures the technical and political features of energy policy as well as the broader notion of a fragmented policy arena in which there is a high dispersion of resources (authority, information, material resources) required to address governance challenges. *Coordination* involves the management of patterns of multi-level interaction and is concerned fundamentally with the form and effectiveness of coordination between different actors and levels involved in multi-level energy policymaking. *Capacity,* finally, is the ability of jurisdictions and institutional arrangements to meet the substantive challenges of today's energy world, including the technical ability to make energy systems effectively deliver the needed mix of energy services.

The three-part framework also reflects the key issues and debates raised at the Transatlantic Energy Conference in which this book originated. *Complexity* emerged as a common theme of a set of presentations that dealt with the nature of the current energy challenge and

Table 15.1 Framework for energy multi-level regulatory governance:
A German-Canadian comparison

Framework element	Germany	Canada
Complexity (1) Material complexity: Large technical systems with high potential for politicization (2) Institutional complexity: Fragmented policy arena (high degree of dispersion of resources, authority, information, material resources) results in complex layering of regulatory regimes across territorial levels and traditional sectors	(1) Electricity supply involves real-time complex synchronization of components, de-integration and rearrangement as artificial markets are prone to design flaws – Structured without full consideration of market concentration and of incumbent privileges – Short-term wholesale markets versus long-term capital intensive commitments; (2) International regulation and market integration vis-à-vis EU and Russia; role of Länder in regulatory governance – Horizontal regimes for competition and environment affect energy sector equally	(1) Electricity supply involves real-time complex synchronization of components, de-integration and rearrangement as artificial markets are prone to design flaws – Structured without full consideration of what happens when energy prices rise to politically unacceptable levels – Short-term wholesale markets versus long-term capital-intensive commitments (2) International regulation and market integration vis-à-vis U.S.; provincial autonomy – Horizontal regime for trade has so far stronger impact on governance of energy sector than environmental regime – Absence of interprovincial electricity market/network
Coordination Negotiation as dominant mode in multi-level systems with dispersed authority, outcomes shaped by power relations, actor strategies, and institutional rules	– Germany and EU offer a constellation of actors and institutional settings more conducive to consensual conflict management – Germany not endowed with natural energy resources and thus fewer cleavages between producer and consumer regions – Has political and institutional system geared to consensus-building mixed with some stalemate – Has corporatist-style relationships between government and industry and cross-sector associations	– Canada and NAFTA offer set of actors and institutional setting that militate against high levels of coordination – Canada is endowed with natural energy resources and thus has major cleavages between producer and consumer regions – Has conflict-prone mix of partisan politics and 'executive federalism' that privileges bilateral bargaining between federal level and individual provinces

Table 15.1 (*continued*)

Framework element	Germany	Canada
	– Greater balance of power among EU countries in general and on energy matters – Dense networks between national energy regulators instead of centralization of regulatory authority in Brussels	– NAFTA 'constitutionalized' Canada-U.S. energy free trade – Asymmetrical power relations between the U.S. and Canada in general and vis-à-vis energy, despite Canada's great resource endowments
Capacity Ability of jurisdictions and institutional arrangements to meet the substantive challenges of energy provision and resource management, including the properties of new and old energy sources and the technical ability to make energy systems effectively deliver the needed mix of energy services	– Ability to meet three key goals that are often in conflict: (a) deliver useable and reliable energy at reasonable prices to all citizens, (b) provide sustainable energy and reduced energy use per capita, (c) economic efficiency mainly through market disciplines – Lack of resource endowment has compelled early and strong capacity for alternative energy – Strong emphasis on energy security (also on EU level), but dependence vis-à-vis Russia remains unresolved – Strong Kyoto emissions reductions due half to regulatory will and capacity and half to closure of East German industries as it integrated into a reunited Germany; – Domestic and EU market liberalization has not resulted in competitive, efficient markets (domination by incumbents)	– Ability to meet four key goals that are often in conflict: (a) deliver useable and reliable energy at reasonable prices to all citizens, (b) provide sustainable energy and reduced energy use per capita, (c) economic efficiency mainly through market disciplines, (d) national unity among producer and consumer regions/provinces – Large and diverse resource endowment has resulted in weak capacity on renewable energy – Energy security not a problem, although physical security is, given proximity to terrorist threat against U.S. – Weak Kyoto performance due to strong federal and provincial desire to develop Alberta oil sands and increase oil and gas exports to U.S. and to weak regulation to reduce greenhouse gases – Stalled electricity market reforms, reasonably competitive in oil and gas

German institutions and EU directives in table: Bundesministerium für Wirtschaft und Technologie (Federal Ministry of Economics and Technology); Bundeskartellamt-FCO (Federal Cartel Office); Bundesnetzagentur für Elektrizität, Gas, Telekommunikation, Post und Eisenbahnen (Federal Network Agency); Gesetz zur Neuregelung des Energiewirtschaftsrechts vom 24 April 1998 (E-Directive 96/92 EC implemented by the *Energy Industry Act* 1998); Zweites Gesetz zur Neuregelung des Energiewirtschaftsrechts vom 7.7.2005 (E-Directive 2003/55 EC implemented by the *New Energy Industry Act* 2005).

with how recent domestic and international market reforms had transformed the energy landscape, and met with different regulatory responses and processes, in Germany and Canada respectively. *Coordination* was the common concern of a second group of papers that addressed key features of multi-level governance in Europe and North America and that noted major differences between the EU and NAFTA frameworks in particular. The concept of *capacity*, finally, evolved from a final session entitled 'Strategies towards Sustainability: Canada and Germany,' which raised the question of how to account for the stark contrast between Canada and Germany in environmental sustainability. This led to broader reflections on what the notion of energy governance capacity should entail and how to evaluate it in comparative perspective.

Complexity

We approach complexity along two dimensions. First, we discuss complexity as a feature inherent in the technical nature of the substantive policy area. Second, we look at complexity as the result of increasing vertical and horizontal differentiation or fragmentation of the policy arena.

Most, if not all, areas of today's public policy may lay claim to the label of complexity, to the extent that they involve a high number of interrelated, and often conflicting, sets of issues and goals, interests, and actors on different levels of decision-making. What makes energy policy particularly complex? We argue that from a regulatory perspective *energy policy combines high technical complexity or 'systemness' with high issue salience or potential for politicization* (Eisner, Worsham, and Ringquist 2000, 29).

Under these circumstances, the management of change is exceptionally risk-prone. The delivery of energy to individuals and companies depends on sophisticated, 'large technical systems' (Hughes 1987). Electricity supply, which is the empirical focus of most chapters in part 1, rests on the real-time, complex synchronization of components (generation plants, transmission lines, distribution networks), whereas the oil and (less so) gas infrastructures have traditionally been more amenable to decomposition into elements along the value chain and to governance by decentralized (mostly market) mechanisms.

Traditionally, the systemic character and prevailing technologies (large-scale generation) in electricity were viewed as resulting in important economies of scale and scope. This favoured tight integration under a monopoly model. Electricity restructuring or 'deregulation' decomposed this integrated system into natural monopoly elements (grids and wires) versus potentially competitive elements (generating plants and supply), in order to enhance economic efficiency.

However, this rearrangement of the electricity system, with a multiplication of actors and transactions, made system coordination more – not less – complex. Given the nature of the industry, the introduction of market elements required more – not less – regulatory intervention. As chapters 3 and 10 by Dewees and Theobald on electricity industry restructuring in Canada and Germany respectively show, regulatory reforms are all plagued by the complexities of what Dewees rightly describes as 'artificial markets with extensive rules for all participants arising from the complex interconnections of the electricity network' (71).

The introduction of market mechanisms requires careful design. Design errors in one area can have important ripple effects that may destabilize the entire system, or at least undermine the achievement of reform goals. The California electricity crisis is only the most extreme example of design flaws potentially leading to disastrous consequences (Duane 2002; Jaccard 2002). The fact that there was little previous experience with the intricacies of competitive industry restructuring in electricity contributed to design flaws, and to unexpected and undesirable results. Policymakers often emulated (Anglo-American) reform templates, with insufficient attention to specific local circumstances and differences in 'starting points' (Dewees) of regulatory reform.

Policymakers also underestimated the trade-offs and tensions that would arise, not by design flaw but by necessity, between the different elements and logics of a restructured, de-integrated system. If prices are effectively set by short-term wholesale markets, private investment in new generation capacity, that involves long-term and capital-intensive commitments, is forthcoming only at a higher risk premium, or not at all if regulatory risk or instability is regarded as too high (Levy and Spiller 1996). In such a complex design context, the introduction and monitoring of sustainable competition can be very costly in itself.

More generally, both Canadian and European evidence presented in these chapters underscores the observation that it is very difficult to create and sustain truly competitive electricity markets. There is a strong tendency for companies to seek vertical (re-)integration, and for markets to gravitate towards concentration (Dewees 2005; Finon and Midttun 2004). Theobald's analysis in chapter 10 demonstrates with evidence from the German case that the fight against market concentration in generation may well be a far greater challenge than the natural monopoly regulation of wires and pipelines, to which the reform orthodoxy pays so much attention.

Regulatory reforms of energy systems are not only technically complex, they are also *highly political* as they affect, at least in the utility realm, an essential, non-substitutable service for all citizens. Dewees' account of the botched 'deregulation' reforms in Ontario is a perfect illustration of the fact that politics constantly interferes with, and mostly overrules, technical market design. When energy prices in Ontario rose to politically unacceptable levels following market opening, the provincial government responded to the public outcry by introducing price freezes for residential consumers, thereby effectively disabling market signals, with disastrous effects on incentives for investment in urgently needed new generation capacity (Trebilcock and Hrab 2005).

Price volatility and the possibility of price spikes are inherent in a market with very low demand elasticity. Even the European poster child of successful liberalization, the North European wholesale market Noordpool, came under political pressure by retail consumers when it delivered massive price spikes of more than 600 per cent within six months, basically as a result of extreme weather conditions affecting the availability of hydro-generation (von der Fehr et al. 2005). Finally, the 2003 series of blackouts in both North America and Europe, although not directly attributable to industry restructuring, have further undermined public confidence in industry reforms.

A second key dimension of complexity is less linked to the substance of energy policy but can be found in other industries and sectors as well. Its source is the increasing *vertical and horizontal differentiation of the policy arena that generates a high level of fragmentation and, potentially, conflict.* Differentiation means that policy resources and functions are more widely distributed, among actors and levels, in the governance of the energy system.

It is true that the boundaries of the energy policy arena are less clearly delineated than in other industries or sectors to begin with. Energy use has cross-sector properties as it reaches into areas as diverse as transport, research and development, and land use, not to mention the environmental impacts of energy use. Hence, we can expect a higher number of issues, interests, and actors to be involved.

Looking more specifically at the distribution of policymaking powers in the Canadian and German institutional context, energy policy has always been multi-layered, as discussed in chapter 1. The federal division of powers introduces a fundamental vertical layering of governance in both cases, but with a much stronger decentralization to the sub-national level in the Canadian federation.

Horizontal layering plays a large role as well, as the numerous substantive links to other areas, and especially the energy-environment nexus, would suggest. Doern and Gattinger (2003) convincingly show for the Canadian case that energy regulatory governance involves a discrete sector regime, but also, and increasingly, it involves horizontal regimes for the environment, and for competition and trade, within which the energy sector is but one industry.

It can be argued that *both vertical and horizontal processes of layering of regulatory regimes have become much more prominent, thus adding to complexity.* In a vertical perspective, both German and Canadian regulatory regimes are increasingly shaped by international levels and processes, in particular by regional or continental energy market integration. Clarkson in his chapter shows how Canada's oil and gas resources and markets (much more than Mexico's) have progressively been integrated with U.S. markets, under the quasi-constitutional free-trade arrangement of NAFTA, that was underpinned by market-friendly policies in both countries.

Likewise, recent developments of the German regulatory regime that is moving from industrial self-regulation towards sector-specific public regulation can be attributed to the supranational push for market opening and regulated market integration, as detailed in the chapters 6 and 10 by Froschauer and, indirectly, Theobald. At the same time, domestic regimes do not simply converge on international patterns. Froschauer shows how Canada and Germany implemented nationally distinct reform policies in the electricity industry, even though momentum and direction of regulatory reform were essentially 'downloaded' from the international level.

Furthermore, there is no zero-sum game logic at work in the layering. While the most important dimension of vertical layering is internationalization, local and regional energy governance levels do not, by the same token, become less important. In the Canadian case of natural resource development in the North, for example, indigenous communities play an increasingly important role. And the expansion of decentralized, renewable sources of electricity generation in Germany (such as wind farms) brings the land planning powers of local authorities into play.

Horizontal layering is also on the rise, on different territorial levels. As a matter of fact, regional or continental market integration under EU or NAFTA rules could be interpreted as the extension of horizontal competition and trade regimes into the energy sector.

The most significant horizontal regime for energy policy, however, is the environmental regime. Environmental regulation of energy use and impact has been on the rise for some time now, especially in Germany, which introduced strict limitations on all emissions from large combustion plants as early as 1983. As a matter of fact, the current pioneer role of Germany in climate policy can be traced back to these early efforts at emissions control, as demonstrated by the Weidner and Eberlein (chapter 12).

Mez in his chapter on renewable energy policy in Germany shows how, since the first oil crisis in 1974, environmental advocacy, policies, and regulations have contributed to a significant shift in the German palette of fuels and sources that contribute to electricity generation, with the share of renewable sources rising from under 4 per cent in 1990 to 10.2 per cent in 2005.

It is true that most environmental regulation continues to be developed and implemented on the national level, which accounts for the possibility of stark national differences, such as between Canadian inertia and German leadership in climate change policies, as revealed in the two chapters by Rivers and Jaccard and Weidner and Eberlein, respectively. However, increasingly, international agreements and regimes at least set environmental standards and regulatory targets, with, of course, the Kyoto Protocol as the most prominent and relevant example.

To some extent, these processes of vertical and horizontal layering reflect the fact that current energy challenges such as energy security and the fight against global warming cross national and sector boundaries and call for more integrated governance arrangements. Yet processes of layering *do not necessarily mitigate the incongruence between the trans-border nature of governance challenges and jurisdictional divisions.* They seldom conveniently allocate authority and resources at the most 'appropriate' (in terms of externalities) territorial level, or streamline horizontal and sector regimes goals and policies. Rather, they tend to contribute to fragmentation of policy resources in a more complex multi-level setting.

In the EU, for example, the horizontal competition and trade regime is supranational, while energy policy in sector terms rests largely under the control of twenty-seven member states with veto powers. As Cameron details in chapter 7, EU framework rules need to be implemented and monitored on the national or sub-national level by regulatory agencies. The chapter by Rivers and Jaccard provides illustration from the Canadian context. The federal government exercised its sole authority to sign international treaties and made the commitment under the 1997 Kyoto Protocol to reduce Canada's greenhouse gas emissions by 6 per cent from 1990 levels (averaged over the 2008–12 period). But the government lacks legal and political powers domestically to impose burdens of adjustment on those provinces (Alberta and Ontario) with the highest share of total Canadian greenhouse gas emissions. Federal climate change policies, they note, 'require cooperation from the provinces, little of which has been forthcoming' (300).

The dispersion of authority and policy resources typical for layered, multi-level energy governance raises the question of if and how the ensuing tensions generated by interdependence and fragmentation can be managed by some form of coordination.

Coordination

'Multi-level policy-making occurs when actors from different levels are dependent on each other in fulfilling their tasks and have to coordinate their policies' (Benz 2003, 2). A key concern of multi-level governance studies is the form, extent, and effectiveness of coordination under conditions of dispersed authority (Bache and Flinders 2004; Hooghe and Marks 2003).

In theory, policy coordination can take various forms: reciprocal adaptation ('mutual adjustment'), competition, hierarchy, or negotiation. Which type of coordination will be prevalent in a given multi-level system depends on the 'constellations of actors' (players, preferences, options, and strategies) and the material and ideational incentives and constraints provided by the institutional setting in which they interact (Scharpf 1997).

In most multi-level systems, (pure) hierarchical steering is not a practically available option, as a result of veto positions of actors in systems of divided powers. In intergovernmental relations, procedural rules often limit the exclusive use of competition or mutual adjustment. Typically, negotiation is the most prominent form of coordination in multi-level systems, in variable combinations with elements (or 'shadows') of competition, hierarchy, or mutual adjustment.

Gattinger in chapter 8 uses a descriptive spectrum of coordination that is more interested in outcomes, ranging from 'conflict' (resulting in a lack of coordination) on the one hand and to 'harmonization' on the other hand. The assumption is that a higher level of coordination will produce higher regulatory convergence between levels, thus reducing the tensions generated by fragmentation.

On the basis of comparison of the German and the Canadian multi-level regulatory regimes presented in chapter 1, we argue that *Germany and the EU offer a constellation of actors and an institutional setting that is more conducive to the consensual management of multi-level tensions than the Canadian and the NAFTA framework*. We first review the domestic arrangements before including the supranational or continental context in our comparison.

As Gattinger points out, 'In Canadian energy regulatory governance, the institutions, regimes, and structural underpinnings of multi-level governance militate against high levels of coordination' (214).

First, regarding the structural features shaping energy policy, the unequal distribution of (large) energy reserves, population, and economic activity across Canada have resulted in profound conflicts between major energy producing regions/provinces (especially Alberta) and other more populous consumer regions, provinces, and interests (especially Ontario and Quebec). The redistributive nature of this divide makes any negotiation between the provinces, and agreements on joint directions of energy policy, particularly difficult. The 'have' provinces such as Alberta for oil and gas (or Quebec for hydropower) have little incentive to coordinate and integrate more closely (and share) with provincial counterparts, unless they have good commercial reasons. However, it is much more attractive for them to sell into the high-demand U.S. market over existing inter-ties than to invest in east-west grids or pipelines.

Pineau's contribution underscores these structural obstacles to closer electricity market integration in Canada, notably the stark differences, and the high degree of isolation, between provinces in generation and ownership, and infrastructural, regulatory, and commercial integration. At the same time, Pineau maintains that functional pressures (energy and environment challenges) might eventually focus provincial and federal attention on limited, mutually beneficial areas of further integration, such as an enhanced role of the National Energy Board in fostering interprovincial trade and transmission grids. These kinds of changes, however, would require a major reorientation of the federal-provincial dynamic.

Germany, by contrast, is uniformly, and poorly, endowed with natural resources. Hence, it does not feature major cleavages between producer and consumer regions, with the exception of regionally concentrated subsidies for coal mining. Rather, the absence of abundant oil and gas resources (and Germany's larger exposure to environmental risks) has favoured a consensus on the search for wider energy options (including renewable sources) to secure energy supply.

A second factor that militates against high levels of coordination is that the constitutional division of powers over energy and environment in Canada grants individual provinces a strong veto position in interprovincial and federal-provincial negotiations. The traumatic legacy of the National Energy Policy (NEP 1980–4), when the Trudeau government, following the 1979 oil crisis, massively intervened in energy markets and profoundly alienated Western energy interests, continues to influence federal-provincial dynamics in the energy domain, effectively excluding any federal energy policy leadership.

Furthermore, the nature of Cabinet-parliamentary government, with majority governments as the norm and no federal body to adequately represent provinces and regions collectively at the federal level, results in energy and other political disputes being fought out in a conflict-prone combination of partisan party politics and 'executive federalism,' privileging bilateral bargaining between the federal level and individual provinces. Pluralist patterns of government-industry relations dominated by issue-based lobbying of individual companies further accentuate the fragmented and conflict-prone character of Canadian energy regulatory governance.

Germany's political and institutional system, by contrast, is more geared towards consensus-building, but also stalemate. 'Cooperative federalism' grants direct representation and federal co-decision powers to the sixteen Länder via the Bundesrat, the upper house of parliament, which feeds regional demands into the core of federal decision-making.

At the same time, the federal government still has a lead role under the constitutional arrangement for energy and environment matters.

Coalition governments contribute to the need to engineer cross-partisan, national compromises. Also, corporatist-style relationships between the government and industry and cross-sector associations traditionally helped to foster consensus on the governance of the industry. All this is not to suggest that the German regime is devoid of conflict of interests or power struggles. *Yet the German energy policy regime is structurally less prone to tensions between levels, and it provides more institutional avenues for multi-level management than the Canadian regime.*

The contrast between Canada and Germany as milieus for multi-level coordination is further reinforced if we consider the embedding of domestic regimes in the regional integration context of NAFTA and EU respectively. Clarkson's chapter cautions us against looking at NAFTA as the 'embryonic, institutionally lighter version' of the EU, or as a 'European-Union-in-the-making' (99). Notwithstanding certain similarities in size, culture, or economic weight, the European Union and NAFTA are separated by durable, structural features that affect the coordination capacity of multi-level interaction. The common observation that integration in North America is largely market-driven and institutionally 'thin,' whereas as European integration is politically driven and institutionally 'deep,' is a good starting point but needs to be refined.

Firstly, regional integration under NAFTA is fundamentally asymmetrical, containing two distinct bilateral relationships between the regional (and global) hegemon, the United States, and two much less powerful neighbours. This contrasts with a greater balance of power among the twenty-seven EU members. Secondly, NAFTA has developed only a thin layer of transnational authority that is limited to economic norms, such as national treatment, but virtually 'constitutionalizes' free trade, including energy trade, between Canada and the United States (Clarkson 2005; Hoberg 2002; Hufbauer and Schott 2005). The relative weakness, or absence, of political and legal institutions (legislative, executive, and adjudicatory mechanisms) gives more room to market-driven or power-based patterns of interaction, and less to legal or negotiated ones – since issue-based interaction patterns are not nested in larger, institutionalized norms and contexts.

This makes negotiated bilateral policy coordination that respects partners as equals much more difficult. At the same time, virtually every aspect of Canadian energy policy depends in some way on U.S. conditions and actions. Traditionally, Canadian policy has needed U.S.

energy markets, U.S. energy capital, or even U.S. energy regulatory approval before key projects could proceed. More recently, increasing cross-border energy integration includes the need to better manage the reliability of the North American electricity grid (post–2003 blackout), and the need to have Canadian climate change policies take into account that fact that the United States was not a Kyoto signatory and thus its industries had a comparative advantage over Canadian firms. Canadian policy also needs to deal with the aggressive drive for supply security under the Bush administration's National Energy Policy that saw Canada's oil and gas reserves as a key part of America's continental plan.

The EU, by contrast, has developed a complex set of economic, political, and legal institutions that deeply penetrates domestic arrangements and constrains the sovereignty of all members. Supranational law and intergovernmental treaties developed around the core concept of building a common market, but they also protect a broader set of social and political rights. Most importantly, a culture of negotiated consensus permeates the entire EU institutional fabric and provides multiple avenues for the management of differences and tensions (such as Héritier 1999; Kohler-Koch and Eising, 1999; Wallace 2005). As a result, energy policymaking in the EU, while also driven to a considerable extent by the 'economic constitution' of the single market, is much more institutionalized, symmetrical, and consensus-based than under NAFTA.

As chapter 7 by Cameron shows, the single energy market remains a controversial process that needs to accommodate the jealously guarded jurisdiction of member states over energy resources and policies, which results in a decentralized regulatory model. At the same time, the legal-institutional depth of the supranational framework has stronger transformational potential for domestic governance arrangements. Berlin is certainly one of the key players in EU energy policymaking, but it also finds its regulatory regime substantially transformed by EU rules, as recent developments in German energy regulation, detailed in Theobald's chapter, demonstrate.

Clarkson in his chapter insists on the driving role of private-sector, corporate interests and U.S. hegemony in North America's energy governance. It is important to note, though, that key political decisions and multi-level institutional constellations in Canada were crucial for the emergence of a 'constitutionalized' free trade energy regime between the United States and its northern neighbour. To begin with, after the failure of the interventionist National Energy Policy, federal energy policy after 1984 was decidedly pro-market and welcomed the continentalization of energy trade. But it also was geared towards reconciling Western energy interests. As a matter of fact, continental integration with the United States conveniently combined the agenda of market reform with the need for the federal government, after the NEP trauma, to tread very carefully and show respect for provincial claims to leadership in energy matters, and for their concern to enjoy free access to U.S. markets (Doern and Toner 1985).

The Canada-U.S. Free Trade Agreement and later NAFTA were essentially based on a core energy bargain between the oil and gas producing provinces and the federal government, and the United States. It ensured energy pro-market free trade and pro-rated security of supply for the U.S. For Alberta in particular the free trade agreement provided a guarantee that federal interventionism NEP-style could never occur again, and that, essentially, provinces would decide on the international trade of their energy resources on a commercial basis.

A similar constellation of provincial leadership and federal retreat is revealed in Froschauer's analysis of the ongoing integration of electricity markets between Canada and the United States (also see Gattinger 2005; Griffin Cohen 2004). The pro-market and pro-provincial-autonomy orientation of federal energy policy plus the North American free trade framework contributed to a reduction of federal oversight over the provincial export of electricity, visible, for example, in the relaxation of export hearings by the National Energy Board. In the absence of a Canadian federal framework for extra-provincial trade, grid connections, or regulatory reform in general, provinces took the lead in all these areas.

As a consequence, electricity-exporting provinces are increasingly drawn instead into the orbit of U.S. regulatory changes and requirements. For example, provincial utilities that wish to sell into the deregulated (and generally higher-priced) U.S. wholesale market are required to comply with the U.S. electricity regulator FERC's 'reciprocity requirements,' which include reciprocal access to transmission grids. This obliges participating provincial utilities to separate ('unbundle') transmission networks from the generation and supply businesses. Under cross-border wholesale arrangements, provincial transmission entities join regional transmission organizations (RTOs) with their U.S. counterparts. The 2004 IEA energy policy review of Canada, quoted by Froschauer, notes 'major impacts on the policy and regulation of electricity grids and markets in Canada through FERC's control of access of Canadian utilities to the US market' (IEA 2004, 148).

Hence, not only the asymmetrical nature of the U.S.-Canadian relationship but also the domestic fragmentation of Canadian energy regulatory governance contributes to a *more market-driven and unbalanced system of bilateral, continental governance* under which energy-rich Canada seems to be more of a rule-taker than a rule-maker, and where *policy coordination occurs more through market pressures and unilateral adaptation than through balanced negotiation.*

Notwithstanding these fundamental differences in multi-level dynamics between EU and North America energy governance, we should also note areas of potentially converging practices designed to enhance multi-level coordination. While the capacity of EU institutions to produce supranationally coordinated policies is generally much higher than in North American governance, the delicate balance of power between supranational institutions and member states precludes any centralization of regulatory authority in Brussels.

Rather, as discussed in detail by Cameron, dense networks between national regulatory agencies, charged with the national implementation of EU market rules, provide a key, bureaucratic, and partly informal channel for the coordination of energy policy (Eberlein and Newman 2008). Technocratic management of tensions between different regulatory interests and approaches helps to defuse political conflicts, but also raises issues of political legitimacy (Eberlein and Grande 2005).

Disaggregated, trans-governmental cooperation (Slaughter 2004) between energy-policy experts and officials, below the diplomatic-political radar, plays a role in the North American context as well. For example, energy department experts from Canada, Mexico, and the United States cooperate in a number of subgroups under the North American Energy Working Group (NAEWG), instituted by the political leaders to foster information exchange and policy cooperation.

Yet sub-state energy regulatory networks and 'committee governance' mechanisms more generally, have a much stronger capacity for regulatory convergence and harmonization in the dense institutional context of the EU than under the NAFTA framework, which is more dominated by bilateral, governmental exchanges, in stricter respect of jurisdictional divisions (Gattinger 2005).

How do these contrasting patterns of multi-level coordination affect the capacity of Canada and Germany to address today's energy policy challenges? Does a higher capacity to manage multi-level fragmentation and tension translate into a higher capacity to meet the substantive challenges of energy policy?

Capacity

To assess the capacity of different jurisdictions and institutional arrangements to master the challenges of today's complex energy world, as mapped in chapter 2, is probably the most daunting analytical task.

First and foremost, the question is how to define the 'deliverables.' At one level, there is a consensus on the fundamental goals of energy policy, which can be represented as a magic triangle of three key goals. Firstly, energy policy is expected to deliver useable and reliable energy, at reasonable prices, to all citizens of a given jurisdiction. A broader notion of energy security includes the physical security of infrastructures (grids, pipelines) and the security and functioning of the entire supply chain that can be affected by physical threats but also by political or economic risk, such as the dependence on supply from politically volatile regions (Yergin 2006).

Secondly, the paradigm of sustainability requires that energy use does at least not further erode the state of the environment and the ecosystem (Lafferty and Meadowcroft 2000). Sustainable development in energy terms is often tested against the basic concept of whether countries or regions have made progress in reducing energy use on a per capita basis, or as evidenced by other measures of energy efficiency. With the increasing prominence of the climate change challenge, the reduction or avoidance of greenhouse gas emissions has also become a test for sustainability.

Thirdly, and finally, energy use and supply is expected to meet the standard of economic efficiency, meaning that producers and consumers of energy should, wherever possible and appropriate, be subject to the unconstrained discipline of market mechanisms on a level playing field that signals and rewards the most efficient use of fully costed resources, including their environmental cost.

The problem is, of course, that these three goals are not only interrelated but often also in conflict with each other, so it becomes difficult to assign separate scores of performance on these three goals or indicators. It is true that economic efficiency and environmental efficiency or sustainability, in a system that fully costs external effects, can actually point in the same direction. However, trade-offs and conflicts between the goals abound. The most secure energy source for a given country, such as Germany, may be domestic coal. But the use of coal (under given technology) may have environmentally unsustainable consequences. And instead of burning expensive domestic coal it may be economically more efficient to import cheaper coal or gas from other regions to meet the same demand.

Ultimately, therefore, energy policy choices, such as the one to burn domestic coal, involve political decisions about relative preferences and the ranking of desired policy outcomes. And empirically, of course, we know that decision-making is shaped by power relations and conflicting interests. However, this is not to suggest that policy decisions cannot be held against certain standards. As set out in chapter 2, a reasonable yardstick for an optimal energy system that most energy economists would subscribe to could be based on a scenario of level-playing-field competition between all, fully costed energy sources and supplies, in a market that is transparent and rigorously regulated in its trade, competition, and environmental dimensions (Helm 2003, 2005). The relative approximation of such an optimal system could serve as an indicator of high capacity to meet energy challenges. Yet, in political terms, it is best to think of capacity as *the intelligent management of tensions that arise between the different goals that energy policy is expected to meet.*

The question then becomes what explains the relative capacity of countries like Canada and Germany to arrive at balanced energy policy decisions, or to come closer to a best-practice energy system. How we can account for differences in performance to meet certain standards? In essence, we argue that two key factors come into play: firstly, and evidently, *the structural properties of the substantive energy field, and the resource endowment of a country or region in particular*, define the specific challenges and priorities as well as the range of options available to policymakers. Secondly, *the multi-level, institutional framework of energy policymaking, including the constellation of interests and power relationships*, affects what one could call the *institutional capacity* of energy policy, much of which necessarily overlaps with what we have already discussed under the theme of coordination.

A logical starting point for a brief assessment of energy policy capacity in Canada and Germany, that complements the more detailed comparative information given in chapter 2, is the striking contrast between Canadian and German resource endowment. On the one side, we have an energy resource-rich country, with Saudi-Arabia-sized oil sand reserves, that is also rich in natural gas, uranium, and hydroelectric power. On the other side, we have a poorly endowed country that has few, economically and environmentally less attractive, domestic fuel sources (mainly coal) but that at least enjoys a central location in, and easy access to, broader European markets.

Given these conditions, we would expect that Canada finds it easy to guarantee energy security at reasonable prices to its citizens and, in addition, to generate economic wealth for the country from its energy riches. However, the story, as we have seen, is more complex. To begin with, energy reserves and economic gains are concentrated in the West, whereas higher energy prices affect the industry in the rest of Canada – although the Alberta energy boom boosts the entire economy. More importantly, however, *the asymmetrical nature of Canada's free-trade relationship with the powerful and energy-hungry United States, the conflicting interests of producer versus consumer regions within Canada, and the fragmented character of domestic energy governance, with the provinces in the driver's seat, combine to grant Canada less control over its energy riches than it might otherwise enjoy.* The lack of federal leadership in energy matters gives market forces, and U.S. policy, a large role in Canadian energy policy.

Energy security is the major challenge for and concern of German energy policy. Energy dependence on foreign supply, especially on Russian natural gas and oil, has not been reduced. Rather, it is on the rise. Berlin, followed to some extent by Brussels, has sought to construct a – rather controversial – privileged partnership with Russia, and has built energy security into its foreign policy priorities, such as by giving government support to the North European Gas Pipeline (NEGP) project between Russian monopolist Gazprom and German partners E.ON and BASF. It remains to be seen if this strategy will actually enhance supply security or rather lock Germany into a dangerous dependency trap (*Economist* 2007).

At the same time, however, the poor fuel-resource endowment has spurred, beginning with the 1974 oil crisis, sustained efforts to diversify supply sources and to enhance energy efficiency, as documented in the chapters by Mez and Weidner/Eberlein. These initiatives could build on a public consensus on energy policy needs, the consensual nature of German institutions, and the corporatist character of the political economy that, different from Canada, reduced potential conflicts between energy suppliers and consumers.

As discussed in more detail by Mez and Doern in chapter 5, nuclear energy for electricity generation has been an important, though increasingly contested, component of this diversification strategy until it was definitely discredited in German public opinion after the 1986 Chernobyl disaster. Given the looming demand-supply squeeze and sharp price increases, however, political pressures to revisit the 2002 decision to phase out nuclear energy use by 2025 have intensified.

The success story of diversification, of course, is the impressive expansion of renewable energy sources for electricity generation, as the Mez analysis in chapter 14 shows. As a matter of fact, diversification, in view of security of supply, and the drive for environmental sustainability worked in tandem. Germany is now the world leader in installed wind-power capacity and ranks first in photovoltaics as well, although natural conditions are far less favourable than in many other countries (Reiche 2005). As Mez shows, the success of renewables is due to effective public policy, the 'positive discrimination' of alternative energy sources, under the guaranteed feed-in tariff legislation that has been an effective incentive for investment. The federal government has the ambitious plan to raise the share of renewable sources in electricity generation from 10.1 per cent (2005) to at least 20 per cent by 2020 (IEA 2007, 67–8). Moreover, the achievements in the area of climate policies, detailed in the Weidner and Eberlein chapter, and a reduction of energy use per capita, add to a rather positive assessment of German capacity to move towards environmental sustainability.

This positive performance holds especially true in comparison to Canada, a clear laggard on all these environmental fronts. Alternative, renewable energy sources (with the exception of hydro) have been marginal so far, and per capita energy use has actually increased (Lipp 2007).

Climate change policies offer the greatest contrast. As discussed by Rivers and Jaccard, Canada is among the worst offenders among the Kyoto signatories (and among many non-signatories), having increased, not reduced, its greenhouse gas emissions by 245 per cent in 2005, compared to 1990 levels.

To some extent, of course, this is due to the fact that Canada's energy riches are a blessing for energy security, but a burden when it comes to environmental sustainability. As Rivers and Jaccard remind us, Canada as energy producer and host to energy-intensive industries, prime among them the mining and resource-extracting industries themselves, thrives as a high carbon economy. The Alberta oil sand production is the single most important emitter of Canadian green-house gases. Higher than European population and economic growth (fuelled by immigration) also significantly contributes to the current increase in energy use and emissions. But this is only part of the story.

A host of factors that in Germany have underpinned a better environmental sustainability performance are absent or much weaker in Canada, such as the need to diversify supplies, geographical/population density, environmental risk and awareness, advocacy, and the political strength of Green parties. But at the same time, the institutional context is, as in the case of energy security, of prime importance to understand Canadian underperformance: the lack of federal leadership and leverage opportunities (and activities) in the energy and environment field; competitive disadvantage of environmental regulations for Canadian companies who compete on the U.S. market; the focus of federal policy on oil, gas, or nuclear, to the detriment of alternative energy sources; and the general pro-market policy framework throughout the 1980s and 1990s, which was not conducive to government intervention in favour of renewables.

A good example for the ineffectiveness of weak federal leadership is climate policy. The federal government has relied almost exclusively on non-compulsory greenhouse gas reduction mechanisms, in a desire, as Rivers and Jaccard note, to 'minimize political resistance.'

How do Canada and Germany perform in economic efficiency and level-playing-field competition? In both countries, market mechanisms have played an increasing role in energy governance over the last two decades, mainly under the impulse of internationalization and regional trade integration.

Under the EU single energy market framework, Germany moved, in 1998, from monopoly to full market liberalization, including retail, in electricity and gas markets. However, the legacy of corporatist arrangements in the energy sector has been a barrier to the development of effective competition. Industrial self-regulation continued to play an important role in network access regulation to electricity grids and gas pipelines, resulting in the discrimination against and exit of new market entrants.

Sector-specific regulation was introduced only in 2005, under heavy EU pressure. As Theobald's analysis in chapter 10 shows, the federal government has done little to fight against rapid market concentration. The controversial decision, in 2003, to approve the mega-merger between E.on and Ruhrgas, against the advice of both the Federal

Cartel Office and the Monopolies Commission, seemed to indicate that the government was more concerned about the ability of large German companies to dominate European markets, and to negotiate favourable supply deals with Russian Gazprom and other major suppliers, than about competition at home. Interpreted in a benign way, one could say that security of supply concerns triumphs economic efficiency and competition principles.

The federal government has also not been shy to intervene in energy markets in the area of environmental regulation and taxation, as Mez shows in his chapter, and to favour certain energy sources over others. However, environmentalists would respond to level-playing-field critics that the recent aggressive promotion of renewable energy sources did less than offset the level of long-standing subsidization enjoyed by traditional fuels such as coal, and especially nuclear, whose environmental costs were never fully costed.

In Canada, as seen earlier, market forces have dominated much of energy policy since the mid-1980s, with the progressive North American integration of oil and natural gas markets. The introduction of competition in electricity is, however, much less advanced than in Germany, partly because of provincial prerogatives, partly because of mixed experiences with market reforms.

Unlike in Germany, there was no supranational constraint for provinces to stick with specific market models, and reforms could thus stall, or be reversed, more easily. However, as discussed above, U.S. influence over regulatory design of increasing cross-border trade of electricity leads to some spill-over of U.S. deregulation patterns into provincial electricity policies.

In contrast to those in Germany and Europe, market forces in Canada have progressed less by design (the EU Single Market) and more by default, and in a disjointed way. While the pro-market and pro-continentalization approach to energy governance was a federal political choice, it also very much reflected the reality of U.S-Canadian and federal-provincial relations and pressures. Nonetheless, for most of the period from 1985 until very recently, energy markets in Canada were broadly competitive and reasonably efficient. High oil and gas prices and electricity supply problems in recent years would yield a somewhat more sceptical verdict on the competition and efficiency front.

It is clear that both countries do considerably diverge from the optimal system of a true level-playing-field competition between fully costed energy sources, governed by rigorous competition and environmental regulation. The competition between carbon or nuclear sources and alternative, renewable sources remains skewed in favour of the former in various ways, but perhaps less so in Germany, where fuel-producer interests are less strong. Germany has not enough competition but a lot of environmental regulation, while Canada has some of both but is hardly exemplary.

Looking at how the two countries balance the fundamental goals of energy policy in response to their specific challenge, we have seen that Germany gives top priority to security of supply (without having achieved top results), and that it performs rather well in environmental sustainability. Both goals seem to override economic efficiency concerns. Canada's priorities, by contrast, have been to exploit its energy riches and to ensure access to U.S. markets. Environmental sustainability is only a very recent concern.

Finally, what does this comparative overview tells us about how structural properties of the energy field and the multi-level institutional framework of energy policymaking combine to affect national capacity in our two countries? In a nutshell, *Canada's favourable resource endowment is coupled with weak institutional capacity*. Political fragmentation under Canadian federalism and the asymmetrical character of regional trade integration contribute to relative under-performance in security of supply and to poor performance in environmental sustainability. *Germany, by contrast, enjoys stronger institutional capacity that has helped to mitigate (not compensate) the effects of poor resource endowment, by developing a more diverse and environmentally sustainable supply basis.*

Conclusions

We have presented a three-part analytical framework to capture the key issues and features of contemporary energy regulatory governance in the two contrasting cases of Canada in NAFTA and Germany in the EU (also see table 15.1). The analytical concepts of complexity, coordination, and capacity have allowed us to organize and interpret our authors' contributions in an integrated manner. This framework has also served as a productive tool to address the substantive aspects of the energy challenge and its governance in the two jurisdictions, thus bringing together institutional regulatory analysis and substantive energy policy content. Furthermore, this simple yet robust framework can guide future comparative research on energy policy across more jurisdictions and also multi-level regulatory governance in other policy fields.

In this concluding section, we highlight key empirical findings and theoretical implications but also point to remaining puzzles and research desiderata. We conclude also with an assessment of which of the two countries might be better positioned to master emerging energy challenges.

A first result of our study is that energy policy is confronted with a very complex technical system in a highly political environment. The study of market liberalization and integration in the two 'most different systems' of Germany and Canada delivers similar results, so that our findings can be generalized to other advanced industrialized countries: the typical features of energy policy invite design flaws, ad-hoc political intervention, and unintended consequences, which often translate into disappointing reform outcomes.

A second key insight about energy policy is its truly multi-level character. Energy policymaking in both Canada and Germany involves practically all territorial levels, from international trade and market integration under NAFTA and EU respectively down to the local community or municipal level of land-use management or alternative energy use. Again, notwithstanding the distinct federal character of our two case countries, we would expect to find similar constellations in most other jurisdictions of the 'OECD' world as well.

Energy policy is also highly multi-level in functional terms, as it reaches into and is in turn affected by multiple policy regimes: environment and trade are most prominent, but other areas include consumer, Aboriginal, and regional policies. This complex territorial and functional layering of levels and policy regimes involves cooperation and collision between different actors and domains, raising the question of how the tensions of 'complex interdependence' can, if at all, be managed.

Third – and this time in view of identifying key institutional differences that explain contrasting policy processes and outcomes – our comparison of institutional coordination mechanisms in the two jurisdictions reveals that Germany and the EU offer a constellation of actors and institutional rules and norms that is more conducive to consensual and productive management of multi-level tensions than Canada and NAFTA. In the latter case, both the asymmetrical nature of U.S.-Canadian relations and the domestic institutional setting (a conflict-prone mix of partisan politics and executive federalism with federal-provincial bilateralism) militate against high levels of coordination. Conflicts are exacerbated by major cleavages between energy producer and consumer regions.

In contrast, Germany has, for lack of abundant natural resources, avoided these producer-consumer cleavages, And, more importantly, it features an institutional system geared to patient consensus-building – although the corporatist style of government-industry relations can be a source of stalemate, and tensions between the energy provision regime and the environmental regime are far from absent. The EU, finally, is an international arena with a much greater balance of power and higher capacity to manage conflicts than NAFTA. And, unlike Canada, Germany has been able to upload many of its concerns and policy models onto the supranational level.

Fourth, our study finds that this marked difference in institutional capacity to deal with the multi-level nature of energy policy has a significant impact on the ability to meet substantive challenges of energy provision and resource management. Two types of capacity determine the overall ability to meet the energy challenge: first, the material capacity that is mainly a function of resource endowment but also includes the properties of energy sources as well as energy-specific expertise and innovative capacities of a country; and, second, the political-institutional capacity of multi-level management.

We find Canada and Germany at opposite ends in a two-by-two comparison of the countries and the two kinds of capacity. *Whereas Germany combines low material capacity (in terms of resource endowment) with high institutional capacity, Canada shows the reverse combination. Germany has been able to leverage its high institutional capacity to mitigate its inherent absence of abundant oil and gas resources* (while energy dependence on foreign suppliers, Russia in particular, loom large). As a matter of fact, Germany's poor natural resource base compelled it earlier to search for wider energy options and build strong institutional and environmental capacities, to develop alternative energy technologies in particular.

Canada's poor institutional capacity, by contrast, has led to relative under-performance, considering its strong material resource base. In fact, abundance of resources may also present a burden and inhibit the development of new (material and institutional) capacities, especially when it comes to innovative climate policy. Canada's energy riches have not only fuelled conflicts between producer and consumer regions that have surfaced again over the issue of burden-sharing regarding the reduction of Canada's GHG emissions. Canada's abundant resource base, combined with a strong orientation towards securing market-driven exports to the United States, has also deflected attention from exploring alternative energy options (except for nuclear energy). In this perspective, our study underscores the observation that energy riches do not necessarily translate into strong capacity or successful energy policy. These implications of different combinations of material and institutional capacity can inform the future analysis of energy governance capacity in other jurisdictions as well.

In theoretical terms, then, our study highlights, first, the need for analytical frameworks such as the one developed here to capture the complex dynamics of contemporary regulatory governance. Such frameworks can help add more subtlety to neo-institutional theory as it seeks to capture and understand both inertia and change in energy and other policy fields.

While the energy domain can be considered an extreme case of multi-level regulatory complexity and coordination challenges, modern governance more generally needs to be understood as negotiated exchange between different actors across multiple, interdependent, and overlapping functional arenas and territorial levels, as further developed in our introductory chapter. Therefore, our conceptual framework can help to better understand policy dynamics in other multi-level domains as well.

Second, and crucially, the three-part analytical framework integrates the institutional analysis of interaction dynamics between actors and levels with the substantive 'realities' of the policy domain. As the discussion of capacity in energy policy demonstrates, it is imperative to analyse institutional dynamics in their interaction effects with the structural properties of a policy area, in order to explain process and outcome of regulatory governance in specific policy fields. Our study thus revives and refines the neglected dictum that 'policy determines politics' for contemporary multi-level institutional analysis that tends to neglect the structural properties and substantive determinants of policymaking.

This being said, puzzles and open questions remain: how to determine the relative importance of substantive policy features versus multi-level institutional settings of incentives and constraints? And how to establish the interaction effects between the two? In particular, we need to better understand under which conditions structural properties of a policy area may encourage or inhibit the development of relevant institutional capacities.

Examples here are not hard to find. Germany's greater success in fostering alternative renewable energy sources can be traced back to its poor fossil fuel resource base that compelled it early on to search for alternative technologies. At the same time, the very success of this policy may now generate new governance challenges such as possible limits on suitable or acceptable sites for wind power and related approaches. From an institutional vantage point, Canada in the context of North American energy integration faces serious problems of coordination and economic costs should it now make more energetic moves towards a low-carbon resource economy. These costs can arise from the development of several different 'cap-and-trade' systems involving regional subgroups of American states and Canadian provinces without any overall national approach on either side of the border. In North America and Europe, both countries face serious policy puzzles rooted in energy resource properties, such as the encouragement and greater use of biofuels, which, though useful in some respects as substitutes for oil and gas, are already showing signs of increasing food costs and even global food shortages.

A second key area is the stability and adaptability of multi-level arrangements, raising the question of institutional change and inertia. Under which conditions and to which extent can and do institutional arrangements adapt to international and domestic pressures for change? Will, for example, Canada adjust its climate policy path (and underpinning institutional rules and norms) to respond to the mounting international pressures, in the aftermath of the Stern report, the June 2007 G8 Summit in Germany, and the December 2007 UN Bali Conference? Which drivers of change will be most significant?

Hence, this question links our study to the larger questions of explaining and understanding change and inertia.

Looking ahead, this book cautiously suggests that Germany is better equipped to master emerging energy challenges. It has developed, over many years, significant institutional and technological capacities that have begun already to bear fruit in the current transition to a low-carbon economy. For Germany the largest concern is still with energy security, particularly in its major Russian supplies of natural gas. Also, the challenge of replacing nuclear capacity (under the phase-out policy) without recourse to high-carbon coal- or gas-fired generation remains unresolved.

For Canada, the main dilemma is how to actually give alternative energy sources a serious opportunity to compete and to not be seduced again into thinking that its huge resource endowments are themselves its automatic answer to matters of energy production and demand and to its difficult and conflictual underlying energy politics.

REFERENCES

Bache, Ian, and Matthew Flinders, eds. 2004. *Multi-level governance*. Oxford: Oxford University Press.

Benz, Arthur. 2003. Mehrebenenverflechtung in der Europäischen Union [Multilevel governance in the European Union]. In *Europäische Integration*, ed. Markus Jachtenfuchs and Beate Kohler-Koch, 94–112. 2nd ed. Berlin: Leske + Budrich UTB..

Clarkson, Stephen. 2005. The primitive realities of North America's transnational governance. In *Complex sovereignty: Reconstituting political authority in the twenty-first century*, ed. Edgar Grande and Louis W. Pauly, 168–94. Toronto: University of Toronto Press.

Dewees, Donald N. 2005. Electricity restructuring in Canada. In *Canadian energy policy and the struggle for sustainable development*, ed. Bruce Doern, 128–50. Toronto: University of Toronto Press.

Doern, G. Bruce, ed. 2005. *Canadian energy policy and the struggle for sustainable development*. Toronto: University of Toronto Press.

Doern, G. Bruce, and Monica Gattinger. 2003. *Power switch: Energy regulatory governance in the 21st century*. Toronto: University of Toronto Press.

Doern, G. Bruce, and Glen Toner. 1985. *The politics of energy*. Toronto: Methuen.

Duane, Timothy P. 2002. Regulations rationale: Learning from the California energy crisis. *Yale Journal of Regulation* 19 (2): 471–540.

Economist. 2007. European energy security: A bear at the throat. 14 April.

Eberlein, Burkard. 2005. Regulation by cooperation: The 'third way' in making rules for the internal energy market. In *Legal aspects of EU energy regulation*, ed. Peter Cameron, 59–88. Oxford: Oxford University Press.

Eberlein, Burkard, and Edgar Grande. 2005. Beyond delegation: Transnational regulatory regimes and the EU regulatory state. *Journal of European Public Policy* 12 (1): 89–112.

Eberlein, Burkard, and Abraham Newman. 2008. Escaping the international governance dilemma? Incorporated transgovernmental networks in the European Union. *Governance* 21 (1): 25–52.

Eisner, Marc Allen, Jeff Worsham, and Evan J. Ringquist. 2000. *Contemporary Regulatory Policy*. London: Lynne Rienner.

Finon, Dominique, and Atle Midttun, eds. 2004. *Reshaping European gas and electricity industries*. London: Elsevier.

Gattinger, Monica. 2005. Canada–United States electricity relations: Policy coordination and multi-level associative governance. In *How Ottawa spends 2005–2006: Managing the minority*, ed. Bruce Doern, 143–62. Montreal and Kingston: McGill-Queen's University Press.

Griffin Cohen, Marjorie. 2004. International forces driving electricity deregulation in the semi-periphery: The case of Canada. In *Governing under stress: Middle powers and the challenge of globalization*, ed. Marjorie Griffin Cohen and Stephen Clarkson, 175–94. Toronto: Fernwood.

Helm, Dieter. 2003. *Energy, the state and the market: British energy policy since 1979*. Oxford: Oxford University Press.

– 2005. European energy policy: Securing supplies and meeting the challenge of climate change. Discussion paper prepared for the UK presidency of the European Union. http://www.fco.gov.uk/Files/kfile/PN%20papers_%20energy.pdf.

Héritier, Adrienne. 1999. *Policy-making and diversity in Europe: Escape from deadlock*. Cambridge: Cambridge University Press.

Hoberg, George, ed. 2002. *Capacity for choice: Canada in a new North America*. Toronto: University of Toronto Press.

Hooghe, Liesbet, and Gary Marks. 2003. Unraveling the central state, but how? Types of multi-level governance. *American Political Science Review* 97 (2): 233–43.

Hufbauer, Gary, and Jeffrey Schott. 2005. *NAFTA revisited: Achievements and challenges*. Washington: Institute for International Economics.

Hughes, Thomas P. 1987. The evolution of large technological systems. In *The social construction of technological systems: New directions in the sociology and history of technology*, ed. Wiebke E. Bijker, Thomas P. Hughes, and Trevor J. Pinch, 51–82. Cambridge, MA: MIT Press.

IEA. *See* International Energy Agency.

International Energy Agency. 2004. *Energy policies of IEA countries: Canada*. Paris: International Energy Agency.

– 2007. *Energy policies of IEA countries: Germany*. Paris: International Energy Agency.

Jaccard, Mark. 2002. *California shorts a circuit: Should Canadians trust the wiring diagram? C.D. Howe Institute Commentary* 159.

Kohler-Koch, Beate, and Rainer Eising, eds. 1999. *The transformation of governance in the European Union*. London: Routledge.

Lafferty, William M., and James Meadowcroft, eds. 2000. *Implementing sustainable development*. Oxford: Oxford University Press.

Levy, Brian, and Pablo T. Spiller. 1996. A framework for resolving the regula
tory problem. In *Regulations, institutions, and commitments: Comparative
studies of telecommunications*, ed. Brian Levy and Pablo T. Stiller, 1–35. Cambridge: Cambridge University Press.

Lipp, Judith. 2007. Renewable energy policies and the provinces. In *Innova-
tion, science, environment: Canadian policies and performance 2007–2008*, ed.
Bruce Doern, 176–99. Montreal and Kingston: McGill-Queen's University
Press.

Reiche, Danyel, ed. 2005. *Handbook of renewable energies in the European Union:
Case-studies of the EU-15 states*. 2nd ed. Berlin: Lang.

Scharpf, Fritz W. 1997. *Games real actors play: Actor-centered institutionalism in
policy research*. London: Westview / Harper Collins.

Slaughter, Anne-Marie. 2004. *A new world order*. Princeton: Princeton University Press.

Trebilcock, Michael J., and Roy Hrab. 2005. Electricity restructuring in
Ontario. *Energy Journal* 26 (1): 123–46.

Wallace, Helen. 2005. An institutional anatomy and five policy modes. In
Policy-making in the European Union, ed. Helen Wallace, William Wallace,
and Mark A. Pollack, 49–90. Oxford: Oxford University Press.

von der Fehr, Nils Henrik M., Eirik S. Amundsen, and Lars Bergman. 2005.
The Nordic market: Signs of stress? *Energy Journal* 9 (3): 71–98.

Yergin, Daniel. 2006. Ensuring energy security. *Foreign Affairs* 85 (2): 69–82.

Glossary

Alternative or renewable energy Alternative energy sources to oil, natural gas, and nuclear energy. It includes low-impact renewables such as some biofuels, wind, solar, biomass, and small hydro (with big hydro often excluded as a 'renewable' because of its major impacts in creating huge hydro dams).

Baseload plants Electricity generation plants that have high capital cost and low operating cost. They can be nuclear, run-of-the-river hydroelectric, or coal-fired thermal plants.

Merit based plants Electricity generation plants that have moderate capital and operating costs. They are usually coal- or oil-fired steam turbine plants, or combined cycle gas turbines.

Merit order The principle that governs how most electric utilities dispatch plants, starting with the lowest-marginal-cost plants, which minimize the cost of generation.

Multi-level governance Non-hierarchical, negotiated exchange between actors across multiple, interdependent, and overlapping (functional) arenas or territorial levels. It explicitly recognizes the participation of non-state, private actors in public policymaking, and it includes informal dimensions of decision-making.

Multi-level regulation Regulation making and regulatory compliance involving the coordinated or conflicting actions of regulatory bodies at different levels of government (national, sub-national, international, and local) as well as modes of self- and co-regulation initiated and managed by business interest groups and NGOs through the use of voluntary codes and related approaches.

Neo-Institutional theory Posits that formal and informal institutions are rule systems that mediate processes and outcomes of political behaviour and policymaking. There are several varieties of this theory. Rational choice institutionalism views institutions as intervening variables, offering incentives and imposing constraints on actors in pursuit of exogenous preferences. Sociological institutionalism considers institutions rather as independent variables, shaping or even constituting actors' preferences and normative orientations. Historical institutionalism is concerned with how institutional configurations emerge from historical processes (at critical junctures) and are sustained through sequencing and lock-in effects, resulting in path-dependent trajectories.

Peak oil Some energy forecasters argue that oil reserves are depleting. The evidence for this claim is partly that big oil firms are finding it difficult to replace reserves.

Peaking plants Electricity generation plants that have low capital cost and high operating cost and often rely on a simple gas turbine or storage hydroelectric power. The aggregate marginal cost curve for a typical fleet of plants rises gradually over a range of output as baseload and mid-merit plants are used but rises rapidly as capacity is approached and peaking plants must be run.

Public interest theory A theory of policy and regulation making, which posits/assumes that government agencies try to determine what will maximize public welfare and then pursue policies to achieve this end.

Proportionality clause The provision in Article 605 of the Canada-U.S. Free Trade Agreement, which requires that in any export restrictions justified on the basis of conservation, price stabilization, and supply shortage, 'the share of total supply available for export purchase may not fall below the average level in the previous 36 months.' In other words, neither country may reduce the *proportion* of the energy or petrochemicals it exports to the other party.

Regulatory capture The theory of regulation that argues that regulators are captured by the industries they are regulating. Such capture can occur gradually or can exist from the outset of the creation of a new regulatory body.

Subsidiarity principle The principle in the governance of the European Union whereby the EU does not take action (outside of its areas of exclusive competence) unless it is more effective than action taken at the national or sub-national level. This principle is thus recognizes the diversity of circumstances in policy mixes among the member states and the diverse priorities in national policies.

Sustainable development policy A policy whose intent is to ensure in any number of areas of governance that the environment and its ecosystems are left in at least as good a state for the next generation as they were for the current generation. Cast somewhat more broadly, such a policy is often defined as one that takes into consideration in a balanced way the economic, social, and environmental effects of policies, sometimes referred to as the 'triple bottom line.'

Wholesale spot price The price that is set when fully competitive use bids by electricity generators are submitted. It reflects the price-setting bid for that hour. If generators cannot exercise market power, this spot price should represent the short run marginal cost of generation.

Contributors

Peter D. Cameron is a professor of international energy law and policy, and is director of research at the Centre of Energy, Petroleum, and Mineral Law and Policy, University of Dundee. Since 2002, he has also been part-time professor at the Robert Schuman Centre for Advanced Studies, European University Institute (EUI) in Florence, Italy. He organizes and chairs the annual EU Energy Law Workshop at the EUI. His most recent publication is *Legal Aspects of EU Energy Regulation: The Implementation of the Electricity and Gas Directives across the EU* (Oxford University Press 2005).

Stephen Clarkson is a professor of political economy in the Department of Political Science at the University of Toronto and directs the Program on the Governance of North America. His current research focuses on the impact of globalization and trade liberalization on the Canadian state and on the evolution of North American governance under NAFTA. His recent books include *Uncle Same and Us: Globalization, Neoconservatism, and the Canadian State* (University of Toronto Press 2002) and (edited with Marjorie Griffin Cohen) *Governing under Stress: Middle Powers and the Challenge of Globalization* (Zed Books / Fernwood 2004).

Donald N. Dewees is a professor of economics and a professor of law at the University of Toronto. During 1998 he served as the vice-chair of the Ontario Market Design Committee, which advised the government on the introduction of competition into the electricity market in Ontario. He has written several books and numerous book chapters and scholarly articles in the fields of environmental economics, law and economics, and electricity restructuring.

G. Bruce Doern is a professor in the School of Public Policy and Administration, Carleton University, and served as director of the Carleton Research Unit on Innovation, Science, and Environment. He also holds a joint research chair in public policy in the Politics Department, University of Exeter. He has written a number of books on aspects of energy policy, regulatory governance, and comparative public policy. Recent books include *Red Tape, Red Flags: Regulation for the Innovation Age* (Conference Board of Canada 2007), *Canadian Energy Policy and the Struggle for Sustainable Development* (edited, University of Toronto Press 2005), and *Rules, Rules, Rules, Rules: Multi-Level Regulatory Governance* (edited with Robert Johnson, University of Toronto Press 2006).

Burkard Eberlein is an assistant professor of policy at the Schulich School of Business, York University, where he is also a researcher at the Canadian Centre for German and European Studies. His research interests include comparative public policy, especially economic regulation and the governance of markets, and international governance, with a special focus on the EU. His current research projects deal with comparative energy market regulation in Canada and the EU, transgovernmental networks and international organizations, business responses to climate change, and the globalization of accounting standards. His work has been published in journals such as *Governance, Journal of European Public Policy, Journal of Public Policy*, and *Journal of Common Market Studies*.

Karl Froschauer is an assistant professor of sociology and director of the Centre for Canadian Studies, Department of Sociology and Anthropology, Simon Fraser University. As part of his research on hydroelectric resources, he wrote *White Gold: Hydroelectric Development in Canada* (UBC Press 1999). He has also published on Niagara Falls Privatization Reversal, Canada's failed national electricity network, and regional electricity sector integration comparisons in the NAFTA, the EU, and the Mercosur regions. He is co-editor of *Convergence and Divergence in North America: Canada and the United States* (Centre for Canadian Studies, SFU, forthcoming).

Monica Gattinger is an associate professor in the School of Political Studies, University of Ottawa. Her research interests pertain to public policy, public administration, and governance. Her work focuses on the influence of integration on public policy and public administration, the implications of broader shifts from government to governance, and the involvement of non-government actors in policy and regulatory processes. She is co-author with G. Bruce Doern of *Power Switch: Energy Regulatory Governance in the Twenty-First Century* (University of Toronto Press 2003) and co-editor of *Accounting for Culture: Thinking Through Cultural Citizenship* (University of Ottawa Press 2005).

Mark Jaccard is an associate professor and director of the Energy and Materials Research Group in the School of Resource and Environmental Management at Simon Fraser University. He served as chair and CEO of the BC Utilities Commission from 1992 to 1997. He was a member of the Intergovernmental Panel on Climate Change (IPCC) from 1993 to 1996 for the production of the IPCC's Second Assessment Report. He has chaired several task forces and inquiries in areas such as electricity market reform, gasoline pricing, and greenhouse gas emission policies. He co-authored *The Cost of Climate Policy* (UBC Press 2002). His most recent book is *Sustainable Fossil Fuels* (Cambridge University Press 2006).

Lutz Mez is a senior associate professor in the Department of Social and Political Sciences, Free University of Berlin, and deputy director of the Environmental Policy Research Centre. His major research area is environmental and energy policy, with particular reference to nuclear and electricity policy. He is author of numerous articles and chapters in internationally edited books on these topics. He has contributed most recently to *Reshaping European Gas and Electricity Markets* (Elsevier 2004, edited by Dominique Finon and Atle Midttun).

Pierre-Olivier Pineau is an associate professor in the Department of Management Sciences at École des hautes études commerciales in Montreal. His work focuses on electricity market reforms and investment problems in an international context. He has studied the Nordic electricity market, the Cameroon electric utility privatization, and the Peruvian electricity market. He has published articles in *Energy Policy, Energy Studies Review,* and *Annals of Operations Research,* and many chapters in edited books.

Nic Rivers is a research associate at the Energy and Materials Research Group in the School of Resource and Environmental Management at

Simon Fraser University. He has published on energy and environmental policies in journals such as *Energy Economics, Energy Journal,* and the *Energy Policy Journal.*

Christian Theobald is a lawyer and partner of Becker Büttner Held, a law firm specializing in infrastructure law. He is also a lecturer at the Technical University of Berlin and chairman of the Regulation of Network Industries study group at the University of Bonn. He has published on German and European energy and utilities law. He is the editor of the multi-volume *Energie und Infrastrukturrecht* (Energy and infrastructure law) and the monthly journal *InfrastrukturRecht – Energie, Verkehr, Abfall, Wasser* (Infrastructure law: Energy, transport, waste, water), both published by Beck, Munich. He has served as expert counsel for the German parliament (Economic Committee) during the legislative drafting of the EnWG (Energy Act).

Helmut Weidner is a senior researcher, Research Unit 'Civil Society and Transnational Networks,' Social Science Research Centre, Berlin, and private lecturer, Faculty of Political Science, Free University of Berlin. He has published widely in the area of environmental policy. His major research areas are cross-national comparison of environmental policy, global climate change policy and equity issues, and alternative dispute resolution. He is author of numerous articles and books on these topics. He is co-editor (with Martin Jänicke) of *Capacity Building in National Environmental Policy: A Comparative Study of 17 Countries* (Springer 2002).

Hans-Joachim Ziesing is a former senior executive, Department of Energy, Transport, and Environment, at the German Institute for Economic Research in Berlin. He also teaches at the Free University of Berlin. His research areas include the evaluation of energy and environmental policy strategies, scenarios for climate protection, and instruments for the implementation of sustainable development. Dr Ziesing was a member of the select committee, Sustainable Energy Supply in Times of Globalization and Liberalization (commissioned by the German parliament), and a member and chair of the Berlin Energy Advisory Board. More recently, he has assisted the Federal Ministry of Environment with the preparation and implementation of the National Allocation Plan for Germany's emission allowances under the EU Emission Trading System.